A MERE MACHINE

A MERE MACHINE

The Supreme Court,
Congress, and
American Democracy

Anna Harvey

Yale UNIVERSITY PRESS

New Haven and London

Published with assistance from the Mary Cady Tew Memorial Fund.

Yale University Press books may be purchased in quantity for educational,
business, or promotional use. For information, please e-mail sales.press@
yale.edu (U.S. office) or sales@yaleup.co.uk (U.K. office).

Set in Galliard type by Newgen North America.
Printed in the United States of America.

The Library of Congress has cataloged the hardcover edition as follows:

Harvey, Anna L. (Anna Lil), 1966–
    A mere machine : the Supreme Court, Congress, and American
democracy / Anna Harvey.
        p. cm.
    Includes bibliographical references and index.
    ISBN 978-0-300-17111-2 (clothbound : alk. paper)
    1. United States. Supreme Court.   2. Judicial power—United
States. 3.   Judicial independence—United States.   4. Separation of
powers—United States.   5. Political questions and judicial power—
United States.   I. Title.
    KF8742.H375 2013
    347.73'26—dc23
                                                              2013013064

ISBN 978-0-300-20577-0 (pbk.)

A catalogue record for this book is available from the British Library.

10 9 8 7 6 5 4 3 2 1

Darwin
Riley
Finn

Let mercy be the character of the law-giver, but let the judge be a mere machine.
—Thomas Jefferson, 1776

CONTENTS

PREFACE: "A MERE MACHINE"

On June 28, 2012, the Supreme Court ruled for the first time in seventy-five years that Congress had exceeded the limits of its powers under the Spending Clause, the clause of Article I, Section 8, empowering the Congress "to pay the Debts and provide for the common Defence and general Welfare of the United States."[1] Striking a key component of the Patient Protection and Affordable Care Act, signed by President Barack Obama in March of 2010, the Court ruled that Congress could not withhold all federal Medicaid funds from states choosing not to participate in the substantial expansion of Medicaid envisioned by the Act. Instead, states choosing not to participate in the program's expansion would simply lose the additional federal monies available under the Act to partially fund that expansion. In effect, the Court made the states' participation in the Affordable Care Act's Medicaid expansion, an expansion that had been predicted to extend health insurance to approximately 22.3 million previously uninsured low-income individuals, a purely voluntary choice.[2]

The Court's Spending Clause ruling initially attracted little attention from observers focused on its ruling, in the same case, that Congress could levy a penalty on certain categories of individuals choosing not to purchase private health insurance. But the significance of the Court's Medicaid ruling soon became apparent. Within days of the ruling the Republican governors of some of the states with the largest populations of potential recipients under the proposed Medicaid expansion had announced that they would resist any efforts to participate in that expansion, a resistance that would have been virtually unthinkable prior to the Court's ruling.[3] Other governors announced that they might consider participating in Medicaid's expansion, but only under broad waivers from program requirements that would allow them to limit recipients' eligibility and benefits; the Court's ruling had given these governors the leverage to demand such waivers.[4] The emboldened opposition to Medicaid's expansion in these states began to put pressure on neighboring states, which would likely face an influx of potential Medicaid recipients should they expand eligibility and benefits while their neighbors did not.[5] The growing resistance to Medicaid's expansion also began to put pressure on hospitals, which had agreed to lower Medicaid reimbursement rates in return for an expected increase in the number of (paid) Medicaid patients, but which now faced a much smaller than expected Medicaid population as a consequence of the Court's ruling; the American Hospital Association began to float proposals to roll back the renegotiated reimbursement rates.[6] To make matters worse, the Urban Institute reported that approximately 80 percent of the potential recipients under the proposed Medicaid expansion, or 17.8 million uninsured individuals, had incomes below the federal poverty line, implying their ineligibility for health insurance subsidies available under other provisions of the Affordable Care Act.[7] Should states choose not to participate in the Medicaid expansion, that Act would perversely provide financial assistance only to those uninsured individuals with incomes above the federal poverty line, while denying assistance to those below it.

In short, despite headlines trumpeting the Court's endorsement of the Affordable Care Act (the *New York Times*'s print headline read, "Justices, By 5–4, Uphold Health Care Law; Roberts in Majority; Victory For Obama"), the Court in fact had dealt a significant blow to the signature policy achievement of Barack Obama's presidency. One conservative commentator likened Chief Justice John Roberts's opinion in the case to that of Chief Justice John Marshall in *Marbury v. Madison*, 5 U.S. 137 (1803), noting that Marshall had similarly won a major policy victory while appearing to defer to his partisan opponents. Marshall had appeased (and distracted) the Jeffersonian Republicans by refusing to implement William Marbury's judicial commission, while securing for the Federalist majority on the Court a precedent supporting the Court's exercise of judicial review. Roberts likewise appeared to have appeased (and distracted)

Democrats by upholding the Affordable Care Act's penalty for failing to purchase private insurance, while potentially gutting the Act's Medicaid expansion.[8]

As the significance of the Court's ruling on Medicaid slowly became apparent, liberals and conservatives fell into predictable patterns of reaction. Conservatives celebrated the ruling, asserting that the justices in the majority had appropriately followed the Court's Spending Clause precedents prohibiting federal spending that coerces, rather than incentivizes, the states into serving federal policy agendas.[9] Liberals, by contrast, ridiculed the notion that the Court's ruling had been guided by precedent, suggesting more darkly that the Republican-appointed justices in the majority had instrumentally used Spending Clause precedent in order to gut the Affordable Care Act's redistributive policy agenda.[10]

But neither explanation for the Court's Medicaid ruling was entirely convincing. The conservatives' doctrinal argument could not explain why, given that the Court had never articulated the line separating coercive spending from incentivizing spending, the Affordable Care Act's Medicaid expansion had ended up on the wrong side of that line. In fact, in surveys conducted prior to the issuance of the Court's ruling, only about 20 percent of former Supreme Court clerks and attorneys who had argued cases before the Court believed that a majority of the justices would find the Medicaid expansion to be on the wrong side of the Spending Clause line.[11]

On the other hand, the liberals' explanation based on partisan policy preferences over redistribution could not explain why the Court's Medicaid judgment had been supported not only by the five justices on the Roberts Court appointed by Republican presidents, but also by two of the four justices appointed by Democratic presidents (Justices Stephen Breyer and Elena Kagan).[12] Nor could it account for the support of Republican-appointed Justices William Rehnquist and Antonin Scalia for apparently coercive federal spending in the most prominent prior Spending Clause case, *South Dakota v. Dole*, 483 U.S. 203 (1987) (upholding the withholding of federal highway monies from states with drinking ages below 21).

Perhaps the weaknesses of these explanations for the Court's ruling lay in their common assumption that the justices are free to decide cases as they see fit. Both liberal and conservative observers of the Court's ruling at least implicitly presumed that, insulated from elected branch influence by their life tenures and guaranteed salaries, the justices had the liberty to decide *National Federation of Independent Business* using whatever combination of legal doctrines, policy preferences, and interpretive strategies seemed most appropriate to them at the time. These observers disagreed only on the weights that the justices appeared to assign to these influences.

This common assumption of judicial independence, widely shared by observers of the Court, may be deeply flawed. For it does not appear to be the case that our Constitution created a purely independent Supreme Court, with justices free to issue rulings at will. Instead, our constitutional design makes the justices' tenures, salaries, budgets, and more dependent on the will of congressional majorities. Moreover, that design gives to the House of Representatives particularly important gatekeeping roles in both impeachment and appropriations, the two processes on which the justices' tenures, salaries, and budgets depend. This design incentivizes the justices to defer to the preferences of majorities in the House of Representatives. And, whether the justices are aware of them or not, those incentives appear to work. At least in the data analyzed here, the justices of the U.S. Supreme Court do not appear to decide constitutional cases independently of elected branch preferences. Instead, they are extraordinarily deferential to those preferences, in particular to the preferences of majorities in the House of Representatives. This deference does not appear to be merely the spurious product of changes in the justices' own preferences, or judicial responsiveness to trends in public opinion, socioeconomic conditions, or public policy. Moreover, it is even more evident when we control for the selection bias in the Court's docket.

The Court's Medicaid ruling in *National Federation of Independent Business* may illustrate this finding. For although it was something of an inconvenient truth for those who had supported the passage of the Affordable Care Act in 2010, the Democratic majorities that had enabled the Act's passage vanished only a few months after President Obama signed it into existence. Given the choice between supporting Democratic congressional incumbents whose signature policy achievement over the previous two years had been the Affordable Care Act, and Republican challengers who promised to repeal "Obamacare," voters overwhelmingly chose the latter. The Democrats lost 63 seats in the House of Representatives, their largest seat loss in the House since the 1938 elections, and also lost their near-filibuster-proof majority in the Senate.

Of course, in all likelihood voters in the 2010 congressional elections knew very little about the specifics (or even the broad contours) of the Affordable Care Act. And there were many other factors at play in those elections, including an economy that stubbornly refused to recover from the 2008 financial crisis. Still, the consequence of those elections was that the House ended up in the control of a sizable majority of Republican incumbents committed to the repeal of the Affordable Care Act.

The results reported in this book suggest that this Republican House majority may have been instrumental to the Court's anti-Medicaid ruling in *National Federation of Independent Business*. Whether the justices are consciously aware of the Constitution's incentives or not, it appears to be the case that they systematically defer to the preferences of House majorities in their constitutional rulings on federal statutes. Their anti-Medicaid ruling in *National Federation* was at a minimum consistent with this pattern. By contrast, when the Court had upheld the use of federal highway monies to induce the states to adopt higher legal drinking ages in *South Dakota v. Dole* (1987), the House had been controlled by a liberal Democratic majority. Facing this liberal House majority, even conservative justices had found themselves willing to endorse an expansive federal spending authority.

The Court's apparent responsiveness to the preferences of House majorities implies that we, as voters, may ultimately bear a large part of the responsibility for the Court's rulings. Perhaps, instead of parsing the justices' motives so closely, we should be parsing our own.

Understanding the extent to which the Court defers to elected branch preferences, while intrinsically important as a purely descriptive matter, may also help us to better understand the consequences of that deference. Are we better or worse off because the Court appears to defer to the preferences of majorities in the House of Representatives? After all, most of us have been taught that independent courts are critical for the protection of individual rights and liberties. Perhaps we should be concerned that the Supreme Court (and presumably the lower federal courts it supervises) appears to be so lacking in independence.

On the other hand, most of us have also been taught that the protection of civil rights and liberties in the United States has been substantially due to our independent Supreme Court. But this proposition appears to be incorrect. If the Supreme Court is not independent of the elected branches, then it cannot be the case that rights protections in the United States have been, even in part, due to an independent Supreme Court. Instead, the rights protections that we enjoy, to the extent that they have been due to the actions of the Supreme Court, must have been the product of an apparently democratically accountable court.

And looking cross-nationally, right protections in the United States are relatively high. So perhaps the more general claim is also incorrect, namely that independent courts increase rights protections, relative to their more accountable counterparts. It turns out that, at least in the data analyzed here, this hunch appears to be supported by the evidence. As reported in this book's last chapter, democracies with more accountable courts have higher levels of economic and political rights than do those whose courts are less accountable (and more independent). Although this may seem surprising, perhaps it should not be. Around the world more democratic accountability generally means more public goods provision, across a range of policy domains (including that of economic and political rights). We should perhaps have expected the same to be true of courts, namely that more democratically accountable courts would produce more rights protections and other public goods than would their less accountable counterparts. We would likely have fewer protections for economic and political rights, and fewer public goods more generally, were our federal courts more independent from the elected branches. We are then fortunate that they are not.

For despite the Court's anti-Medicaid ruling in *National Federation of Independent Business*, when congressional majorities have retained their hold on public office after enacting important federal statutes, the Court generally has upheld those statutes. While the Democrats retained their congressional majorities during and after the New Deal and Great Society years, the Court upheld their most important policy achievements. The Wagner Act, the Social Security Act, Medicare, Medicaid, the Civil and Voting Rights Acts of 1964 and 1965, and many other important federal statutes were all upheld by the Court under the condition of sustained

Democratic congressional majorities. Had the Court been less responsive to congressional majorities, and more independent, it might well have been less deferential to these statutes.

That the Court was not similarly deferential to the Medicaid expansion contained in the Affordable Care Act was likely more our responsibility than it was the Court's. For whatever reasons, in the 2010 elections we conspicuously voted out the party whose members had provided the only votes for that Act, and voted in the party whose members had loudly opposed it. Had we instead expressed our support for congressional Democrats, we likely would be enjoying the full scope of the Act as written.

And yet, the findings reported in this book's final chapter also indicate that our apparently democratically accountable Supreme Court may not have an entirely benign effect on public policies providing rights protections and other public goods. Those findings suggest that, although democratically accountable courts produce more extensive rights protections than do their unaccountable counterparts, courts that are not permitted to exercise judicial review outperform them both. After all, even a court that is leashed by democratically elected majorities may sometimes take advantage of the slack in that leash. The Supreme Court's decision in *Citizens United v. Federal Election Commission*, 558 U.S. 50 (2010), for example, striking key provisions of the Bipartisan Campaign Finance Reform Act of 2002, was issued during the same congressional term that saw the enactment of the Affordable Care Act by an unusually large Democratic congressional majority. In the data analyzed here, *Citizens United* is one of the handful of cases that is not well predicted by the preferences of House majorities. To the extent that even democratically leashed courts can sometimes issue rulings that are at odds with the preferences of democratically elected majorities, protections for economic and political rights and other public goods may be fewer than if those rulings were simply prohibited.

But there may be another, more insidious, reason why the practice of judicial review, even as exercised by democratically accountable courts, may lead to fewer rights protections and other public goods. Courts cannot generally enact comprehensive public policies providing public goods, but they can veto them. So even democratically accountable courts may respond more to elected branch preferences to strike previously enacted policies, than to their preferences to see new policies enacted. In the case of the Supreme Court, for example, when majorities in the House of Representatives want to enact a policy, but fail to also win 60 votes in the Senate and/or the president's assent, the Court cannot respond by enacting that policy itself. But when majorities in the House of Representatives want to repeal a previously enacted policy, but fail to also win 60 votes in the Senate and/or the president's assent, a responsive Court can repeal the policy on its own.

Once again, the recent example of *National Federation of Independent Business* may illustrate this pattern. After the 2010 midterm elections, the newly ascendant Republican House majority immediately began efforts to repeal the Affordable Care Act. While bills implementing such a repeal repeatedly passed the House, they as repeatedly failed of passage in the still-Democratic Senate (not to mention failing to win support from still-President Obama). In the absence of judicial review, even the Republican victories in 2010 still would have failed to result in any reduction in the scope of the Affordable Care Act. But because of the presence of judicial review, even as exercised by an apparently democratically accountable court, an important component of the Act was eliminated.

In other words, judicial review in democracies, even when exercised by democratically accountable courts, may operate something like a one-way ratchet, disproportionately reducing public goods provision relative to that in comparable democracies not possessing the institution of judicial review. This ratchet effect may be most pronounced under institutional designs like that of the U.S. Constitution, which requires support in three separate elected branches in order for policies to be either enacted or repealed, but which incentivizes judicial deference to only one branch in particular. Under this constitution, the exercise of judicial review may offer to majorities in the House of Representatives a fast track enabling the repeal of previously enacted public goods. But there is no analogous fast track enabling the enactment of new public goods.

The findings reported here must be understood as provisional. As with any work of social science, they are limited to the specific data I have collected, and to my choices of measurement and specification. Even in my own limited data, I cannot precisely identify which causal mechanisms are driving the patterns I identify (to the extent that those patterns are real and not a product of my own choices). I can only suggest plausible mechanisms that are consistent with these patterns. Others may find alternative mechanisms more convincing (or may question the existence of the patterns in the first place).

But the findings reported here, provisional and limited as they may be, seem sufficient at least to prompt a reconsideration of both the existence and the value of independent courts exercising judicial review. Perhaps we have been mistaken in our belief that the Supreme Court of the United States is free to decide cases independently of elected branch preferences. More ominously, perhaps we have also been mistaken in our belief that independent courts exercising judicial review are even a good idea in the first place.

Perhaps, that is, Thomas Jefferson was wise to trust in the democratically elected legislator or lawgiver, rather than in the unaccountable judge. Jefferson advised in 1776, "Let mercy be the character of the law-giver, but let the judge be a mere machine." Perhaps somewhat like a "mere machine," our Supreme Court is systematically and predictably deferential to elected branch preferences, in particular to those of majorities in the House of Representatives. Perhaps we are better off as a result of this deference. But perhaps we would be better off still if we eliminated judicial review altogether.

During the many years I have been working on this book, I have incurred numerous debts. My colleagues at New York University, both in the Department of Politics and in the School of Law, have been enormously generous with their time and intellectual energy. I would particularly like to thank Jonathan Nagler, Pat Egan, Sandy Gordon, Michael Woodruff, Barry Friedman, Lewis Kornhauser, and John Ferejohn. Many colleagues at other institutions also offered advice, data, and opportunities to present the work as it evolved. My editor at Yale University Press, William Frucht, shepherded the manuscript through the publication process with skill and aplomb.

But I owe the largest debt to my family, whose understanding and encouragement enabled me to complete this project. My parents, Richard and Karen Harvey, have always been unwavering in their support, for which I have always been thankful. To Darwin, Riley, and Finn I am especially grateful. I could not have written this book without your help. I promise to try to make it up to you.

1

—

THE SUPREME COURT, CONGRESS, AND AMERICAN DEMOCRACY

Americans are routinely exhorted to take pride in their independent federal judiciary. Protected by life tenure and guaranteed salaries, federal judges in the United States are said to resolve disputes free from the political intimidation that exists in other, less fortunate, countries. The late Chief Justice William H. Rehnquist declared, for example, that "the performance of the judicial branch of the United States government for a period of nearly two hundred years has shown it to be remarkably independent of the other coordinate branches of that government," and that "the creation of an independent constitutional court" was "probably the most significant single contribution the United States has made to the art of government."[1] Retired Justice Sandra Day O'Connor has asserted that the "independent" federal judiciary in the United States is the "envy of the world."[2] Justice Stephen Breyer has written that "judicial independence . . . offers meaningful protection for the fundamental political rights that every American enjoys . . . that independence is a national treasure."[3]

Because of their independence, federal judges in the United States are said to be able to exercise a robust check on the elected branches, whose members are frequently tempted to undermine economic and political rights. Harvard University Professor of Law Cass Sunstein has written, for example, that the "insulation" of the federal judiciary has enabled federal judges successfully to pursue democracy's "internal morality, which constrains what a majority may do."[4] New York University Professor of Law Ronald Dworkin asserted that "the United States is a more just society than it would have been had its constitutional rights been left to the conscience of majoritarian institutions."[5] The American Bar Association has likewise claimed that "the longevity and continuing vitality of our Constitution is attributable in significant measure to an independent judiciary."[6] The nonprofit organization The Constitution Project has told us that, "were it not for an independent judiciary, America would be a very different place. Judges have acted courageously to make unpopular decisions throughout our history knowing that, to an extent, they would be protected by the federal or a state constitution. A wide array of constitutional and civil rights have been recognized and upheld only because of an independent judiciary."[7]

These claims have an impressive pedigree in the postwar years alone. Eugene Rostow wrote in 1952 of the benefits Americans derived from having "responsible and independent judges act as important constitutional mediators."[8] Robert McCloskey asserted in 1960 that without the benefit of the "longer view" provided by the "independent judiciary," "surely American democracy would be poorer."[9] Charles Black Jr. wrote in 1961 of the value of the Supreme Court's independence in protecting "the moral basis of democracy" from the "dominant majority."[10] Alexander Bickel wrote approvingly in 1962 of the Court's "insulation," characterizing the Court as "an institution which stands altogether aside from the current clash of interests, and which, insofar as is humanly possible, is concerned only with principle."[11] Philip Kurland wrote in 1970 of a Court that, because it was "essentially antidemocratic," could "protect the individual against the Leviathan of government and . . . protect minorities against oppression by majorities."[12]

A belief in the independence of the federal judiciary has not been limited to the legal academy. Social scientists have supported this belief with rigorous quantitative evidence. Numerous econometric studies of the Supreme Court have demonstrated, apparently conclusively, that the justices decide constitutional cases independently of elected branch preferences.[13] These quantitative studies have bolstered the arguments of those who have attributed an array of good outcomes to the apparent independence of the federal courts.

Many have looked beyond the context of the United States and asserted the superiority of independent courts as a general principle. Justice Stephen Breyer has written, for example, that, "without an independent judiciary . . . basic constitutional protections for the minority can become merely empty rhetoric."[14] Justice Anthony Kennedy has asserted that "if you believe in judicial independence, you believe in freedom."[15] Retired Justice Sandra Day O'Connor has instructed us that judges require independence from popular majorities so that they may "enforce the rule of law and protect individual freedoms."[16]

Naturally the justices prefer to be unconstrained in their decision making; as federal appellate judge Richard A. Posner has observed, "Judges are biased in favor of judicial autonomy."[17] But a belief in the general superiority of independent courts is widely shared. University of Michigan Professor of Law Steven P. Croley has written, for example, that "electoral independence goes far to safeguard constitutional rights from majoritarian encroachment."[18] University of California, Irvine, Professor of Law Erwin Chemerinsky has argued that only if a judiciary is "insulated from electoral politics" can it be "the proper institution for constitutional interpretation."[19] Northwestern University Professor of Law Martin Redish has claimed that, "absent an independent judiciary free from basic political pressures and influences, individual rights intended to be insulated from majoritarian interference would be threatened."[20] New York University Professor of Law Ronald Dworkin asserted that "the majority should not always be the final judge of when its own power should be limited to protect individual rights."[21] Dworkin's colleague New York University Professor of Law Burt Neuborne has claimed that judicial independence is a "safeguard against majoritarian tyranny" and "has proved superior to any alternative form of discharging the judicial function that has ever been tried or conceived."[22]

These claims have been endorsed by influential policy organizations. The United Nations has declared judicial independence to be a "Human Rights Priority," appointing a Special Rapporteur to focus on its promotion.[23] It is one of the policy goals of the U.S. Agency for International Development.[24] Its supporters include the League of Women Voters, the American Bar Association, the American Judicature Society, The Century Foundation, The Constitution Project, the National Center for State

Courts, the Committee for Economic Development, and the Brennan Center for Justice at the New York University School of Law. Funds for its promotion have been provided by the Open Society Institute and the Carnegie Corporation of New York.[25]

In recent years prominent development economists have joined the ranks of those who promote the benefits of independent courts. Drawing inspiration from Friedrich von Hayek, who asserted that only independent courts could restrain majorities bent on redistribution, they tout the ability of such courts to protect both economic and political rights from majoritarian threat, leading ultimately to increased economic development.[26] Their cross-national empirical studies, which assign the highest level of judicial independence both to the Supreme Court of the United States and to other courts operating under constitutional provisions like those of Article III, have confirmed that more independent courts are in fact associated with large increases in both economic and political rights.[27]

But Is Any of It True?

These claims are widely accepted. But it is unclear whether any of them are actually true. They rest on a chain of inferences based on the presumption that Article III guarantees the independence of the federal judiciary in the United States. The robust rights protections observed in that country are then thought to follow from, at least in part, the independence of its federal courts. Courts in other countries operating under constitutional provisions like those of Article III are likewise presumed to be independent of the policymaking branches in their countries. The high levels of rights protections observed in many of these countries are then thought to follow from the independence of their courts. Cross-national quantitative studies of judicial independence have adopted these presumptions.

But what if the premise is wrong? What if federal courts in the United States are not in fact independent of the elected branches? What if they are instead democratically accountable courts, courts that are incentivized to defer to the preferences of the majoritarian elected branches? If this is the case, then we may have made a series of grave inferential errors. We may have misattributed the robust rights protections found in the United States to independent federal courts, when those courts were not in fact independent. We may have incorrectly assumed that courts operating under constitutional provisions like those governing federal courts in the United States are also independent, when those provisions do not in fact produce judicial independence. And we may then have misattributed the high levels of rights protections found in many of these countries to independent courts, when those courts were not actually independent either.

This book interrogates the premise of an independent federal judiciary in the United States, focusing on the Supreme Court's constitutional rulings on federal statutes between 1953 and 2004. Its findings are perhaps surprising. At least in the sample of cases analyzed here, the justices do not appear to decide cases independently of elected branch preferences. Instead, they appear to be extraordinarily deferential to those preferences, in particular to the preferences of majorities in the House of Representatives. Any protections for individual rights secured by the Court in these cases must presumably have been a product not of their independence from elective majorities, but rather of their deference to those majorities.

By extension, any courts around the world operating under constitutional rules like those governing federal courts in the United States are likely to be similarly deferential to the policymaking branches in their countries. Empirical studies coding such courts as independent may then have reported dangerously misleading results. In fact, a cross-national analysis using a perhaps more appropriately coded measure of judicial independence, reported in this book's last chapter, indicates that in countries with democratic policymaking institutions, more independent courts actually *reduce* rights protections by substantively large amounts. If this analysis is correct, then we would likely have fewer protections for individual rights in the United States if our federal courts were more independent of the elected branches. We could possibly have even more robust rights protections than we currently enjoy, were we to eliminate judicial review altogether.

How Independent Are Our Federal Courts?

But why would we ever think that the federal courts in the United States are *not* independent of the elected branches? After all, as we are repeatedly instructed, Article III of the U.S. Constitution guarantees to

federal judges life tenure and salaries protected from elected branch manipulation. In his recent best-selling account of the Supreme Court, for
example, Jeffrey Toobin described the Court as "a fundamentally anti-
democratic institution," the justices' "life tenure" giving them "no reason to cater to the will of the people."[28] Legal academic Scott Gerber
likewise began his recent history of the idea of judicial independence in
the United States by simply assuming the independence of Article III
courts: "Of course, the federal Constitution drafted in 1787 made the
federal judiciary independent."[29] The textbook I use for my introductory
class in American politics at New York University similarly characterizes
the Supreme Court as "independent and powerful," the result of "constitutional guarantees of life tenure and stable salaries."[30]

But these claims, though often repeated, are simply incorrect. Article III does not in fact endow federal judges with "life tenure." Instead,
federal judges in the United States serve only on the condition of "good
Behaviour."[31] As we will see in greater detail in Chapter Two, some
have suggested that this constitutional provision empowers the elected
branches to enact procedures enabling the removal of federal judges for
"bad" behavior.[32] At a minimum we know that under the Impeachment
Clause, federal judges may be removed from the bench for "high Crimes
and Misdemeanors" by the joint action of a majority in the House and a
two-thirds majority in the Senate.[33]

Moreover, Article III does not in fact guarantee "stable salaries" for
federal judges. The Compensation Clause states merely that the justices
"shall, at stated Times, receive for their Services, a Compensation, which
shall not be diminished during their Continuance in Office."[34] This phrasing permits the justices' salaries to be decreased in real terms if either
House majorities, Senate majorities, or the president reject judicial salary
increases (unless two-thirds majorities in both congressional chambers
override the presidential veto in the last case).

Either or both of these constitutional provisions may incentivize the
justices to defer to elected branch preferences. Alexander Hamilton asserted as much when he wrote that the congressional impeachment
power, an "important constitutional check," provides a "complete security" against the danger that the justices might act as free agents: "There
never can be danger that the judges, by a series of deliberate usurpations

on the authority of the legislature, would hazard the united resentment of the body entrusted with it, while this body was possessed of the means of punishing their presumption by degrading them from their stations."[35] Hamilton also observed that it would be at the "discretion of the legislature" to increase the justices' salaries (or not), noting as well that "a power over a man's subsistence amounts to a power over his will."[36]

These constitutional provisions may induce particular judicial deference to the preferences of majorities in the House of Representatives. Impeachment, for example, is an unusual constitutional procedure in that it is explicitly sequential and does not require presidential assent. Article I, Section 2 gives to the House the "sole" power to initiate potentially embarrassing impeachment investigations of the justices. There are no formal constraints on how House majorities may interpret the constitutional standard for impeachment, nor limits on their powers to investigate justices suspected of having violated it.[37] House majorities are consequently not prohibited from going on fishing expeditions targeted at justices with divergent preferences. These fishing expeditions may reveal judicial improprieties sufficiently serious to increase the likelihood that even friendly Senate majorities vote for conviction. Conversely, even hostile Senate majorities cannot initiate impeachment proceedings against a justice in the absence of support in the House. The agenda setting power of the House in the impeachment process may then give the justices powerful incentives to defer to the preferences of House majorities.

The Origination Clause likewise gives the House a particularly important role in initiating appropriations bills that may provide for judicial salary increases.[38] While a Senate majority can block such a bill, and while the president can use his veto power to increase the size of the congressional majorities required to pass such a bill, it is the prerogative of the House to initiate appropriations bills. The justices may then have particular incentives to defer to the preferences of House majorities in order to facilitate the introduction of bills increasing judicial salaries.

These potential incentives to defer to elected branch preferences are possibly reinforced by multiple other constitutional provisions. The elected branches allocate the budgets for the federal courts under the Article I appropriations power; House majorities again have a particularly prominent role in proposing appropriations bills under the Origination

Clause. To the extent that federal judges prefer larger budgets in order to maintain and renovate the physical spaces housing their courts, to hire more and better-quality staff members, including the law clerks who can significantly reduce judges' workloads, and to purchase upgraded technology on a regular basis, the appropriations power gives elected branch majorities, particularly majorities in the House of Representatives, yet another tool to induce judicial deference to elected branch preferences.

The jurisdiction of the federal courts is likewise subject to the discretion of elected branch majorities. Article III specifies only a very limited original jurisdiction for the Supreme Court; all other federal jurisdiction is granted to the federal courts only "with such Exceptions, and under such Regulations as the Congress shall make."[39] To the extent that federal judges prefer more to less power, the ability of elected branch majorities to strip them of their ability to decide cases may also induce judicial deference to elected branch preferences. Article III similarly does not specify the size of the Supreme Court, implying that elective majorities may add and/or subtract seats on the Court at will. Because this power gives to the elected branches the ability to convert intransigent majorities on the Court into vulnerable minorities, justices who prefer majority to minority status will have incentives to defer to the preferences of elected branch majorities. Finally, all "inferior" federal courts exist only "as the Congress may from time to time ordain and establish."[40] The power to simply eliminate existing federal courts gives elected branch majorities another means beyond impeachment to remove lower federal judges from office. In short, the U.S. Constitution provides many different means by which elected branch majorities, perhaps particularly majorities in the House of Representatives, may be able to induce judicial deference to elected branch preferences.

Some may object that any interpretation of these constitutional provisions permitting elected branch majorities to compel judicial deference to elected branch preferences violates the original intent of the framers of the Constitution. These men, many assert, believed in the principle of judicial independence. Legal academic Scott Gerber, for example, characterizes John Adams's 1776 pamphlet, *Thoughts on Government*, as "the final step in the political theory of an independent judiciary eventually embodied in Article III."[41] The historically correct interpretation of these constitutional provisions would prohibit elected branch majorities from using them to intimidate federal judges.

Of course, it is not at all clear that elected branch majorities are in any way restrained by what political elites may or may not have believed over two hundred years ago. But, as will be discussed at greater length in Chapter Two, it is also not clear that the objection is even correct. One of the grievances of the colonial assemblies during the pre-Revolutionary years was precisely their lack of influence over royally appointed judges. These judges typically served at the pleasure of the Crown or its agents, and were widely suspected of deference to royal preferences as a result. Good behavior tenure, which protected judges from removal at the Crown's pleasure, was long pursued by colonial reformers, as it had been by earlier parliamentary reformers, as a way to reduce this perceived judicial deference to antimajoritarian royal preferences. But good behavior tenure, in both Britain and North America, did not protect judges from removal by majoritarian legislatures. Instead, good behavior tenure was seen as a complement to legislative powers of impeachment or address, powers enabling legislative majorities to remove judges from office for only vaguely defined offenses. Just as "at pleasure" tenure was thought to induce judicial deference to royal preferences, the combination of good behavior tenure and legislative removal powers was widely thought to induce judicial deference to legislative preferences. Recall Hamilton's assertion that the Good Behavior and Impeachment Clauses of the U.S. Constitution would provide a "complete security" against the threat of antimajoritarian judges.[42]

Indeed, a Constitution that provides for democratically accountable judges seems much more consistent with the writings of the framers than one that does not. These men generally distrusted unaccountable, "independent" power. James Madison in fact warned in Federalist 51 that, from a misguided desire to secure individual rights, societies might be tempted to create "a will in the community independent of the majority."[43] "This, at best, is but a precarious security," he wrote, "because a power independent of the society may as well espouse the unjust views of the major as the rightful interests of the minor party, and may possibly be turned against both parties."[44] Thomas Jefferson had earlier written in 1776 that judicial decision making uncabined by majoritarian preferences would give free rein to "the eccentric impulses of whimsical, capricious designing man." But judicial deference to majoritarian legislatures would instead ensure that "the mercies of the law will be dispensed equally and impartially to every description of men."[45] John Adams had likewise declared in *Thoughts on Government* that, just as the judicial power should serve as a check upon the legislative and executive powers, so "both should be checks upon that."[46] To that end Adams had endorsed the legislative impeachment power as a means to remove appointed judges, and in his draft of the 1780 Massachusetts Constitution specified not only the power of impeachment, but also the power of legislative majorities to request judicial removal at will (legislative address).[47] Although some high Federalists had a more favorable opinion of independent courts, it is not at all clear that their views were widely shared.

Others may object that, even if some (if not most) of the framers intended that the federal courts would be policed by the elected branches, the design of those branches makes such policing very difficult. The House, the Senate, and the presidency were designed to represent different electoral constituencies, on different clocks, with different degrees of responsiveness to the preferences of those constituencies. By design, the preferences represented in these three institutions are rarely perfectly aligned. Yet the Constitution requires that majorities in both congressional chambers, as well as the president, agree on statutory policy changes. The sheer difficulty of coordinating cross-institutional agreements to police federal judges via statutory means may liberate those judges to act as de facto free agents.

But as already noted, the elected branches do not have to enact statutes in order to police federal judges. Impeachment, for example, does not require statutory action. Given the power of the House to investigate and publicize previously hidden judicial improprieties through the impeachment process, it may require only a determined House majority in order to effectively cabin judicial discretion. In the case of judicial salaries, the elected branches may be able to cabin judicial discretion simply by doing nothing, given the ongoing real deterioration in those salaries in the absence of affirmative elected branch action. The onus may instead be on federal judges to convince elected branch majorities, perhaps at least in part through their rulings, that they are deserving of salary increases. And just as in the case of impeachment, federal judges may be particularly solicitous of House majorities in order to get judicial salary and budget increases on the appropriations agenda.

Yet others may object that judicial and elected branch preferences should only rarely be out of alignment, given that federal judges are selected by the joint action of the president and Senate majorities. If this is case, then the question of whether the Constitution incentivizes judicial deference to elected branch preferences is largely moot; that question should only arise when judicial preferences diverge from those of the members of the elected branches.

However, there is considerably more turnover in the elected branches than there is on the federal bench. Incoming electoral majorities can easily find the federal bench stacked with opposing party judges possessing divergent preferences. Moreover, if federal judges have particular incentives to defer to the preferences of House majorities, rather than to those of Senate majorities or the president, then the objection loses even more of its force. Federal judges appointed by presidents and confirmed by Senate majorities will not necessarily mirror the preferences of House majorities. In fact, as we will see in Chapter Three, modern estimates of judicial and elected branch preferences reveal periods of quite striking divergence between the preferences of Supreme Court justices and those of majorities in the House of Representatives. One such period occurred in the 1980s and early 1990s, as the Court grew increasingly more conservative after repeated appointments by Republican presidents, while House majorities grew increasingly liberal. These estimates suggest that the question of federal judicial deference or independence is not in fact mooted by the argument from judicial preferences.

But others will argue that we only rarely see the elected branches attempting to cabin the justices' decisions. No justice has been impeached, for example, since the impeachment of Justice Samuel Chase in 1805. The absence of explicit elected branch attempts to discipline the justices, it is argued, indicates that elected branch majorities must reject the appropriateness of such attempts. Even if judicial independence was not embraced by the framers of the Constitution, it is a principle that has come to be endorsed by successive elected branch majorities over time.[48]

But the evidence in support of this argument is not entirely persuasive. The fact that the elected branches rarely exercise their powers to check the federal courts does not imply that elected branch majorities

are unwilling to use those powers, if necessary. Maybe the mere existence of the Constitution's checks on the federal judiciary is sufficient
to induce judicial deference to elected branch preferences. Parliamentary and colonial reformers evidently believed that the Crown's power to
remove judges from office during the pre-Revolutionary years induced
judicial deference to royal preferences, even if the actual instances of removal were rare. Again, recall Hamilton's prediction that "there never
can be danger that the judges, by a series of deliberate usurpations on
the authority of the legislature, would hazard the united resentment of
the body entrusted with it, while this body was possessed of the means
of punishing their presumption by degrading them from their stations."[49]
Maybe Hamilton was right. Maybe precisely because the mere existence
of the Constitution's checks on the judiciary are so effective, they are only
infrequently used. And maybe we have incorrectly inferred that, because
the elected branches only rarely exercise their powers to discipline federal
judges, those judges must be free to decide cases independently of elected
branch preferences.

At this point some may object that there exist numerous econometric studies of the Supreme Court demonstrating that the justices do not
in fact defer to elected branch preferences in their constitutional judgments.[50] These studies have virtually all led to the conclusion that the
tools possessed by the elected branches to ensure the Court's deference
do not in fact produce that outcome. As we will see in Chapter Three,
replicating the design of these studies, it is true that there is no evidence
of judicial deference to elected branch preferences between 1953 and
2004, the period spanning the Warren, Burger, and Rehnquist Courts. It
is perhaps particularly damning that we can find no evidence of such deference during the Rehnquist Court terms, when a relatively stable conservative majority on the Court faced first a series of liberal Democratic
Congresses, and then, after the 1994 congressional elections, a series of
conservative Republican Congresses. Because of this variation in congressional preferences, while judicial preferences remained relatively constant,
these terms present a near ideal opportunity to test the hypothesis of the
Court's responsiveness to congressional preferences. And during these
terms the Court is clearly unresponsive to those preferences. Small wonder that most social scientists who study the Court have concluded that,

even if the Court was designed to be a democratically accountable institution de jure, it has turned out to be an unaccountable institution de facto.

But, strangely, these quantitative findings about the Rehnquist Court do not jibe with what close observers of that Court reported. As we will see in Chapter Four, those who read the Rehnquist Court's opinions and followed its doctrinal evolution saw a very different Court from the one portrayed in the quantitative literature. They saw a Court whose jurisprudence was oddly moderate, even liberal, during its first eight terms, from the 1986 through the 1993 terms. Then, in the second half of the 1994 term, something happened. Nobody really knew what. But quite suddenly observers witnessed a Court that was jettisoning decades of constitutional jurisprudence in favor of radically more conservative doctrines. Many divided the Rehnquist Court into two eras: the "first" Rehnquist Court of the 1986 through the 1993 terms and the "second" Rehnquist Court from the 1994 through the 2004 terms. But virtually nobody suggested that the 1994 congressional elections might have been responsible for this sudden change in the Court's behavior.[51]

These two very different portraits of the Rehnquist Court indicate that we should perhaps take a second look at the quantitative studies of the Supreme Court's independence. Chapter Five explores one difficulty worth a second look, namely the subjectively coded measure of the Court's judgments used in nearly all the quantitative studies of the Court's decision making. Subjectively coded measures are susceptible to contamination from coders' prior expectations. In particular, in the context of widespread beliefs in the Court's independence, we might see subjectively coded judgment measures reflecting coders' expectations about the kinds of judgments that might generally issue from more liberal and more conservative courts, *under the assumption of independence from elected branch preferences.* These measures might then understate the magnitude of the Court's deference to those preferences.

It turns out that the judgment measure used in virtually all quantitative studies of the Court's independence, a measure that subjectively codes a judgment as either "liberal" or "conservative," does in fact appear to incorporate expectations about the kinds of judgments typically issued by liberal or conservative courts—under the hypothesis of judicial independence. This measure, reported in the United States Supreme

Court Database, considerably understates the effects of elected branch preferences on the Court's judgments, relative to objectively coded judgment measures. Using several different objectively coded measures of the Court's judgments in cases involving constitutional challenges to federal statutes, we in fact observe considerable judicial deference to elected branch preferences from the Warren through the Rehnquist Courts.

More specifically, the justices' decisions throughout this period are strongly and consistently responsive to changes in the preferences of majorities in the House of Representatives. However, they are largely unresponsive to changes in the preferences of majorities in the Senate or the president. The specificity of the justices' deference is striking, suggesting that they respond to the specific constitutional provisions giving the House of Representatives an agenda-setting role in the impeachment and appropriations processes, rather than to more general political trends.

The deference of the Court to House majorities is particularly evident during the early Rehnquist Court terms, when the conservative majority on the Court faced liberal Democratic majorities in the House. Using the objectively constructed judgment measure for which we have the most observations, and controlling for both judicial and other elected branch preferences, as well as for several case-specific covariates, between its 1986 and 1993 terms the Rehnquist Court is predicted to issue conservative judgments in cases involving constitutional challenges to federal statutes with an average probability of only .13. But had the justices instead faced House majorities with preferences identical to their own, the average predicted probability of a conservative judgment during these terms rises to .62. The differences between these two sets of predicted probabilities are significant in each term at conventional levels of statistical significance.[52]

The effect of House majorities on the Rehnquist Court then largely disappears after the 1994 congressional elections, as a result of this chamber's rightward shift toward the most preferred rule of the median justice. Between the 1994 and 2004 terms, the average predicted probability of a conservative judgment by the Rehnquist Court remains at .62; the only slightly less conservative preferences of the Republican House majorities facing the Court during these terms have no effect on the Court's judgments. However, had the House during these terms remained as liberal as it had been during the 103d Congress, the last liberal Democratic

Congress before the 1994 elections, the average predicted probability of a conservative judgment decreases to .15. Again, the differences between these two sets of predicted probabilities are significant at conventional thresholds in each term between 1994 and 2004.

These estimates, which are robust to alternative measurement and specification strategies, suggest that observers' impressions of "two" Rehnquist Courts were not unfounded. There does indeed appear to have been a "first" Rehnquist Court that was relatively liberal through the 1993 term, and a "second" Rehnquist Court that moved sharply to the right in the 1994 term. The estimates reported in Chapter Five also indicate that this rightward shift in the Rehnquist Court's jurisprudence was most likely the product of a shift in the preferences of House majorities. This Court likely would have been considerably more conservative between 1986 and 1993, had it not deferred to more liberal congressional preferences. And had the Congress not shifted rightward in the 1994 elections, the Court's rulings likely would not have shifted rightward either.

The estimates reported in Chapter Five can also be used to interrogate one of the more prominent claims made about the second Rehnquist Court, namely that it was the product of an apparently newfound interest by the conservative majority in federalism or states' rights. Presumably, if the federalism interpretation were correct, the Rehnquist Court would have been equally likely to strike both liberal and conservative federal statutes. All federal statutes should have been similarly at risk during the second Rehnquist Court, as the justices sought to free state governments from burdensome federal regulations.

But this is not what we observe. Federal statutes enacted by the unified Republican Congresses sitting between 1995 and 2004 were significantly less likely to be struck by the second Rehnquist Court, relative to statutes enacted by unified Democratic Congresses, even controlling for statute age. While the average predicted probability that a liberal federal statute would be struck by the second Rehnquist Court was .62 between 1994 and 2004, the predicted probability that this Court would strike a conservative federal statute ranged between only .36 and .39. These predicted probabilities, which are distinct in each term at conventional thresholds, suggest that the federalism explanation for the second Rehnquist Court does not hold much water. That Court had few problems with federal statutes enacted by conservative Republican Congresses. It was only statutes enacted by liberal Democratic Congresses that the Court found objectionable.

The estimates reported in Chapter Five also permit us to make counterfactual predictions for periods when the preferences of majorities on the Court and in the House did not diverge as much as they did in the 1980s and early 1990s. For most of the Warren and Burger Court terms, for example, the preferences of the median justice and the median representative diverged only slightly. The liberal Warren Court justices faced relatively liberal Democratic House majorities during all but that Court's first term. While these House majorities are estimated to have had somewhat less liberal preferences than the majority on the Court, the magnitude of the resulting conservative constraint on the Court is nonetheless relatively small, particularly after the 1964 congressional elections. The Burger Court majority, which remained moderately liberal until the early 1980s, likewise faced Democratic House majorities during all of that Court's terms. These House majorities are estimated to have been slightly less liberal than the Court's majority until the 1974 congressional elections, and then slightly more liberal than the Court's majority through the remaining Burger Court terms. But again, the magnitude of the constraint thereby influencing the Court's judgments remains relatively small until the early 1980s.[53]

But had the preferences of House majorities diverged more significantly from those on the Court during these terms, the Court's rulings might well have looked quite different. Had the liberal Warren Court justices faced Republican House majorities with preferences as conservative as those of the 104th House majority, the majority elected in the 1994 elections, in every term they are predicted to be most likely to issue conservative judgments in cases involving constitutional challenges to federal statutes.[54] The Warren Court was then perhaps not the "independent and aggressive guarantor of constitutional rights" it has been widely reputed to be, including recently in Jeffrey Toobin's *The Nine*.[55] Rather, the Warren Court's liberalism appears to have been enabled by generally liberal Democratic House majorities. Had those majorities instead been relatively conservative, it is unlikely that the Warren Court justices could have sustained their preferred liberal course.

Likewise, during the 1970s the moderate liberalism of the Burger Court appears to have been contingent on the liberalism of the House of Representatives. Had the Burger Court between the 1969 and 1979 terms faced a House majority as conservative as that of the 104th House, the probability that it would issue conservative rulings in cases involving constitutional challenges to federal statutes is predicted to not fall below .50 in any term. Many liberal federal statutes would have been at risk during these terms under this counterfactual condition. But because the Burger Court instead faced liberal Democratic House majorities during these terms, these statutes were most likely to be upheld.[56]

These findings would seem to provide fairly compelling evidence of the Court's deference to elected branch preferences. But some may suspect that these results are being driven not by the justices' deference to elected branch preferences, but rather by their deference to public opinion. Perhaps the justices care most not about their own survival in office, nor about their salaries or budgets, but rather about compliance with their decisions. Lacking the power to enforce their rulings, they may tailor their decisions to come as close as possible to their most preferred decisions, while yet inducing widespread voluntary compliance. In this case we should expect a direct, unmediated relationship between public opinion and the Court's decisions. Because elected branch preferences are at least partially correlated with public opinion, the findings reported here may simply be a spurious result of that correlation.

Others may wonder whether even public opinion trends might mask the real influences on the Court's judgments. Perhaps the justices respond directly to the economic, social and policy trends that appear to drive movement in public opinion over time. If this is the case, then the correlations between these more fundamental socioeconomic forces, public opinion, and elected branch preferences might result in spurious associations between both public opinion and elected branch preferences and the Court's judgments.

These possible alternative explanations are hard to square with the specificity of the Court's deference. The justices appear to defer only to the preferences of majorities in the House of Representatives, not to those of Senate majorities or the president. This is the case even though, over the period examined here, the estimated preferences of both Senate majorities and the president are more closely linked to public opinion (and thereby also to the factors that drive public opinion) than are those of House majorities. If the justices were simply responding to general trends in public opinion or socioeconomic indicators, we would have no reason to expect them to defer more to the House than to the Senate or the president. The fact that the justices do appear to be more sensitive to the preferences of House majorities would seem to indicate that they are responding to the specific incentives created by the Constitution, rather than to broad currents in public opinion or socioeconomic indicators.

Nonetheless, Chapter Six reports the results of several tests of these alternative hypotheses, employing the most widely used index of public opinion as well as measures of the socioeconomic factors most consistently associated with that index. In both case-based and time-series analyses there is no evidence that any of the findings reported in Chapter Five are simply the spurious results of more fundamental associations between the Court's judgments and public opinion, unemployment, inflation, the homicide rate, federal military spending, or the overall liberalism of federal public policy. In fact, none of these alternative causal factors have any consistent association with the Court's rulings in cases involving constitutional challenges to federal statutes, regardless of the specification used. While it may still be the case that our measurements of these alternative factors are flawed, or that there remain some unidentified factors that are "really" driving the apparent association between the preferences of House majorities and the Court's judgments, the currently available data do not support any of the plausible alternative explanations.

The findings of judicial deference reported in Chapters Five and Six are enabled by the use of objective measures of the Court's judgments, measures free from possible contamination by expectations of the Court's independence. But there is another way in which these expectations may have affected analyses of the Court's decision making, including even the analyses reported here. The standard practice in the empirical literature, a practice followed in Chapters Five and Six, is to estimate the Court's deference to elected branch preferences using only the sample of cases selected by the justices for review. But this sample is not likely to be a random sample of the population of disputes that the justices could have reviewed. If the Court is indeed constrained by elected branch preferences in its final rulings, then its selection of cases may likewise be constrained by those preferences. When the Court faces a hostile House majority with preferences distant from its own, for example, the justices may choose not to take cases wherein they would likely be compelled to endorse outcomes far from their own most preferred outcomes. Of particular relevance for the empirical analyses reported in Chapters Five and Six, a conservative Court majority confronting a population of recently enacted liberal federal statutes may choose not to hear challenges to those statutes while a liberal Democratic majority retains control of the House of Representatives. Moreover, litigants anticipating the Court's decisions may not even bring such challenges to the Court in the first place, given the likelihood that the Court will either decline to hear these challenges or uphold the challenged statutes.

During periods of significant divergence between the preferences of House majorities and majorities on the Court, then, the Court may have a substantial "missing" docket, a docket that we don't observe. And the cases missing from the Court's docket during these terms may undermine our ability to accurately estimate the effect of House majorities on the Court's judgments. We may end up underestimating this effect, perhaps even concluding that no such effect exists, simply because we have too few relevant cases in our sample from terms wherein the Court faced hostile House majorities.

Using a known population of potential cases, however, we can attempt to address this problem of selection bias in the Court's docket. Chapter Seven reports the results of such an analysis, using the population of all "landmark" federal statutes enacted between 1987 and 2002, and available for review by the Rehnquist Court between 1987 and 2004.[57] This analysis consists first of estimating the probability that constitutional challenges to liberal landmark statutes enacted between 1987 and 1994 make it onto the Rehnquist Court's docket in each term, as a function of both judicial and elected branch preferences, controlling for statute age. It is then possible to estimate the number of such challenges that the Rehnquist Court would have heard in each term, had it not faced elected branch constraint.

It turns out that the early Rehnquist Court's docket was very responsive to the preferences of liberal majorities in the House of Representatives, although not to those of majorities in the Senate or the president.

In fact, the estimates from this analysis indicate that the first Rehnquist Court's docket of constitutional challenges to liberal landmark statutes was reduced by approximately 93 percent between its 1987 and 1993 terms, relative to the docket we would have observed had this Court not faced liberal House majorities. Between its 1994 and 2004 terms, however, the presence of conservative Republican House majorities freed the Court's docket from any elected branch constraint.

The problems created by this selection bias in the early Rehnquist Court's docket are clear when we look at the Rehnquist Court's dispositions of constitutional challenges to landmark federal statutes enacted between 1987 and 2002. When we estimate the effect of elected branch preferences on these dispositions, using only the sample of challenges actually docketed by the Court, we find no evidence that any such effect exists. This result mirrors the many null findings for the effect of elected branch preferences on the Court's constitutional decisions, reported in the existing empirical literature.

However, our estimates indicate that the Rehnquist Court's docket of challenges to liberal landmark statutes was reduced by approximately 93 percent during the terms wherein it faced liberal House majorities. We can simulate what the Court's likely dispositions would have been in these "missing" cases by again resorting to the full population of landmark statutes enacted between 1987 and 2002. We first estimate the probability that any given statute in this population will be struck by the Rehnquist Court in any given term, as a function of both judicial and elected branch preferences, again controlling for statute age. These population-based estimates are unaffected by the evident selection bias in the Court's docket. Aggregating over the terms wherein the Rehnquist Court faced liberal House majorities, these estimates tell us approximately how many statutes the Court would have struck during these terms, had there been no selection bias in its docket. We can then apply these estimates to the statutes "missing" from the Court's docket.

We can in this way attempt to "restore" the Rehnquist Court's missing docket of constitutional challenges to liberal landmark statutes between its 1987 and 1993 terms. When we do so, we find that the preferences of House majorities in fact have a large effect on this "restored" docket: holding all other variables constant, the average predicted probability that one of the liberal landmark statutes on the Rehnquist Court's "restored" docket will be struck is only .20 between the 1987 and 1993 terms, but rises to .89 between the 1994 and 2004 terms, solely as a function of the changed preferences of the median member of the House of Representatives. Meanwhile, the probability that one of the docketed conservative landmark statutes will be struck between the 1995 and 2004 terms averages only .25.

In short, null results for the hypothesis of judicial deference to elected branch preferences may simply be the result of selection bias in the Court's docket. More generally, the estimated effects of elected branch preferences on the Court's judgments in its docketed cases likely understate the magnitude of those effects. Only by correcting for the selection bias in the Court's docket might we be able to get accurate estimates of the extent of the justices' deference to elected branch preferences.

Finally, some may object that the findings reported here, estimated using samples of cases from the Warren, Burger and Rehnquist Courts, may not apply to the current Supreme Court, led by Chief Justice John Roberts. This court, some say, is qualitatively different from its predecessors. It is more extreme, more ideological, more aggressive, and perhaps less likely to defer to elected branch preferences than were previous courts. Perhaps the constitutional sanctions designed by the framers to cabin the Supreme Court will not work on the Roberts Court.[58]

But these speculations are not supported when we look at the constitutional challenges to federal statutes heard by the Roberts Court during its first four full terms, all terms wherein it faced liberal Democratic majorities in the House of Representatives. As reported in Chapter Eight, like the Rehnquist Court when it faced an oppositional House, the Roberts Court heard few of these challenges. In its first four full terms it heard only about half the number of constitutional challenges to federal statutes heard during an equivalent number of terms by the post-1993 Rehnquist Court. Moreover, despite the fact that the preferences of its median justice had clearly shifted to the right, relative to those of the Rehnquist Court median, the Roberts Court was particularly deferential to liberal federal statutes. It heard only 42 percent of the number of constitutional challenges to liberal statutes heard by the second Rehnquist Court during the equivalent number of terms. Finally, the Roberts Court struck only

40 percent of the number of liberal federal statutes struck by the post-1993 Rehnquist Court during the equivalent number of terms. These differences are all significant at conventional thresholds. At least for this population of cases, the Roberts Court was not the ultra-conservative court it had been expected to be. And it was not evidently less deferential to elected branch preferences than had been previous courts.

These findings would seem to suggest that the Supreme Court of the United States is not the exemplar of judicial independence it has been reputed to be. To the extent that this court is the "envy of the world," in the words of former Justice O'Connor, it should perhaps serve as an example of the merits of a democratically accountable court, one that is incentivized to defer to the majoritarian elected branches.

There are, of course, limitations to the findings reported here. For example, many prominent decisions made by the Court, including those involving constitutional review of state and local actions, lie outside the samples of cases analyzed here. We have no estimates of the effects of elected branch preferences on the Court's rulings in these cases. Several of these cases, generally involving constitutional rulings by the Warren Court on state and local actions, are frequently cited as evidence of the Court's independence. Ronald Dworkin, for example, cited *Brown v. Board of Education of Topeka*, 349 U.S. 294 (1954), and *Griswold v. Connecticut*, 381 U.S. 479 (1965), as "shining examples" of the Court's independence.[59] Justice Stephen Breyer points to *Cooper v. Aaron*, 358 U.S. 1 (1958), as an example of an "unpopular" decision that could only have been made by an independent court.[60] It is possible that our estimates of the Court's deference to elected branch preferences do not generalize to such cases.

But although it is possible, it is perhaps not very probable. The elected branch powers to discipline and reward the justices are not limited to cases involving constitutional rulings on federal statutes. These cases are used here simply because they present easily measurable outcomes. But we have no obvious reason to think that the judicial deference to elected branch preferences reported here is limited to these cases.

Of course, low salience cases that elected branch majorities don't care about likely won't result in elected branch sanctions or rewards, no matter what the Court decides. But the cases frequently cited as evidence of the Court's independence would be hard to characterize in these terms. Instead, these cases drew significant national attention and had national policy impacts. They probably generated more attention than did many cases involving the constitutional review of federal statutes. It is difficult to imagine that the Court would have deferred to elected branch preferences in the latter cases, but not in the former. Nonetheless, there is no direct evidence of such deference reported here.

The evidence reported here also does not include any decisions from "inferior" federal courts, those established by federal statute. The judges sitting on these courts are subject to the same constitutional sanctions as are the justices of the Supreme Court. In fact, they are subject to an additional sanction to which the justices are not, namely the power of elected branch majorities to dissolve their courts. Their decisions, moreover, may be appealed to the Supreme Court and thereby modified or even overruled by justices apparently deferential to elected branch preferences, as least in cases involving federal judicial review. We have no evident reason to suspect that the constitutional sanctions available to elected branch majorities would induce deference among the justices of the Supreme Court, but not among the judges of the inferior federal bench. But again, no direct evidence of such deference will be reported here.

Finally, the period analyzed here is limited to the modern Supreme Court between its 1953 and 2004 terms. This period includes the entire Warren, Burger, and Rehnquist Courts, with a partial analysis of the early Roberts Court. Many consequential jurisprudential developments occurred over this fifty-year span. Still, we may wonder whether the justices' apparent deference to elected branch preferences over this period generalizes to earlier Courts. Future research may be able to address this question.

What's So Great About Independent Courts, Anyway?

That the modern Supreme Court of the United States appears to defer to majorities in the House of Representatives in cases involving federal judicial review does not necessarily tell us whether such deference is a good or a bad thing. But the fact of that deference does seem to undermine the claim that the relatively high levels of rights protections observed in the United States are a product of independent federal courts. Instead, the findings reported here suggest that when rights have been protected by federal courts in the United States, it has been because House majorities have supported their protection. As reported in Chapters Five and Six, for example, the Warren Court's famous rulings endorsing the landmark federal civil rights statutes of the 1960s appear to have been conditional on the support of liberal Democratic majorities in the House of Representatives.[61] The same can be said for the Burger Court's rulings endorsing extensions to those statutes enacted during the 1970s.[62] Moreover, there have been long stretches when, had the Court been left to its own devices, civil rights and liberties likely would have been considerably less protected. During the early Rehnquist Court terms, for example, the conservative majority on the Court was demonstrably hostile to federal statutes enacted by liberal Democratic Congresses, including the Civil Rights Act of 1964, the Voting Rights Act of 1965, and later amendments reinforcing and extending the protections contained in those statutes. But these statutes appear to have been protected from the Court by the presence of liberal House majorities possessed of the power to discipline the justices, should they attempt to act as free agents. During these terms, civil rights and liberties likely would have been *less* protected had the Court been more independent of House majorities.

Some may object that cross-national empirical studies have reported evidence that more independent courts in fact increase civil rights and liberties.[63] Perhaps, despite the findings reported here, we would see even more extensive rights protections in the United States were our federal courts made truly independent of elected branch majorities.

But existing cross-national studies of judicial independence are not entirely persuasive. In perhaps the most prominent of these studies, courts are coded largely by the length of their judges' tenures; longer tenures are thought to lead to greater independence from the policymaking branches. Constitutional provisions enabling elected branch majorities to remove judges from office and/or to adjust judicial salaries are dismissed as irrelevant. The justices of the Supreme Court of the United States, for example, are coded in these studies as possessing "life tenure," and thus as enjoying the highest level of independence from the policymaking branches. The constitutional provisions enabling the elected branches both to remove the justices from the bench and to control their salaries are not incorporated into the tenure-based measure of judicial independence.[64]

But the evidence reported here suggests that they should be. The constitutional provisions enabling House majorities to initiate both impeachment proceedings and bills proposing judicial salary increases appear to have large effects on that court's decisions. By implication, we should expect that other constitutions enabling policymaking branches to control either judicial removal or judicial salaries (or both) likewise induce considerable judicial deference to policymakers' preferences.

Perhaps, then, existing cross-national studies of judicial independence have miscoded many constitutions. Assuming that the U.S. Constitution guarantees independence to its federal courts, researchers have dismissed the provisions of that constitution incentivizing judicial deference to elected branch majorities. They then have dismissed similar provisions found in other constitutions, assuming that the judges operating under these constitutions are likewise free to decide cases independently of the policymaking branches. High levels of rights protections have been attributed to what were thought to be independent courts, when those courts were perhaps in fact accountable, deferential courts.

If it turns out to be the case that it is in fact accountable courts that increase rights protections, rather than independent courts, we should perhaps not be too surprised. It is actually difficult to understand the logic by which independent courts are thought to provide rights protections superior to those provided by electoral majorities. After all, political leaders who are held accountable to such majorities provide significantly higher levels of civil rights and liberties than do their more "independent" counterparts. For example, the nonprofit organization Freedom House has rated the levels of civil liberties and political rights found in about 140 countries since 1972. Even after controlling for other factors that might affect the provision of these rights and liberties, moving from the least to the most democratic policymaking institutions increases both civil liberties and political rights from 4 to 6 points on the 7-point Freedom House scales.[65]

These increases in rights protections are apparently made possible by political institutions that compel the holders of public office regularly to seek the approval of electoral majorities. Far from being a threat to economic and political rights, such majorities generally prefer more robust rights protections. In the words of political scientist Bruce Bueno de Mesquita and his colleagues, "Whatever else is found in the basket of public goods provided by government, the benefits of civil liberties [and] political rights . . . seem to be of universal desirability among residents of a state."[66] By contrast, when political leaders are not held accountable to electoral majorities, we find few protections for economic and political rights. The fewer supporters a political leader requires in order to survive in office, the less extensive are the rights protections provided to that country's citizens.

What then is the mechanism by which unaccountable, independent judges are thought to be incentivized to provide rights protections superior to those provided by judges accountable to electoral majorities? Those who advocate judicial independence rarely address judicial incentives, or explain why they believe that unaccountable judges can be trusted to protect individual rights and liberties. Some appear to assume that judges are simply immune from the need to be incentivized into good behavior, or that judges are somehow intrinsically different from other holders of public office. In the words of constitutional theorist Alexander Bickel, independence from the elected branches permits judges to "follow the ways of the scholar" and to "appeal to men's better natures, to call forth their aspirations."[67] New York University Professor of Law Burt Neuborne has described independent judges as "neutral arbiter[s] willing and able to listen to arguments from both sides before making a decision."[68] Indiana University Professor of Law Charles Gardner Geyh has asserted, "What has distinguished judges from other elected officials is their capacity to uphold the rule of law by deciding cases impartially on the basis of facts as they find them and law as they construe it to be written, without regard to the popularity of the decisions they make."[69] The American Bar Association's 1997 *Report on an Independent Judiciary* noted, "We expect a great deal from our judges. Not only are they charged with the grave responsibility of exercising impartial judgment in their judicial role, but they have to fashion their lives so as to avoid even the appearance of partiality."[70] One is reminded of William Howard Taft's opinion of judges: "I love judges, and I love courts. They are my ideals. They typify on earth what we shall meet hereafter in heaven under a just God."[71]

Of course, these claims strain credulity. It seems significantly more plausible that judges are not so different from other political actors. As University of Texas Professor of Law Frank B. Cross has observed, "An independent, unchecked judiciary may simply decide cases according to its own whims and predilections, rather than according to the rule of law . . . Saintliness is not a historic precondition to becoming a judge, nor does the process of doffing [sic] judicial robes magically make one saintly."[72] University of Virginia Professor of Law Saikrishna Prakash has likewise cautioned that "life tenure does not . . . make constitutional fidelity more likely. Instead, the corrupting influence of life tenure might make constitutional *in*fidelity more probable."[73]

Constitutional theorist Ronald Dworkin assured us that we should not be troubled by the prospect that unaccountable judges might predate our rights and liberties, for democratically accountable legislatures pose the same danger: "Certainly it impairs democracy when an authoritative court makes the wrong decision about what the democratic conditions require—but not more than it does when a majoritarian legislature makes a wrong constitutional decision that is allowed to stand. The possibility of error is symmetrical. So the majoritarian premise is confused, and it must be abandoned."[74] But the possibility of "error" is not in fact symmetrical. Majoritarian legislators may be removed from office for having violated our civil rights and liberties. Our power to so relieve them of their positions gives them powerful incentives *not* to violate those freedoms. But what gives antimajoritarian judges incentives to protect those freedoms?

Development economists studying judicial independence have suggested that independent judges may simply be relatively more protected from the pressures inducing legislators and executives to predate economic and political rights. Legislators and executives with uncertain tenures face incentives to give preferential treatment to their supporters, and to silence their opponents; these survival-directed incentives may induce them to expropriate private property and/or suppress dissent. Judges whose tenures are relatively more secure face these incentives to a lesser degree; they may therefore be more supportive of enforcing individuals' economic and political rights.[75]

Importantly, this argument does not assume that judges sincerely prefer more robust rights protections than do legislators and executives. Legislators, executives, and judges in any given country may, on average, prefer greater or fewer protections for economic and political rights relative to the legislators, executives, and judges in some other country. But within any single country, there is no reason to expect sincere judicial preferences over rights to be any different from sincere legislative and/or executive preferences over rights.

The institutional rules governing these officials' survival in office, however, may well induce office-specific differences in *revealed* rights preferences. Legislators and executives, whose tenures in office depend on cultivating supporters and undermining opponents, may be induced to choose lower levels of rights protections, regardless of their sincere preferences. Judges whose tenures in office in turn depend on retaining the support of these legislators and/or executives may be induced to endorse their rights choices, again regardless of their sincere preferences. But independent judges with guaranteed tenures will be insulated from the need to cultivate support, and will therefore be relatively freer to decide cases on the basis of their sincere preferences. On average, controlling for country-specific differences in rights preferences, independent judges should choose higher levels of rights protections, relative to those chosen by survival-constrained legislators and executives.

Because this argument does not assume that judges are inherently more supportive of rights than legislators and executives, it offers a perhaps more plausible account of the potential for judicial independence to increase rights protections. But, surprisingly, the argument does not distinguish between the threats to rights posed by policymakers operating under more or less majoritarian political institutions. Both antimajoritarian and majoritarian policymakers are said to significantly endanger individual rights. And so the empirical analyses testing the argument do not control for policymaking institutions, nor do they permit the effects of independent courts on rights to vary across different policymaking institutions.[76]

But we know that not all legislators and executives face equally compelling incentives to predate individual rights; empirical evidence indicates that more majoritarian legislators and executives are in fact significantly more protective of rights than their less majoritarian counterparts. And by the very logic of the argument for more independent courts, we might expect the effects of these courts to vary as a function of a country's policymaking institutions. When policymakers are constrained by their circumstances to predate rights more extensively than they might otherwise prefer, as in the countries with the least majoritarian policymaking institutions, we might indeed expect more independent courts to increase rights protections. Increasing the independence of courts from the policymaking branches in these countries should enable judges to decide cases more frequently on the basis of their sincere preferences. On average, independent judges in these countries should choose more rights protections, relative to survival-constrained executives and legislators. That is, for the subset of countries with the least majoritarian policymaking institutions, the economists' story should be correct.

But when policymakers are instead constrained to protect rights more extensively than they might otherwise prefer, as in the countries with the most majoritarian policymaking institutions, we might expect more independent courts actually to *decrease* rights protections. Again, increasing the independence of courts from the policymaking branches in these countries should enable judges to more frequently decide cases on the basis of their sincere preferences. On average, independent judges in these countries should choose *fewer* rights protections, relative to survival-constrained executives and legislators.

That is, by its own logic the argument for more independent courts fails in countries with majoritarian policymaking institutions. In these countries, the argument implies that more independent judges will actually undermine the rights protections favored by majoritarian legislators and executives. Because the U.S. House of Representatives is a majoritarian institution whose members are elected in open, contested, and competitive elections, for example, we should expect judges dependent on House majorities for their survival in office to cater to majoritarian preferences for civil rights, liberties, and other core public goods. We should expect federal judges in the United States to protect civil rights and liberties not because they are independent of legislative majorities, but rather precisely because they are dependent on those majorities for their political survival. And we should expect that releasing these judges from their dependence on elected majorities should only decrease their incentives to defer to these majorities' preferences for robust rights protections.

Although these expectations seem to fly in the face of the widely repeated conventional wisdom, this is not the first time they have been put to paper. Thomas Jefferson made essentially the same conditional prediction in a letter to a colleague in 1816, writing that, "where judges were named and removable at the will of an hereditary executive, from which branch most misrule was feared, and has flowed, it was a great point gained, by fixing them for life, to make them independent of that executive. But in a government founded on the public will, this principle operates in an opposite direction, and against that will."[77]

Chapter Nine reports results from a test of Jefferson's prediction, using a cross-national measure of judicial independence that incorporates the possibility of judicial removal by the policymaking branches into the tenure-based measure. These results suggest that the benefits of instituting more independent courts are in fact sharply limited to those countries with the least majoritarian policymaking institutions. Even among these countries, the increases in rights that could be realized by instituting more independent courts are dwarfed by those that would result from keeping deferential courts, while democratizing these countries' policymaking institutions. And among the countries with the most democratic policymaking institutions, more independent courts actually produce *lower* levels of rights protections than their less independent counterparts. If these results withstand further scrutiny, they imply that we would actually have fewer protections for individual rights in the United States were our federal courts more independent.

The Rehnquist Court's constitutional rulings on federal statutes may illustrate this finding. As reported in Chapters Five through Seven, during the "first" Rehnquist Court, a conservative majority on the Court largely pulled its constitutional punches in its rulings on liberal federal statutes. Facing a liberal Democratic majority in the House of Representatives during its first eight terms, the conservative Rehnquist Court either avoided reviewing liberal federal statutes, or largely upheld the constitutionality of those statutes. The best explanation for these decisions appears to be that the Court was deferring to the preferences of liberal Democratic House majorities. The Court's apparent democratic accountability thus led to outcomes preserving numerous public policies providing rights protections and other public goods. Had the Court been less democratically accountable, the estimates reported here indicate that many of these policies would have been struck.

But the results reported in Chapter Nine also suggest that we could possibly have even more robust rights protections and more extensive public goods, were we to eliminate judicial review altogether. Rights protections appear to be maximally provided under democratic constitutions that flatly prohibit courts from overruling elected branch policy decisions. In part this may be because even well-designed incentives are unlikely to be perfectly effective. If our goal is to secure maximal judicial deference to elected branch preferences, then presumably the most effective way to achieve that goal is simply to prohibit courts from overruling elected branch decisions.

But in part the apparently negative consequences of judicial review, even as exercised by democratically accountable courts, may stem from the nature of judicial review as an institutional practice. Crudely speaking, the exercise of judicial review generally involves examination of a statute or an executive branch action in order to determine whether that statute or action is, in the opinion of the sitting judges, in conformity with a constitution. If the reviewing judges agree that it is, then the statute or action stands; the status quo is maintained. If they agree that it is not, then the statute or action falls; the status quo reverts to that obtaining before the statute's enactment or the action's implementation.

Courts can, of course, operate with more subtlety than may be implied by the foregoing crude description of judicial review. In the case of *National Federation of Independent Business* (2012), for example, Justice Roberts's controlling opinion on Medicaid struck the portion of the Affordable Care Act directing the Secretary of Health and Human Services to withhold all of a state's Medicaid funds, should it choose not to participate in the statute's expansion of the Medicaid program. However, Roberts's opinion endorsed the withholding of only those federal Medicaid funds available under the expansion, a withholding not explicitly envisioned by the statute. The joint dissent protested that Roberts's opinion rewrote the statute, going beyond the permissible limits of judicial review. Roberts protested in return that his opinion simply struck one constitutionally impermissible application of the statute, while allowing other applications to stand.

Still, regardless of these subtleties, it is generally the case that the impact of judicial review in democracies is either to uphold elected branch actions, thereby preserving the status quo ex ante, or to strike elected branch actions, thereby causing the status quo to revert to that obtaining before those actions. What judicial review cannot generally do is to produce new policies providing rights protections or other public goods. In other words, the impact of judicial review on public goods provision is generally either to preserve the same provision of public goods that would have existed even in the absence of judicial review, or to reduce that provision. Even when judicial review is exercised in response to elected branch preferences, it may still have an asymmetric negative effect on public goods provision.

Judicial review, that is, even when exercised by democratically accountable courts, may have a downward ratchet effect on the public goods preferred by electoral majorities. This negative ratchet effect may be most pronounced under constitutions like that of the United States, which requires the coordinated action of three separate elected branches in order to either enact or repeal policies providing federal public goods, but which incentivizes judicial responsiveness to only one of those branches. Under the U.S. Constitution, federal courts may be responsive to the preferences of House majorities desirous of repealing previously enacted federal statutes, while remaining unresponsive to those majorities' desires to see new policies enacted.

Again, the Rehnquist Court's constitutional rulings may illustrate this finding. As previously noted, the estimates reported in Chapters Five through Seven indicate that the Court's apparent democratic accountability resulted in the preservation of numerous rights protections and other public goods during the Rehnquist Court's first eight terms. During these terms a democratically accountable court appears to have preserved rights protections and other public goods considerably more than would have been the case under a more independent court. But at the same time, even the democratically accountable Rehnquist Court was unable during these terms to respond to Democratic House majorities' preferences for even more rights protections and other public goods, preferences that in many cases likely went unfulfilled due to the presence of a Republican president until 1993. Enacting comprehensive public policy is not on the menu of what a court can accomplish, even a court possessed of the power of judicial review. Instead, the effect of democratic accountability during these terms of the Rehnquist Court appears to have been limited to the preservation of the existing status quo.

Between its 1994 and 2004 terms, however, the Rehnquist Court struck numerous federal statutes that had previously been enacted by liberal Democratic Congresses. The best explanation for these strikes appears to lie in the Republican victories of the 1994 congressional elections and beyond, victories that enabled the Republican Party to maintain control of the House of Representatives through the 2004 term. This was still a democratically accountable court, now responding to Republican majorities' preferences for smaller government and fewer public goods. But at the same time, it is unlikely that, had the Court lacked the power of judicial review, the Republican House majorities sitting between at least 1995 and 2003 would have been able to repeal liberal statutes on their own. During these years the Republican House shared power with either a Democratic president or a Democratic-majority Senate, whose preferences likely would have protected previously enacted liberal statutes. The presence of judicial review made it easier for previously extended public goods to be rolled back during the second Rehnquist Court terms, relative to the likely outcomes that would have prevailed in the absence of judicial review.

The Rehnquist Court thus may illustrate both the apparently positive effect of a democratically accountable court on rights protections and other public goods, relative to a democratically unaccountable court, and the apparently negative effect of judicial review on those public goods, relative to the absence of judicial review, even where that review is exercised by a democratically accountable court. Had the Supreme Court been designed to be a more fully independent institution, the first Rehnquist Court likely would have struck many more liberal federal statutes than it actually did, while the second Rehnquist Court likely would have behaved about the same. But had the Supreme Court lacked the power of judicial review, we likely would have seen about the same outcomes during the Rehnquist Court's first eight terms as we actually saw, while seeing many more liberal public policies preserved during that Court's remaining eleven terms.

If the findings reported here are to be believed, then democracies are better off with deferential courts than with independent courts, and are best off with courts prohibited altogether from exercising judicial review. If this is in fact the case, then the attempts of the United States, the United Nations, and numerous NGOs to promote judicial independence and judicial review around the world are not destined to produce higher levels of rights protections. At least for those countries with relatively democratic policymaking institutions, they may in fact have precisely the opposite effect.

James Madison famously wrote in Federalist 51, "If men were angels, no government would be necessary." But because men are men, not angels, institutional constraints must remedy "the defect of better motives."[78] Our federal judges, unelected and long-tenured as they are, nonetheless appear to have been closely bound by such constraints. We appear to be better off as a result. And we might be better off still were we to tighten their leashes even further.

2

THE SUPREME COURT, THE ELECTED
BRANCHES, AND THE CONSTITUTION

Today many regard it as implausible that the federal elected branches in the United States exercise any meaningful checks on the federal courts. Some assert that the Constitution's textual guarantees of life tenure and protected salaries create an "independent and powerful federal judiciary," in the words of a prominent college-level textbook on American politics.[1] Others claim that, even if the text of the Constitution permits elected branch checks on the federal courts, the founders nonetheless intended to secure independent federal courts. Some point to the difficulty of coordinating cross-institutional action under the Madisonian constitutional design, arguing that this difficulty enables at least de facto judicial independence. Others suggest that, because of their appointment by the joint action of the president and Senate majorities, federal judges' preferences will rarely diverge from those of the elected branches. And yet others argue that, because federal elected officials and/or majorities of their constituents endorse the principle of independent courts, constitutionally available checks on the federal courts are never used in practice.

If the evidence in support of any of these arguments were conclusive, we could pack up and go home. The question of the independence of the federal courts would be settled. For any or all of these reasons, we could conclude that federal judges in the United States are free to decide cases independently of elected branch preferences.

The point of this chapter is simply to suggest that we shouldn't call it a day quite yet. While there is some suggestive evidence supporting each of these claims, this evidence is far from conclusive. While the Constitution's text does provide federal judges with some protections from the elected branches, for example, it also appears to leave considerable room for elected branch majorities to punish divergence from and reward deference to elected branch preferences. Likewise, while some founding-era political elites appear to have endorsed independent courts, many others appear to have preferred deferential and accountable courts. Moreover, the structure of the Constitution's provisions regulating the federal courts may make it far easier for the elected branches to induce judicial deference than is commonly believed. There may be more periods of divergence between elected branch and judicial preferences than we have previously suspected. And the most frequently cited evidence in support of the claim that elected officials do not seek judicial deference, namely that the elected branches rarely attempt to check the federal courts, is consistent with multiple interpretations.

In short, none of these arguments, or the evidence adduced in their support, conclusively establish the independence (or lack thereof) of the federal courts in the United States. At the end of the day, this remains an open question.

The Textual Argument

One of the most widely repeated arguments supporting the claim of federal judicial independence is that the text of the Constitution clearly secures that independence. More specifically, Article III is frequently said, both in the popular press and in the legal academy, to guarantee "life tenure" and protected salaries to federal judges.[2]

Yet Article III in fact guarantees neither life tenure nor fully protected salaries to federal judges. With respect to federal judicial tenure, what Article III actually says is that federal judges "shall hold their Offices during good Behaviour."[3] The tenure of federal judges in the United States is contingent; they possess what should more properly be called "good behavior tenure," not "life tenure." The Good Behavior clause does not further define what constitutes "good" behavior, but presumably its existence implies a category of "bad" behavior for which a judge can be removed from office. Article II, Section 4 explicitly provides a procedure for the removal of federal judges, specifying that congressional majorities may remove from office "civil officers of the United States" for "Treason, Bribery, or other High Crimes and Misdemeanors."[4]

Legal academics have argued at some length about how the Good Behavior and Impeachment Clauses should be interpreted, both as to the appropriate proceedings for judicial removal, and as to the appropriate standards to be applied in those proceedings.[5] For example, because Article III does not specify the procedures by which badly behaving federal judges, however defined, are to be removed from office, some have suggested that the Congress may use its powers under the Necessary and Proper Clause to create such procedures.[6] Others have asserted that federal judges may be removed from office only through the impeachment proceedings specified in Article II.[7] Some have argued that restricting judicial removal to Article II impeachment proceedings narrows the range of offenses for which judges can appropriately be removed.[8] Others have asserted that the "high crimes and misdemeanors" language of Article II is permissive enough to sanction judicial removal under a broad range of circumstances, possibly even including removal for the substance of judicial decisions.[9]

For our purposes, the significance of these interpretive disputes is simply their implication that the Good Behavior and Impeachment Clauses are sufficiently vague to permit varying interpretations by congressional majorities. Should congressional majorities face a hostile federal bench, it would appear to be at least possible for those majorities to interpret these clauses expansively. In this context congressional majorities might seek to intimidate opposing-party judges by asserting that impeachment should be available for relatively minor infractions. In 1936, for example, despite having been acquitted of all the specific charges of judicial misconduct brought against him, Republican-appointed District Judge Halsted L. Ritter was impeached and convicted by the Democratic-majority Congress on the sole charge of having brought his court "into scandal and disrepute."[10]

But should congressional majorities face a friendly federal bench, there would appear to be room for narrower interpretations of these clauses. In this context congressional majorities might seek to protect same-party judges by declaring that the scope of impeachable offenses should be very carefully restricted. In 1970, for example, a Democratic-majority subcommittee of the House Judiciary Committee recommended a conclusion to any further impeachment proceedings against Democrat-appointed Associate Justice William O. Douglas, asserting that "the independence of the Judiciary" and "the exalted station assigned to the Judge by our society" required that judicial impeachment be restricted to "serious derelictions of duty."[11]

The inference that the Good Behavior and Impeachment Clauses permit considerable congressional discretion is strengthened by the refusal of the Supreme Court to impose any limits on that discretion. On two occasions the Court has been asked to consider such limits. In 1936, after having been impeached and removed from office for "disrepute," Judge Ritter brought suit in the U.S. Court of Claims on the grounds that his removal could not be justified under the standard of "Treason, Bribery, or other High Crimes and Misdemeanors."[12] The Court of Claims dismissed Ritter's case, ruling that the federal courts have no jurisdiction to review the constitutionality of impeachment actions, the Constitution having given the House the "sole" power to impeach, and the Senate the "sole" power to try impeachments. The Supreme Court declined to review the case.[13]

In 1993 the Supreme Court did review a challenge to a congressional impeachment action. District Judge Walter L. Nixon, who had been impeached and removed from office for having been convicted of federal perjury charges, challenged his removal on the grounds that the Senate had delegated his impeachment trial to an ad hoc committee. Nixon argued that the Senate's action violated the Impeachment Clause's prescription that the Senate "try" impeachments. The Rehnquist Court's majority dismissed Nixon's claim as nonjusticiable, adopting essentially the same argument as had been made earlier by the Court of Claims. The majority opinion also noted that "judicial involvement in impeachment proceedings, even if only for purposes of judicial review, is counterintuitive, because it would eviscerate the 'important constitutional check' placed on the Judiciary by the Framers."[14]

Of course, it remains an open question whether congressional majorities have actually sought to use the Good Behavior and Impeachment Clauses to induce judicial deference to congressional preferences. But the existence of interpretive disputes over the scope of these clauses, and the refusal of the federal courts to impose any limits on their interpretation, would appear at least to enable such use.

Article III likewise does not fully protect judicial salaries, specifying merely that federal judges "shall, at stated Times, receive for their Services, a Compensation, which shall not be diminished during their Continuance in Office."[15] The Compensation Clause does not require the elected branches regularly to increase judicial salaries, but rather only to not decrease those salaries. This wording implies that, in the presence of inflation, judicial salaries will decrease in real terms unless majorities in the House and the Senate, with the consent of the president, take affirmative action to increase those salaries. Whether the elected branches in fact choose to protect judicial salaries from real decreases is at the discretion of those branches.

The wording of Article III's Compensation Clause would thus appear to permit the elected branches to use the lure of salary increases as a means to induce judicial deference to elected branch preferences. The same can presumably also be said of the power of the elected branches to allocate the budgets for the federal courts, which are also at the discretion of those branches.

Beyond the powers of impeachment and appropriations, there are several other constitutional provisions giving the elected branches powers to affect the federal courts. Article III specifies only a very limited original jurisdiction for the Supreme Court; all other federal jurisdiction is granted to the federal courts only "with such Exceptions, and under such Regulations as the Congress shall make."[16] The Exceptions Clause permits the elected branches to use the threat of jurisdiction-stripping to induce federal judicial deference to elected branch preferences. Article III similarly does not specify the size of the Supreme Court, implying that the elected branches may add and/or subtract seats on the Court at will. This textual omission enables the elected branches to construct a friendly majority on the Supreme Court, should the existing Court majority fail to defer sufficiently to elected branch preferences. Finally, all "inferior" federal courts exist only "as the Congress may from time to time ordain and establish."[17] The power to simply eliminate existing federal courts gives the elected branches another means beyond impeachment to remove lower federal judges from the bench.

In short, the Constitution's text provides the elected branches with a variety of tools that may potentially be used to induce federal judicial deference to elected branch preferences. To the extent that federal judges want to keep their jobs, see their salaries and budgets increased, not have their jurisdiction stripped, not have seats added or subtracted from their courts, and not have their courts simply eliminated, the existence of these tools may give them powerful incentives to keep federal elected officials happy.

The Argument from Original Intent

Some argue that, even if these constitutional provisions can be interpreted so as to enable elected branch policing of federal judicial decision making, this interpretation violates the intent of those who crafted these provisions. Judicial independence was a core value of those who framed the Constitution, it is said, and the framers never intended that the elected branches would be able to influence the decisions made by federal judges. Good behavior tenure in particular, it is argued, was long sought by colonial and revolutionary leaders as a means to protect judges from arbitrary removal by the executive, thereby demonstrating these leaders' commitment to the principle of judicial independence.[18] Yet while the claim about good behavior tenure appears to be at least partially true, the broader claim about the founders' unconditional belief in the value of judicial independence is, at a minimum, open to question.

Prior to the Revolution colonial judges in North America generally served *quam diu nobis placuerit*, or at the pleasure of the king, and could be dismissed by him (or his agents) at will.[19] Despite the fact that the vast majority of judges so appointed were allowed to remain in office, many reformers believed that the ability of the sovereign to remove judges at his pleasure induced judicial deference to royal preferences.[20] "At pleasure" judicial tenure was thus said by colonial reformers to be "dangerous to the liberty and property of the subject."[21]

Its alternative was tenure *quam diu se bene gesserint*, or tenure held during good behavior, a privilege enjoyed by English judges after the 1701 Act of Settlement but one not generally available in the North American colonies. Under British common law, a judge appointed on the condition of good behavior could not be removed by the monarch at will, but rather only through the submission of a writ of *scire facias*, or a writ to show cause, before an appropriate court. The production of such a writ essentially constituted an allegation of judicial misbehavior, which would then result in an evidentiary trial before the court as to whether the alleged misbehavior in fact had occurred. The court would then make a determination as to whether the misbehavior, had it been found to occur, was sufficiently serious as to violate the accused judge's condition of appointment.[22]

Because good behavior tenure protected judges from arbitrary removal by the sovereign, it was thought to free judges from the need to defer to royal preferences. It was consequently repeatedly sought by colonial political reformers, who feared the consequences of unlimited royal power over judicial decision making.[23] Their efforts, however, were just as repeatedly repudiated by the Crown and its agents.[24] While some colonial governors extended isolated offers of good behavior judicial appointments, they were under no obligation to continue this practice, once begun, and most opted for at pleasure appointments.[25] By 1761 the Crown had decided to prohibit even voluntary good behavior appointments made by its agents. In that year the British Board of Trade wrote King George III that extending good behavior tenure to the colonial judiciary would be "subversive of that Policy by which alone Colonies can be kept in a just dependence upon the Government of the Mother Country."[26] The King in Council then declared that the Crown would no longer tolerate even isolated instances of colonial judicial appointments made on the condition of good behavior tenure, characterizing such appointments as "contrary to the express directions of the instructions given to the said governors or other chief officers by us or by our royal predecessors," and forbidding royal governors from making any further such appointments "upon pain of being removed from your government."[27]

John Dickinson later lamented, "In the colonies, how fruitless has been every attempt to have the judges appointed 'during good behavior?'"[28] Dickinson and other colonial reformers had to wait until after independence to see the widespread adoption of good behavior judicial appointments in the new state constitutions.[29]

If that were all there were to the story, one might reasonably conclude that it supported the claim that judicial independence was an important value for revolutionary era thinkers. Good behavior tenure protected judges from arbitrary removal by the Crown (and later, by the executive branch), thereby promoting judicial independence. Colonial and revolutionary era leaders sought to replace at pleasure tenure with good behavior tenure, thereby demonstrating their commitment to the principle of judicial independence. Thwarted in their efforts by the Crown's agents during the colonial period, these reformers succeeded in institutionalizing good behavior tenure (and thus judicial independence) in the new state constitutions.

However, that is not all there is to the story. While colonial and revolutionary era reformers sought to insulate judges from arbitrary removal by the executive, they did not seek corresponding protections from removal by the legislative branch. To the contrary, they actively sought to increase legislative powers of judicial removal during the same period that they were seeking to reduce executive powers of judicial removal. Moreover, they jealously guarded the colonial assemblies' powers to set and fund judicial salaries, powers believed to cabin the decision making of appointed judges.

Their model appears to have been the precedent set by earlier English reformers, who had secured not only good behavior judicial tenure in the 1701 Act of Settlement, but also the parliamentary right to impeach royally appointed judges without the possibility of royal pardon.[30] The Act had moreover empowered the Parliament to remove judges essentially at will, "upon the Address of both Houses of Parliament."[31] Impeachment was an exclusively legislative power to remove judges from office, while legislative address became one.[32] Although good behavior tenure precluded the monarch's ability to remove judges at will, it did not protect those judges from parliamentary removal through either impeachment or legislative address.

These legislative powers of judicial removal were understood at the time to have a broad reach. The power to impeach had originally been sought by the British Parliament in the late fourteenth century as a means to check the exercise of unfettered judgment by the royally appointed holders of public office.[33] The King himself, protected by his connection to the divine, was considered to be untouchable by parliamentary action. But the King's appointed ministers and judges, responsible for implementing his policies, were increasingly held to be accountable for the consequences of those policies. When those consequences were, in the eyes of parliamentary majorities, injurious to the public good, the King's appointees became liable to parliamentary impeachment efforts.[34]

Importantly, impeachment in this early context had no association with ordinary criminal behavior, or crimes committed against individuals. Impeachment for "high crimes and misdemeanors," a common ground for parliamentary impeachment, did not refer to ordinary criminal acts.[35] "High crimes" were understood to be political crimes committed against the commonwealth, or failures to act on behalf of the public good. "High misdemeanors" were likewise understood in a more literal translation to be instances of bad demeanor, or misbehavior, by the holders of public office.[36] In the words of University of North Carolina Professor of Law Michael Gerhardt, "impeachment was considered a political proceeding, and impeachable offenses were political crimes."[37] As an example of such a political crime, eighteenth-century British legal scholar Richard Wooddeson cited the case of "the judges mislead[ing] their sovereign by unconstitutional opinions."[38]

There were no limits to parliamentary impeachment powers in this early context; Parliament retained the sole right to define the scope of impeachable offenses.[39] In the seventeenth century, the Parliament exercised this discretion by using impeachment "as an instrument for striking at unpopular royal policies."[40] Royally appointed judges and ministers were impeached for supporting the King's increasingly onerous tax policies, along with other policies believed by parliamentary majorities to be "pernicious to the realm," and for having given "bad advice" to the King.[41] In 1680 Chief Justice Scroggs was impeached for having introduced "arbitrary and tyrannical government against law," or more particularly for having favored Catholics and royalists in the cases before his court.[42] The codification of the parliamentary powers of impeachment and legislative address in the Act of Settlement of 1701 was a victory for parliamentary reformers, who sought greater control over judicial and executive policymaking. But the Act of Settlement did not apply to the British colonies in North America. The colonial assemblies there were not empowered to remove royal appointees, including judges, either by impeachment or by legislative address.[43]

If colonial reformers had fully embraced the principle of judicial independence, presumably they would have sought only to reduce royal powers to remove judges from office. But they also sought to increase legislative powers to remove judges from office. On several occasions colonial assemblies sought to assert the power of impeachment against royally appointed judges.[44] These efforts were roundly rebuffed by the Crown, which declared in a 1759 case originating in Pennsylvania that, "this unusual power could not be tolerated in inferior assemblies in the Colonies."[45] In 1768, Josiah Quincy Jr. called for the general establishment in the colonies of the parliamentary right to impeach royally appointed judges for "subverting the fundamental laws and introducing arbitrary power."[46] According to historians of colonial impeachment, as the Revolution neared, impeachment became a highly visible act of protest against monarchical rule in the colonies.[47]

While the colonial assemblies did not possess the power to impeach, they did have the power to fund judicial salaries. This power was thought to give the assemblies some degree of influence over judicial decisions. At least in the opinion of the Board of Trade, the assemblies' control over judicial salaries rendered colonial judges vulnerable to the assemblies' "Factious will and Caprice."[48] In 1767 the Crown consequently stripped the assemblies of their power to set and fund judicial salaries, occasioning uproar in the colonies.[49] John Adams protested that the Crown's action rendered the Massachusetts Bay Colony's judges "independent of the grants of the commons of this province," as a result of which "our lives and properties will be rendered very precarious."[50] When in 1774 the Crown's Chief Justice in the colony had the temerity to accept his royal salary as ordered, the Massachusetts Bay assembly sought his impeachment, echoing Adams's denunciation of "independent" judges: "any one of [the Justices of the Superior Court] who shall accept of, and depend upon the pleasure of the crown for his support, independent of the grants and acts of the General Assembly, will discover to the world, that he has not a due sense of the importance of an impartial administration of justice; that he is an enemy to the constitution, and has it in his heart to promote the establishment of an arbitrary government in the province."[51]

This episode probably led directly to the complaint voiced in the Declaration of Independence that the King had "made Judges dependent on his Will alone, for the Tenure of their Offices, and the Amount and Payment of their Salaries."[52] George III's offense was not that he had made colonial judges dependent *per se,* but rather that he had made them exclusively dependent on royal preferences. The absence of any institutional mechanisms incentivizing those judges to defer to majoritarian legislative preferences rendered the colonists vulnerable to arbitrary, antimajoritarian royal power.

Yet pure judicial independence was clearly not the answer for colonial political leaders. As historian Gordon Wood has written, the colonists had "a profound fear of judicial independence and discretion."[53] Thomas Paine in 1776 famously decried political leaders who were "independent of the people," and who thereby "contribute[d] nothing towards the freedom of the state."[54] The author of the 1776 pamphlet *The People the Best Governors* warned that judicial discretion would lead judges to "assume what is in fact the prerogative of the legislature, for those, that made the laws ought to give them a meaning, when they are doubtful."[55] Thomas Jefferson in the same year warned that giving life tenure to any public official would be destructive of "that regard to the public good that otherwise they might perhaps be induced by their independence to forget."[56] Jefferson went on to suggest that elected legislators would dispense "the mercies of the law . . . equally and impartially to every description of men," while unelected judges would succumb to "the eccentric impulses of whimsical, capricious designing man." In consequence Jefferson recommended, "Let mercy be the character of the law-giver, but let the judge be a mere machine."[57]

Unsurprisingly, the state constitutions written in the wake of the Declaration opted for majoritarian courts, endowing state legislatures with the power of judicial removal, through impeachment and/or legislative address, and with control over judicial salaries.[58] In the words of Gordon Wood, "These constitutional provisions giving control of the courts and judicial tenure to the legislatures actually represented the culmination of what the colonial assemblies had been struggling for in their eighteenth century contests with the Crown. The Revolutionaries had no intention of curtailing legislative interference in the court structure and in judicial functions, and in fact they meant to increase it."[59]

The Massachusetts Constitution of 1780, for example, drafted largely by John Adams and reputed to be a model for the delegates to the later federal Constitutional Convention, declared, "All power residing originally in the people, and being derived from them, the several magistrates and officers of government, vested with authority, whether legislative, executive, or judicial, are their substitutes and agents, and are at all times accountable to them."[60] This constitution provided that judges in the Commonwealth of Massachusetts would be removable by the state legislature through both impeachment and legislative address, and that they would see salary increases only at the discretion of legislative majorities.

By the time of the drafting of the federal Constitution, then, the principle of majoritarian legislative control over judicial removal had been institutionalized in every state constitution. But many revolutionary era reformers became less enamored with the legislative branch in the decade preceding the Constitutional Convention. As state legislatures printed inflationary paper money, forgave revolutionary war debts, defaulted on their own debt obligations, and generally displayed little respect for the property rights of the landed and wealthy, prominent political thinkers sought strategies to check the legislative branch.[61] Perhaps during this period reformers began to turn to independent courts as a means to protect individual rights from the predatory actions of majoritarian legislatures. Perhaps Article III's at least partial protections for judicial tenures and salaries should be understood in this context, as institutional strategies to secure more independent courts.

Alexander Hamilton's arguments in Federalist 78 for "the complete independence of the courts" are typically cited in this context, to support the claim that the delegates to the Constitutional Convention fully endorsed the principle of independent federal courts.[62] Hamilton asserts that judicial "permanency in office" is essential to secure "the general liberty of the people" from "the encroachments and oppressions of the representative body."[63] In Federalist 79 Hamilton goes on to claim that a "fixed provision" for judicial salaries is also necessary to guarantee "the independence of the judges."[64]

But it is not clear how widely shared were Hamilton's views on the merits of independent courts. James Madison's Federalist essays, for example, articulate a constitutional design for the protection of individual rights wherein independent courts play virtually no role. Madison identifies instead an extensive representative republic wherein policymaking institutions are separated both vertically (that is, via federalism) and horizontally (that is, via a bicameral legislature and a separately elected executive endowed with veto power), as the set of institutional arrangements most likely to lead to the protection of individual rights. Under such a constitution, "the society itself will be broken into so many parts, interests and classes of citizens, that the rights of individuals, or of the minority, will be in little danger from interested combinations of the majority."[65] Instead of relying on independent courts to check policymaking majorities, Madison's design makes it exceedingly difficult for those majorities to form in the first place.

Madison in fact explicitly rejects the idea of independent courts. In Federalist 48, he argues that each branch must be checked by the others; no branch of government should be able to operate independently: "unless these departments be so far connected and blended as to give to each a constitutional control over the others, the degree of separation which the maxim requires, as essential to a free government, can never in practice be duly maintained."[66] As examples of "constitutional controls" exercised by the legislative branch over the judicial, he cites favorably the provisions for judicial removal via legislative address and impeachment found both in England and in many of the new state constitutions, including those of Massachusetts, Pennsylvania, and Delaware, also noting with approval the ability of legislatures to impeach appointed officeholders under the constitutions of New Hampshire, New York, and New Jersey. For Madison, the ability of these legislatures to remove judges from office did not endanger the protection of individual rights. Instead, the legislative power of judicial removal in fact helped to secure rights from possible predation by the judicial branch.

Madison actually considers and rejects, as a means to protect individual rights, the creation of "some power altogether independent of the people" that would have authority to make policy. In Federalist 51 he warns that this would be, "at best, but a precarious security," because "a power independent of the society may as well espouse the unjust views of the major as the rightful interests of the minor party, and may possibly be turned against both parties."[67]

Madison, then, considered by many to be the primary architect of the Constitution's design, envisioned literally no role for independent courts in protecting individual rights. Indeed, he cautioned against a facile reliance on the utopian notion that "some power altogether independent of the people" could be trusted to protect the people's rights. Commenting at approximately the same time on Jefferson's draft constitution for the state of Virginia, Madison wrote that judges should not even be given the power of judicial review: "This makes the Judiciary Department paramount in fact to the Legislature, which was never intended and can never be proper."[68]

Although we do not know with any certainty how prevalent Madison's views were, we at least know that, even after the bloom was starting to come off the rose of legislative supremacy, he was not alone in preferring accountable to unaccountable courts. In an address to his fellow South Carolinians, for example, an anonymous author asked bluntly in 1783, "What people in their senses would make the judges, who are fallible men, depositaries of the law?"[69] Thomas Jefferson likewise reaffirmed his commitment to judicial deference in 1785, writing, "Relieve the judges from the rigour of text law, and permit them, with pretorian discretion, to wander into its equity, and the whole legal system becomes incertain."[70] The courts, declared the *Providence Gazette* in 1787, were properly regarded as the "servants" of the people.[71]

Similar sentiments were expressed during the Constitutional Convention itself. The initial language proposed for the Impeachment Clause, for example, would have permitted impeachment for "neglect of duty, malversation [misbehavior by public officials], or corruption."[72] When language was proposed limiting impeachable offenses to treason and bribery, George Mason objected that impeachment should be available for "attempts to subvert the Constitution."[73] He proposed expanding the Impeachment Clause first by adding "maladministration" as an impeachable offense, and then, more successfully, by adding the phrase "other High Crimes and Misdemeanors."[74] University of North Carolina Professor of Law Michael Gerhardt suggests that this phrasing was understood to include non-criminal offenses against the public trust, "the kinds of abuses of power or injuries to the Republic that only could be committed by public officials by virtue of the public offices or privileges they held."[75]

That this phrase invited congressional discretion appeared to be clear to the delegates. For example, Madison expressed concern that the executive and judicial officers subject to the Impeachment Clause would be rendered "improperly dependent" on the Congress "for any act which might be called a misdemeasnor [sic]"; they would hold office "at pleasure" of the House and Senate.[76] Nonetheless, or perhaps because of the opportunity for such dependence, Mason's amendment was approved by the Convention.

And despite his claim in Federalist 78 that judges should have "permanent" tenures, even Alexander Hamilton appeared to endorse the use of impeachment as a political check on judicial and executive officers. In Federalist 65 Hamilton described impeachment as "a bridle in the hands of the legislative body," characterizing as "political" the standard to be used for federal impeachments.[77] This standard would encompass "those offenses which proceed from the conduct of public men, or, in other words, from the abuse or violation of some public trust. They are of a nature which may with peculiar propriety be denominated POLITICAL, as they relate chiefly to injuries done immediately to the society itself."[78] Hamilton also noted that the Congress could not be "tied down" by narrow rules "either in the delineation of the offense by the prosecutors or in the construction of it by the judges."[79]

In Federalist 81 Hamilton even argued approvingly that the congressional impeachment power would thwart what some saw as the potential for a dangerously independent federal judiciary. He paraphrased this objection to the federal Constitution as follows: "The power of construing the laws according to the *spirit* of the Constitution will enable [the Supreme Court] to mould them into whatever shape it may think proper; especially as its decisions will not be in any manner subject to the revision or correction of the legislative body. This is as unprecedented as it is dangerous . . . the usurpations of the Supreme Court of the United States will be uncontrollable and remediless."[80]

Hamilton characterized the objection as a "phantom," "made up altogether of false reasoning upon misconceived fact."[81] The Court would *not* in fact impose its own preferences on the Congress, because the congressional impeachment power would provide what Hamilton called "precautions for [the justices'] responsibility."[82] He elaborated: "The inference [of judicial deference] is greatly fortified by the consideration of the important constitutional check which the power of instituting impeachments in one part of the legislative body, and of determining upon them in the other, would give to that body upon the members of the judicial department. This is alone a complete security. There never can be danger that the judges, by a series of deliberate usurpations on the authority of the legislature, would hazard the united resentment of the body entrusted with it, while this body was possessed of the means of punishing their presumption by degrading them from their stations."[83]

Despite his frequently quoted claim in Federalist 78 that the Constitution secures "the complete independence of the courts of justice," in Federalist 81 Hamilton appears confident not only that the congressional impeachment power would provide a majoritarian check on federal judicial decision making, but also that the Congress would never need to actually use this power in order for it to be effective. Federal judges would anticipate the Congress's "united resentment" should they attempt "deliberate usurpations" of congressional authority, and would not risk the resulting congressional punishment.

It is equally hard to read the framers' intentions concerning the Constitution's other provisions regulating the federal judiciary as unconditional endorsements of judicial independence. For example, it is true that Hamilton claimed in Federalist 79 that Article III's Compensation Clause secures a "fixed provision" for judicial salaries. But others of the founders acknowledged that this clause actually permits considerable elected branch discretion over judicial salaries. An early proposal in the Constitutional Convention in fact would have precluded any elected branch influence on judicial salaries, foreclosing upward as well as downward adjustments in judicial pay. A proposed amendment to this provision permitted the elected branches to adjust judicial salaries upward. In the debates over this proposal Madison pointed out that giving the elected branches the power to hand out periodic salary increases might produce judicial deference to elected branch preferences. He noted that "whenever an increase is wished by the Judges, or may be in agitation in the legislature, an undue complaisance in the former may be felt toward the latter," and that "it will be improper even so far to permit a dependence."[84] Madison advocated instead a constitutionally mandated indexing of judicial salaries, but his motion to implement this feature was defeated.[85] The convention then passed the amendment permitting elected branch discretion over judicial salary increases.

And in Federalist 79, despite his claim that the Compensation Clause would provide a "fixed provision" for judicial salaries, Hamilton took note of the elected branches' discretion to increase judicial salaries, observing, "It may well happen . . . that a stipend which would be very sufficient at their first appointment would become too small in the progress of their service."[86] He notes that in that event judges would be dependent on the "discretion of the legislature" for salary increases, a dependence likely to lead to judicial deference to legislative preferences, since "a power over a man's subsistence amounts to a power over his will."[87]

Hamilton also recognized, and drew attention to, the fact that Article's III's jurisdictional provisions invited elected branch discretion. He pointed out in Federalist 80 that the Exceptions Clause gives elected branch majorities "ample authority" to tailor federal jurisdiction to their preferences.[88] Hamilton went on in Federalist 81 to note that this clause "carefully restricted" the scope of federal judicial authority; beyond a small class of cases, "of a nature rarely to occur," assigned to the Supreme Court's original jurisdiction, federal jurisdiction would be subject to elected branch discretion.[89] He observed approvingly that the Exceptions Clause enabled the elected branches "to modify [federal jurisdiction] in such a manner as will best answer the ends of public justice and security."[90]

In Federalist 82, Hamilton also pointed out that the jurisdiction of any lower federal courts that the elected branches might see fit to create, whether original or appellate, would also be entirely at "the discretion of the legislature."[91] As the prominent Antifederalist "The Federal Farmer" observed with approval, "the inferior federal courts are left by the Constitution to be instituted and regulated altogether as the legislature shall judge best."[92]

Finally, Hamilton noted that the Supreme Court is dependent on the elected branches for "the efficacy of its judgments."[93] He addressed the judiciary's lack of enforcement power in Federalist 78: "The judiciary . . . will always be the least dangerous to the political rights of the Constitution; because it will be least in a capacity to annoy or injure them . . . The judiciary . . . has no influence over either the sword or the purse; no direction either of the strength or of the wealth of the society, and can take no active resolution whatsoever. It may truly be said to have neither FORCE nor WILL but merely judgment; and must ultimately depend upon the aid of the executive arm even for the efficacy of its judgments."⁹⁴

In short, many of those who participated in the drafting and ratification of the Constitution appeared to believe that several of its provisions enabled elected branch influence over judicial branch decisions. Their evident acceptance of this potential outcome would appear to imply their approval of judicial deference to elected branch preferences. This reading of the founders' intentions is then difficult to square with accounts asserting their unconditional support for independent courts.

Of course, it is impossible to know with any certainty what influential men of the 1780s *really* thought about judicial independence. Still, in response to the claim that the nation's founders unconditionally endorsed independent, antimajoritarian courts, it does seem worth pointing out that there is at least as much evidence that they instead endorsed majoritarian checks on the federal judiciary. John Adams did write approvingly of the "independence" of the judiciary in his influential pamphlet *Thoughts on Government*, written contemporaneously with the Declaration in 1776; legal academic Scott Gerber characterizes *Thoughts* as "unequivocal in its commitment to an independent judiciary."⁹⁵ But it is clear that Adams' view of judicial independence encompassed majoritarian checks on the judiciary: "The dignity and stability of government in all its branches, the morals of the people, and every blessing of society depend so much upon an upright and skillful administration of justice, that the judicial power ought to be distinct from both the legislative and executive, and independent upon both, that so it may be a check upon both, *as both should be checks upon that.*"⁹⁶

In *Thoughts on Government* Adams endorsed the legislative impeachment power as a means to "check" judges, and in his draft of the 1780 Massachusetts Constitution gave the legislature the power to remove judges not only through impeachment, but also through legislative address.⁹⁷ As Gordon Wood has written, "Most of the early constitution-makers had little sense that judicial independence meant independence from the people."⁹⁸

Some believers in the existence of an independent federal judiciary have expressed their bewilderment that many of those who endorsed majoritarian courts in the early state constitutions went on to endorse an apparently antimajoritarian federal judiciary. Musing on the provision of "life tenure" to federal judges, for example, legal academic Saikrishna Prakash has remarked, "How truly odd and perverse it is that our Constitution explicitly promises republican governments to the peoples of the several states but implicitly denies such a right to the people of the United States . . . Why Hamilton and other members of the founding generation blithely assumed that fidelity to the Constitution rather than the self-indulgent pursuit of one's own preferences would follow from life tenure is a mystery."[99]

But it is not at all clear that the framers thought that they were in fact granting unchecked "life tenure" to federal judges. Rather, it seems considerably more likely that they believed that elected branch checks on the federal courts would cabin the "self-indulgent pursuit of one's own preferences." Most of these men appeared to believe that political institutions should not permit public officials to exercise unchecked authority. Federal judges who could interpret the Constitution at will, without fear of reprisals, would have violated the guiding principle animating the entire Constitution.

It is perhaps small wonder, then, that Hamilton called this view of the Court's constitutional role "made up altogether of false reasoning upon misconceived fact."[100] Many of Hamilton's contemporaries likewise shared his view that "the judiciary is beyond comparison the weakest of the three departments of power."[101] Several of the Antifederalists, for example, pointed to the Court's institutional dependence on the federal elected branches as a potential problem. They feared that, when faced with conflicts between the federal and state elected branches, the Court would naturally rule in favor of the former because of the evident deference the justices would have toward federal elected officials. During the ratification debates in Virginia, for example, Patrick Henry referred to the recent willingness of Virginia's judges to defy their state legislature as a "land-mark" signifying judicial independence from legislative preferences: "Yes, Sir, our Judges opposed the acts of the Legislature. We have this land-mark to guide us. They had fortitude to declare that they were the Judiciary and would oppose unconstitutional acts. Are you sure that your Federal Judiciary will act thus? Is that Judiciary so well constructed, and so independent of the other branches, as our State Judiciary? Where are your land-marks in this government? I will be bold to say you cannot find any in it."[102]

Perhaps Henry could not find any such landmarks because majorities at the Constitutional Convention had not in fact endorsed the idea of unconditional judicial independence. As Supreme Court Justice James Wilson was later to write about the U.S. Constitution, "The executive and judicial powers are now drawn from the same source, are now animated by the same principles, and are now directed to the same ends, with the legislative authority: they who execute, and they who administer the laws, are so much the servants, and therefore as much the friends of the people, as those who make them."[103]

In the end it may be impossible to infer with any certainty the framers' beliefs about independent courts. But we can perhaps at least rule out the possibility that judicial independence was universally and unconditionally endorsed by those who drafted and ratified the Constitution. While some of the leaders of the founding generation may indeed have preferred more independent courts, many others apparently preferred courts that deferred to the majoritarian elected branches. As legal academics Saikrishna Prakash and Steven D. Smith observed, "If judicial independence had been an unqualified value or purpose of Article III, the Constitution could simply have given judges an absolute life tenure, unconstrained by any good-behavior condition—or even, for that matter, the possibility of impeachment."[104]

The Feasibility Argument

Some suggest that, even if the Constitution's text permits elected branch policing of judicial decision making, and even if these textual provisions were intended to enable such policing, effective elected branch policing of the federal judiciary depends on the feasibility of these policing actions. Under the Madisonian constitutional design it can be very difficult to assemble simultaneous bicameral majorities while also securing presidential consent. This difficulty of coordinating cross-institutional action may leave federal judges with considerable leeway to pursue their own preferences, free from the possibility of elected branch sanctions.

However, we may have overestimated elected branch difficulties in policing the judicial branch. First, the effective use of impeachment may not in fact require complicated cross-institutional action. The impeachment power is unusual under the U.S. Constitution in that the chambers act sequentially and do not require presidential assent. The House of Representatives initiates the impeachment process, and the Constitution requires only a simple majority in the House to impeach a federal judge. Importantly, it also takes only a simple majority in the House to initiate an impeachment investigation of a federal judge. There are no constitutional or other requirements that evidence of judicial misconduct must be provided in advance of such an investigation.[105] There are also no constitutional or other limitations on what the House may investigate, once a majority has decided to target a federal judge. As noted earlier, the Constitution gives to the House the "sole" power of impeachment, and the federal courts have declined to set limits on this power.

The enormous discretion House majorities have to conduct impeachment investigations enables these majorities to go on fishing expeditions targeted at judges with divergent preferences. In these fishing expeditions judges' personal lives, as well as those of their family members, friends, and acquaintances, are fair game. A judge's financial records, his marital status, where he lives and with whom, his employment of domestic help, his associations with political figures and organizations, his connections, however tangential, to any parties appearing before his court: any of these areas could reveal minor improprieties that nonetheless, in the right hostile political context, could lead to a majority for impeachment in the House.[106]

The Constitution also requires a two-thirds majority in the Senate to actually remove a federal judge from the bench. If the impeachment process were not sequential, it would require only a friendly minority of slightly more than one third of the Senate to protect a federal judge from being removed from office. But because the impeachment process is sequential, the House may be able to turn the votes of senators disposed to be friendly to a judge's case. If the House is able to uncover any evidence of judicial misconduct in the course of its potentially lengthy investigations, it may be able to force the hand of these senators. Presented with

a documented and publicized record of judicial improprieties, even senators sympathetic to a judge's preferences might be induced to vote for
removal, if only to avoid public condemnation for voting to keep him on
the bench.[107]

Conversely, a two-thirds Senate majority hostile to a judge's preferences cannot use impeachment as a check on judicial discretion as long as
the judge enjoys a friendly majority in the House of Representatives. The
Senate can move on impeachment only after the House has moved. From
the perspective of a federal judge, then, deterring impeachment may primarily imply keeping House majorities happy. When a House majority
is happy, impeachment cannot go forward. But when a House majority is not happy, even a friendly Senate may not be able to save a judge
from being removed from the bench.

In the case of impeachment, consequently, the effective policing of
judicial decision making may not require complicated cross-institutional
action. Instead, it may simply require majorities in the House of Representatives willing to police judges' decisions. While subsequent chapters
will test this hypothesis using quantitative evidence, there is anecdotal evidence in the historical record of impeachment in both England and North
America that is at least consistent with it. The historians Peter Hoffer and
N. E. H. Hull report of English impeachments, for example, "On many
occasions the Commons did not even prosecute—the impeachment itself
was sufficient warning or inconvenience to the accused."[108] To the extent
that this statement is accurate, it implies that majorities in the House of
Commons may have been able to police judicial decision making irrespective of the preferences of members of the House of Lords. Given that the
impeachment process embodied in the U.S. Constitution was modeled
on that used in England, it is perhaps reasonable to expect that the same
would be true in the United States.[109]

There is also some evidence that, when both methods were available,
legislative majorities preferred impeachment to legislative address as a
means of policing judges. During the Jeffersonian period, for example,
when many states' constitutions provided for judicial removal via both
impeachment and legislative address, it was apparently not uncommon
to see legislative majorities eschewing the seemingly simpler procedure
of legislative address for that of impeachment proceedings.[110] Under leg-

islative address, bicameral legislative majorities can remove an appointed judge essentially at will, without having to show cause. On its face this might seem like an easier way for legislators to remove judges, thereby enabling greater legislative control over judicial decision making. But when a chamber votes for a judge's removal without showing cause, its action is presumably less likely to lead to an increased probability of a vote for removal in a second chamber, relative to impeachment proceedings. The requirement under legislative address of bicameral majorities is then a real requirement, in the sense that a vote for removal in one chamber will not necessarily increase the likelihood of a vote for removal in a second chamber. A friendly majority in one chamber can consequently protect a threatened judge from removal by legislative address simply by not voting for removal. It may then actually be more difficult for a legislature to police judicial decision making using legislative address, relative to using impeachment proceedings. This may at least partially account for the apparent preference for impeachment among legislative majorities during the Jeffersonian period.

In short, it is at least possible that the sequential and investigatory nature of the impeachment process gives House majorities a pivotal agenda-setting role in the removal of federal judges, independent of the preferences of Senate majorities If this is the case, then it may be much easier for the Congress to cabin judicial discretion than previously believed.

It may also be the case that the wording of the Compensation Clause makes it easier for the elected branches to police judicial decision making than has been previously thought. As we saw earlier, this wording specifies that federal judges "shall, at stated Times, receive for their Services, a Compensation, which shall not be diminished during their Continuance in Office." The Compensation Clause prohibits the elected branches from explicitly reducing judicial salaries during a judge's term in office, but it does not require elected officials to provide regular salary increases. This wording permits the elected branches, in the presence of inflation, to reduce judicial salaries simply by doing nothing. If the elected branches do not provide for regular salary increases, in the presence of inflation judicial salaries will automatically decrease in real terms.

This state of affairs implies that, instead of the elected branches needing to coordinate cross-institutional action in order to police federal judges, the shoe is actually on the other foot. It is federal judges who need to coordinate cross-institutional elected branch action in order to preserve their salaries from being automatically reduced. Federal judges must go cap in hand to the elected branches every year in an effort to assemble majorities supportive of judicial salary increases. This effort may very well serve to induce at least partial judicial deference to elected branch preferences, even in the complete absence of elected branch action.

Moreover, the combined impact of Article III's Compensation Clause and Article I's Origination Clause may again focus federal judges' attention on the House of Representatives. Just as the Impeachment Clause gives the House an agenda-setting role in the impeachment process, so too does the Origination Clause give the House an agenda-setting role in the appropriations process. While the Origination Clause specifies merely that bills for "raising Revenue" must originate in the House of Representatives, House majorities have historically interpreted this provision as applying to appropriations bills as well. As a consequence it is not uncommon for the House to reject appropriations measures originating in the Senate simply because these bills violate this interpretation of the Origination Clause.[111]

Federal judges must then first cultivate supportive majorities in the House in order to realize salary increases. Even if federal judges enjoy a Senate majority disposed to increase judicial salaries, the Senate cannot take appropriations action without prior action by a supportive majority in the House. Conversely, once a judicial salary increase has been added to an appropriations bill by the House, this action sets the agenda for the Senate. At that point it requires affirmative action by the Senate in order to remove the judicial salary increase from the appropriations agenda. Moreover, the agenda-setting role of the House extends as well to annual appropriations for the federal courts. Federal judges may then have particular incentives to cater to the preferences of House majorities in order to facilitate the introduction of bills increasing judicial salaries and budgets.

In sum, it may be considerably easier for the elected branches to police federal judicial decision making than has previously been believed. In the case of impeachment, it may require only a determined House majority in order to cabin judicial discretion, given the power of the House to investigate and publicize previously hidden judicial improprieties through the impeachment process. In the case of judicial salaries, the elected branches may be able to cabin judicial discretion simply by doing nothing, given the ongoing real deterioration in those salaries in the absence of affirmative elected branch action. The onus may instead be on federal judges to convince elected branch majorities, perhaps at least in part through their rulings, that they are deserving of salary increases. And just as in the case of impeachment, federal judges may be particularly solicitous of House majorities in order to get judicial salary and budget increases on the appropriations agenda.

The Argument from Judicial Preferences

Some have suggested that, even if it is feasible for the elected branches to police federal judicial decision making, or at least more feasible than we have previously believed to be the case, most of the time judicial preferences will not diverge significantly from those of the elected branches.[112] Federal judges are nominated by presidents and confirmed by Senate majorities. Consequently we might expect judicial preferences to closely mirror elected branch preferences. If this is case, then the question of whether the Constitution incentivizes judicial deference to elected branch preferences is largely moot; that question arises only when judicial preferences diverge from those of the members of the elected branches.

However, there is considerably more turnover in the elected branches than there is on the federal courts. Incoming electoral majorities can easily find the federal bench stacked with opposing party judges possessing divergent preferences, as was the case with the Jeffersonian Republicans in the early 1800s, the Jacksonian Democrats in the 1830s, the Republicans in the 1860s, the Democrats during Woodrow Wilson's presidency, and the Democrats again in the 1930s. Moreover, if federal judges have particular incentives to defer to the preferences of House majorities, rather than to those of Senate majorities or the president, then the objection loses even more of its force. The House, the Senate, and the presidency were designed to represent different electoral constituencies, on different clocks, with different degrees of responsiveness to the preferences of those constituencies. Federal judges appointed by presidents and confirmed by Senate majorities will not necessarily mirror the preferences of House majorities.

In fact, as we will see in Chapter Three, modern estimates of judicial and elected branch preferences in fact reveal periods of quite striking divergence between the preferences of Supreme Court justices and those of majorities in the House of Representatives. One such period occurred in the 1980s and early 1990s, as the Court grew increasingly more conservative after repeated appointments by Republican presidents, while House majorities grew increasingly liberal. These estimates suggest that the question of federal judicial deference or independence is not in fact mooted by the argument from judicial preferences.

The Argument from Normative Beliefs in Judicial Independence

Even if there is divergence between the preferences of elected branch and judicial majorities, however, in order for this divergence to matter it still must be the case that elected branch majorities *want* to police federal judicial decision making. And here there appears to be a consensus that in fact elected branch majorities do not want to be in the business of policing federal judges. Elected officials or their constituents or both, it is said, believe that it is inappropriate for federal judges to be policed by the elected branches. Former Associate Justice Sandra Day O'Connor has written, for example, that "impeachment for a judge's judicial acts has been politically taboo since the failure of Justice Samuel Chase's impeachment back in 1805."[113] University of Pennsylvania Professor of Law Stephen Burbank has likewise asserted that "from the conclusion of the proceedings against Justice Chase to the present it has remained the general view, including of most people in the political branches, that invocation of the impeachment process is not an appropriate response to unpopular judicial decisions."[114] If these claims are correct, then even if many of the framers intended that the federal courts would be checked by the elected branches, and even if it is relatively easy for elected officials to implement these checks, and even if there are divergent preferences between the elected and the judicial branches, the Constitution's checks on the federal judiciary largely go unused because of widespread normative beliefs in the value of independent courts.

The primary evidence cited in support of this claim is the infrequency with which these checks are implemented. Impeachment in particular is a constitutional check on the federal judiciary noted for the rarity of its use. As reported in Table 2.1, only one Supreme Court justice has ever been impeached (Justice Samuel Chase, impeached in 1805), and only fourteen other federal judges have ever been impeached. Because the impeachment of federal judges is so rarely pursued, surely we can infer that elected officials are reluctant to pursue impeachment proceedings.

But this inference does not necessarily follow. The fact that the elected branches use their powers to check the federal courts only rarely (or not at all) does not imply that elected officials are unwilling to use those powers. It might instead imply that federal judges are sufficiently deferential to elected branch preferences so as to effectively deter elected branch sanctions. Imagine a thief holding a gun on his victim in the course of an armed robbery. The gun is not discharged during the robbery. We would not then want to infer that the thief never intended to fire his weapon, and ignore its presence during subsequent criminal proceedings. It is at least as plausible that the victim might well have been shot, had he failed to comply with the thief's demands.

Likewise, it is at least possible that the constitutional checks on the federal courts do not have to be used in order to be effective. As long as federal judges believe that the checks *would* be used, were their decisions to diverge from elected branch preferences, elected officials will never have to actually use any of their powers to discipline the federal courts. We would not then want to infer from the infrequency of their use that elected officials are opposed to their use, and that federal judges are therefore free to defy elected branch preferences.

Colonial judges in North America, for example, remained on the bench only at the pleasure of the Crown's agents. Those agents rarely exercised their powers to remove judges from the bench. But it was apparently widely believed that colonial judges disproportionately deferred to royal preferences, at least in part because removal was a distinct possibility, were judges to be too sympathetic to the colonists' preferences. That is,

Table 2.1: **House Impeachments**

	Party of Appointing President	Majority Party of Impeaching House
House-Initiated Impeachments		
Judge John Pickering	Federalist (George Washington, 1795)	Jeffersonian Republican (1803)
Justice Samuel Chase	Federalist (George Washington, 1796)	Jeffersonian Republican (1804)
Judge James H. Peck	Jeffersonian Republican (James Monroe, 1822)	Jacksonian Democrat (1830)
Judge West H. Humphreys	Democrat (Franklin Pierce, 1853)	Republican (1862)
Judge Mark W. Delahay	Republican (Abraham Lincoln, 1863)	Republican (1873)
Judge Charles Swayne	Republican (Benjamin Harrison, 1890)	Republican (1904)*
Judge Robert W. Archbald	Republican (William Howard Taft, 1910)	Democrat (1912)
Judge George W. English	Democrat (Woodrow Wilson, 1918)	Republican (1926)
Judge Harold Louderback	Republican (Calvin Coolidge, 1928)	Democrat (1933)
Judge Halsted Ritter	Republican (Calvin Coolidge, 1929)	Democrat (1936)
Judiciary-Initiated Impeachments		
Judge Harry E. Claiborne	Democrat (Jimmy Carter, 1978)	Democrat (1986)
Judge Alcee Hastings	Democrat (Jimmy Carter, 1979)	Democrat (1988)

Judge Walter L. Nixon	Democrat (Lyndon B. Johnson, 1968)	Democrat (1989)
Judge Samuel B. Kent	Republican (George H. W. Bush, 1990)	Democrat (2009)
Judge G. Thomas Porteous	Democrat (Bill Clinton, 1994)	Democrat (2010)

---

* 87% of the votes in favor of Judge Swayne's impeachment on the grounds that he had falsified his expense accounts came from House Democrats; 98% of those opposed came from House Republicans. Bushnell (1992), 192.

colonial reformers evidently did not infer from the infrequency of judicial removal that the Crown's agents were reluctant to remove judges from the bench, and that those judges were therefore free to give the colonists impartial and fair hearings in the colonial courts. Instead, they made the perhaps more realistic inference that the willingness of the Crown's agents to invoke judicial removal induced judicial deference, even if actual instances of removal only rarely occurred.[115]

While it is far from conclusive, there is at least suggestive anecdotal evidence that elected officials have likewise been willing to use the Constitution's checks to induce federal judicial deference. During the immediate post-founding period, for example, the historians Peter Hoffer and N. E. H. Hull report that impeachment proceedings were "designed solely to remove partisan or unpopular incumbents on grounds of their partiality and politically unacceptable views."[116] During this period impeachment was apparently pursued primarily as a means to "discredit . . . opposing politicians": "resignation of the defendant or a change in his policies ended the matter. There was no attempt to pursue the charges into the regular courts, for no crimes were alleged."[117] When opposing party majorities controlled a legislature, "no officeholder, whatever his status, was truly safe from impeachment." Hoffer and Hull see in this period's impeachments "the same characteristics that were coming to mark major electoral campaigns—hoopla, press coverage, popular rhetoric preached to the mass of voters . . . the objective of proving a charge became less important than the objective of discrediting an entire party."[118]

Looking beyond the immediate post-founding period one can find similarly suggestive evidence of elected officials' willingness to police federal judicial decision making. For example, while federal judicial impeachments have indeed been rare, there is yet a suspicious pattern of partisanship in House-initiated judicial impeachments. Table 2.1 reports the fifteen realized instances of judicial impeachment in the House of Representatives, including the year of judicial appointment, the party of the appointing president, the year of impeachment, the identity of the majority party in the impeaching House, and whether the impeachment was initiated by the House or was referred to the House by the Judicial Conference of the United States.[119] In eight of the ten House-initiated judicial impeachments, the impeached judge was appointed by a president belonging to a party different from that of the majority party in the impeaching House of Representatives. In another of these impeachments, that of Judge Charles Swayne, appointed by Republican President Benjamin Harrison in 1890, Republicans held a narrow majority in the impeaching House. As reported in the note to Table 2.1, the votes for Judge Swayne's impeachment came overwhelmingly from House Democrats; Republicans largely opposed impeachment.[120]

Rarely were divergent preferences cited as the grounds for impeachment in the House-initiated impeachments. However, that does not imply that divergent preferences played no role in these impeachments. Many of these judges were impeached for perhaps not entirely uncommon offenses like alcohol abuse, using profanity in the courtroom, padding expense accounts, and giving preferential treatment to friends in the distribution of their courts' business.[121] Others were impeached for somewhat questionable rulings, including the use of contempt citations. In the words of Hoffer and Hull, members of House majorities looked for "palpable mistakes or expressions of prejudice and expand[ed] them . . . into impeachable offenses."[122] Presumably one could find infractions of similar severity among judges belonging to the same party as that of the House majority in any given Congress. Yet disproportionately it has been opposing party judges who have been impeached for these kinds of minor offenses.

The partisan pattern in federal judicial impeachments disappears after 1980. In this year the Congress passed the Judicial Conduct and Disability Act, creating procedures whereby complaints against federal judges may be brought to administrative councils within the appellate circuits. These councils are empowered to investigate such complaints as they see fit, and to forward the evidentiary records from these investigations to the Judicial Conference of the United States. The Judicial Conference can then recommend to the House that it begin impeachment proceedings against judges whose conduct is considered to be particularly egregious.

Because the 1980 Judicial Conduct and Disability Act empowered the federal circuits to internally investigate allegations of judicial misconduct, the Act ended the previous monopoly on impeachment investigations held by the House of Representatives. Now candidates for impeachment can be presented to the House by the Judicial Conference of the United States after thorough investigation, and with substantial supporting documentation. At that point even friendly House majorities, that is, those whose preferences are close to those of the targeted judge, can do little other than finish the process. The initiation of the five post-1980 judicial impeachments by the judicial councils of the federal circuits likely accounts for the absence of a pattern of partisanship in these impeachments.[123]

Of course, the rarity of House-initiated judicial impeachments makes it impossible to make reliable inferences. Although there is an apparent pattern of partisanship in these impeachments, there are too few observations for this pattern to be anything more than suggestive. Yet the House-initiated impeachment process is still available to House majorities. And despite widespread popular deference to the ideal of judicial independence, one place where that ideal is not often defended is in the House itself. In 2005, for example, the spokesman for then-House Judiciary Committee chairman F. James Sensenbrenner (R-Wisconsin) told the *New York Times*, "There does seem to be this misunderstanding out there that our system was created with a completely independent judiciary."[124]

The Republican Congresses sitting between 1995 and 2007 were particularly fond of using the impeachment threat to assert congressional supremacy over the federal bench. In 1996, for example, a pamphlet entitled "Impeachment! Restraining an Overactive Judiciary" received wide circulation among Republican members of Congress. It instructed those members that the threat of impeachment could be just as effective as the real thing: "Even if it seems that an impeachment conviction against a certain official is unlikely, impeachment should nevertheless be pursued. Why? Because just the process of impeachment serves as a deterrent. A judge, even if he knows that he is facing nothing more than a congressional hearing on his conduct, will usually become more restrained in order to avoid adding 'fuel to the fire' and thus giving more evidence to the critics calling for his removal."[125]

Republican House Majority Leader Tom DeLay became a particularly impassioned advocate of the impeachment threat. In 1997 DeLay announced, "I advocate impeaching judges who consistently ignore their constitutional role, violate their oath of office, and breach the separation of powers . . . The framers provided the tool of impeachment to keep the power of the judiciary in check."[126] DeLay reported that his staff was reviewing the voting records of federal judges to see which of them would make good impeachment targets: "You have to be a good candidate for impeachment in order to make it stick. We are doing a lot of research on judges' records to see what kinds of attitudes they have."[127] DeLay later told the *Houston Chronicle*, "It is my opinion that anybody can be impeached for anything."[128]

In 2004 DeLay established a House Working Group on Judicial Accountability, boasting that the group would "take no prisoners."[129] That spring, House Republicans considered the Reaffirmation of American Independence Resolution, a measure with dozens of sponsors. The resolution declared that "inappropriate judicial reliance on foreign judgments, laws or pronouncements threatens the sovereignty of the United States, the separation of powers and the president's and the Senate's treaty-making authority."[130] The measure was directed at recent decisions from the Supreme Court that had cited foreign law. Florida Republican Representative Tom Feeney, one of the resolution's main sponsors, said upon its introduction that judges who based decisions on foreign precedents would risk the "ultimate remedy" of impeachment.[131]

Congressional impeachment threats increased in intensity during the 2005 battle over Terri Schiavo, the gravely injured Florida woman whose husband sought the removal of her feeding tube. Elected officials in both Florida and Washington became embroiled in the legal struggle over whether Schiavo's husband should be granted permission to pursue this course of action. After Schiavo passed away, House Majority Leader Tom

DeLay asked the House Judiciary Committee to investigate the federal judges who had refused to issue an order to reinsert Schiavo's feeding tube. DeLay was quoted as saying that Congress "for many years has shirked its responsibility to hold the judiciary accountable. No longer. We will look at an arrogant, out of control, unaccountable judiciary that thumbed their nose at Congress and President when given jurisdiction to hear this case anew and look at all the facts . . . We want to define what good behavior means, and that's where you have to start . . . The time will come for the men responsible for this to answer for their behavior."[132] The chief of staff to Oklahoma Republican Senator Tom Coburn likewise told a gathering of conservatives, "It is tenure for life as long as you behave well . . . as I know that Justice Kennedy and Justice Souter and Justice Breyer and Justice Ginsburg and the rest of that crowd have not done . . . I'm in favor of mass impeachment if that's what it takes."[133] He also recommended judicial removal for misbehavior: "Then the judge's term has simply come to an end. The president gives them a call and says, 'Clean out your desk, the Capitol Police will be in to help you find your way home.'"[134] Pennsylvania Republican Senator Rick Santorum mused, "Should we look at situations where judges have decided to go off on their own tangent and disobey the statutes of the United States of America?" Santorum answered his own question in the affirmative: "I think that's a legitimate area for oversight, sure."[135]

Congressional Republicans also took note of the Ninth Circuit's ruling in 2003 that public schools could not lead students in the Pledge of Allegiance without violating the Establishment Clause.[136] Former Speaker of the House Newt Gingrich wrote in 2005 that the judges joining that opinion "could be considered unfit to serve and be impeached."[137]

These impeachment threats weren't just cheap talk. In 2003 the Congress enacted a bill requiring special scrutiny of federal judges who issued sentences shorter than those called for by the federal sentencing guidelines. Known as the Feeney Amendment, for its sponsor Florida Republican Representative Tom Feeney, the bill instructed the United States Sentencing Commission to maintain judge-by-judge records of downward sentencing departures and to send these records to the Attorney General, who was in turn directed to provide the information to both chambers' Judiciary Committees. The chairman of the House Judiciary Committee,

Wisconsin Republican Representative F. James Sensenbrenner Jr., explicitly acknowledged that the bill "resulted from a policy dispute between Congress and the judiciary."[138] The late Senator Edward Kennedy excoriated the statute's evident aim to bring federal judges' sentencing behavior into conformity with the Republican congressional majority's preferences, denouncing the statute as "blacklisting."[139]

Federal judges took note of congressional Republicans' efforts to remind them of their vulnerability. Testifying before the American Bar Association's hearings on judicial independence in 1996, former Second Circuit Judge John M. Walker reported, "Judges are human, and thus, perhaps depending on the thickness of a particular judge's skin, are not invulnerable to the influence of political pressure."[140] Federal District Judge Louis Pollack likewise told the Commission, in response to a question about whether there were any effects on federal judges from elected branch criticism, "I think what I would sense is caution. It would be nice to make a decision that doesn't necessarily get closer than about page 23 to anybody's attention who is reading the next day's newspapers."[141] The Commission also noted a 1996 speech by District Judge Gerald Rosen, who warned, "What those of us in the judiciary must always remember is that if we begin to exceed our limited constitutional role of interpreting the laws and the Constitution and becoming super-legislators, invading the provinces of the policy branches of government by blithely striking down statutes, regulations and popular referenda . . . we will without question engender a response from policy makers and the people. The response may at first be incremental, aimed only at specific judicial action itself. But, if judicial excesses come to be viewed as commonplace, I believe the response will be systemic and broad-based."[142]

The justices of the Supreme Court also clearly registered congressional Republicans' efforts to intimidate federal judges. In 1998 Justice Anthony Kennedy issued a call for help in defending the Court, which he declared to be "under attack."[143] Justice Ruth Bader Ginsburg noted the threat posed to the liberal justices on the Court by Representative DeLay's impeachment campaign: "I suppose I might someday end up on his list of impeachment targets."[144] After the passage of the Feeney Amendment in 2003, then-Chief Justice Rehnquist characterized it as "an unwarranted and ill-considered effort to intimidate individual judges in the performance of their judicial duties."[145] Justice O'Connor called the Reaffirmation of American Independence Resolution of 2004 "very worrisome," and characterized the relationship between Congress and the federal courts as "more tense than at any time in my lifetime."[146] In 2006, Justice Ginsburg said of congressional impeachment proposals, "it is disquieting that they have attracted sizeable support."[147]

There is likewise suggestive anecdotal evidence that congressional majorities have been willing to use the Constitution's other checks on the federal judiciary. Recall Madison's concern that congressional majorities might strategically fail to increase judicial salaries, or perhaps cut the judiciary's budgets, should judicial decisions not be to their liking. Republican Representative Steve King instantiated Madison's fears in 2005, when he told the *Miami Herald:* "When [the Supreme Court's] budget starts to dry up, we'll get their attention . . . If we're going to preserve our Constitution, we must get them in line."[148]

Federal judges seem to be quite aware of congressional control of their purse strings. In testimony before the American Bar Association, for example, Appellate Judge John Walker noted that "there can be no doubt that the reduction in purchasing power that results from inflation is a real pay cut," and protested that "it leads to the unseemly practice of judges having to implore Congress to restore fair compensation at the very same time that these judges are sitting in review of congressional enactments and interpreting legislation."[149] Judge Walker went on to complain, "The necessary reliance by the judiciary on the political branches of government for its sustenance creates the potential for the weakening of the judiciary as an institution."[150] District Judge Joseph H. Rodriguez corroborated this concern, noting, "If the problem of judicial pay is not fixed, judges will have to implore Congress to take the politically untenable position of voting for unpopular, huge, catch-up increases, an intolerable situation that inappropriately places a non-political judiciary in the center of a hostile public controversy."[151] District Judge Richard Arnold likewise wrote, "Essentially, the courts have no substantial money of their 'own,' barring admission fees from lawyers. We have to get money from somewhere if the judges are to be compensated, if the lights are going to turn on in the courtroom, if the doors are going to open and if the rent is going to be paid. We get money, of course, from Congress."[152]

These concerns have also been expressed by the justices. Speaking at the University of Florida in the fall of 2005, Justice O'Connor demonstrated that Representative King did indeed have her attention, expressing her concern about congressional threats to the Court's budget: "When I hear a threat to cut judicial budgets . . . I get really worried."[153] That same year Justice O'Connor observed, "In all the years of my life, I don't think I've ever seen relations as strained as they are now between the judiciary and some members of Congress . . . For one thing, Congress has not seen fit to have judicial salaries keep pace with what would be expected of people in equivalent professions."[154]

Bills to strip the Court's jurisdiction, or that of the federal courts more generally, also regularly surface in, and sometimes pass, one or even both houses of Congress.[155] In 1996, for example, the Congress passed the Prison Litigation Reform Act, limiting the discretion of federal judges in cases involving the conditions of state prison systems. Prior to the passage of the Act, federal judges could use consent decrees to place state prison systems in the hands of court-appointed special masters, to ensure that conditions improved on schedule. The Act imposed time limits on these consent decrees, limited pay for the special masters, and restricted the ability of judges to issue preliminary injunctions in these cases.[156] Likewise, in the Illegal Immigration Reform and Immigrant Responsibility Act of 1996, Congress eliminated the jurisdiction of the federal courts to hear class action suits challenging certain practices of the Immigration and Naturalization Service. The statute also eliminated judicial review of discretionary deportation decisions by the Attorney General.[157]

Jurisdiction stripping bills continue to be popular in the Congress. In 2004 the House passed a bill to prevent the federal courts from hearing challenges to the 1996 Defense of Marriage Act, the federal statute that permits states to withhold recognition of same-sex marriages performed in other states; the measure failed to clear the Senate. In 2006 the House passed a bill that would have eliminated the jurisdiction of the Supreme Court to review any challenges to the constitutionality of the phrase "under God" in the Pledge of Allegiance; again the bill failed of passage in the Senate. Other jurisdiction stripping bills recently introduced in the Congress include bills limiting or eliminating federal jurisdiction to review cases involving the death penalty, voter referenda, any actions by governmental officials concerning "the acknowledgement of God as the sovereign source of law, liberty, or government," the display of religious texts and imagery on government property, abortion, sexual practices, same-sex marriage, and state laws regulating pornography.[158]

Characterizing such jurisdiction-stripping proposals as "threats for retribution against judges for certain decisions," the retired Justice O'Connor objected to such congressional intimidation: "Let's deprive [the Supreme Court] of jurisdiction over certain kinds of cases . . . I mean, that's contrary to every notion of judicial independence that we know, from the time that the Constitution was adopted."[159] Then-Chief Justice Rehnquist likewise noted the frequency of bill proposals to "limit the jurisdiction of the federal courts to decide constitutional challenges to certain kinds of government action," proclaiming loftily, "Let us hope that the Supreme Court and all of our courts will continue to command sufficient public respect to enable them to survive basic attacks on the judicial independence that has made our judicial system a model for much of the world."[160]

The congressional power to alter the size of the Supreme Court is perhaps referred to less frequently, but has nonetheless not gone unused. During the Civil War, the size of the Supreme Court was for a time increased to ten justices, later reduced to eight, and then restored to nine, as the Radical Republican Congress sought to manipulate the composition of the Court to its liking.[161] In 1937 President Franklin Delano Roosevelt somewhat famously proposed, "Whenever a judge or justice of any federal court has reached the age of seventy and does not avail himself of the opportunity to retire on a pension, a new member shall be appointed."[162] Roosevelt's proposal was widely understood as an effort to "pack" the conservative Supreme Court with new liberal members.[163]

Members of Congress have also not been shy about threatening to use the congressional power to establish, or disestablish, the lower federal courts. Indeed, this power was used not long after the Constitution's ratification. A lame duck Federalist congressional majority had passed the Judiciary Act of 1801, establishing sixteen new appellate court judgeships. Outgoing Federalist President John Adams promptly filled these courts with Federalist judges. The newly elected Jeffersonian Republicans then sought the Act's repeal, hoping to relieve the newly appointed

Federalist judges of their short-lived jobs. The Federalist congressional minority protested that the Repeal Act would inappropriately incentivize the remaining federal judges to be particularly solicitous of the Republican majority's preferences: "What will be the effect of a desired repeal? Will it not be a declaration to the remaining judges that they hold their offices subject to your will and pleasure?"[164] Nevertheless, the Repeal Act passed, and was subsequently upheld by the Supreme Court in *Stuart v. Laird,* 5 U.S. 299 (1803).[165]

More recently, the Ninth Circuit Court of Appeals, known as a particularly liberal appellate court, became a frequent target for elimination by Republican congresses. After the Circuit's 2003 ruling that recitation of the Pledge of Allegiance in a public school constituted an unconstitutional establishment of religion, congressional lawmakers threatened to reconstitute the Ninth Circuit, in what was widely described as punishment for the Pledge ruling.[166] Likewise, after the Terri Schiavo case in 2005, Republican Representative Steve King was quoted as saying, in a clear warning to the federal courts, "We have the constitutional authority to eliminate any and all inferior courts."[167]

These anecdotes, of course, are far from being conclusive evidence that congressional majorities have consistently been willing to use the constitutionally available tools to police federal judicial decision making. While members of Congress not infrequently threaten federal judges with constitutional checks, and while federal judges express concern about these threats, the threats rarely come to fruition. Perhaps they are mostly cheap talk, posing few credible constraints on the decisional authority of federal judges.

Or perhaps not. The question of the willingness of the elected branches to use the constitutionally available tools to police federal judicial decision making cannot be resolved by competing anecdotes. Instead we must turn to the decisions of federal judges. If it is both feasible and likely that elected officials will discipline federal judges, should the latter not defer to elected branch preferences in their rulings, then we should expect federal judges to defer to elected branch preferences in their rulings. If it is either infeasible for elected officials to discipline the federal courts (for example, because it is too difficult to coordinate cross-institutional action) or unlikely that elected officials will want to use the disciplinary measures available to them (for example, because either those officials or their constituents, or both, believe in the principle of independent courts), then we should not expect federal judges to defer to elected branch preferences in their rulings. The key question is, then, do federal judges in fact defer to elected branch preferences in their rulings? This is the empirical question to which we turn in subsequent chapters.

The Elected Branches That Did Nothing in the Night-Time

Many today regard it as simply implausible that federal judges defer to elected branch preferences. Some assert that the Constitution's text protects federal judges from the need to do so. Others claim that, even if the Constitution can be read to permit elected branch checks on the federal courts, this is not the reading that was intended by those who wrote and ratified that document. Some suggest that, even if some or perhaps most of the framers intended that the elected branches would check the federal courts, under the Madisonian design the difficulty of coordinating cross-institutional action precludes those branches from implementing such checks. Still others suggest that, even if these checks are feasibly implemented, most of the time judicial preferences will not diverge from elected branch preferences. Yet others maintain that, even if judicial and elected branch preferences frequently diverge, norms of judicial independence constrain elected officials from seeking to check the federal courts.

As a result of some combination of these factors, most observers of the federal courts today seem to believe that these courts enjoy at least de facto judicial independence. Northwestern University Professors of Law Steven Calabresi and James Lindgren assert, for example, that "impeachment has been of no use whatsoever for controlling the behavior of Supreme Court Justices."[168] University of Virginia Professor of Law Saikrishna Prakash likewise writes that "impeachment can never be used as a means of keeping judges accountable . . . Impeachment is a phantom menace."[169] The Wikipedia entry on the Supreme Court of the United States, probably the modal source of information about the Court, declares confidently: "The term 'good behavior' is well understood to mean Justices may serve for the remainder of their lives, although they can voluntarily resign or

retire."[170] Indiana University Professor of Law Charles Gardner Geyh has
asserted more generally that all routes for holding federal judges accountable to the elected branches "have been systematically closed,"[171] while
Calabresi and Lindgren have written that the Constitution's checks on
the federal judiciary "can hardly be considered effective means of rendering the Court democratically accountable."[172]

The central point of this chapter is simply that we should not be so
persuaded by any of these arguments that we call it a day and go home.
First, the plain words of the Constitution's text appear to enable multiple
elected branch checks on the federal courts. The Constitution provides
for elected branch control over federal judges' tenures, salaries, budgets,
jurisdictions, and whether they will be in the majority or the minority on
their courts. While constitutional theorists argue about the appropriate
scope of these provisions, the very existence of these interpretive disputes
seems to indicate that elected majorities have the opportunity to interpret
these provisions more broadly or more narrowly, as circumstances require.

Second, there is considerable evidence in the historical record that
many colonial and revolutionary era reformers actually preferred deferential to independent courts, and that they sought elected branch control
over judicial tenures and salaries precisely in order to induce judicial deference to elected branch preferences. These institutional practices were
then included in the post-independence state constitutions and in the
United States Constitution, with the Impeachment Clause of the latter subsequently defended during the ratification debates as providing a
"complete security" against the threat of antimajoritarian judges.[173] While
this evidence is not conclusive as to the private beliefs of those who voted
for the Constitution's provisions (as no evidence probably ever will be), it
should at least be sufficient to reject as conclusive the argument that the
founders never intended to induce judicial deference to elected branch
preferences. The alternative hypothesis, that majorities in the Constitutional Convention and in the ratification conventions did in fact intend
to secure federal judicial deference to elected branch preferences, should
at least remain alive as a possibility.

Third, there is also considerable reason to reject as determinative the
argument that, even if the Constitution's provisions regulating the federal judiciary were in fact intended to induce judicial deference to elected

branch preferences, those provisions have proved too difficult for elected officials to implement. Upon closer examination, both the impeachment and the appropriations powers would appear to require considerably less of elected officials than commonly believed. An effective impeachment threat may require only House majorities willing to investigate rumors of improprieties committed by judges possessing divergent preferences. An effective appropriations threat may require only House majorities willing to refrain from including judicial salary increases in annual appropriations bills, unless and until judicial decisions conform to their preferences.

Fourth, there are both logical and empirical reasons to reject as conclusive the argument that judicial and elected branch preferences will only rarely diverge. Because elections are more frequent than federal judicial appointments, there is considerably more turnover in elected branch preferences than in judicial preferences. The latter can easily lag the former by several years, if not decades. Moreover, if it is the case that federal judges have particular incentives to defer to the preferences of majorities in the House of Representatives, divergence is even more likely to occur, given that the House plays no role in federal judicial appointments. Finally, the preference estimates reported in the next chapter indicate that, at least between 1953 and 2004, there have been several periods of considerable divergence between the preferences of majorities in the elected branches and those on the Supreme Court.

Fifth, and finally, we can't make any reliable inferences about the willingness of elected officials to police federal judicial decision making from the frequency with which policing is observed. The fact that the elected branches rarely levy overt sanctions against the federal courts could be because either elected officials or their constituents, or both, are opposed on normative grounds to the use of such sanctions. Or it could be because federal judges are sufficiently deferential in their rulings so as not to induce these sanctions. We simply cannot know whether the possible threat of elected branch sanctions affects federal judicial decision making without looking at federal judicial decisions.

We may, in short, have made an inferential error not unlike that committed by the hapless Inspector Gregory in the Arthur Conan Doyle story "Silver Blaze." A famous racehorse has disappeared on the eve of an important race. The Scotland Yard detective assigned to the case, Inspector

Gregory, has a suspect in custody (incorrectly, it turns out), but has not been able to locate the horse. So the services of Sherlock Holmes are requested. After Holmes identifies several important but overlooked aspects of the case, Inspector Gregory asks, "Is there any other point to which you would wish to draw my attention?" Holmes replies, "To the curious incident of the dog in the night-time." Inspector Gregory responds, puzzled, "The dog did nothing in the night-time." Says Holmes, "That was the curious incident."[174]

Like Inspector Gregory, perhaps we have misread the curious incident of the elected branches that did nothing in the night-time. From the relative infrequency with which federal judges are sanctioned by the elected branches, we inferred that those judges are largely safe from elected branch sanctions. Yet there was another inference that could have been drawn. Perhaps federal judges are infrequently sanctioned by the elected branches precisely because those judges are *not* safe from elected branch sanctions. Being vulnerable to elected branch sanctions, perhaps federal judges take care in their decisions not to, in the words of Justice O'Connor, "make the president or Congress really, really angry."[175]

Perhaps, that is, Hamilton was right when he predicted that "[t]here never can be danger that the judges, by a series of deliberate usurpations on the authority of the legislature, would hazard the united resentment of the body entrusted with it, while this body was possessed of the means of punishing their presumption by degrading them from their stations."[176] Hamilton believed that the mere possession of the power to punish would be sufficient to induce federal judicial deference to elected branch preferences. The elected branches would never need to use their disciplinary powers, because judges would tread very carefully. If Hamilton was right, then even were federal judges never sanctioned by the elected branches, the federal judiciary still might not be independent of those branches. It might merely serve its masters well.

3

ESTIMATING THE EFFECT OF ELECTED BRANCH PREFERENCES ON SUPREME COURT JUDGMENTS

As we saw in the last chapter, the United States Constitution gives to the elected branches numerous powers to check the decision making of federal judges. Two of these powers, namely impeachment and appropriations, give a prominent role to majorities in the House of Representatives. The existence of these powers may give federal judges powerful incentives to defer to the preferences of elected branch majorities, perhaps particularly to majorities in the House.

However, we rarely see the elected branches exercising their powers over the federal courts. As a consequence, the conventional wisdom is that federal judges in the United States are free to disregard the possibility of elected branch sanctions. But it is at least possible that the conventional wisdom is mistaken. Perhaps the mere existence of these powers is sufficient to induce judicial deference to elected branch preferences, even in the absence of their use.

The frequency of elected branch attempts to sanction the federal courts is thus not a reliable measure of the efficacy of those sanctions.[1] Instead, the empirical question we want to ask is, irrespective of the frequency of elected branch sanctions, do federal judges defer to elected branch preferences in their decisions?

This is the question to which the next several chapters now turn. In these chapters we narrow our focus from the federal courts in general to the Supreme Court in particular. As the highest court in the federal judicial hierarchy, and the only federal court actually established by the

Constitution, the Supreme Court occupies a uniquely important position. Because federal appellate and district courts are bound to follow the rules issued by the Supreme Court (or risk reversal on appeal), it is those rules that we would most like to understand. If we do find an effect of elected branch preferences on this Court's decisions, we might then expect that this effect would also be found on the decisions made in the lower federal courts.

In recent years legal historians have engaged in a lively debate over whether the justices of the Supreme Court defer to elected branch preferences in their decisions.[2] This debate has undoubtedly broadened our understanding of the particular political circumstances attending the Court's deliberations in several important cases. It is unlikely, however, that qualitative history will be able to conclusively resolve the question of the Court's independence. It is often difficult to assess the reliability of inferences drawn from historical narratives, given issues of selection, sample size, and the need to control for alternative explanations.

For these reasons social scientists generally rely on quantitative analyses of the Court's judgments. These analyses permit us to look for patterns in large numbers of the Court's decisions, leveraging the power of statistical inference, while controlling for alternative explanations. Recently major strides have been made in the measurement of the "revealed preferences" of both the justices and members of the elected branches, further enabling the quantitative analysis of the Court's hypothesized independence from elected branch preferences.

And the news is good for proponents of the claim of the Court's independence. Quantitative studies of the Court's decisions generally have failed to find any support for the hypothesis of judicial deference to elected branch preferences (also known as the "separation-of-powers" hypothesis in the quantitative literature). Indeed, some quantitative analysts believe the question of the Court's independence to be conclusively settled. Reviewing the empirical literature on the Court's independence, political scientists Jeffrey Segal and Harold Spaeth write, "Recent years have witnessed an explosion in quantitative analyses of the separation-of-powers model. The findings are overwhelming in their lack of support for the model . . . the empirical evidence refutes the model."[3]

In this chapter we will look at how quantitative analysts have approached the empirical question of estimating the Court's independence (or lack thereof) from elected branch preferences. As we will see, there is indeed good reason to agree with Segal and Spaeth's conclusion: using the measures and research designs widely adopted in the quantitative literature, there is no evidence of judicial deference to the preferences of elected branch majorities, from the Warren through the Rehnquist Courts. It is particularly striking that we can find no evidence of such deference during the Rehnquist Court terms, when a relatively stable conservative majority on the Court faced first a series of liberal Democratic Congresses and then, after the 1994 congressional elections, a series of conservative Republican Congresses. Instead, the Court's judgments closely tracked the estimated preferences of the Court's median justice.

But as we will then see in Chapter Four, this quantitative account of the Rehnquist Court does not square with the narrative accounts of that court related by the journalists and legal academics who watch the Court for a living. Despite the difficulties inherent in drawing reliable inferences from qualitative narratives, the sheer consistency of these narrative accounts should raise a red flag for quantitative analysts. Either scores of close observers of the Court's jurisprudence have been collectively deceived, or something is wrong with the quantitative analyses.

Modeling the Court's Decisions

Most quantitative studies of the Court's putative independence from the elected branches follow a common research design. First, the researcher assumes that both the justices and members of the elected branches care about the same thing, namely the legal rules endorsed by the Court in its opinions. These rules govern the dispositions not only of the instant cases, but also of future cases presenting similar legal issues. They sort cases, presenting varying fact patterns, into dispositional outcomes: a statute is struck or upheld, a criminal conviction is affirmed or overturned, a firm's conduct is held to have been anti-competitive or not.[4] For example, a legal rule in the area of Interstate Commerce Clause jurisprudence might proscribe congressional regulation of economic activity that does not actually cross state boundaries. Challenged statutes that regulate purely intrastate activity will be struck as unconstitutional, while those regulating clearly interstate activity will be upheld. A more liberal legal rule in this jurisprudential area would permit intrastate activity to be regulated, as long as that activity had substantial effects on the interstate economy. A rule falling in between these two rules might permit the regulation of only "economic" intrastate activity having substantial effects on interstate commerce.[5]

Those studying the question of the Court's independence typically assume that both the justices and members of the elected branches have preferences over these legal rules, such that each individual justice or elected official has a most preferred rule in any area of the law. Satisfaction with a rule peaks at one's most preferred rule, and declines as that rule moves either to the left or the right, away from the most preferred rule.[6]

It is easy to see why the justices would care about these rules; they are the means by which the Court makes policy. Likewise, these rules, particularly if they are constitutional rules, condition the kinds of policies elected officials can enact. An elected official will naturally prefer rules that allow the elected branches to enact her most preferred policies. By the same token, statutes enacted by the elected branches must of necessity at least implicitly embody elected branch preferences over these rules. When the elected branches enact a statute regulating gun possession within school zones, for example, elected branch majorities are clearly expressing their preference for a legal rule governing elected branch power under the Interstate Commerce Clause that endorses the permissibility of this particular bill.

Quantitative analysts of the Court's jurisprudence generally represent these legal rules on a single dimension, ranging from more liberal to more conservative rules. We might hesitate to do this; it is certainly possible for any particular area of the law to have multidimensional rules, or for all the areas of law aggregated together to form a multidimensional space of rules. But when analysts estimate elected branch and judicial preferences over these rules, the vast majority of both roll call votes and the justices' votes in cases can be explained by reference to a single underlying dimension.[7] This is not unusual; almost all institutions of collective decision making within which preferences have been estimated appear to structure those preferences on a single liberal-conservative dimension. From the U.S. Congress to the United Nations to the European Parliament, from very new to very old democracies, it appears to be the case that voting over policy choices tends to be ordered on a single dimension of competition; the Supreme Court provides no exception to this pattern.[8]

The fact that the justices' preferences over rules may be well estimated on a single dimension, much as legislators' preferences may be well estimated on a single dimension, has raised some concerns in the legal academy that these estimates, frequently referred to as measures of judicial "ideology," do not incorporate the possibly profound concern and respect that the justices may have for "law." Quantitative analysts of the Court are seen as claiming that the justices care only about narrowly political or ideological goals, and not about jurisprudential concerns like precedent or theories of interpretation.[9]

However, as others have pointed out, the supposed dichotomy between "ideology" and "law" is a false one.[10] The fact that a justice may have a deep commitment to a philosophy of constitutional interpretation is not likely to be unrelated to the kinds of outcomes that justice would like to see in the world. The possibility that a justice may possess a strong normative belief in the value of precedent does not address the question of which precedents that justice might see as relevant to a given decision. Moreover, the law itself often grants to the justices a considerable degree of discretion in reaching their decisions. As a purely theoretical matter, then, it is quite difficult, and probably counterproductive, to distinguish between ideology and law as separate categories.

In any case, even were there a clearer theoretical distinction between ideology and law, our measures of judicial preferences would give us very little information about which of these sources had generated those preferences, that is, whether they were more a product of ideology or law. All the measures do is reveal a structure to the pattern of votes cast by the justices. This structure aligns the justices on a single dimension, with each justice's estimated position on that dimension being the best empirical representation of that justice's most preferred point, relative to the other justices. These most preferred points are fairly precisely estimated, meaning that there is in fact a good deal of structure in the justices' votes across cases. However, the measures themselves give us little indication of what we should call these most preferred points.

Finally, these estimated preferences do not explain, meaning are not consistent with, every vote cast by the justices. There are clearly other

factors operating on the justices' decisions in cases, beyond the underlying preferences captured by these estimates. It is certainly possible that
many of these factors are legal in nature. However, given the difficulty of
measuring these possibly legal influences on the justices' decisions, they
are typically not included in the models of judicial decision making used
in quantitative studies of the Court's independence.

As noted previously, there is considerable evidence that estimates of
the justices' most preferred rules are closely associated with their votes
over judgments. The question is whether, after controlling for the effects
of judicial preferences, there is any effect of elected branch preferences
on the Court's judgments. To address this question we will estimate the
probability that the Court issues a conservative judgment in a case as a
function of both the estimated most preferred rule of the pivotal justice,
and the estimated most preferred rules of pivotal members of the elected
branches (with pivotality identified by auxiliary theoretical assumptions,
to be discussed below).

If elected branch preferences have no effect on the Court's decisions,
then we expect to find only a relationship between the most preferred rule
of the pivotal justice and the Court's judgments: as this most preferred
rule becomes more conservative, we expect an increase in the probability
that the Court issues a conservative judgment. We would expect to find
no effect on this judgment probability from any variation in the preferences of pivotal members of the elected branches.

But if elected branch preferences in fact have an effect on the Court's
decisions, then we would expect to find predicted effects both from
changes in the preferences of the pivotal justice, and from changes in
the preferences of pivotal members of the elected branches: holding constant the most preferred rule of the pivotal justice, as the most preferred
rules of pivotal members of the elected branches move to the right, we
expect increases in the probability that the Court issues a conservative
judgment. Likewise, still holding constant the most preferred rule of
the pivotal justice, as the most preferred rules of pivotal members of the
elected branches move to the left, we expect corresponding decreases in
the probability that the Court issues a conservative judgment.

Identifying the pivotal members of the Court and the elected branches
requires researchers to say something about how decisions get made

in these institutions. The typical starting point for a model of collective decision making is to emphasize the importance of the median, or middle, voter in a collective that makes decisions via majority rule. For example, imagine that the justices, whom we assume to have single peaked preferences over legal rules on a single dimension, are asked to choose between two proposed rules: one located to the left of the median justice, the other to her right. In the absence of any external constraints on the justices' decisions, we would expect that every justice whose most preferred rule is closer to Option A will vote for A, while those whose most preferred rules are closer to Option B will choose B. The option with the most votes will win; those votes will necessarily include the vote of the median justice.

Now imagine that there exist no constraints on the process of suggesting changes or amendments to these proposed rules, or of proposing alternative rules. There are thus opportunities for some justices to make themselves better off. For any proposed rule to the left of the median justice, there will always exist a majority in favor of an amendment to that proposal which moves it to the right, closer to the most preferred rule of the median justice. Once that amended proposal hits the most preferred rule of the median justice, however, there will no longer be a majority of justices to support amendments moving the proposed rule even further to the right. The same situation exists for any rule proposed to the right of the median justice: there will always be a majority in favor of amendments which move that proposal to the left, but only as far as the most preferred rule of the median justice. In other words, if the justices have single peaked preferences on a single dimension, make decisions via majority rule, and are not constrained in the kinds of opinions they can write, we generally expect proposed opinion alternatives to converge to the most preferred rule of the median justice.[11]

There is not complete agreement among those who study the Court that the median justice is always the Court's pivotal voter. In a world in which writing competing opinions is costly, for example, the justice originally assigned a majority opinion may be able to write, and get a majority to join, an opinion somewhat closer to her own preferences than the median would prefer.[12] However, while research on these questions proceeds, the most preferred rule of the median justice is not a bad starting point to think about how to summarize the Court's preferences in a given case.

Thinking about how to model the collective decision making of the elected branches is somewhat more complicated. First, we have to distinguish between elected branch responses to statutory and constitutional cases. With respect to the former, some have asked whether the Court defers to elected branch preferences in cases involving the interpretation of federal statutes. In these cases the Court simply expresses its views about how federal statutes should be read. After a decision in such a case, the elected branches are free to enact amending legislation rejecting or otherwise qualifying the Court's statutory interpretation. These elected branch responses may make the Court worse off than if it had strategically deferred to elected branch preferences in the first place. In statutory cases, then, we may observe the Court deferring to elected branch preferences not because the justices fear elected branch sanctions or seek elected branch rewards, but rather because the Court does not have the last word in cases involving statutory interpretation.[13]

If it exists, this effect of elected branch preferences in statutory cases should work through the elected branches' power to enact legislation. Empirical studies of this possible effect of elected branch preferences have then grappled with the question of how the bicameral Congress enacts legislation that then must survive the threat of a possible presidential veto. These models of elected branch lawmaking can get quite complicated, specifying possible avenues for committee influence, majority party influence, the possibility of filibusters in the Senate, the potential threat of presidential vetoes, and the role of conference committees.[14]

Evidence of judicial deference in these cases is mixed.[15] But in any case these studies do not conclusively test the hypothesis of institutional constraints on the Court. That hypothesis suggests that the Court will defer to elected branch preferences generally, not just in statutory cases, because the justices fear elected branch sanctions and/or seek elected branch rewards. Should analyses of statutory cases fail to find evidence of elected branch influence on the Court's decisions, those findings would undermine the claim of a possible effect from elected branch sanctions. But should those analyses instead find evidence of elected branch influence, we would still be left with the question of why that influence exists.

Do elected branch preferences affect the justices' decisions in statutory cases because the justices fear elected branch sanctions, or simply because the Court and the elected branches are sequentially making law over time?

For this reason the Court's decisions in constitutional cases are perhaps more valuable for examining the effects of possible elected branch sanctions. The elected branches possess no generally recognized power to amend the Court's decisions in constitutional cases using ordinary legislation.[16] If we find evidence of elected branch constraint in the Court's constitutional cases, then presumably it is due to the justices' anticipation of elected branch punishments or rewards.[17]

The handful of empirical studies that have evaluated the effect of elected branch preferences on the Court's constitutional decisions generally have assumed that the elected branches need to enact legislation in order to punish the Court. These studies have thus imported into the constitutional context the models of elected branch lawmaking used in analyses of the Court's statutory decisions. Because it is relatively difficult to enact legislation in the Madisonian context of separated institutions sharing powers, these models typically generate predictions of a Court that is largely unconstrained: because it is hard for the elected branches to enact legislation, it is unlikely that elected branch majorities will be able to discipline or reward the justices. The few predictions of constraint that are made by these models have found very little evidentiary support in the Court's constitutional decisions.[18]

But the Constitution doesn't require the elected branches to legislate in order to discipline the Court. As we saw in Chapter Two, the impeachment power is unusual in that the congressional chambers act separately and sequentially, and no presidential assent is required. The House acts first, and the Constitution requires of the House only a simple majority vote for impeachment. In order for a justice actually to be removed from office, the Constitution then requires a two-thirds majority in the Senate. But impeachment alone may be a significant sanction, one that in and of itself may constitute an effective threat.

Likewise, sanctioning the justices through the appropriations process requires not that the elected branches enact legislation, but rather that they do not enact legislation. In the presence of inflation, judicial salaries will decrease in real terms if either House majorities, Senate majorities, or the president, acting separately, do not agree to judicial salary increases. Conversely, each branch, acting separately, must agree to judicial salary increases in order to see those increases realized. As in the impeachment process, these salary increases must be initiated by majorities in the House of Representatives.

The justices may then be particularly interested in the preferences of House majorities, or more simply, in those of the median member of the House. Locating legal rules at the most preferred rule of the median representative in the House may be the best way both to deter House impeachment investigations, and to induce the inclusion of judicial salary and budget increases in annual appropriations bills.

The constitutional design of both the impeachment and the appropriations processes thus suggests that House majorities may be able to induce judicial deference even in the absence of cooperation from the other branches. However, there are also constitutionally sanctioned avenues for Senate majorities and the president to influence the justices' decisions as well, for example through the passage of bills increasing the justices' salaries, increasing or decreasing the justices' budgets, stripping or otherwise modifying the Court's jurisdiction, and increasing or decreasing the size of the Court. The analyses to follow will estimate separate effects for the preferences of the median member of the House of Representatives, the median senator, and the president, although we might expect to see particular judicial deference to the preferences of the median representative.

As is the case with those who study the Court, there is not complete consensus among those who study Congress that the chamber or floor medians will always be pivotal. Some argue that committee chairs and/or medians may act as gatekeepers by preventing proposals from reaching the floor, others that majority party leaders and/or medians may structure agendas through the use of restrictive rules. However, there are good reasons to be skeptical of these possibilities. Floor majorities in both chambers may order committees to discharge proposals to the floor, thus preventing committee gatekeeping, and any restrictive voting rules must also be approved by floor majorities. These procedures imply the pivotality of the chamber or floor medians.[19]

Measuring Preferences

To estimate the effects of elected branch preferences on the Court's decisions, researchers need to be able to locate elected branch and judicial preferences over legal rules relative to each other. That is, we have to have some way of bridging our estimates of judicial preferences, generated from the justices' votes on judgments, with estimates of elected branch preferences, generated from roll call votes.

There have been two approaches to this problem in the recent empirical literature. The first approach is to actually estimate these preferences jointly. The data used to estimate the justices' most preferred rules, namely their votes in cases, are expanded to include elected branch "votes" on these same cases. For example, congressional and presidential votes on federal statutes that are challenged before the Court on constitutional grounds are also implicit votes on the Court's dispositions of these statutes; those elected branch officials who voted for the statute at issue presumably would also vote to uphold the statute, while those who voted against would presumably also vote to strike. Members of Congress and the executive branch also often file amicus curiae briefs in litigation before the Court; these briefs can be treated as votes for particular case dispositions. Likewise, in response to judicial decisions, members of Congress and the president often make statements, propose legislation, and sometimes even vote on such legislation; these actions can be treated as votes comparable to the dispositional votes cast by the justices in the actual decisions. These data points can be used to estimate the most preferred legal rules of members of the elected branches, scaled in the same unidimensional space as those of the justices. This is the approach underlying the crosstemporal and crossinstitutional (XTI) preference estimates reported by Michael Bailey of Georgetown University.[20]

The second approach to this problem has been to try to find a way to link separately estimated judicial and elected branch preferences. This is the approach underlying the "Judicial Common Space" estimates, widely used in the empirical literature.[21] This approach assumes that under certain conditions a president will nominate candidates for vacancies on the Court who share his most preferred legal rule, and that these candidates will then be approved by Senate majorities. More specifically, when the president's most preferred rule lies between that of the median senator and the existing Court median, the president can nominate a candidate for the Court at his own most preferred rule and expect to have that candidate confirmed by a Senate majority. These candidates are then identified empirically, using a variety of preference estimates. Their most preferred legal rules are assumed to be identical to the nominating presidents' most preferred rules. This strategy then provides a link between separately estimated elected branch and judicial preferences.[22]

However, this strategy is somewhat circular, being dependent upon the initial identification of the relative locations of the most preferred rules of justices, median senators, and presidents. These relative locations are identified using a hodgepodge of preference estimates that are not themselves scaled in the same policy space.[23] Consequently, as acknowledged by the creators of the Judicial Common Space (JCS) estimates, accepting the validity of these estimates is at least partially "a matter of faith."[24]

The Bailey XTI preference estimates are then perhaps preferable to the JCS estimates, having been directly and simultaneously estimated from a common set of votes, rather than produced from two separately estimated series linked together by a reasonable, but not ironclad, assumption. However, all the analyses in Chapters Three, Five, and Six are replicated using both sets of preference estimates.

One issue with both these sets of preference estimates is that they are derived from models of decision making that assume away any systematic external effects on votes; both elected branch officials' and justices' votes are assumed to result only from their own preferences. If this assumption is violated, then the preference estimates may incorporate these external effects. The justices' preference estimates in particular may already incorporate the effects of elected branch preferences on their votes. When we attempt to estimate the effects of elected branch preferences on the justices' votes, while controlling for judicial preferences, we might not find any effect from the former, simply because that effect would already have been incorporated into our estimates of judicial preferences. For this reason it would be preferable to have estimates of judicial preferences purged of any effects from elected branch preferences. But even if the effects of elected branch preferences are already incorporated into our estimates of judicial preferences, this will mitigate against finding any independent effects of elected branch preferences on the justices' votes, because we would have already captured those effects in our estimates of judicial preferences. Any independent effects from elected branch preferences that we do find, then, should be viewed as a lower bound estimate of the "true" effects of those preferences.[25]

Figures 3.1 and 3.2 report the Bailey XTI estimated most preferred rules for the median justice, the median representative, the median senator, and the president between 1953 and 2004.[26] These preferences are increasing in conservatism; larger positive values indicate preferences for more conservative legal rules, while larger negative values indicate preferences for more liberal legal rules. Looking first at Figure 3.1, there are clearly periods when the estimated preferences of the House and Senate medians are relatively close to those of the median justice, and when

Figure 3.1. Supreme Court and Congressional Medians, 1953–2004
Source: Bailey (2007). Estimated ideal points are increasing in conservatism.

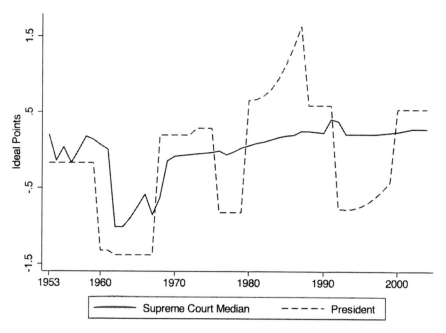

Figure 3.2. Supreme Court and Presidential Preferences, 1953–2004
Source: Bailey (2007). Estimated ideal points are increasing in conservatism.

the effect of congressional constraint on the Court, even if it existed, would have been slight. These periods correspond to the conventional wisdom that the degree of divergence between the elected branches and the Court is likely to be small.

However, there are also two periods between 1953 and 2004 when there are sizable differences between the most preferred rules of the two congressional medians and that of the median justice: the period of the late Warren and early Burger Courts, from approximately the 1962 through the 1973 terms, when the median justice's most preferred legal rule was significantly to the left of those preferred by the House and Senate medians, and the period of the late Burger and early Rehnquist Courts, from approximately the 1982 through the 1993 terms, when the median justice's most preferred legal rule was significantly, and increasingly, to the right of those preferred by the House and Senate medians. Replicating this figure using the Judicial Common Space preference estimates also highlights these two periods of divergent preferences.

The second period of divergence, in the 1980s and early 1990s, may be particularly helpful for testing the hypothesis of congressional constraint on the Court's decisions. During the 1960s and early 1970s, both the Court and the Congress moved in a more liberal direction; the Court simply moved more to the left than did the House or the Senate. Yet the liberal Warren and early Burger Court justices still enjoyed Democratic majorities in both the House and the Senate.

But during the 1980s and early 1990s, congressional and judicial preferences move in opposite directions. The estimated most preferred rule of the median justice continued to move in a conservative direction, as the Court experienced three appointments made by a Republican President and confirmed by a Republican Senate: the appointment of Sandra Day O'Connor in 1981, the elevation of Justice William Rehnquist to the position of Chief Justice in 1986, and the appointment of Antonin Scalia, also in 1986. Moreover, the estimated most preferred rule of Justice Byron White, one of the more centrist justices, also moved in a conservative direction throughout this period.

By contrast, the estimated preferences of the House and Senate medians moved in a more liberal direction, particularly after the 1982, 1986, and 1990 midterm elections. As can be seen in Figure 3.1, by 1986, the first term of the Rehnquist Court, the most preferred legal rules of the House and Senate medians are estimated to have been considerably to the left of that of the median justice, and remained so through the 1993 term. The most preferred rules of the congressional medians then shifted sharply to the right as a result of the 1994 congressional elections, while that of the median justice remained relatively stable.

The Rehnquist Court thus presents a near ideal opportunity to test the hypothesis of congressional constraint on the justices' decisions. As a result of plausibly exogenous electoral forces, during this Court's terms the most preferred rules of the House and Senate medians first moved steadily to the left, away from that of the median justice, and then jumped abruptly to the right in the 1994 term. But the estimated most preferred rule of the median justice remained consistently conservative. Although we don't have the luxury of being able to randomly assign preferences to the Court and the Congress in order to test the hypothesis of the Court's independence, these electorally induced shifts are perhaps the next best thing.

Figure 3.2, reporting the estimated most preferred rules of the median justice and the president over the same time period, reveals a different pattern of convergence and divergence. In this figure the presidencies of Jimmy Carter and Bill Clinton stand out as episodes when the president's preferences were significantly to the left of those of the median justice. During the presidency of Ronald Reagan, by contrast, presidential preferences were significantly to the right of those of the Court. These episodes provide us with opportunities to test the hypothesis that presidential preferences affect the Court's judgments.

Measuring Judgments

In order to estimate the effects of elected branch preferences on the Court's decisions, however, we still need to address a final measurement issue: how to measure those decisions. The hypothesis of judicial deference to elected branch preferences predicts that the legal rules announced by the Court in its opinions will respond not only to changes in the most preferred rule of the median justice, but also to changes in the most preferred rules of pivotal elected officials. The competing hypothesis of judicial independence predicts instead that the Court's endorsed rules will be unresponsive to variation in the latter.

Ideally we would measure the exact location of the rules announced in the Court's decisions, in the same way that we measure the locations of the justices' most preferred rules. However, the two measurement problems are not symmetric. In the latter case we have many votes that we can use to infer the location of a justice's most preferred rule, relative to those of other justices. But we do not easily have access to analogous data giving us information about the precise location of a particular legal rule, relative to other rules in the same area of law.[27]

Instead, the measure of choice in the quantitative literature on the question of the Court's independence has been a measure of the direction of the Court's judgments, as reported in the United States Supreme Court Database.[28] This measure codes dispositional outcomes, and the votes in favor of or opposed to those outcomes, as either liberal or conservative, according to a set of issue-specific decision rules. Essentially, a coder for the Supreme Court Database reads a majority opinion, assigns to it an issue code (for example, antitrust), then consults the decision rule for coding judgments in that issue area. In the case of opinions assigned antitrust issue codes, these decision rules specify that judgments that are "pro-competition" are to be coded as liberal judgments; all other judgments are to receive conservative judgment codes.[29]

Even though this measure codes only the Court's judgments, not the rules announced in its opinions, we can still use it to test hypotheses that make predictions about the expected locations of those rules. Recall that legal rules sort cases presenting varying fact patterns into dispositional outcomes. As a legal rule shifts in a more conservative (liberal) direction, we would expect a greater (lesser) proportion of cases to fall into the conservative dispositional bin. For example, in the area of interstate commerce clause jurisprudence, a rule that challenged statutes must not only have substantial effects on interstate commerce, but also be "economic" in character, will prohibit more federal regulatory action than a rule that challenged statutes need only have substantial effects on interstate commerce. Most legal commentators would agree that the first rule is a more conservative rule than the second rule, in that it restricts more governmental regulation of the economy, relative to the second rule. Some regulatory statutes that, under the first rule, would receive "strike" dispositions, would have received "uphold" dispositions under the second rule. Under the Supreme Court Database decision rules for coding judgments in the area of interstate commerce clause jurisprudence, these "strike" dispositions will be coded as conservative judgments. We should then observe a greater proportion of these conservative judgments as the Court's rule shifts to the right.

If the Court is not constrained by elected branch preferences, then we would expect that as the most preferred legal rule of the Court's median justice shifts in a conservative direction, either through changes in the Court's membership, or through changes in the preferences of the median justice, we will find an increased probability that the Court issues judgments coded as conservative in the Supreme Court Database. But we would not expect to find any variation in the probability of a conservative judgment as a function of variation in the preferences of elected officials. If the Court is constrained by elected branch preferences, however, then we should find that the Court's judgments respond not only to shifts in the most preferred rule of the median justice, but also to shifts in the most preferred rules of elected officials.

Some researchers have attempted to estimate the effects of elected branch preferences on the individual justices' votes over the Court's judgments, rather than on the judgments themselves.[30] However, it is not clear that we have as firm predictions for the justices' votes, as we do for the Court's judgments. When the preferences of the median justice diverge from those of elected officials, the justices face a kind of coordination problem. Any justice who votes to join an opinion implementing the most preferred rule of the median justice may be subject to the wrath of elected branch majorities. But once five justices have voted to join an opinion implementing a rule closer to the most preferred rules of elected branch majorities, the remaining justices are free to not join this opinion; elected branch majorities are assumed to care about outcomes, not expression. And we do not have particularly strong theory to suggest how the median justice and her brethren most distant from the elected branches solve the problem of identifying who will join majority opinions deferring to the elected branches, and who will remain free to express their sincere preferences. Consequently it seems most reasonable to focus on the Court's judgments, rather than on the justices' votes.

Using the Supreme Court Database judgment data, we can immediately see a strong connection between the estimated preferences of the median justice and the Court's judgments. Figure 3.3 graphs the annual percentage of decisions receiving a conservative judgment code in the Supreme Court Database, along with the Bailey XTI estimated most preferred rule of the Court's median justice, for the terms between 1953 and 2004.[31] The correlation between these two series is very strong, at .74 (a correlation of 1 would indicate perfect correlation). As the most preferred rule of the median justice gets more liberal, the Court's judgments get more liberal; as the most preferred rule of the median justice Court gets more conservative, the Court's judgments get more conservative as well. The correlation for the analogous series produced using the Judicial Common Space preference estimates is .63.

By contrast, we see no obvious connections between the estimated preferences of pivotal elected officials and the Court's judgments. Recall

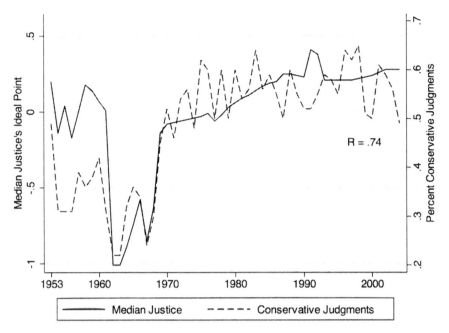

Figure 3.3. Judicial Preferences and Judgments, 1953–2004
Sources: Bailey (2007), United States Supreme Court Database. This figure reports all cases in the Supreme Court Database to which a directional judgment code is assigned.

the hypothesis that, if elected branch constraint on the Court exists, it is most likely to be exercised by majorities in the House of Representatives, possessed of agenda control in both the impeachment and the appropriations processes. But there is no evident connection between the estimated preferences of the median representative and the Court's judgments, using either the Bailey XTI or the JCS preference estimates. Figure 3.4 graphs the Bailey XTI estimated most preferred rule of the median representative against the percentage of decisions receiving a conservative judgment code between 1953 and 2004. The two series are actually negatively correlated at −.21, although the correlation is not significant at standard thresholds.[32] The series of median representatives' estimated most preferred rules reported by the Judicial Common Space is also uncorrelated with that of the Court's judgments.[33]

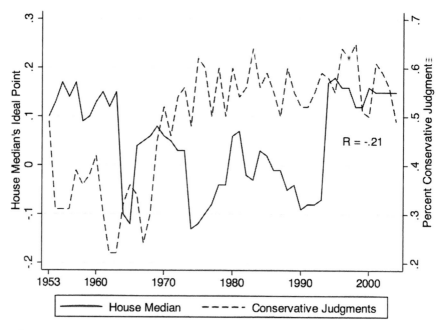

Figure 3.4. House Median's Preferences and Judgments, 1953–2004
Sources: Bailey (2007), United States Supreme Court Database. This figure reports all cases in the Supreme Court Database to which a directional judgment code is assigned.

The descriptive evidence for relationships between the estimated preferences of the median senator, the president, and the median justice is somewhat more mixed. Using the Bailey XTI preference estimates, the median senator's preferences for more conservative legal rules are not positively correlated with the frequency of conservative judgments at conventional levels of statistical significance, but using the JCS preference estimates, they are.[34] Using the Bailey XTI preference estimates, the president's preferences for more conservative legal rules are positively correlated with the frequency of conservative judgments at conventional levels of statistical significance, but using the JCS preference estimates, they are not.[35]

Estimating Judgment Probabilities

We can test the hypothesis of elected branch constraint on the Court more precisely by directly estimating the impact of both judicial and elected branch preferences on the propensity of the Court to issue a conservative judgment over this period. Conservative judgments are coded as one in these analyses; liberal judgments are coded as zero. Because both the Bailey XTI and the Judicial Common Space preference estimates are increasing in conservatism, positive coefficients on any of the preference variables in the tables reported here would indicate that as that actor's preferences become more conservative, the probability that the Court issues a conservative judgment increases. Negative coefficients on the preference variables would indicate perverse effects, such that as an actor's preferences become more conservative, the probability that the Court issues a conservative judgment actually decreases.

We can also control for case-specific covariates that may affect the justices' decisions. The Supreme Court reverses more lower court judgments than it affirms; a liberal lower court ruling has a higher probability of resulting in a conservative judgment by the Court than does a conservative lower court ruling.[36] For cases wherein a winning party can be identified, the Supreme Court Database reports the direction of lower court judgments, coded as a function of the Court's judgments. For example, a case coded as resulting in a liberal judgment by the Supreme Court, wherein the petitioner was the winning party, will also be coded as having had a conservative lower court judgment. The direction of the lower court judgment is included in the following analyses, with conservative lower court judgments coded as zero and liberal lower court judgments coded as one; given its coding we would expect this variable to have a positive relationship with the probability that the Court issues a conservative judgment.

The Court is also more likely to decide a case in favor of the U.S. government if the latter is a party to a case.[37] In the analyses to follow two variables are included to capture this tendency: one denoting cases wherein the United States is a party to a case and argues for a liberal judgment, and one denoting cases wherein the United States is a party to a case and argues for a conservative judgment. Each variable is coded as one when the United States is a party to a case arguing for a particular judgment, and zero otherwise. We expect the former variable to decrease the probability of a conservative judgment by the Court, and the latter to increase that probability.

Tables 3.1 and 3.2 report the results of these probit regressions, using both the Bailey XTI and the Judicial Common Space preference estimates. In neither regression is there any effect of elected branch preferences on the Court's decisions in the predicted direction. In fact, in the regression using the Bailey XTI preference estimates, increases in the conservatism of the Senate median are actually significantly associated with decreases in the probability that the Court issues a conservative judgment, although this perverse effect disappears in the regression using the JCS preference estimates.

By contrast, in both regressions there are large increases in the probability of a conservative judgment as the median justice's most preferred rule moves in a conservative direction. Using the results reported in Table 3.1 for the Bailey XTI preference estimates, moving from the most liberal of the median justice's most preferred rules (estimated in the 1962 and 1963 terms) to the most conservative (estimated in the 1991 term) results in an increase in the average predicted probability that the Court will issue a conservative judgment from .27 to .58.[38] Using the results reported

Table 3.1: **Estimating the Probability of a Conservative Judgment: Bailey XTI Judicial and Elected Branch Preferences, 1953–2004**

	Coefficient	SE	95% CI
Conservatism of SCOTUS Median	.59	.07	(.44, .73)
Conservatism of House Median	−.18	.24	(.66, .30)
Conservatism of Senate Median	−.49	.13	(−.74, −.23)
Conservatism of President	−.02	.03	(−.08, .05)
Liberal Lower Court Judgment	.65	.04	(.56, .73)
US Liberal Party	−.44	.06	(−.55, −.32)
US Conservative Party	.34	.05	(.25, .43)

N = 6908
Wald chi^2 = 561.97

Note: Probit regression; robust standard errors reported, clustered by term. Intercept term not reported. Italicized variables are statistically significant at the .10 level (two-tailed). Dependent variable is the Supreme Court Database "Decision Direction" variable. All cases are included excepting memoranda and those whose judgments, in either the Supreme Court or the lower court, are not assigned a direction in the Supreme Court Database.

Table 3.2: Estimating the Probability of a Conservative Judgment: Judicial Common Space Judicial and Elected Branch Preferences, 1953–2004

	Coefficient	SE	95% CI
Conservatism of SCOTUS Median	1.06	.16	(.74, 1.37)
Conservatism of House Median	−.35	.31	(−.96, .25)
Conservatism of Senate Median	.33	.41	(−.48, 1.13)
Conservatism of President	−.04	.06	(−.16, .08)
Liberal Lower Court Judgment	.67	.04	(.59, .76)
US Liberal Party	−.46	.06	(−.58, −.35)
US Conservative Party	.31	.05	(.22, .40)

N = 6908
Wald chi^2 = 442.97

Note: Probit regression; robust standard errors reported, clustered by term. Intercept term not reported. Italicized variables are statistically significant at the .10 level (two-tailed). Dependent variable is the Supreme Court Database "Decision Direction" variable. All cases are included excepting memoranda and those whose judgments, in either the Supreme Court or the lower court, are not assigned a direction in the Supreme Court Database.

in Table 3.2 for the Judicial Common Space estimates, moving from the most liberal of the median justice's most preferred rules (estimated in the 1968 term) to the most conservative (estimated in the 1972 and 1988 terms) increases the average predicted probability of a conservative judgment from .33 to .56.[39] The two sets of predictions are both distinct from one another at conventional thresholds of statistical significance.

Figure 3.5 graphs the predicted probability of a conservative judgment as a function of the median justice's most preferred rule, along with the 95 percent confidence intervals, for the Bailey XTI preference estimates, holding all other variables at their mean values. The estimated most preferred rules of the median justice and median representative are also shown for reference. The 95 percent confidence interval around the predicted probabilities reported in Figure 3.5 is quite narrow, indicating that the judgment data are very closely associated with the median justice's estimated most preferred rule. By contrast, the predicted probability of a conservative judgment clearly has no relationship with the estimated most preferred rule of the median representative.

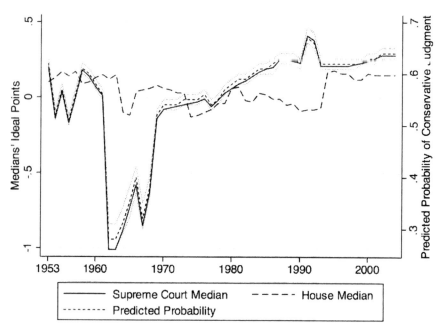

Figure 3.5. Probability of a Conservative Judgment, 1953–2004
Sources: Bailey (2007), United States Supreme Court Database. This figure reports the predicted probability of a conservative judgment and associated 95 percent confidence interval, using the estimates reported in Table 3.1. All variables other than the Supreme Court median's ideal point are held at their mean values.

Figure 3.6 reports these predicted probabilities for the Rehnquist Court only. Recall that it is the Rehnquist Court terms that would seem to offer the best opportunity to test the claim of the Court's independence from congressional preferences. The results of this test appear to be conclusive: the Rehnquist Court's judgments are unresponsive to the dramatic changes in congressional preferences effected by the 1994 elections, represented here by the estimated preferences of the House median. They instead hew closely to the consistently conservative preferences of the Court's median justice during these terms. These results do not change when we use the Judicial Common Space preference estimates.

These null results are obviously not supportive of the hypothesis that the Court defers to elected branch preferences. But the sample we have been using includes all the Court's cases from the Warren through the Rehnquist Courts, to which judgment codes are assigned in the Supreme

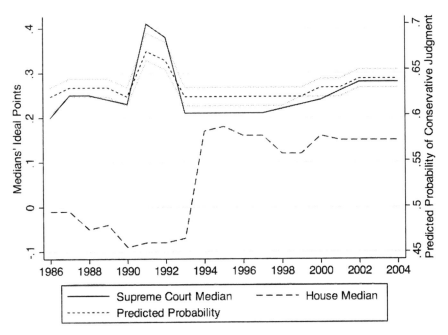

Figure 3.6. Probability of a Conservative Judgment, 1986–2004
Sources: Bailey (2007), United States Supreme Court Database. This figure reports the predicted probability of a conservative judgment and associated 95 percent confidence interval from Figure 3.5, for the Rehnquist Court terms only.

Court Database (for the dispositions of both the lower court and the Supreme Court). And we are particularly interested in the Court's decisions in constitutional cases. Perhaps isolating these constitutional cases will reveal different results.

But no dice. As reported in Tables 3.3 and 3.4, when we restrict the sample to only those cases involving constitutional review of federal or state actions, there is still no evidence of any elected branch constraint in the predicted direction, using either the Bailey XTI or the Judicial Common Space preference estimates.[40] As with the full sample, an increasingly conservative Senate median is associated with a decrease in the probability of a conservative judgment using the Bailey XTI preference estimates, but this perverse effect disappears using the JCS estimates. Similarly, an increasingly conservative House median is associated with a decrease in the probability of a conservative judgment using the JCS preference

Table 3.3: Estimating the Probability of a Conservative Judgment: Bailey XTI Judicial and Elected Branch Preferences, 1953–2004, Constitutional Cases Only

	Coefficient	SE	95% CI
Conservatism of SCOTUS Median	.80	.15	(.50, 1.09)
Conservatism of House Median	−.03	.49	(−.99, .93)
Conservatism of Senate Median	−.48	.21	(−.89, −.08)
Conservatism of President	−.01	.05	(−.11, .09)
Liberal Lower Court Judgment	.72	.05	(.62, .82)
US Liberal Party	−.40	.13	(−.66, −.15)
US Conservative Party	.59	.09	(.43, .76)

N = 2344
Wald chi^2 = 395.09

Note: Probit regression; robust standard errors reported, clustered by term. Intercept term not reported. Italicized variables are statistically significant at the .10 level (two-tailed). Dependent variable is the Supreme Court Database "Decision Direction" variable. All cases involving constitutional review are included excepting memoranda and those whose judgments, in either the Supreme Court or the lower court, are not assigned a direction in the Supreme Court Database.

Table 3.4: Estimating the Probability of a Conservative Judgment: Judicial Common Space Judicial and Elected Branch Preferences, 1953–2004, Constitutional Cases Only

	Coefficient	SE	95% CI
Conservatism of SCOTUS Median	1.63	.23	(1.17, 2.09)
Conservatism of House Median	−.62	.34	(−1.29, .04)
Conservatism of Senate Median	.84	.53	(−.19, 1.87)
Conservatism of President	−.09	.08	(−.25, .07)
Liberal Lower Court Judgment	.75	.05	(.65, .85)
US Liberal Party	−.39	.13	(−.64, −.14)
US Conservative Party	.58	.09	(.41, .75)

N = 2344
Wald chi^2 = 384.81

Note: Probit regression; robust standard errors reported, clustered by term. Intercept term not reported. Italicized variables are statistically significant at the .10 level (two-tailed). Dependent variable is the Supreme Court Database "Decision Direction" variable. All cases involving constitutional review are included excepting memoranda and those whose judgments, in either the Supreme Court or the lower court, are not assigned a direction in the Supreme Court Database.

estimates, but this perverse effect is absent when we use the Bailey XTI estimates.

There remain, however, very large effects from changes in the estimated most preferred rule of the median justice under both sets of preference estimates. Using the Bailey XTI preference estimates, moving from the most liberal of these rules to the most conservative increases the average predicted probability of a conservative judgment from .20 to .62. The same movement using the JCS preference estimates increases the average predicted probability of a conservative judgment from .26 to .61.[41] As with the full sample, these predictions are distinct at conventional significance levels.

When we further restrict the sample to only those cases involving constitutional review of federal action, as reported in Tables 3.5 and 3.6, the results remain the same. There is still no evidence of any elected branch constraint on the Court's decisions in the predicted direction, using either the Bailey XTI or the JCS preference estimates. There is no longer a

Table 3.5: **Estimating the Probability of a Conservative Judgment: Bailey XTI Judicial and Elected Branch Preferences, 1953–2004, Constitutional Review of Federal Action Only**

	Coefficient	SE	95% CI
Conservatism of SCOTUS Median	.74	.28	(.19, 1.30)
Conservatism of House Median	−.21	.99	(−2.15, 1.73)
Conservatism of Senate Median	−.71	.49	(−1.67, .25)
Conservatism of President	−.03	.09	(−.21, .15)
Liberal Lower Court Judgment	.53	.11	(.32, .73)
US Liberal Party	−.51	.17	(−.85, −.17)
US Conservative Party	.49	.15	(.19, .78)

N = 652
Wald chi² = 86.74

Note: Probit regression; robust standard errors reported, clustered by term. Intercept term not reported. Italicized variables are statistically significant at the .10 level (two-tailed). Dependent variable is the Supreme Court Database "Decision Direction" variable. All cases involving constitutional review of federal action included excepting memoranda and those whose judgments, in either the Supreme Court or the lower court, are not assigned a direction in the Supreme Court Database.

Table 3.6: Estimating the Probability of a Conservative Judgment: Judicial Common Space Judicial and Elected Branch Preferences, 1953–2004, Constitutional Review of Federal Action Only

	Coefficient	SE	95% CI
Conservatism of SCOTUS Median	1.36	.46	(.46, 2.27)
Conservatism of House Median	−1.40	.82	(−3.02, .21)
Conservatism of Senate Median	1.01	.96	(−.87, 2.89)
Conservatism of President	−.16	.15	(−.45, .13)
Liberal Lower Court Judgment	.56	.10	(.36, .76)
US Liberal Party	−.51	.17	(−.86, −.17)
US Conservative Party	.48	.15	(.19, .77)

N = 652
Wald chi² = 91.17

Note: Probit regression; robust standard errors reported, clustered by term. Intercept term not reported. Italicized variables are statistically significant at the .10 level (two-tailed). Dependent variable is the Supreme Court Database "Decision Direction" variable. All cases involving constitutional review of federal action included excepting memoranda and those whose judgments, in either the Supreme Court or the lower court, are not assigned a direction in the Supreme Court Database.

perverse effect on the Court's judgments from the Senate median's preferences using the Bailey XTI preference estimates, although an increasingly conservative House median is still associated with a decreased probability of a conservative judgment using the JCS preference estimates. But moving from the most liberal to the most conservative of the median justice's estimated most preferred rules over this time period increases the average predicted probability of a conservative judgment in these cases from .33 to .72 using the Bailey XTI estimates, and from .41 to .70 using the JCS estimates.[42] These predictions remain distinct at conventional significance thresholds.

Finally, restricting the sample to only those cases involving the constitutional review of federal statutes also does not produce different results, as reported in Tables 3.7 and 3.8. Using these cases we again get significant predictive power from the median justice's preferences, but find no evidence of any elected branch constraint in the predicted direction, or even any perverse effects from elected branch preferences, for either set of

Table 3.7: Estimating the Probability of a Conservative Judgment: Bailey XTI Judicial and Elected Branch Preferences, 1953–2004, Constitutional Review of Federal Statutes Only

	Coefficient	SE	95% CI
Conservatism of SCOTUS Median	1.70	.30	(1.11, 2.29)
Conservatism of House Median	.15	1.15	(−2.11, 2.40)
Conservatism of Senate Median	−1.02	.64	(−2.28, .23)
Conservatism of President	−.05	.12	(−.29, .18)
Liberal Lower Court Judgment	.15	.17	(−.19, .49)
US Liberal Party	−.26	.33	(−.91, .39)
US Conservative Party	1.08	.25	(.60, 1.57)

N = 294
Wald chi^2 = 80.16

Note: Probit regression; robust standard errors reported, clustered by term. Intercept term not reported. Italicized variables are statistically significant at the .10 level (two-tailed). Dependent variable is the Supreme Court Database "Decision Direction" variable. All cases involving constitutional review of federal statutes included excepting memoranda and those whose judgments, in either the Supreme Court or the lower court, are not assigned a direction in the Supreme Court Database.

Table 3.8: Estimating the Probability of a Conservative Judgment: Judicial Common Space Judicial and Elected Branch Preferences, 1953–2004, Constitutional Review of Federal Statutes Only

	Coefficient	SE	95% CI
Conservatism of SCOTUS Median	2.83	.68	(1.50, 4.16)
Conservatism of House Median	−1.01	1.21	(−3.38, 1.36)
Conservatism of Senate Median	1.83	1.52	(−1.15, 4.81)
Conservatism of President	−.18	.19	(−.54, .19)
Liberal Lower Court Judgment	.24	.18	(−.11, .60)
US Liberal Party	−.25	.33	(−.89, .39)
US Conservative Party	1.07	.25	(.58, 1.55)

N = 294
Wald chi^2 = 69.16

Note: Probit regression; robust standard errors reported, clustered by term. Intercept term not reported. Italicized variables are statistically significant at the .10 level (two-tailed). Dependent variable is the Supreme Court Database "Decision Direction" variable. All cases involving constitutional review of federal statutes included excepting memoranda and those whose judgments, in either the Supreme Court or the lower court, are not assigned a direction in the Supreme Court Database.

preference estimates. Moving from the most liberal to the most conservative of the median justice's estimated most preferred rules dramatically increases the average predicted probability of a conservative judgment in these cases from .06 to .78 using the Bailey XTI estimates, and from .17 to .74 using the JCS preference estimates.[43] These predictions continue to be distinct at conventional significance levels.

An Independent Supreme Court?

These estimates provide compelling evidence that, in the words of political scientists Jeffrey Segal and Harold Spaeth, "the empirical evidence refutes the [separation-of-powers] model."[44] Segal and Spaeth go on to write, "the federal judiciary was designed to be independent, so we should not be surprised that it in fact is."[45] We have certainly found no evidence that contradicts these claims. We used two different measures of elected branch and judicial preferences, and looked at several subsets of the Court's judgments. We looked in particular at what seemed like a gift-wrapped opportunity to find evidence of elected branch constraint on the Court, namely the Rehnquist Court terms between 1986 and 2004. Perhaps Segal and Spaeth are correct. Perhaps the case of the Court's independence from the elected branches is indeed closed.[46]

Before we accept this conclusion, however, we should perhaps listen to what journalists and constitutional scholars had to say about the Rehnquist Court. They seemed to observe an entirely different Court from the one portrayed in Figure 3.6. Their observations may induce us to take another look at our data.

4

THE PUZZLE OF THE TWO REHNQUIST COURTS

According to rigorous econometric studies of the Supreme Court, the justices do not alter their decisions in response to changes in elected branch preferences, including changes in the preferences of House majorities. A perfect example of this appears to be provided by the Rehnquist Court, which faced both liberal and conservative House majorities, while remaining consistently conservative itself. Presumably, had the preferences of those majorities mattered to the Court, we would have seen some changes in its decisions as those preferences varied. The Court should have pulled its conservative punches during its first eight terms, but then let those punches fly after the 1994 elections.

The fact that we see no such effect in the econometric results might seem like conclusive evidence in support of the Court's independence. However, there is something odd about these results. The oddity is that observers of the Rehnquist Court in both the popular press and the legal academy saw a Court that was unexpectedly moderate, even liberal, during its first eight terms, yet inexplicably became sharply more conservative midway through its 1994 term. The differences between these two periods were so marked, and spanned so many areas of constitutional law, that many legal academics took to characterizing the pre-1994 Court as the "first" Rehnquist Court and the post-1993 Court as the "second" Rehnquist Court.[1]

These narrative accounts of the Rehnquist Court should perhaps give us pause. As noted in Chapter Three, it is admittedly difficult to assess the reliability of such accounts. Historical narratives of the Court's jurisprudence focus our attention on some cases, but not on others, perhaps because the highlighted cases best support the particular story being told. The many narrative accounts of the apparent jurisprudential break between the "first" and "second" Rehnquist Courts may well be guilty of this selection bias. Nevertheless, the sheer frequency with which observers narrated the same pattern in the Rehnquist Court's jurisprudence indicates that, at a minimum, we should take a second look at our econometric studies.

The "First" Rehnquist Court

In the summer of 1986, conservative judicial activists finally appeared to be on the brink of achieving their long-sought goal of moving the Court's jurisprudence to the right. Despite the fact that Republican appointees held seven out of nine seats on the Court, those Republican justices had, in the eyes of many conservatives, failed to significantly shift the Court's jurisprudence away from the precedents set by the liberal Warren Court.[2] The Burger Court was widely thought to be "the counter-revolution that wasn't."[3]

But the announced departure of Chief Justice Warren E. Burger at the close of the 1985 term appeared to bring the counter-revolution within reach. The Reagan Justice Department, responsible for overseeing the process to fill the vacancy on the Court, had been given a tune-up after the 1984 reelection landslide. Under Attorney General Edwin Meese III and Solicitor General Charles Fried, it was now being run by activists said to be committed to a more aggressively conservative jurisprudence.[4]

The Reagan administration's choice to put forward Associate Justice William H. Rehnquist for the position of Chief Justice was a bold one. Rehnquist, appointed to the Court in 1972, had consistently provided a lone voice of conservative dissent on the Burger Court. Despite the fact that his elevation to the office of Chief Justice would not itself change the composition of the Court, it was not without controversy; that position was widely anticipated, with either hope or dismay, to offer him enhanced abilities to "persuade" his colleagues to support his conservative positions.[5]

His successor as Associate Justice was likewise thought to be considerably more doctrinal than previous Republican appointees. Antonin Scalia had been named to the United States Court of Appeals for the District of Columbia in 1982, and in his writings both before and after that appointment had advocated positions "almost perfectly consistent with the Reagan administration's conservative legal and political agenda, and considerably more so than the judicial opinions of Chief Justice Warren E. Burger."[6] Scalia had reportedly been kept under close watch by conservative activists in the Reagan Justice Department: "They liked virtually everything they saw and have long listed him as a leading Supreme Court prospect. These officials view his planned elevation as a capstone of their efforts—which experts call the most systematic by any Administration in modern history—to reverse the course of the Federal judiciary."[7]

Even though the identity of the median justice was likely not changing with the substitution of Scalia for Rehnquist/Burger, Court observers predicted nonetheless that with the elevation of Rehnquist and the appointment of Scalia, the ideological balance on the Court was "likely to shift perceptibly to the right; the two selected today are said by most students of their records to be more consistent, more energetic and more intellectually formidable advocates of conservative views, and of judicial restraint, than Chief Justice Burger has been."[8]

And yet, the counterrevolution was still not to be. In increasingly puzzled commentary, observers of the Rehnquist Court saw its jurisprudence remain apparently unaltered by these changes in its membership. As early as January 1987, reports were appearing that, despite the cherished hopes of conservative legal theorists, a "more complex picture" was emerging from the Rehnquist Court.[9] Apparently "to Reagan's consternation," in its first term the Rehnquist Court issued moderate, even liberal, decisions in prominent cases involving affirmative action, pregnancy leave, political asylum, and discrimination against AIDS patients.[10] In his end-of-term summary, *New York Times* Supreme Court reporter Stuart Taylor Jr. observed that "the decisions of the 1986–87 term showed little deviation from the Court's direction in Warren E. Burger's 17 years as Chief Justice. The rulings were moderate to liberal on social issues like racial and sexual discrimination, abortion and church-state relations . . . and moderate and pragmatic in [their] basic instincts."[11]

Despite this disappointment, conservative judicial activists received some much welcomed good news at the close of the 1986 term: the retirement of Justice Lewis Powell. Justice Powell was widely believed to be the median or "swing" justice on the Court, the justice whose vote was pivotal in determining the character of the Court's opinions.[12] Observers could now rationalize the lack of change on the Court during the 1986 term by pointing to the lack of change in the location of the median justice: a conservative justice, to the right of the median, had simply been replaced by another conservative justice, to the right of the median. But Justice Powell's resignation presented the Reagan administration with a clear opportunity to move the identity of the median justice to the right. This could dramatically affect the Court's jurisprudence.[13]

Seeing important Warren Court precedents within their grasp, the Reagan Justice Department chose Robert Bork as the administration's nominee. As has been well chronicled elsewhere, Bork failed to win confirmation from the Democratic Senate majority. The second nominee for this seat, D.C. Circuit Court Judge Douglas Ginsburg, withdrew after reports of prior marijuana use. The third nominee was Judge Anthony M. Kennedy, a Ford appointee to the Ninth Circuit in 1975. Although he did not have the ideological reputation of Robert Bork, Kennedy was nonetheless thought to be "well to the right of center" on the Ninth Circuit, a judge who, in the eyes of many, would "move the Court in a more conservative direction."[14] Liberals worried that "Justice Kennedy may cement the most consistently conservative five justice voting bloc in recent history."[15] Some speculated that liberals might even have been better off with Bork than with Kennedy, "who may wind up being more conservative than Bork in some areas and better at building bridges to others because he's easier to get along with."[16]

With the addition of Justice Kennedy there were now five seemingly reliable conservative votes on the Court: Chief Justice Rehnquist and Associate Justices Scalia, White, O'Connor, and Kennedy. Yet this apparently conservative majority handed the Reagan administration several widely publicized losses during the 1987 term, a term variously characterized as "astonishing," "striking," and "jolting."[17] The most prominent of these setbacks was the "crushing defeat" of *Morrison v. Olson*, 487 U.S. 654 (1988), wherein Justices Rehnquist, White, and O'Connor joined the more liberal justices to uphold the constitutionality of the Independent Counsel Reauthorization Act of 1987. The Act had been challenged by the Reagan Justice Department, three of whose members were being investigated by an independent counsel appointed under the Act's provisions. This investigation had been instigated at the request of the Democratic-majority House Judiciary Committee, whose members suspected the Justice Department officials of having inappropriately interfered with a House inquiry into the failure of Reagan's Environmental Protection Agency to enforce the Superfund statute. The Justice Department officials had challenged the Act on the grounds that it unconstitutionally limited executive power.[18]

The Court's rejection of the Reagan administration's executive power claim was characterized by a Court "insider" as "one of the most important cases in all of constitutional jurisprudence."[19] Moreover, on the same day that *Morrison* was announced, the Court rejected the administration's position in four of five other cases. The *Times* reported, "Each time another loss was announced, Solicitor General Charles Fried, the Government's lawyer, seemed to slump a bit deeper in his chair."[20]

By the end of the 1987 term it was clear that the administration had "lost more of the political blockbuster cases than it ha[d] won."[21] Commentary focused on the failure of the administration's efforts to change the Court: "This term show[s] the limits of a President's power to shape the law of the land through his appointments to the Supreme Court."[22] Even the Chief Justice's previously undisputed conservative beliefs were called into question, given his authorship of the independent prosecutor decision; those beliefs were apparently proving to be "less uniformly conservative than was expected when Mr. Reagan promoted him from Justice in 1986."[23]

There were various ad hoc explanations proffered for the failure of the predicted conservative majority to form during the 1987 term. Some suggested that the Chief Justice had adopted moderation in an effort to become more statesmanlike in his elevated position; this theory would be discredited in about seven years time. Others hypothesized that the Chief was voting with the more liberal justices in order to be able to control opinion assignments; this theory failed to explain how the liberals had come to have a majority of votes in the first place.[24]

Whatever the reason, the conservative majority on the Court continued to disappoint. In its 1988 term, to the dismay of Justice Scalia and
other conservatives, the Court reaffirmed *Roe v. Wade*, 410 U.S. 113
(1973), as still the governing precedent for cases involving abortion rights
(*Webster v. Reproductive Health Services*, 490 U.S. 492 [1989]). Justice
O'Connor deserted the conservative majority to achieve *Webster*'s result.[25]

Justice O'Connor's vote in *Webster* seemed inexplicable. In two earlier abortion cases she had expressed her apparently extreme dislike of
Roe. In *City of Akron v. Akron Center for Reproductive Health*, 462 U.S.
416 (1983), O'Connor had written in dissent that there was "no justification in law or logic" for the "unworkable" trimester framework adopted in *Roe*.[26] In *Thornburgh v. American College of Obstetricians and
Gynecologists*, 476 U.S. 747 (1986), O'Connor had protested in dissent
that the Court's abortion precedents had "worked a major distortion in
the Court's constitutional jurisprudence," had again characterized *Roe*
as "unworkable," and had declared that "the Court is not suited to the
expansive role it has claimed for itself in the series of cases that began
with *Roe v. Wade*."[27] But in neither *Akron* nor *Thornburgh* had there
been five votes to overrule *Roe*. It was fairly costless to excoriate *Roe*
when there were at least five solid votes in favor of upholding it. In *Webster*, by contrast, O'Connor could have provided the critical fifth vote to
finally overturn this "unworkable" precedent. Yet this she unexpectedly
declined to do.[28]

The 1988 term Rehnquist Court also reaffirmed the Establishment
Clause precedent set by *Lemon v. Kurtzman*, 403 U.S. 602 (1971), requiring the city of Pittsburgh to remove a crèche from the steps of the
Allegheny County Courthouse in *Allegheny County v. Greater Pittsburgh
ACLU*, 492 U.S. 573 (1989). Again it was Justice O'Connor's defec-
tion to join the more liberal justices that produced this ruling. And once
again, her vote puzzled. She had expressed a vehement dislike of *Lemon*
in her dissent in the earlier Establishment Clause case *Aguilar v. Felton*,
473 U.S. 402 (1985). Yet, just as with the earlier abortion cases, the
conservatives had been in the minority in *Aguilar*. Advocating *Lemon*'s
demise in that case had had no practical effect. But faced with the opportunity to provide the fifth vote at least for a substantial revision of the
"*Lemon* test," O'Connor inexplicably refused.

The 1988 term Rehnquist Court also extended the congressional power to subject states to suit in federal courts for violating federal statutes in *Pennsylvania v. Union Gas Co.*, 491 U.S. 1 (1989); in this case it was Justice White who defected to the liberal camp. *Union Gas* involved the question of the scope of the Eleventh Amendment to the U.S. Constitution. This amendment, adopted in 1795 to address the states' concerns about being sued over their Revolutionary War debts, protects a state from being sued in federal courts by citizens of another state. The Court had historically interpreted the Amendment's language broadly to imply state immunity from suits by a state's own citizens as well, unless that immunity was explicitly abrogated by a permissible federal statute. Prior to *Union Gas*, the Court had held only that federal statutes enacted under the authority of Section 5 of the Fourteenth Amendment (the provision of that Amendment giving power to the Congress to "enforce" the Amendment's provisions) could abrogate state sovereign immunity.[29] In *Union Gas*, the Court authorized the Congress to abrogate that immunity in statutes enacted under the authority of the Interstate Commerce Clause, upholding the application of the Superfund statute to the state of Pennsylvania.

In its 1989 term the Rehnquist Court continued to defy expectations. A unanimous Court ruled that it must defer to congressional judgments about the extent of congressional authority under the Interstate Commerce Clause, even when federal statutes are aimed at such seemingly noncommercial ends as promoting the "enjoyment and appreciation of the open-air, outdoor areas and historic resources of the Nation" (*Preseault v. ICC*, 494 U.S. 1 [1990], at 17–18, quoting the statute). Justice White joined the four liberals on the Court in ruling that the federal government has more constitutional freedom to implement affirmative action programs than do state governments, upholding minority ownership preferences implemented by the Federal Communications Commission (*Metro Broadcasting v. FCC*, 497 U.S. 547 [1990]). These five justices also ruled that federal judges may order local governments to increase taxes to remedy constitutional violations like race-segregated schools, "one of the major surprises of the term" (*Missouri v. Jenkins*, 495 U.S. 33 [1990]). Meanwhile, Justice O'Connor deserted the conservatives in another abortion case, reaffirming *Roe v. Wade* as the governing precedent when evaluating state statutes restricting access to abortions (*Hodgson v. Minnesota*, 497 U.S. 417 [1990]). The legal director for the liberal group People for the American Way reported regarding the term "with a measure of relief."[30]

And yet conservative judicial activists would get two more shots at remaking the Court. At the close of the 1989 term came the retirement announcement of one of the Court's most reliable liberals, Justice William Brennan, followed only one term later by that of another of the Court's most prominent liberals, Justice Thurgood Marshall. The Bush administration, while perhaps not as populated with judicial ideologues as had been the prior administration, nonetheless nominated apparently solid conservatives to these vacant seats. The Bush White House chief of staff, former Governor of New Hampshire John H. Sununu, assured conservatives that Judge David H. Souter, nominated and confirmed in 1990 to the seat formerly held by Justice Brennan, would be a "home run."[31] And there was not much doubt that Justice Clarence Thomas, nominated and confirmed in 1991 to Thurgood Marshall's seat, would be an advocate for a more conservative jurisprudence.[32]

We now know that Justice Souter was not in fact destined to be viewed as a "home run" by conservative judicial activists. It was, then, perhaps not that surprising that the Court in its 1990 term continued its moderate, even liberal, jurisprudence. However, what is striking with the hindsight of history is that, by the start of the 1991 term, the five-member conservative majority of what would become the "second" Rehnquist Court was in place: Chief Justice Rehnquist and Justices Scalia, Thomas, Kennedy, and O'Connor. There was even a spare conservative vote in the person of Justice White. In this term, surely, reported the *Times*, we would see "the arrival of a firmly consolidated conservative majority," a majority that would find themselves "in the saddle at the Supreme Court."[33]

Liberals were particularly worried about the fate of *Roe v. Wade* (1973). While Justice O'Connor had backed away from the precipice when the chips were down in *Webster*, there had still been four votes in that case for the use of a rational basis test in evaluating state statutes restricting abortion, an approach wholly inconsistent with *Roe*. Edward Lazarus reports that Justice Kennedy, who had provided one of these votes, had even circulated a memo to the other conservative justices during the deliberations over *Webster* declaring his willingness to vote to overrule *Roe*.[34] These four justices had now been joined by Clarence Thomas, widely believed to provide a fifth vote for overturning *Roe*. And there was a case on the Court's calendar in its 1991 term that would provide these five justices with their opportunity, namely *Planned Parenthood of Southeastern Pennsylvania v. Casey*, 505 U.S. 833 (1992).

But even before the result in *Casey* was announced on June 29, 1992, there were indications that the 1991 term, yet again, was not going to come close to meeting conservatives' expectations. In May the Court issued several moderate-to-liberal decisions in less prominent cases, leading the *Times* to report, "If the last few weeks are any indication, the term could turn out to be considerably more ragged, and perhaps even more unpredictable, than appeared likely when it began last fall."[35] At the end of June, "defying almost all expectations," the Court delivered two quite "startling setbacks" to Bush administration positions on habeas corpus and religion. In *Wright v. West*, 505 U.S. 277 (1992), the Court rejected Bush administration efforts to restrict the ability of federal judges to review habeas corpus appeals from state prisoners *de novo*, without deferring to previous state court rulings. Both Justices Kennedy and O'Connor joined the three more liberal justices in rejecting such restrictions.[36] And in *Lee v. Weisman*, 505 U.S. 577 (1992), the Court ruled that prayers at public school commencements are unconstitutional, reaffirming the liberal Establishment Clause precedent *Lemon v. Kurtzman* (1971). Justices Kennedy and O'Connor again voted with the three more liberal justices to reach this outcome.

Constitutional scholars were particularly surprised by Justice Kennedy's opinion in favor of the constitutional challenge in *Lee v. Weisman*.[37] In *Allegheny County* (1989) Justice O'Connor had defected from her earlier willingness to modify *Lemon*, voting with the liberal justices to endorse the precedent. Her vote in *Lee v. Weisman* was then perhaps not entirely unexpected. But Justice Kennedy had authored the joint dissent in *Allegheny County*, writing that "persuasive criticism of *Lemon* has emerged" and that "substantial revision of our Establishment Clause doctrine may be in order."[38] In his majority opinion in *Allegheny County* Justice Blackmun had gone so far as to accuse Justice Kennedy of "gut[ting] the core of the Establishment Clause."[39] In *Lee v. Weisman* Justice Kennedy now had the five votes to carry out this gutting, thanks to the substitution of Justice Thomas for Justice Marshall. But instead he voted with Justice O'Connor and the liberals.

Kenneth W. Starr, the Bush administration's Solicitor General, called the Court's ruling in *Lee v. Weisman* "just stunning": "If there is one thing I'm not doing, it's downplaying it. It says something very significant about the mood of the Court. It's really a new Court . . . There's a Kennedy-Souter center to the Court now, and that's a cautious center. As Kennedy and Souter go, so goes the Court, and I see in them the spirit of Lewis Powell."[40] The *Times*, characterizing the Court's habeas corpus and school prayer decisions as "remarkable" and "unexpected," noted the surprising moderation of O'Connor and Kennedy, characterizing their jurisprudence as "cautious," "hesitant," and marked by "a distaste for aggressive arguments."[41]

And then, on the last day of the 1991 term, the Court issued its opinion in *Casey*, reaffirming the central holding *of Roe v. Wade* (1973) that a woman's right to pursue an abortion is "fundamental." Once again it was Justices Kennedy and O'Connor who cast their votes with the three more liberal justices. As had been the case in *Lee v. Weisman*, Justice Kennedy's critical vote to uphold *Roe v. Wade* seemed inexplicable. Justice O'Connor had already risen to *Roe*'s defense when it had fallen to her to cast the pivotal vote to overrule *Roe* in *Webster* (1989). But in *Casey*, the conservative majority no longer needed O'Connor's vote to overturn the critical precedent guaranteeing a fundamental right to an abortion. Kennedy's vote would suffice. But when push came to shove, Kennedy withheld that vote.

The decision seemed to be the nail in the coffin for the conservative judicial project. University of Pittsburgh Professor of History and Law David J. Garrow was later to write, "*Casey* . . . signaled the unexpected failure of the right-wing judicial counterrevolution that the Reagan and Bush Administrations had hoped to bring about by naming staunch conservatives to the Federal bench."[42] Harvard University Professor of Law Laurence H. Tribe said of *Casey* that it "puts the right to abortion on a firmer jurisprudential foundation than ever before."[43] Overall, the Court's "moderate turn" in the 1991 term was characterized by the *Times* as "surprising" and "fascinating" in its reaffirmations of "some of the Court's most important modern precedents."[44] In the words of Laurence Tribe, this was "a fundamentally unadventuresome and cautious Court."[45]

Judicial conservatives were dealt yet another blow with the election of Bill Clinton in the fall of 1992. The *Times* opined that, now, "Chief Justice Rehnquist may never compile the working majority he needs, and clearly lacked last term, to overturn the liberal precedents he scorns and to stamp the law in a lasting way with his own vision."[46]

It would turn out to be the case that Rehnquist in fact had his majority already. It just wasn't willing to "work" yet. But the *Times*'s prediction seemed to be an accurate one at the close of the 1992 term, when Justice Byron White announced his retirement. Appointed to the Court by President Kennedy in 1962, White had in fact proven to be a "reliable conservative."[47] He had dissented in key liberal precedents from the Warren and Burger Courts, like *Miranda v. Arizona* (384 U.S. 436 [1966]) and *Roe v. Wade* (1973). He had written an opinion full of contempt for the idea of gay rights in *Bowers v. Hardwick*, 478 U.S. 186 (1986). Most recently he had voted with the conservatives on all the important decisions of the 1991 term, including *Wright v. West* (1992), *Lee v. Weisman* (1992), and *Planned Parenthood v. Casey* (1992). His departure thus appeared to give the Democrats, now holding both the presidency and a majority in the Senate, an opportunity to move the already apparently moderate Rehnquist Court even further to the left, with the first appointment by a Democratic president in twenty-six years.[48]

President Clinton's nominee to replace Justice White, Ruth Bader Ginsburg, had been an architect of the successful legal strategy to eliminate statute-based gender discrimination, and was widely considered to have significantly more liberal preferences than Justice White. The *Times* predicted that Ginsburg would be "substantially more liberal" than Justice White, thereby likely moving the Court median to the left.[49]

Prior expectations about the likely conservatism of the Rehnquist Court now seemed to have been completely overcome. At the start of the 1993 term, the *Times*'s Linda Greenhouse predicted that Justice Ginsburg's influence on the court "is likely to be felt quickly . . . Justice Byron R. White, whom she succeeded, often voted for narrow interpretations of Federal anti-discrimination laws; Justice Ginsburg is likely to cast more liberal votes in those cases . . . Her vote could also make an important difference in the criminal area."[50] The next day the *Times*'s editorial page wrote in agreement that Justice Ginsburg, "a pioneering women's rights advocate and former Federal appellate judge, is expected to be a more liberal justice than Mr. White."[51]

Indeed, the 1993 term was hailed by the *Times* as providing final confirmation of "the failure of the conservative revolution."[52] But expectations were to shift even further to the left. At the close of the 1993 term, Justice Harry Blackmun announced his retirement from the Court; the Democrats would have yet another opportunity to forestall a conservative shift on the Court for many more years to come. Although Justice Blackmun had been appointed to the Court by Richard Nixon in 1970, he had moved in a steadily more liberal direction since his arrival. His replacement, Justice Stephen Breyer, had clerked for Justice Arthur Goldberg, one of the more liberal justices to serve on the Court, had served as chief counsel for the Senate Judiciary Committee under the chairmanship of Senator Edward Kennedy, and had been nominated to the First Circuit Court of Appeals by Jimmy Carter and confirmed by a Democratic Senate. In the words of author Jeffrey Toobin, "Breyer arrived at the Court bearing an uncynical love of government. He believed that government existed to serve people and solve problems, and to a great extent, that it did."[53]

The National Right to Life Committee said at the time that it was "perfectly clear" that Breyer fully supported abortion rights, while Republican Senator Trent Lott voted against his nomination on the grounds that Breyer "lacked a commitment to fundamental rights such as private property."[54] The *Times* predicted that Breyer's votes "will almost certainly please liberals most of the time."[55]

Since a liberal would be exchanged for a liberal, few expected the location of the median justice to shift to the left as a result of Justice Breyer's appointment. Still, court watchers seemed to think that the appointment would nonetheless lend new energy to the Court's left/center group of Justices. In anticipation of the 1994 term, the *Times* wrote, "Justice Breyer . . . is in a position to make a fast start. From his more than 13 years as a Federal appeals court judge in Boston, he is familiar with most of the issues before the court . . . [He] is widely expected to add his voice to argument sessions that, with the arrival last year of Justice Ruth Bader Ginsburg, were already the liveliest in years."[56]

The start of the 1994 term marked the first time that the Rehnquist Court would sit with two justices newly appointed and confirmed during a time of unified Democratic control of the Presidency and Senate. A bench that was already widely considered to be fairly moderate had been joined by two justices predicted to be quite liberal in their votes. The Court was thus expected to turn even further to its left during the 1994 term.[57]

In hindsight it was the height of irony that, by the fall of 1994, professional observers of the Court appeared to have finally and fully released their expectations that the Rehnquist Court would ever live up to its ultraconservative reputation. After eight years of moderation from the Court, that train had left the station. The only thing anybody expected now was for the Court to move even further to the left. Instead, Court watchers finally got the conservative counter-revolution they had finally stopped expecting.

The "Second" Rehnquist Court

The big decision came first. In late April 1995, the Court struck a federal statute on the grounds that it exceeded congressional power under the Interstate Commerce Clause, the first time it had done so since 1936 (*U.S. v. Lopez*, 514 U.S. 549 [1995]). The statute, the Gun-Free School Zones Act of 1990, had made it a federal criminal offense for "any individual knowingly to possess a firearm at a place that the individual knows, or has reasonable cause to believe, is a school zone."[58] The lower court had declared the statute unconstitutional on the narrow grounds that Congress had made no findings about the connection between possession of a gun near a school and interstate commerce. But in affirming the lower court's judgment, the Court reached for a much more sweeping constitutional argument.[59]

From *NLRB v. Jones & Laughlin Steel Corporation*, 301 U.S. 1 (1937), to *Lopez*, the Court's doctrinal standard for authorizing federal statutes under the Interstate Commerce Clause had been whether the regulated activity generated "substantial effects" on interstate commerce, even if the activity itself was purely intrastate in nature. In implementing this standard, the Court had generally deferred to congressional judgments, employing a "rational basis" test: as long as members of Congress could have had a rational basis for believing that a practice generated substantial effects on interstate commerce, that is, long as the congressional judgment did not appear to be completely arbitrary, the Court would defer to Congress and uphold the statute.[60] In the words of Laurence Tribe, the Court's interpretation of the Commerce Clause after 1937 made "striking down a congressional attempt to invoke the commerce power as outside the affirmative scope of that power . . . a de facto impossibility."[61]

The Rehnquist Court had adhered to this approach as recently as 1989, during its first incarnation, reaffirming the use of the rational basis test for evaluating the presence of "substantial effects" on interstate commerce in *Preseault v. ICC* (1990). Justices Rehnquist, Scalia, Kennedy, and O'Connor had all joined the majority opinion in that case. But all four of these justices voted for a new doctrinal approach in *Lopez*. Now federal statutes would have to clear an additional hurdle: a federal statute would exceed congressional power under the Interstate Commerce Clause if it did not explicitly regulate a "commercial activity."[62] The Gun-Free School Zones Act of 1990 failed this test: "Section 922(q) is a criminal statute that by its terms has nothing to do with 'commerce' or any sort of economic enterprise, however broadly one might define those terms."[63] Possession of a gun in a school zone, said the majority, did not belong to a class of activities "that arise out of or are connected with a commercial transaction."[64]

As both the dissenting justices and observers of the Court were quick to point out, never before had the Court sought to use the commercial character of an activity (or lack thereof) as a criterion for evaluating whether Congress could regulate that activity. Justice Breyer, reading portions of the joint dissent from the bench, said that the decision "threatens legal uncertainty in an area of law that, until this case, seemed reasonably well settled."[65] Justice Stevens called the majority opinion "extraordinary."[66] Christopher Schroeder of Duke Law School later wrote, "Nothing in the Court's opinions prior to *Lopez* pointed to the specific distinction the Court has erected to police those Commerce Clause boundaries."[67] Laurence Tribe described the Court's opinion in *Lopez* as constituting a

"new focus on 'economic' activity" justified by a "post-hoc reconfigura-
tion" of prior precedents.[68]

Meanwhile, conservatives were ecstatic. Roger Pilon, director of the
Center for Constitutional Studies at the Cato Institute, enthused, "The
Court is reaching the question at the heart of it all: Did we authorize all
this government? When you ask the question 'by what authority?' you are
asking the most fundamental question in law and in politics."[69] Many believed that the Court was resurrecting the "Constitution-in-exile," a set
of principles of constitutional interpretation embodying a severely limited
federal government, thought to have been rejected with finality during
the New Deal.[70]

The *Times*, calling the decision "stunning," noted that in its opinion
the Court was "repudiating one of the fundamental principles underlying
the modern understanding of the commerce clause: that the power of the
Federal Government grows necessarily, almost organically . . . in place of
that longstanding view, the Court would be reinserting itself into a role it
explicitly renounced in a landmark decision 10 years ago: that of guardian
of the Federal-state balance."[71] Jeffrey Toobin wrote in *The New Yorker*
that the Court had "proposed a radical reorientation of governmental
power away from the federal government and toward the states."[72] Jonathan L. Entin of Case Western Reserve Law School called the decision "a
distinct surprise . . . a major development portending significant change
in constitutional doctrine."[73]

There followed a series of rulings reversing course on affirmative action, school desegregation, racial gerrymandering, and religion. All of
these decisions were 5–4, with Justices O'Connor and Kennedy voting
with the conservative majority. In *Adarand Constructors Inc. v. Pena*, 515
U.S. 200 (1995), "an important doctrinal shift for the Court," the Court
overruled *Metro Broadcasting* (1990), decided during the first Rehnquist
Court, holding that federal affirmative action programs must be subjected
to the same strict scrutiny as state programs.[74] In *Missouri v. Jenkins*, 515
U.S. 70 (1995), the Court ruled that federal courts couldn't require the
state of Missouri to pay for magnet schools in Kansas City intended to
attract out-of-district white students, essentially overruling its 1990 ruling in *Missouri v. Jenkins*, 495 U.S. 33, that they could.[75] In *Miller v.
Johnson*, 515 U.S. 900 (1995), the Court declared that race could not

be a "predominant factor" in drawing congressional district lines absent compelling justification.[76]

Finally, in *Rosenberger v. University of Virginia*, 515 U.S. 819 (1995), the conservative majority ruled that the University of Virginia would not violate the Establishment Clause by subsidizing an evangelical student magazine.[77] *Rosenberger* marked yet another Establishment Clause reversal for both Justices O'Connor and Kennedy. When a liberal majority had existed for an aggressive defense of the Establishment Clause, Justice O'Connor had been willing to express her unhappiness with this jurisprudence (for example, as in her dissent in *Aguilar v. Felton*, 473 U.S. 402 [1985]). But when her vote had been necessary to sustain that jurisprudence in both *Allegheny County* (1989) and *Lee v. Weisman* (1992), both Establishment Clause cases decided during the first Rehnquist Court, Justice O'Connor had been willing to provide that vote. Yet she refused to vote with the liberal justices in *Rosenberger* (1995). Likewise, Justice Kennedy had expressed his dissatisfaction with the liberals' robust defense of the Establishment Clause in *Allegheny County* (1989), when his vote was not needed to sustain that defense, but had joined the liberal justices and Justice O'Connor in *Lee v. Weisman* (1992). Now he also was willing to vote with the conservatives.

Court watchers were stunned. Writing in the *Times*, Linda Greenhouse characterized the 1994 term as a "riveting," "radical," "gaudy show of zero-based jurisprudence": "The birth struggle of a new era is not a pretty sight. It is messy, it is unstable, it is riveting. It was the Supreme Court during the 1994–95 term that ended on Thursday . . . [It] was surprising, given the arrival of President Clinton's two nominees, Ruth Bader Ginsburg and Stephen G. Breyer, both pragmatic moderates who easily won confirmation with strong bipartisan support and who were widely expected to help anchor a strong central bloc. But there turned out to be virtually no center for these two experienced Federal judges to anchor."[78] Charles Fried's end-of-term summary in the *Harvard Law Review* likewise proclaimed, "The opinions in the 1994 Term of the Supreme Court were redolent of first principles and revolutionary gesture."[79] John G. Kester wrote in the *Wall Street Journal* that "the court of 1995 mirrors the court of 1935, with the politics reversed," while Timothy M.

Phelps of *Newsday* saw "a revolutionary states-rights movement within the court."[80]

Yet nobody seemed quite sure why the Court had taken such a dramatic turn. While lamenting "this sudden lurch to the right and backward in time," the *Times* could say only that "radical change is under way at the Supreme Court, only three years after its center held against a strong right-wing campaign to overturn the Court's 1973 abortion decision. The changed atmosphere is driven largely by justices who were on the Court in 1992 when a majority adhered to the *Roe v. Wade* precedent."[81] But journalists had few explanations for why these justices had had such a change of heart.

The Court's aggressive conservatism continued in the 1995 term, signaling that the 1994 term had not been just a fluke. In March the five-justice conservative majority handed down its decision in *Seminole Tribe of Florida v. Florida*, 517 U.S. 44 (1996), striking a federal statute on Eleventh Amendment grounds and overruling its 1989 precedent in *Union Gas*. In *Union Gas* the Court had extended the congressional power to abrogate state sovereign immunity to statutes enacted under the authority of the Interstate Commerce Clause.[82] But in *Seminole Tribe* the Court changed its mind.

At issue in *Seminole Tribe* was the Indian Gaming Regulatory Act, enacted under Congress's Indian Commerce Clause authority in 1988, making states liable in federal court for failing to negotiate "in good faith" with an Indian tribe over the establishment of an Indian-operated gaming enterprise within a state. A lower court had struck the statute on the narrow grounds that the Congress has more limited authority to abrogate state sovereign immunity under the Indian Commerce Clause than under the Interstate Commerce Clause. But in affirming the lower court's judgment, as it had done in *Lopez*, the Court made a much more sweeping constitutional argument. The *Seminole* majority explicitly rejected the *Union Gas* ruling of the "first" Rehnquist Court: "We feel bound to conclude that *Union Gas* was wrongly decided and that it should be, and now is, overruled."[83]

The *Times* reported that "the significance of today's decision extends far beyond the particular context of the case, raising questions about whether individuals can use the courts to force states to abide by a variety of Federal laws . . . It is evident now that the *Lopez* decision was a signal that the current majority is in the process of revisiting some long-settled assumptions about the structure of the Federal Government and the constitutional allocation of authority between Washington and the states."[84] Justice Stevens called the majority's opinion "shocking," and "a sharp break with the past."[85] Justice Souter characterized the Court's decision as "amazing" and compared it to the decisions issued by the Court at "the nadir of its competence" in the *Lochner* era.[86]

The *Times* reported that the 1995 term provided "abundant evidence of the extent to which the Court's discourse has shifted to the right."[87] In sharp contrast to characterizations of the first Rehnquist Court, Chief Justice Rehnquist was now portrayed as the "general" in charge of a constitutional war, a war he was clearly winning.[88] Justice Kennedy was now characterized as an exemplar of "libertarian jurisprudence," a Justice who was "emphatically not a squishy moderate."[89]

The 1996 term followed with yet another blockbuster win for judicial conservatives, in yet another important area of constitutional law. This time the target was Section 5 of the Fourteenth Amendment. Section 1 of this Amendment, ratified in 1868, prohibits states from depriving any person of "life, liberty, or property, without due process of law" or "the equal protection of the laws." Section 5 of the Fourteenth Amendment provides that "Congress shall have power to enforce, by appropriate legislation, the provisions of this article."[90]

Until its 1996 term, the Court had construed congressional power under Section 5 quite broadly. In *Ex parte Virginia*, 100 U.S. 339 (1879), a majority for the Court had declared that Congress could enact any "appropriate" enforcement legislation under Section 5. In subsequent cases the Court had deferred to congressional judgments as to just what constituted "appropriate" enforcement legislation through the same "rational basis" test used in Interstate Commerce Clause litigation.[91]

Not only did the Court defer to congressional judgments about the "appropriateness" of enforcement legislation under the Fourteenth and Fifteenth Amendments; its jurisprudence also permitted the Congress to go further in enacting enforcement legislation than the Court was willing to go itself in litigation arising under those Amendments.[92] In at least two cases the Court had upheld federal statutes prohibiting conduct found by the Court in previous decisions to have been constitutional.[93]

But then came *Boerne*. In *City of Boerne v. Flores*, 521 U.S. 507 (1997), the Court evaluated the constitutionality of the Religious Freedom Restoration Act of 1993. That statute prohibited governmental actors from "substantially burdening" a person's religious practice, even if the burden resulted from a rule of general applicability, unless the government could demonstrate that the burden both served a compelling governmental interest, and was "the least restrictive means of furthering that compelling governmental interest."[94] A church in Boerne, Texas, had invoked the act in response to the city's denial of a building permit for the church's expansion into an area zoned for historic preservation. In response, the city had challenged the act on the grounds that it exceeded Congress's Section 5 powers to enforce the guarantees of the First Amendment's Free Exercise Clause upon the states. The United States Court of Appeals for the Fifth Circuit had upheld the statute.

The five-justice conservative majority in *Boerne* declared that the previous standard of "appropriateness" used to evaluate Section 5 statutes would be replaced by a new standard of "congruence and proportionality." Statutes enacted under Section 5 authority must now possess "a congruence and proportionality between the injury to be prevented or remedied and the means adopted to that end."[95] Moreover, the Court signaled that it would not defer to congressional judgments as to what constituted "congruent and proportional" Section 5 legislation. Case in point, the Religious Freedom Restoration Act of 1993, which did not meet the Court's new standard.

The Court's decision in *Boerne* was characterized as "one of its most important modern-day rulings on the sources and limits of Congressional power," a "new departure" that limited the ability of Congress to define rights protections more aggressively than the Court itself had done.[96] Observers of the Court pointed out that the Court's new Section 5 jurisprudence amounted to telling Congress that it could not go beyond judicial determinations of what constituted violations of Section 1: "The 'proportionality and congruence' test has arguably come to mean that Congress's powers under Section 5 are coextensive with the Court's authority to declare government conduct unconstitutional under Section 1."[97] Robert

Post and Reva Siegel of the Yale University School of Law characterized the decision as adding "an entirely new chapter" to the Court's Section 5 jurisprudence, one that is "entirely alien to the spirit and intention of earlier precedents."[98]

Boerne was followed by a 5–4 ruling overturning the Brady Handgun Violence Prevention Act of 1993 on the grounds that requiring state officials to conduct background checks of prospective handgun purchasers violated state sovereignty (*Printz v. United States*, 521 U.S. 898 [1997]). Senator Charles Schumer noted that the decision had "huge implications": "If you take the Scalia opinion to its logical extreme, you could go back to the 1890's."[99] Paul Gewirtz of Yale Law School commented, "The Supreme Court is redesigning the basic institutional architecture of our public lives. The Court's insistence on certain structures of power has enormous consequences."[100] The *Times* asserted that the decision "would have been inconceivable to many people only a few years ago."[101]

The 1996 term was rounded out by another Establishment Clause case wherein Justices O'Connor and Kennedy again backed away from their votes cast during the first Rehnquist Court to enforce that clause. In *Agostini v. Felton*, 521 U.S. 203 (1997), both O'Connor and Kennedy voted to overrule the Burger Court precedent *Aguilar v. Felton*, 473 U.S. 402 (1985), joining a five-justice majority to rule that New York City did not violate the Establishment Clause by providing additional educational services on the premises of parochial schools. The *Times* asserted that "the single most important fact" about the Court's 1996 term was "how important it was."[102] The 1996 term provided "a powerful reminder of the extent to which the Court's center of gravity has shifted to the right in recent years . . . arguments that not so many years ago would have flowed comfortably, even if not successfully, from the mainstream of legal thought now appear to be little more than liberal delusions."[103]

By the Rehnquist Court's 1998 term, there was no more talk of a moderate Court. Yet there was still some skepticism about how far the Court was willing to take its own logic. In that term, the Court was hearing a series of cases wherein lower courts had aggressively applied the Court's recent federalism rulings. Thomas Merrill of Columbia Law School commented that these cases pushed the federalism envelope to such an extent that "I can't help but think is going to make the swing votes on the Court a little queasy."[104]

But it turned out that the justices had strong stomachs. In three major cases the five-justice majority further limited the ability of the federal government to protect individual rights from the actions of state governments. In a pair of cases involving federal statutes making states liable for damages caused by unremediated patent infringement or unfair practices such as false advertising, the Court reaffirmed its new Section 5 jurisprudence as established in *Boerne* (1997) (*College Savings Bank v. Florida Prepaid*, 527 U.S. 666 [1999], *Florida Prepaid v. College Savings Bank*, 527 U.S. 627 [1999]). The Court declared that the challenged statutes had to meet the hurdle of "congruence and proportionality" between the injury to be prevented and the means of prevention provided in the statute. In the Court's judgment, which was apparently the only judgment that mattered, the challenged statutes did not meet this hurdle.

The five-justice majority also extended its Eleventh Amendment jurisprudence to state courts, ruling that states could not be sued by their own residents in their own courts for violating federal statutes passed under the congressional power to regulate interstate commerce. In this case employees of the state of Maine were prohibited from suing the state for violating the minimum wage and maximum hours provisions of the Fair Labor Standards Act of 1938 (*Alden v. Maine*, 527 U.S. 706 [1999]). The doors of federal courts had already been closed to such suits by the Court's ruling in *Seminole Tribe* (1996). Now, the only way to enforce such statutes against the states would be for the federal government to bring every enforcement suit. However, it was quite clear to observers at the time that the federal government did not have the manpower to be the sole enforcement mechanism for all federal statutes.[105]

The decisions, characterized by the *Times* as "the most powerful indication yet of a narrow majority's determination to reconfigure the balance between state and Federal authority," were announced in a "scene of extraordinary drama."[106] After the author of each of the three majority opinions summarized his opinion, one of the four dissenters spoke, with reportedly unusual passion. Justice Stevens said that the Court had returned constitutional jurisprudence to "the brief period of confusion and crisis when our new nation was governed by the Articles of Confederation."[107]

The concern over these cases went well beyond the particular statutes at issue. The *Times* editorialized, "People with federally protected rights [now] have no realistic way to enforce them against states."[108] Christopher Schroeder of Duke Law School wrote, "Few would have predicted that the Court might uncover the nontextual residual notion of sovereignty that grounds the results in *Seminole Tribe* and *Alden*."[109] The term was characterized as a "triumph" for Chief Justice Rehnquist and his "band of radical judicial activists."[110] The Court had gone too far even for former Solicitor General Charles Fried, the Reagan administration's advocate for a more aggressively conservative jurisprudence. Fried castigated the Court for foreclosing a state employee's right to sue for the infringement of statutorily guaranteed rights in *Alden*, characterizing the majority opinion as "backhanded," "awkward," "absurd," and "bizarre."[111]

Subsequent terms saw more of the same. In its 1999 term the five-justice majority struck the provisions of the federal Age Discrimination in Employment Act permitting state employees to sue for violations of the act by their employers, again applying the new Section 5 standard to the ADEA statute (*Kimel v. Florida Board of Regents*, 528 U.S. 62 [2000]). *Kimel* also reaffirmed the Court's new interpretation of the Eleventh Amendment; even though the statute, as a valid exercise of congressional interstate commerce clause authority, could be enforced in federal courts against private employers, state employees could use neither state nor federal courts to sue their employers for violations of the Act. The *Times* reported that "the difference this time was a notable hardening of tone, with both the majority and dissenting opinions conveying the impression that the two sides, wedded to sharply opposing views of the authentic nature of the federal system, had little left to say to one another across one of the great divides in the court's recent history."[112]

Actually, they did still have a few things left to say to each other. That same term the five-justice majority struck the civil provisions of the Violence Against Women Act of 1994 (*U.S. v. Morrison*, 529 U.S. 598 [2000]). In providing a federal civil remedy for victims of gender-motivated violence, the Act had not been directly targeted at state officials. However, the enacting Congress had amassed considerable testimony documenting bias in state justice systems against victims of gender-motivated violence, bias that arguably prevented those victims from receiving adequate remedies for the crimes perpetrated against them. The appellants in *Morrison* thus argued that the act was justified on Section 5 grounds as a legitimate effort by the Congress to create a substitute for constitutionally inadequate state remedies for gender-motivated violence. But the Court ruled that, because the Act did not directly target state officials, it was too broadly constructed to be justified under Section 5. The Court also ruled that the statute exceeded congressional power to regulate under the Interstate Commerce Clause. As in *Lopez*, the majority asserted that the statute did not have the "commercial" character required under the Court's new Commerce Clause jurisprudence.

Referring to the Court of the early New Deal, the Court that repeatedly struck new federal statutes in an episode with "a pedigree of near-tragedy," Justice Souter's dissent asserted that the majority's opinion in *Morrison* "can only be seen as a step toward recapturing the prior mistakes."[113] Jack Balkin of Yale Law School wrote that, after *Morrison*, "states can now violate many civil rights with impunity."[114] Judith Resnick, also of Yale Law, said that the Court's rejection of congressional power to address gender motivated violence was "a reminder of earlier eras, when the Supreme Court viewed labor-management issues and, even earlier, slavery, as a matter of interpersonal relations, not properly subject to federal intervention."[115] Chris Schroeder of Duke University Law School observed, "The court is reflecting in a bunch of different doctrines the general sense that the federal government is too big, too powerful, too incompetent."[116]

The 2000 term brought *Bush v. Gore*, 531 U.S. 98 (2000), a decision that demonstrated that, even after six terms of consistently aggressive conservative jurisprudence, the five-justice majority of the second incarnation of the Rehnquist Court retained the capacity to shock even well-informed observers.[117] *Bush v. Gore* was followed in the 2000 term by *Board of Trustees of the University of Alabama v. Garrett*, 531 U.S. 356 (2001), wherein the five-justice majority struck the provisions of the Americans with Disabilities Act (ADA) permitting state employees to sue their employers for disability-based discrimination. Like many other federal statutes reviewed by the second Rehnquist Court, the ADA ran afoul of the Court's new Section 5 and Eleventh Amendment doctrinal standards. Democratic Senator Tom Harkin said of *Garrett* that it "undermines every citizen's constitutional right to be protected against irrational and unfair discrimination."[118] Stephen McCutcheon, a lawyer with the conservative Pacific Legal Foundation, said of the decision, "We are very pleased . . . We believe it goes far in helping to restore the Constitution's limits on Congress' power."[119]

Not surprisingly, the *Times* characterized the Court's 2000 term as "distressing."[120] Linda Greenhouse reported, "There is a revolution in progress at the Court, with Chief Justice William H. Rehnquist and Justices Antonin Scalia, Sandra Day O'Connor, Anthony M. Kennedy and Clarence Thomas challenging long-settled doctrines governing state-federal relations, the separation of powers, property rights, and religion."[121]

The 2001 term saw another important Eleventh Amendment ruling by the five-justice conservative majority, namely that federally protected rights could be enforced against the states not only not in federal and state courts, but also not in federal administrative hearings (*Federal Maritime Commission v. South Carolina Ports Authority*, 535 U.S. 743 [2002]). Justice Breyer said that the decision "reaffirms the need for continued dissent," and predicted that the Court's federalism jurisprudence would prove to be "randomly destructive."[122] Cass Sunstein of Harvard Law called the Court's Eleventh Amendment decisions "sweeping" and "remarkable," and characterized *Federal Maritime Commission* as "still more remarkable," noting that the decision would "undermine the enforcement of many laws protecting the health and safety of state employees."[123]

On the last day of the 2001 term, "to the delight of conservatives," the five-justice majority issued a "bombshell" Establishment Clause decision permitting parents to use public money to pay for religious school tuition (*Zelman v. Simmons-Harris*, 536 U.S. 639 [2002]). Voucher advocates called the ruling "the most important Supreme Court education decision since *Brown v. Board of Education*."[124] Voucher opponents claimed that "the strict wall of separation between church and state gradually erected through a series of court rulings in the 1970's and 1980's is now gradually being dismantled."[125]

The 2001 term was described as "the triumph of William H. Rehnquist": "In decision after decision this term, the court, often by a 5-to-4 majority, pushed the law rightward."[126] In a startling indication of just how far rightward the Court had apparently gone, in the summer of 2002 a Reagan-appointed federal appellate judge released a book sharply criticizing the Rehnquist Court's last eight terms of jurisprudence.[127] Judge John T. Noonan argued that the Court had taken the Eleventh Amendment's protection of state sovereign immunity to "ludicrous extremes," permitting states to discriminate or otherwise behave badly virtually at will.[128]

The Court's decision the following term in *Nevada Department of Human Resources v. Hibbs*, 538 U.S. 721 (2003), wherein the Chief Justice deserted the conservative majority to uphold the Family and Medical Leave Act (FMLA) on the grounds that it constituted a valid exercise of congressional power under Section 5 of the 14th Amendment, did little to change perceptions of the Court. The *Times* pointed out that, even though the Court had upheld the FMLA, the Chief Justice's opinion in *Hibbs* reaffirmed the Court's post-1993 Section 5 jurisprudence: "We distinguish appropriate prophylactic legislation from substantive redefinition of the 14th Amendment right at issue."[129] To the *Times*'s editorial staff, *Hibbs* represented "continuity rather than a change": "The last time the Supreme Court paid sustained attention to Section 5 of the 14th Amendment was during the civil rights era of the 1960's, and the difference between then and now is striking. In the earlier decisions, the court's stance toward Congress was one of deference, starting from the presumption that Congress was acting within the scope of its authority not only to enforce but, at least to some degree, also to define the constitutional right at issue. In the Rehnquist court's revisiting of Section 5, the burden has shifted. Now, the presumption is the opposite: that Congress has to prove that it is acting within the scope of its authority, a constricted scope that is limited to enforcement and must stay clear of any effort at definition."[130] The *Times* urged its readers not to overlook "how conservative [the Court] is right now."[131]

The 2003 term raised a few questions in the popular press about whether the conservative judicial revolution was losing some steam, mostly because of the Court's two statutory interpretation decisions protecting the right of "enemy combatants" to contest this classification before a federal judge. In both *Rasul v. Bush*, 542 U.S. 466 (2004), and *Hamdi v. Rumsfeld*, 542 U.S. 507 (2004), the Court ruled that the federal habeas corpus statute applied to those designated as enemy combatants and held at Guantanamo Bay, permitting detainees to bring habeas corpus petitions before federal courts. However, congressional Republicans apparently saw these decisions not as rebukes, but rather as invitations to act.[132] They accepted these invitations, suspending habeas corpus rights for those detained as enemy combatants in the Military Commissions Act of 2006.

In its 2004 term, the last term of the Rehnquist Court, the Court upheld the federal statutory criminalization of marijuana against an Interstate Commerce Clause challenge (*Gonzales v. Raich*, 545 U.S. 1 [2005]). Because the second Rehnquist Court had staked out a considerably higher bar for statutes to clear in order to survive such challenges, the expectation of many was that the Court would apply this same high standard to the provision of the Controlled Substances Act at issue in *Gonzales*. Perhaps somewhat hypocritically, the Court ruled instead that Congress could use its Interstate Commerce Clause authority to regulate the intrastate noncommercial cultivation and possession of marijuana for personal medical use, as recommended by a patient's doctor, and as permitted by California state law. Harvard University Professor of Law Mark Tushnet noted that *Gonzales* "does not necessarily mean a retreat" from the Court's new limits on federal power; the Court appeared to be carving out an exception to those limits simply to achieve its desired outcome in the case.[133]

At the close of the 2004 term Justice Sandra Day O'Connor announced her intention to retire from the Court. On September 3, 2005, Chief Justice William Rehnquist succumbed to thyroid cancer. The second Rehnquist Court was at an end.

The Two Rehnquist Courts

The commitment of the second Rehnquist Court in its last couple of terms to the aggressive conservative jurisprudence of its first nine or so terms came in for some questioning.[134] But it was the sharp break between the first and second Rehnquist Courts that dominated academic commentary on the Rehnquist Court.[135] That break was of "historic importance," wrote University of North Carolina Professor of Law Michael Gerhardt.[136] Former United States Solicitor General Seth Waxman characterized the 1994 term as inaugurating in the Rehnquist Court's jurisprudence "a thoroughgoing paradigm shift."[137] Mark Tushnet asserted that the post-1993 Court had initiated "a new constitutional order."[138] Yale University's Bruce Ackerman characterized the mid-1990s break in the Rehnquist Court's jurisprudence as a transformative constitutional moment, placing the second Rehnquist Court in the same category as the Founding, Reconstruction, and New Deal Courts, an assessment shared by Princeton University Professor Keith Whittington.[139] And many constitutional scholars simply began referring to the "pre-*Lopez*" and "post-*Lopez*" eras.[140]

However, despite the volume of words directed at describing this marked change in the Rehnquist Court's jurisprudence, there were remarkably few explanations for it. Some pointed to the steadily increasing conservatism of the Court since the days of the Warren Court, the result of an unbroken stream of Republican appointees from the Nixon through the George H. W. Bush administrations. The efforts of the Reagan and Bush administrations to appoint more doctrinaire conservatives to the Supreme Court bench drew particular blame from liberal quarters.[141] Duke Law Professor Christopher Schroeder summarized this argument as: "The shifting fortunes of the major political parties have been translated into the appointment of enough conservative Justices to change outcomes on the Court."[142]

But the gradually increasing conservatism of the Court's median justice through the 1970s and mid-1980s cannot account for the sudden emergence of apparently significantly more conservative outcomes in the 1994 term and beyond. As we saw in Figures 3.1 and 3.6, the median justice's estimated most preferred rule was already quite conservative by the 1986 term and did not become appreciably more conservative over the course of the Rehnquist Court. The appointment of Justice Clarence Thomas to Justice Thurgood Marshall's seat in the 1991 term did shift the identity of the median justice rightward (in the Bailey XTI estimates, from Justice O'Connor to Justice Kennedy), but the appointment of Justice Ruth

Bader Ginsburg to Justice Byron White's seat in the 1993 term moved the identity of the Court's median justice back to the left. Between the 1993 and the 1994 terms, using the Bailey XTI estimates, there was no change in either the identity or the estimated preferences of the Court's median justice. Yet by all accounts the Court's jurisprudence became sharply more conservative between these two terms.

Others suggested that the Court's post-1993 jurisprudence was best characterized as an embrace of federalist principles.[143] This characterization generally rested on the Court's decisions in cases involving the constitutionality of federal statutes under the Interstate Commerce Clause, Section 5 of the Fourteenth Amendment, and the Eleventh Amendment. Between the 1986 and 1993 terms, the first Rehnquist Court upheld every federal statute on its docket that was challenged under one of these constitutional provisions. But between the 1994 and 2004 terms, the second Rehnquist Court struck 64 percent of the federal statutes challenged on one of these grounds.[144]

Some suggested that in its reinvigoration of the limits on national regulatory power the second Rehnquist Court was merely following public opinion. Between the 1950s and the 1990s, for example, trust in the national government had declined precipitously. In the words of New York University Professor of Law Barry Friedman, "The justices were following social trends and by doing so were often deciding cases consistent with public opinion . . . the American public was by all accounts well behind the idea of devolving power to the states."[145]

But as we can see in Figure 4.1, most of the decline in trust in the national government had already occurred before the Rehnquist Court's first term. Although there was a small additional decrease in trust in the national government during the first Rehnquist Court terms, trust in the national government began to rise again immediately after the 1994 elections. By 1998, trust in the national government was higher than it had been at the start of the Rehnquist Court. By 2002, trust in the national government was higher than it had been since 1970. Yet the Rehnquist Court continued to strike federal statutes on "federalism" grounds even as public trust in the federal government continued to grow.

Moreover, it is not at all clear that the second Rehnquist Court's jurisprudence is appropriately characterized as "pro-federalism" in any

Figure 4.1. Trust in the Federal Government, 1958–2004
Source: American National Election Studies.

case. Every single federal statute struck by this Court on "federalism" grounds had been enacted by Democratic-majority Congresses.[146] Overall, 82 percent of the statutes enacted by Democratic majority Congresses and reviewed on "federalism" grounds by the second Rehnquist Court resulted in strikes. But this Court struck exactly none of the federal statutes enacted by Republican-majority Congresses and reviewed under one of these "federalism" provisions. The second Rehnquist Court embraced federalism only when it came to the federal statutes enacted by liberal Democratic Congresses. It was apparently happy to tolerate statutes extending federal regulatory power when those statutes had been enacted by conservative Republican Congresses.

   Had there been greater diversity in the kinds of statutes struck and upheld in the second Rehnquist Court's federalism jurisprudence, there would be a more convincing story to tell about the justices' genuine concern with the principle of federalism. In particular, if that Court had struck on federalism grounds even a single federal statute enacted by the Republican Congresses sitting between 1995 and 2004, then the "federalism" story would carry more water. Some of these Republican-enacted statutes had significantly narrowed the scope of the states' legislative authority. For example, the Republican majority 106th Congress had in 2000 amended Schedule I of the Controlled Substances Act, leaving intact the criminalization of the manufacture, distribution, and/or possession of marijuana. The Bush administration had then aggressively enforced this statutory provision even against those using "medical marijuana" in compliance with state statutes legalizing such use. The Court's ruling in *Gonzales v. Raich*, 545 U.S. 1 (2005), had rejected an Interstate Commerce Clause challenge to this federal regulatory scheme, undermining state efforts to devise their own regulations in this contested policy area.

Instead, the Court's "federalism" revolution is perhaps better understood as a revolution in how it would treat liberal statutes enacted by Democratic Congresses. Former Solicitor General Charles Fried may have hit the nail on the head when he said of the Court's federalism argument in *Alden v. Maine* (1999), prohibiting Maine's state employees from suing their employer in state courts for violations of the Fair Labor Standards Act, "I suspect this is a bad case of the tale wagging the dog. The Court's real complaint is with the wage and hours law . . . To remove an employee's right to sue is a backhanded and awkward way to nullify this law, and led to the absurd result we enjoy now."[147]

Others acknowledged that federalism per se might not have been motivating the justices, and proposed that the Court was following a conservative swing in public opinion that had occurred around the time of the 1994 congressional election.[148] But measures of conservative public opinion do not match the patterns in the Court's jurisprudence particularly well. For example, Figure 4.2 reports the index of the conservative "public mood" estimated by James Stimson of the University of North Carolina, by far the dominant measure of public opinion used in the academic literature on the Court.[149] This index is constructed from 139 domestic social and economic policy questions asked in identical form in major public opinion polls in two or more years between 1953 and 2004. From the responses to these questions an annual index of the public "mood" is estimated.[150]

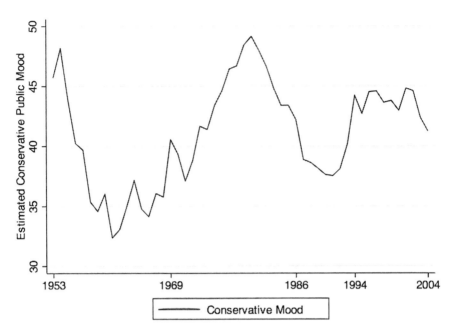

Figure 4.2. Conservative Public Mood, 1953–2004
Source: Stimson (1999), as updated. As reported here, the public mood is increasing in conservatism.

As can be seen in Figure 4.2, between the 1986 and 1994 terms public opinion moved first in a more liberal and then in a more conservative direction, remaining generally stable after 1994. The net result of this movement was essentially zero; by the 1994 term the public mood was no more conservative than it had been at the start of the Rehnquist Court, and was considerably more liberal than it had been in the late 1970s and early 1980s. Yet the Rehnquist Court's jurisprudence became significantly more conservative after 1994 than it had been at its inception. Public opinion does not seem to provide a very good fit to the pattern in the Court's judgments.[151]

Some saw the Court's post-1993 jurisprudence as an inter-institutional battle, claiming that the Court's primary goal in those cases was to "diss" Congress.[152] According to this account, the Court and the Congress were battling for policy supremacy, with the Court having (suddenly) in its 1994 term decided to exercise its power of judicial review to disrespect the Congress: "In acting repeatedly to invalidate federal legislation, the

Court is using its authority to diminish the proper role of Congress. Structurally, the new activist majority has treated the federal legislative process as akin to agency or lower court decision making."[153] Stanford University Law School Dean Larry Kramer likewise saw the second Rehnquist Court as arrogating power to itself in a bid for judicial supremacy, at the expense of Congress.[154] Neal Devins of William and Mary Law School agreed that the distinctive conflict of the second Rehnquist Court was between the Court and the Congress, but argued that by crafting constitutionally sloppy legislation and failing to pay sufficient attention to the Court's rulings, Congress had opened the door to the Court's assertion of judicial supremacy.[155] However, these accounts could explain neither the timing of the Court's apparently newfound dislike of Congress, nor why this dislike manifested itself only when the Court happened to be reviewing statutes enacted by liberal Democratic Congresses.

Finally, Thomas Merrill of Columbia Law School suggested that the stable membership of the Court between the 1994 and 2004 terms enabled the justices better to learn one another's preferences, leading to the formation of the consistent five-justice majority that generated the jurisprudential innovations of the second Rehnquist Court.[156] But University of Louisville Professor of Law Jim Chen, analyzing other periods of stable and fluctuating membership on the Court, failed to find any other evidentiary support for this claim.[157]

The big Republican congressional elephant in the room didn't get much attention. Only a few observers noted the rather striking correlation between congressional election results and the Rehnquist Court's jurisprudence, and these few looked for reasons to dismiss this correlation as unimportant.[158] Their reasons weren't necessarily good ones.[159] But apparently they didn't have to be; the suggestion that the emergence of the second Rehnquist Court could have been a direct result of the Republican electoral landslide of 1994 failed to attract attention in any event. In this intellectual climate, it was even possible to read, in an article attempting to explain the change in the Rehnquist Court jurisprudence, that the Court's 1937 jurisprudential change was likely due to congressional pressure, but never to see that possibility raised with respect to the Rehnquist Court.[160]

The Puzzle of the Two Rehnquist Courts

And so we are left with a rather curious puzzle. The quantitative record depicts a Court unaffected by congressional preferences, including the watershed change in those preferences effected by the 1994 congressional elections. According to quantitative analyses, the Rehnquist Court's constitutional jurisprudence was unresponsive to those elections. Rather, as the most preferred rule of the median justice grew more conservative throughout the 1980s and into the 1990s, the Court's decisions grew steadily more conservative as well.

But the qualitative picture painted by journalists and constitutional scholars conveys a very different characterization of the Rehnquist Court. These observers depict a Court that, between its 1986 and 1993 terms, was strikingly and unexpectedly liberal across a range of important constitutional issues. Those issues included executive power, abortion, the Establishment Clause, affirmative action, school desegregation, habeas corpus, and the congressional powers both to regulate the economy, and to provide for private enforcement actions against the states for failure to comply with those regulations.

These observers then saw a Court that made big doctrinal changes, starting in the second half of the 1994 term. In many areas of the Court's jurisprudence, these changes amounted to outright rejections of doctrines endorsed during the Rehnquist Court's first incarnation. These rejections included decisions on federal affirmative action programs, the role of the federal courts in school desegregation cases, and the powers of the Congress both to regulate under the Interstate Commerce Clause, and to permit private enforcement actions against state violations of those regulations. In the areas of habeas corpus and the Establishment Clause, the second Rehnquist Court backed away from its earlier rulings. And on the question of congressional enforcement of the Fourteenth Amendment, the second Rehnquist Court innovated in an area of jurisprudence it had left untouched during its first eight terms.

As noted at the beginning of this chapter, these narrative accounts of the Rehnquist Court's jurisprudence may well be incomplete or even misleading. But it is nonetheless striking that the pattern identified by journalists and legal scholars in that jurisprudence looks very similar to the one we might expect, had the Court been constrained by congressional preferences. That is, as we saw in Chapter Three, liberal congressional constraint on the Court remained high throughout the 1980s and early 1990s, but dropped into virtual nonexistence as a result of the 1994 elections. If congressional constraint had mattered to the justices, then we would expect to have seen in the Court's decisions precisely the pattern identified by journalists and legal academics.

Those journalists and legal scholars apparently did not believe that the big Republican elephant jumping up and down in the room had anything to do with the dramatic changes in the Court's jurisprudence after 1994. But as the next chapter will demonstrate, there is compelling evidence that both the results from existing econometric studies of the Court and the widely shared belief that congressional elections had nothing to do with the changes in the Rehnquist Court were mistaken.

5

EXPLAINING THE PUZZLE OF THE TWO
REHNQUIST COURTS

The econometric analyses of Chapter Three and the narrative accounts of Chapter Four present two entirely different pictures of the Rehnquist Court. The econometric analyses depict a Court that was consistently and stably conservative between 1986 and 2004, with the predicted probability that the Court would issue a conservative judgment ranging in a narrow band between .62 and .67. This probability remains unchanged by the 1994 elections; in these analyses the Court was as conservative in its pre-1994 terms, when its average predicted probability of a conservative judgment was .64, as it was in its post-1994 terms, when this probability averaged .63.[1]

But journalists and legal academics portrayed a very different Rehnquist Court (or Courts). Their accounts of the Rehnquist Court's constitutional jurisprudence depict a relatively moderate, even liberal, Court that made a "revolutionary" turn to the right in the 1994 term. In these narrative accounts, the "second" Rehnquist Court then remained significantly more conservative than its first incarnation through the remainder of its terms.

The fact that these close observers of the Court's jurisprudence saw such a different Rehnquist Court should perhaps be a red flag for those who engage in more quantitative analyses. Perhaps we need to think a bit harder about the data we have been using to study the question of judicial independence.

Our measures of judicial and elected branch preferences are estimated from hundreds if not thousands of votes cast by legislators and justices; these measures represent the current state of the art in revealed preference estimation.[2] We have seen very similar results using two different versions of these measures. But our measure of the direction of the Court's judgments is a different animal altogether. This measure, as we saw in Chapter Three, is reported in the United States Supreme Court Database (Supreme Court Database), financed by the National Science Foundation and publicly available from the Center for Empirical Research in the Law at Washington University in St. Louis. The Supreme Court Database, often referred to as the "Spaeth" database after its originator and coder, Michigan State University Research Professor of Law Harold Spaeth, has been described as the gold standard for data on the Supreme Court by leading practitioners: "Spaeth's products meet all the aspects of the replication standard . . . The Spaeth databases are so dominating in our discipline that it would certainly be unusual for a refereed journal to publish a manuscript whose data derived from an alternate source. Even in the law reviews, virtually no empirical study of the U.S. Supreme Court produced by political scientists fails to draw on them."[3]

Most of the data reported in the Supreme Court Database comprise relatively objectively coded facts about each case docketed by the Court, such as whether a justice was in the majority or the dissent, whether a justice in the majority joined the majority opinion or merely concurred in the judgment, and so on. But some of the information reported in that database is entirely the product of subjective judgments made by the database's coder. The directional measure of the Court's judgments used in Chapter Three, the measure also used in almost every study failing to find evidence of elected branch constraint on those judgments, is one of these subjectively coded measures.[4]

It is perhaps surprising that so much research on the Supreme Court has been based on a measure so dependent on a coder's discretion, with so little apparent concern for the measure's validity.[5] This discretion prominently enters the Supreme Court Database coding process in the assignment of an "issue code" to each case, a code that will then determine the decision rule for coding the judgment in that case.[6] The Supreme Court Database codebook lists approximately 260 choices for such issue codes, which themselves are grouped into thirteen broader issue areas. There are no rules or even guidelines for this issue coding decision; the Supreme Court Database codebook acknowledges that "criteria for the identification of issues are hard to articulate."[7] Judgments are then coded as "liberal" or "conservative" according to a series of decision rules that are conditional on the prior assignment of an issue code. For example, in cases given antitrust issue codes, judgments that are "pro-competition" are to be coded as liberal judgments. In cases given First Amendment issue codes, judgments that are "pro-civil liberties or civil rights claimant[s]" are to be assigned liberal judgment codes.

The troubling aspect of these coding protocols is that different issue codes may lead to different judgment codes for the same case. Since the coder has considerable discretion in the assignment of issue codes, we might worry that the coder's expectations about how judgments "should" be coded affect his issue coding choices, such that these choices lead to confirmatory judgment codes. In particular, a coder may be improperly influenced by the ex ante expectation that independent liberal courts will generally issue liberal judgments, and that independent conservative courts will generally do the reverse.[8] The Supreme Court Database judgment codes might then reflect not the actual nature of the Court's decisions, but rather the coder's self-fulfilling expectations about those decisions.

It turns out that, looking at a large number of generally comparable cases, issue and judgment code assignments in the Supreme Court Database are indeed systematically conditional on the known preferences of the deciding court. Otherwise identical dispositions are assigned one set of issue codes under liberal courts, and another set under conservative courts. These issue codes then lead to judgment codes confirmatory of the expectations one might have about the kinds of judgments typically issued by such courts, under the assumption of judicial independence.[9]

The apparent confirmation bias in the Supreme Court Database has obvious implications for empirical analyses of elected branch constraint on the Court's decisions. Subjectively assigned Supreme Court Database issue and judgment codes confirm expectations about the kinds of judgments typically issued by more liberal and more conservative courts, under the hypothesis of judicial independence from the elected branches.

They therefore cannot be used to test the validity of that hypothesis itself. To test the hypothesis of the Supreme Court's independence from the elected branches, we need to use objectively coded judgment measures.

Measuring Judgments Objectively

It may not be possible to come up with a strategy for objectively coding all of the Court's judgments. However, we can devise a number of such strategies at least for the subset of the Court's cases involving constitutional challenges to federal statutes. The key to all these strategies is the leveraging of additional information about the federal statutory provisions at issue in these cases. This additional information allows us to make inferences about the direction and impact of the Court's rulings on the challenged provisions.

The most precise information we have about these statutes is derived from the congressional roll call votes over their final passage, if such roll call votes exist. We can use information from these final passage roll call votes to make inferences about the policy direction of the Court's judgments. To do so we turn to the analyses of congressional roll call data reported by political scientists Keith Poole and Howard Rosenthal.[10] Poole and Rosenthal assume a simple model of congressional voting: a bill, located at some point on a left-right continuum of public policy alternatives, proposes a change in some existing status quo policy, located at some other point on that same continuum. Members of Congress each have some most preferred point on that continuum that they would like to see enacted into public policy. Those members whose most preferred public policies lie closer to the proposed bill, than to the status quo, vote for the bill. Those members whose most preferred public policies lie closer to the status quo, than to the proposed bill, vote against the bill.

Along with estimating members' most preferred policies from their roll call votes, Poole and Rosenthal also estimate the cutpoint for each nonunanimous roll call vote, or the estimated point that separates those who voted for and those who voted against a bill, as a function of their policy preferences. These estimated cutpoints are preferable to the actual separation points we observe between those who voted for and those who voted against proposed bills, because the estimated cutpoints reduce the random noise there may be in these votes, allowing us to focus on the effect of members' policy preferences. The cutpoints are estimated with a very low degree of error; they predict actual separation points quite well.[11]

The estimated cutpoints tell us whether a bill moved policy in a liberal or a conservative direction. Essentially, if the estimated most preferred policies of those voting for a bill lie to the left of its estimated cutpoint, then the bill must have been located to the left of the status quo ex ante: those more liberal members whose most preferred policies lay closer to the bill voted "yea," while those more conservative members whose most preferred policies lay closer to the status quo voted "nay." Symmetrically, if the estimated most preferred policies of those voting for a bill lie to the right of its estimated cutpoint, the bill must have been located to the right of the status quo ex ante.[12] When there is a nonunanimous final passage roll call vote on a federal statute, then, we can identify with relative precision whether the statute in question moved policy in a liberal or a conservative direction.

The Court's rulings on constitutional challenges to federal statutes then preserve or reverse these statutes' liberal or conservative movements in the original status quo ex ante. One way to measure the Court's judgments objectively, then, at least for this subset of cases, is to code as liberal those judgments that preserve or produce liberal movements in the original status quo ex ante, and to code as conservative those judgments that preserve or produce conservative movements in the original status quo ex ante.

The sample of constitutional challenges to federal statutes between the 1953 and 2004 terms already compiled in Chapter Three can be used to construct this roll call–based judgment measure.[13] For each case in this sample the enactment date of the statute or statutes at issue was first identified.[14] The final passage roll call vote for each statute in the House of Representatives, if it existed, was then located, and the Poole and Rosenthal roll call estimates for that vote, again if they existed, were retrieved.[15] Statutes were then coded as moving the status quo ex ante in either a liberal or a conservative direction.

The Court's dispositions of the constitutional challenges to these statutes then either preserved the direction of movement of the original status quo (by upholding a statute), or reversed the direction of that movement (by striking a statute, causing policy to revert to the original status quo ex ante). This information was used to construct a dichotomous measure of the direction of the Court's judgments in these cases between the 1953 and 2004 terms.[16]

This roll call–based judgment measure has several obvious disadvantages. It captures neither the magnitude of the movement in the status quo ex ante preserved or produced by a judgment, nor the location of that movement on the policy continuum. It does not incorporate any doctrinal nuances of the Court's opinions, as distinct from its judgments. On the other hand, a judgment measure based on the roll call votes over the statutes challenged in these cases has obvious advantages as well. Most important, it is objectively coded across cases, unlike the Supreme Court Database judgment measure. It measures "liberal" and "conservative" as understood by political actors themselves, most particularly the members of Congress who voted on the challenged statutes. It is specific to the statutory provisions challenged in a given case. And although it measures neither the magnitude of the movements in the status quo ex ante preserved or produced by the Court's judgments, nor the locations of those movements, neither does the Supreme Court Database judgment measure.

Still, the roll call–based judgment measure is available for only slightly more than half of the population of cases involving constitutional challenges to federal statutes between 1953 and 2004, because many statutes are passed via voice votes rather than roll call votes. We may then have concerns about whether analyses using this measure will generalize beyond this limited sample. One strategy to increase the number of judgments in our sample is to leverage Congress-specific rather than statute-specific information about the statutes challenged before the Court.

For example, many of the statutes reviewed between the 1953 and 2004 terms, for which final passage roll call votes are not available, were passed during unified Democratic or Republican control of both houses of Congress.[17] We know that the partisan composition of the enacting Congress is highly correlated with the direction in which bills move the status quo: unified Democratic Congresses are more likely to pass bills moving the status quo in a liberal direction, while unified Republican Congresses are more likely to pass bills moving the status quo in a conservative direction.[18] We can thus use the partisan composition of the enacting Congress to construct a second objective judgment measure for those cases involving constitutional challenges to statutes enacted by unified partisan Congresses. These statutes are coded as liberal if passed by unified Democratic Congresses, and conservative if passed by unified Republican Congresses. If the Court then upholds one of these statutes, the statute's coding is preserved as the Court's judgment code; if the Court strikes a statute, the statute's coding is reversed as the Court's judgment code. This partisan Congress-based judgment measure is available for approximately 86 percent of the population of cases involving constitutional challenges to federal statutes between 1953 and 2004. And despite its apparent crudeness, the Congress-based judgment measure is highly correlated with the more sophisticated roll call–based judgment measure: the two measures agree in 74 percent of the cases for which they are both available.[19]

Estimating Judgment Probabilities

We can now estimate the effects of both judicial and elected branch preferences on these objective measures of the Court's judgments. We essentially want to replicate the analyses performed in Chapter Three, substituting the objective judgment measures for the subjective Supreme Court Database measure used there. Thus we will estimate the effects of the locations of the estimated most preferred rules of the median justice, the median representative, the median senator, and the president on the probability that the Court issues a conservative judgment, using the two samples of cases for which the roll call–based and the Congress-based judgment measures are available. We will also employ the same controls used in Chapter Three: the direction of the lower court judgment, whether the United States was a party to a case arguing for a liberal outcome, and whether the United States was a party to a case arguing for a conservative outcome. In Chapter Three these control variables were constructed relative to the conservative outcome as defined by the Supreme Court Database judgment codes; here they are constructed relative to the conservative outcome as defined by the objectively constructed judgment measures.

Tables 5.1 and 5.2 report the results of analyses of the roll call–based judgment measure, for both the Bailey XTI and the Judicial Common Space preference estimates. Consistent with the results reported in Chapter Three, we see large effects on the Court's judgments from changes in the most preferred rule of the median justice. Using the Bailey XTI preference estimates, increasing the preferences of the median justice from their most liberal value (observed during the 1962 and 1963 terms) to their most conservative value (observed during the 1991 term), while holding other variables at their sample values, increases the average predicted probability of a conservative judgment from .05. to .59.[20] Using the JCS preference estimates, moving from the most liberal median justice to the most conservative (or from the 1968 to the 1988 term), under the same conditions, increases the average predicted probability of a conservative judgment in these cases from .17 to .53.[21] These predicted probabilities are distinct at conventional thresholds.

Also as we saw in Chapter Three, using the Bailey XTI estimates we observe perverse effects from changes in the preferences of the median sena-

Table 5.1: **Estimating the Probability of a Conservative Judgment: Bailey XTI Judicial and Elected Branch Preferences, 1953–2004, Roll Call–Based Judgment Measure**

	Coefficient	SE	95% CI
Conservatism of SCOTUS Median	1.71	.51	(.70, 2.71)
Conservatism of House Median	4.93	1.46	(2.07, 7.79)
Conservatism of Senate Median	−3.08	.88	(−4.80, −1.36)
Conservatism of President	−.37	.14	(−.64, −.10)
Liberal Lower Court Ruling	.42	.24	(−.06, .89)
US Liberal Party	−.17	.37	(−.88, .55)
US Conservative Party	.94	.33	(.29, 1.59)

N = 166
Wald chi^2 = 36.26

Note: Probit regression; robust standard errors reported, clustered by term. Intercept term not reported. Italicized variables are statistically significant at the .10 level (two-tailed).

Table 5.2: Estimating the Probability of a Conservative Judgment: Judicial Common Space Judicial and Elected Branch Preferences, 1953–2004, Roll Call–Based Judgment Measure

	Coefficient	SE	95% CI
Conservatism of SCOTUS Median	2.18	.78	(.65, 3.70)
Conservatism of House Median	2.41	1.16	(.13, 4.70)
Conservatism of Senate Median	−.06	1.45	(−2.90, 2.79)
Conservatism of President	−.34	.28	(−.89, .21)
Liberal Lower Court Ruling	.36	.23	(−.09, .80)
US Liberal Party	−.16	.35	(−.86, .53)
US Conservative Party	.90	.33	(.25, 1.55)

N = 166
Wald chi^2 = 40.60

Note: Probit regression; robust standard errors reported, clustered by term. Intercept term not reported. Italicized variables are statistically significant at the .10 level (two-tailed).

tor and the president; increases in the conservatism of these elected officials' most preferred rules are associated with decreases in the probability that the Court issues conservative judgments. However, these perverse effects disappear when we use the JCS preference estimates. As reported in Table 5.2, using the JCS preference estimates there are no estimated effects on the roll call–based measure of the Court's judgments from changes in the most preferred rules of the median senator or the president.

These results are perhaps no surprise. The surprise comes with the predicted effects of the preferences of the House median on the Court's judgments, using either the Bailey XTI or the JCS preference estimates. Using the estimates reported in Table 5.1, setting the most preferred rule of the House median at the most liberal observed value (in the 1974 term) produces an average predicted probability of a conservative judgment of .20. But setting that rule at the most conservative observed value (in the 1995 term) increases that probability to .62.[22] Likewise, using the JCS-based estimates reported in Table 5.2, moving from the most liberal to the most conservative observed value of the median representative's preferences (or from the 1974 term to the 2004 term) increases the average predicted probability of a conservative judgment from .30 to .58.[23] Both sets of predicted probabilities are distinct at conventional thresholds.

Tables 5.3 and 5.4 report the results of analyses of the partisan Congress-based judgment variable; the control variables in these regressions are coded relative to this new dependent variable. Strikingly, in both analyses we now see no effects on the Court's judgments from changes in the preferences of the median justice. We also see no effects on those judgments from changes in the preferences of the median senator or the president. But we see large effects on those judgments from changes in the preferences of the median representative. Using the Bailey XTI estimates, setting the preferences of the median representative to their most liberal value returns an average predicted probability of a conservative judgment of .10, increasing to .53 when the preferences of the median representative are set to their most conservative value.[24] Using the JCS preference estimates returns average predicted probabilities of .10 and .74, respectively.[25] Both sets of predicted probabilities are again distinct at conventional thresholds.

Table 5.3: **Estimating the Probability of a Conservative Judgment: Bailey XTI Judicial and Elected Branch Preferences, 1953–2004, Partisan Congress-Based Judgment Measure**

	Coefficient	SE	95% CI
Conservatism of SCOTUS Median	−.25	.31	(−.85, .36)
Conservatism of House Median	4.52	1.33	(1.90, 7.13)
Conservatism of Senate Median	.12	.71	(−1.26, 1.50)
Conservatism of President	−.18	.15	(−.48, .11)
Liberal Lower Court Ruling	.08	.20	(−.31, .47)
US Liberal Party	.21	.29	(−.35, .78)
US Conservative Party	.77	.33	(.11, 1.42)

N = 265
Wald chi² = 46.35

Note: Probit regression; robust standard errors reported, clustered by term. Intercept term not reported. Italicized variables are statistically significant at the .10 level (two-tailed).

Table 5.4: Estimating the Probability of a Conservative Judgment: Judicial Common Space Judicial and Elected Branch Preferences, 1953–2004, Partisan Congress-Based Judgment Measure

	Coefficient	SE	95% CI
Conservatism of SCOTUS Median	−.50	.47	(−1.43, .43)
Conservatism of House Median	5.08	1.01	(3.09, 7.07)
Conservatism of Senate Median	−.74	1.15	(−2.99, 1.51)
Conservatism of President	−.25	.20	(−.63, .14)
Liberal Lower Court Ruling	.02	.21	(−.39, .43)
US Liberal Party	.20	.28	(−.34, .74)
US Conservative Party	.61	.35	(−.07, 1.30)

N = 265
Wald chi² = 65.10

Note: Probit regression; robust standard errors reported, clustered by term. Intercept term not reported. Italicized variables are statistically significant at the .10 level (two-tailed).

The effect of the median representative's preferences on the Court's judgments is perhaps easier to interpret by looking at each term between 1953 and 2004. To that end Figures 5.1 through 5.4 display predicted probabilities derived from the estimates reported in Table 5.3. These are the estimates obtained using the larger partisan Congress-based sample of cases and the Bailey XTI preference estimates. Because these estimates generate a smaller predicted effect for the preferences of the median representative, relative to those reported in Table 5.4, they offer perhaps a conservative interpretation of the magnitude of this effect.

Figure 5.1 reports two series of predicted probabilities for each term between 1953 and 2004. One series, the "Actual Constrained Court" series, reports the average predicted probability of a conservative judgment in each term, setting judicial and all elected branch preferences to the correct values for that term. Case-specific control variables retain their sample values for each observation. This series may be interpreted as our best guess for how the justices would have decided cases involving constitutional challenges to federal statutes in a given term, factoring in the effects of both judicial and elected branch preferences.

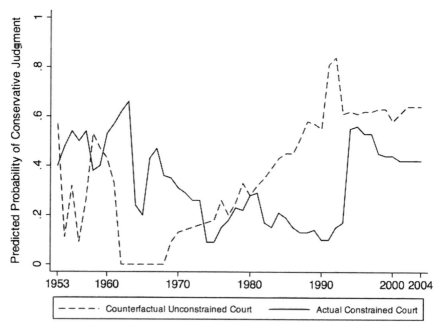

Figure 5.1. Predicted Judgment Probabilities, 1953–2004
Simulated from the estimates reported in Table 5.3. The "Actual Constrained Court"
series uses the actual values of judicial and elected branch preferences; the "Counterfactual Unconstrained Court" series sets the preferences of the median representative
to those of the median justice in each term. Case-specific control variables remain at
their sample values. The two series are distinct with at least 90 percent confidence in
the 1954, 1956–1957, 1962–1971, and 1982–1993 terms.

The second series, labeled the "Counterfactual Unconstrained Court"
series, also reports the average predicted probability of a conservative
judgment in each term, setting the preferences of the median justice,
the median senator, and the president to the correct values for that term,
but counterfactually setting the preferences of the median representative to be identical to the preferences of the median justice in that term.
Case-specific control variables again retain their sample values for each
observation. This series removes any preference divergence between the
Court and the House of Representatives. These predicted probabilities
may consequently be interpreted as our best guess for how the justices
would have decided cases involving constitutional challenges to federal

statutes in a given term, had the Court been completely unconstrained by the House of Representatives.

The differences between the "Counterfactual Unconstrained Court" and the "Actual Constrained Court" series in Figure 5.1 are then a measure of the magnitude of the effect of the preferences of House majorities on the Court's judgments. Perhaps the first thing to notice about this effect is that, as reported in the note to Figure 5.1, it is present at conventional levels of statistical significance in about half the terms between 1953 and 2004. That is, in about half the terms over this approximately 50-year period, the preferences of majorities on the Court and in the House were not sufficiently divergent for the latter to exert a detectable effect on the Court's judgments. These terms include most of the Burger Court terms during the 1970s, when a relatively liberal majority on the Court faced generally liberal majorities in the House, and all of the Rehnquist Court terms between 1994 and 2004, when a conservative majority on the Court faced conservative majorities in the House.

But in the remaining terms between 1953 and 2004, the preferences of House majorities were sufficiently divergent from those of the justices to exercise discernible effects on the Court's judgments. These terms include those of the later Warren and early Burger Courts, when more conservative House majorities appear to have increased the likelihood that the Court would issue conservative judgments, relative to the unconstrained likelihood, and those of the late Burger and early Rehnquist Courts, when more liberal House majorities appear to have decreased the likelihood that the Court would issue conservative judgments, relative to the unconstrained likelihood. These effects of House majorities on the Court's judgments are significant at conventional thresholds between the 1962 and 1971 terms, and again between the 1982 and 1993 terms.[26]

Recall that one objection to the hypothesis of elected branch constraint on the Court is that the preferences of the Court and the elected branches are unlikely to be sufficiently divergent for the elected branches to even want to cabin the Court's judgments. But as we saw in Figure 3.1, there in fact appears to have been considerable divergence between judicial and elected branch preferences between 1953 and 2004. And as we can now see in Figure 5.1, this divergence was sufficiently large for the preferences of House majorities to exercise a detectable pull on the Court's judgments in about half of the Court's terms over this period.

But this pull was more consequential in some terms than in others. House majorities appear to have made less of a difference to the Court's judgments during the later Warren and early Burger Courts, relative to their impact during the late Burger and early Rehnquist Courts. During the former period, a very liberal majority on the Court faced somewhat less liberal Democratic majorities in the House of Representatives. But at least after the 1964 elections, the Court was still most likely to issue liberal judgments in cases involving constitutional challenges to federal statutes, even after factoring in the effects of slightly less liberal House majorities. That is, the conservative effect of House majorities during the later Warren and early Burger Courts appears to have been largely a moderating effect, moving the Court from being extremely unlikely to issue conservative judgments in these cases, to being simply unlikely to issue such judgments.

During the late Burger and early Rehnquist Courts, however, the effect of House majorities on the Court is sufficiently large so as to actually alter the character of the Court's jurisprudence. By the mid-1980s, as a consequence of an unbroken series of appointments made by Republican presidents, the majority on the Court had become sufficiently conservative that, at least in cases involving constitutional challenges to federal statutes, had this majority been free to decide cases at will, it would have been most likely to issue a conservative ruling in any given case. Left to their own devices, the majority of the justices' decisions would have been in a conservative direction, meaning that most of their rulings in these cases would have struck liberal and upheld conservative federal statutes.

But because the conservative majority on the Court was not free to decide cases at will, we in fact saw a very different Court during these terms. We saw a Court that was by far most likely to issue liberal decisions in cases involving constitutional challenges to federal statutes, and that consequently decided only a small proportion of these cases in a conservative direction. Indeed, Figure 5.1 may reveal the nature of conservatives' frustration with the late Burger and early Rehnquist Courts. As we saw in Chapter Four, conservative judicial activists in the Reagan and George H. W. Bush administrations thought that they were engineering a conservative majority on the Court, a majority that would decide cases in a way perhaps well characterized by the "Counterfactual Unconstrained Court" predicted probabilities reported in Figure 5.1. But the House of Representatives remained dominated by liberal Democratic majorities during these administrations. And so conservative judicial activists instead got a Court that decided cases in a way perhaps more accurately characterized by the "Actual Constrained Court" predicted probabilities reported in Figure 5.1.

Overall, then, these estimates suggest not only that the Supreme Court is constrained by the preferences of majorities in the House of Representatives, the institution perhaps most prominently possessed of the power both to punish and reward the justices, but also that between 1953 and 2004 the degree of this constraint was at times sizable enough to effect dramatic changes in the nature of the Court's constitutional jurisprudence. Moreover, as we will see when we examine the Warren, Burger, and Rehnquist Courts in more detail, even during the terms when the magnitude of this constraint was relatively slight, the Court's judgments in cases involving constitutional challenges to federal statutes were still conditional on the presence of friendly House majorities. Had these majorities been less friendly, we could have seen very different decisions in these cases.

The Warren Court, 1953–1968

Although the Warren Court of the 1950s issued a handful of prominent liberal rulings, like the school desegregation decisions in *Brown v. Board* (1954) and *Cooper v. Aaron* (1958), it was not until the 1962 term that this Court had a clear majority of liberal justices. In this term Arthur Goldberg replaced Felix Frankfurter, giving the Warren Court five reliably liberal justices: Chief Justice Earl Warren, Justice William Douglas, Justice William Brennan, Justice Hugo Black, and Justice Goldberg. As we saw in Figure 3.1, in this term the preferences of the median justice shifted sharply to the left, and remained there throughout the remaining Warren Court terms.

We are accustomed to thinking of this later Warren Court, the Court sitting between the 1962 and 1968 terms, as acting as "an independent and aggressive guarantor of constitutional rights," in the words of writer Jeffrey Toobin.[27] And it does at least appear to be true that the effect of House majorities on the later Warren Court was relatively small. We likely would have seen an even more liberal Warren Court in its later terms than the Court we actually saw, had House majorities had no effect on the Court. But even after factoring in the effects of slightly less liberal House majorities, we still saw a pretty liberal Warren Court between 1962 and 1968.

What if, however, the Warren Court justices had faced conservative Republican majorities in the House of Representatives? What if, for example, they had faced House majorities as conservative as the 104th Republican House majority, the majority elected in the 1994 elections? Figure 5.2 reports for the Warren Court terms these counterfactual predicted probabilities, along with the two series of predicted probabilities already reported in Figure 5.1. This new series of counterfactual probabilities, labeled the "Conservatively Constrained Court" series, simulates the average predicted probability of a conservative judgment in each term, setting the preferences of the median representative to their 1995 value. All other preference variables are set at their correct values for each term, while case-specific control variables again retain their sample values.

Now we see a Warren Court that, in each of its terms, is most likely to issue conservative judgments in cases involving constitutional challenges to federal statutes. Even during the later Warren Court terms between 1962 and 1968, the terms wherein the justices are predicted to have decided virtually none of these cases in a conservative direction, had they been unconstrained by House majorities, the Court is predicted to issue conservative judgments with probabilities ranging from .57 to .71. These predicted probabilities are distinct at conventional thresholds from the unconstrained probabilities in each of these later Warren Court terms.

Under the condition of conservative Republican majorities in the House of Representatives, the Warren Court looks very different from the Warren Court of legend. It decides most of its cases in a conservative direction, striking liberal federal statutes and upholding conservative fed-

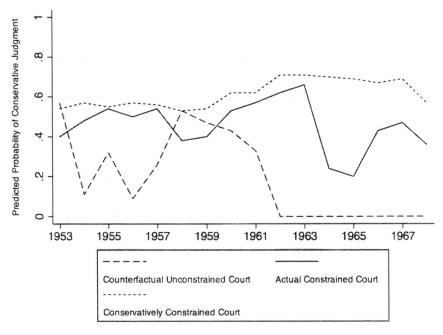

Figure 5.2. Predicted Judgment Probabilities, 1953–1968
Simulated from the estimates reported in Table 5.3. The "Actual Constrained Court"
series uses the actual values of judicial and elected branch preferences; the "Counterfactual Unconstrained Court" series sets the preferences of the median representative to
those of the median justice in each term; the "Conservatively Constrained Court" series sets the preferences of the median representative to their 1995 value. Case-specific
control variables remain at their sample values. The "Conservatively Constrained
Court" series is distinct from the "Counterfactual Unconstrained Court" series with
at least 90 percent confidence in the 1954, 1956–1957, and 1962–1968 terms.

eral statutes. While counterfactual predictions must always be taken with
at least a few grains of salt, those reported here can nonetheless perhaps
offer some insight into the conditional nature of the Warren Court's judgments. For example, in its 1964 and 1965 terms, the Warren Court upheld key provisions of the Civil Rights Act of 1964 and the Voting Rights
Act of 1965. In *Heart of Atlanta Motel v. U.S.*, 379 U.S. 241 (1964),
the Court upheld provisions of the Civil Rights Act of 1964 prohibiting racial discrimination in hotels and motels serving interstate travelers,
while in *Katzenbach v. McClung*, 379 U.S. 294 (1964), the Court upheld

provisions of the same Act prohibiting racial discrimination by restaurants serving food that had moved in interstate commerce. In *South Carolina v. Katzenbach*, 383 U.S. 301 (1966), the Court rejected a challenge to the Voting Rights Act of 1965 by the state of South Carolina, ruling that the Act was well within congressional power under Section 2 of the Fifteenth Amendment; in *Katzenbach v. Morgan*, 384 U.S. 641 (1966), the Court upheld that Act's ban on literacy tests as applied to former residents of Puerto Rico, ruling that the ban was within congressional power under Section 5 of the Fourteenth Amendment.

Both the Civil Rights Act of 1964 and the Voting Rights Act of 1965 had been enacted by unified Democratic majority Congresses; both statutes are also estimated to have moved the status quo in a liberal direction. The Court's rulings upholding these statutes then preserved policy movements in a liberal direction. Using the "Counterfactual Unconstrained Court" predicted probabilities reported in Figures 5.1 and 5.2, had the Warren Court justices been free to decide cases independently of the preferences of House majorities, the predicted probabilities that they would strike these liberal federal statutes would have been less than one percent.

In these terms the Court enjoyed large Democratic majorities in the House of Representatives. The preferences of the median representative during these terms are estimated to have been only slightly less liberal than those of the median justice. Factoring in the effect of these slightly less liberal House medians, the Court is predicted to have issued conservative judgments in its 1964 term with a probability of only .24, and in its 1965 term with a probability of only .20. That is, even after adjusting their decisions to take into account the presence of somewhat less liberal majorities in the House of Representatives, the justices were still very likely to have rejected the challenges to the Civil Rights Act of 1964 and the Voting Rights Act of 1965. However, had the Warren Court faced a House majority as conservative as the 104th House majority, the probabilities of conservative judgments in these cases would have increased to .70 in the 1964 term, and to .69 in the 1965 term. In this different political context, the Court would have been very likely to strike these statutes as unconstitutional.

Similarly, in its 1967 term the Warren Court upheld amendments to the Fair Labor Standards Act of 1938, extending that Act's coverage to state-owned enterprises like schools and hospitals (*Maryland v. Wirtz*, 392 U.S. 183 [1968]). The amendments, enacted in 1966, had been challenged by 28 states on the grounds that they exceeded congressional power under the Interstate Commerce Clause. The 1966 amendments had been enacted by a unified Democratic Congress, and are estimated to have moved policy in a liberal direction. The Court's ruling upholding the amendments then preserved this liberal policy movement. Again, had the Court been completely unconstrained by the House of Representatives in the 1967 term, it would have struck liberal federal statutes like the one at issue in *Maryland v. Wirtz* with a predicted probability of less than one percent. Factoring in the effects of the somewhat less liberal Democratic House, which had moved in a more conservative direction after the 1966 midterm elections, raises this probability to .47. Nonetheless, the Court was still likely to uphold liberal federal statutes challenged during this term. But had the Court faced a House as conservative as the 104th House, the probability of a conservative judgment would have increased to .69, putting such statutes considerably more at risk.

While these counterfactuals should of course be interpreted with caution, they are nonetheless suggestive of how history might have turned out differently. Facing a conservative Republican majority in the House of Representatives, even the famously liberal justices of the later Warren Court are predicted to decide the vast majority of their cases in a conservative direction.

The conventional wisdom is that the later Warren Court terms exemplify the Supreme Court's independence from the elected branches. According to this widely shared belief, during these terms the Warren Court boldly defied the elected branches by protecting individual rights from majoritarian encroachment.[28] Although revisionist historians have challenged the accuracy of this story, it still receives widespread deference.[29] But this story is belied by the predicted probabilities reported in Figures 5.1 and 5.2. These figures suggest that the late Warren Court was permitted to be "an aggressive guarantor of constitutional rights" only by relatively liberal Democratic House majorities. Had those majorities instead been significantly more conservative, it is unlikely that the Warren Court majority would have been able to sustain its preferred liberal course.

The Burger Court, 1969–1985

As we saw in Figure 3.1, during the Burger Court years the most preferred rule of the median justice began to move steadily to the right. Consequently, as reported in Figure 5.1, over these terms the unconstrained predicted probability of a conservative judgment by the Court also grew steadily. While this probability was only .09 in the 1969 term, by the 1985 term it had grown to .45. Meanwhile, the most preferred rule of the median representative was moving steadily to the left. While during the early Burger Court terms the median representative remained to the right of the Burger Court, after the 1974 elections the most preferred rule of the median representative moved to the left of that of the median justice, and remained there throughout the remaining Burger Court terms.

For the first few terms of the Burger Court the slightly less liberal preferences of the median representative exert a detectable conservative constraint on the Court's judgments. However, even after factoring in the effects of this constraint, the predicted probability of a conservative judgment between the 1969 and 1971 terms still ranges only between .29 and .35. The early Burger Court was still very likely to rule in a liberal direction on constitutional challenges to federal statutes, even after factoring in the effects of slightly less liberal House majorities.

As the Court gradually moved to the right during the 1970s, and the House to the left, the preferences of the median justice and the median representative converged sufficiently that the effect of House majorities' preferences on the Court is too small to detect at conventional thresholds. Between the 1972 and 1981 terms there are no effects of House majorities on the Court that are discernable at standard levels of statistical significance. During these terms the unconstrained predicted probability of a conservative judgment grows from .15 to .32; the first slightly more conservative and then slightly more liberal preferences of House majorities have no detectable effects on these predicted probabilities. Both the Burger Court majorities and those in the House of Representatives had moderately liberal preferences, and these predicted probabilities reflect those preferences.

However, had the Burger Court faced a significantly more conservative House, we would likely have seen significantly more conservative rulings. Figure 5.3 reports for the Burger Court terms the same three series of predicted probabilities reported in Figure 5.2. As in Figure 5.2, the "Conservatively Constrained Court" series reports the average predicted probability that the Court issues a conservative judgment in each term, under the condition that it faces a House majority as conservative as the 104th House. This conservatively constrained Burger Court would have been much more likely to have issued conservative judgments throughout the 1970s, relative to the unconstrained Burger Court, with predicted probabilities of a conservative judgment ranging from .50 to .59. Between the 1969 and 1980 terms these predicted probabilities are distinct in every term at conventional thresholds from those predicted for an unconstrained Court.

Again, although these counterfactual predictions are admittedly speculative, they perhaps illustrate the conditional nature of many of the Burger Court's judgments. Between its 1969 and 1980 terms the Burger Court upheld numerous federal statutes enacted by unified Democratic Congresses that are estimated to have moved status quos in a liberal direction. These included the Black Lung Benefits Act of 1972 (*Usery v. Turner Elkhorn Mining Co.*, 428 U.S. 1 [1976]), the 1975 amendments to the Voting Rights Act of 1965, extending that Act's protections to language minorities (*Briscoe v. Bell*, 432 U.S. 404 [1977]), and provisions of the Public Works Employment Act of 1977 requiring that 10 percent of federal funds for public works be given to minority-owned businesses (*Fullilove v. Klutznik*, 448 U.S. 448 [1980]).

As reported in Figure 5.3, the unconstrained predicted probabilities that the Court would strike liberal federal statutes in these terms ranged from .18 to .33. The slightly more liberal preferences of the sitting Democratic House majorities reduced these probabilities to range between only .09 and .22, although the differences between the two sets of predictions are not significant at conventional thresholds. But had the Court faced instead the conservative median representative of the 104th House, the predicted probabilities of conservative judgments in these terms would have ranged instead between .50 and .58. These counterfactual predictions are distinct at conventional thresholds from both the unconstrained and the actual constrained predicted probabilities in each term.

By the Burger Court's 1982 term the justices had become sufficiently conservative, and House majorities sufficiently liberal, that liberal House

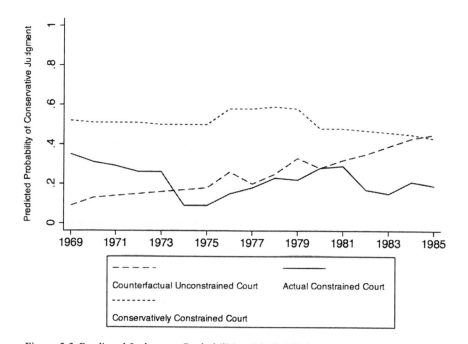

Figure 5.3. Predicted Judgment Probabilities, 1969–1985
Simulated from the estimates reported in Table 5.3. The "Actual Constrained Court" series uses the actual values of judicial and elected branch preferences; the "Counterfactual Unconstrained Court" series sets the preferences of the median representative to those of the median justice in each term; the "Conservatively Constrained Court" series sets the preferences of the median representative to their 1995 value. Case-specific control variables remain at their sample values. The "Conservatively Constrained Court" series is distinct from the "Counterfactual Unconstrained Court" series with at least 90 percent confidence in the 1969–1980 terms.

constraint on the Court had begun to bite. Now the presence of liberal Democratic majorities in the House began to decrease the probabilities of conservative judgments by detectable amounts. As depicted in Figure 5.3, in the Burger Court's last four terms the presence of Democratic House majorities decreased the average predicted probabilities of conservative judgments by magnitudes ranging from 18 to 26 percentage points; these predicted decreases are all significant at conventional thresholds.

During these terms the justices upheld provisions of several federal statutes enacted by unified Democratic Congresses and estimated to have moved the status quo in a liberal direction. These included the 1976 amendments to the Federal Election Campaign Act of 1971, prohibiting corporate political action committees from soliciting contributions from nonmembers (*FEC v. National Right to Work Committee*, 459 U.S. 197 [1982]), Title IX of the Education Amendments of 1972, prohibiting sex discrimination in any educational institution receiving federal funds as applied to students' receipt of federal financial aid (*Grove City College v. Bell*, 465 U.S. 555 [1984]), the "union shop" provisions of the Railway Labor Act of 1951, as applied to union expenditures for conventions, publications, and social activities (*Ellis v. Railway Clerks*, 466 U.S. 435 [(1984]), the minimum wage and overtime pay provisions of the Fair Labor Standards Act, as applied to nonprofit religious organizations (*Tony & Susan Alamo Foundation v. Secretary of Labor*, 471 U.S. 290 [(1985]), and the 1977 amendments to the Social Security Act extending survivors' benefits to wage earners' widowed spouses who remarry after age 60 (*Bowen v. Owens*, 476 U.S. 340 [(1986]).

Had the Court been unconstrained by the Democratic House during these terms, it would have struck liberal federal statutes like these with probabilities ranging from .35 to .45. But because of the presence of liberal House majorities between the 1982 and 1985 terms, the actual probabilities that these statutes would be struck ranged only between .15 and .21. The two sets of predicted probabilities are distinct at conventional thresholds in each term.

The Rehnquist Court, 1986–2004

By the 1986 term, the first term of the Rehnquist Court, the distance between the preferences of the more conservative median justice and those of the more liberal median representative had become substantial. As we already saw in Figure 5.1, between the Rehnquist Court's 1986 and 1993 terms, liberal House majorities decreased the probabilities of conservative judgments by magnitudes ranging from 30 to 71 percentage points; these decreases are all significant at conventional thresholds. Had the Rehnquist Court been unconstrained by the liberal Democratic House between its 1986 and 1993 terms, it would have issued conservative judgments in cases involving constitutional challenges to federal statutes with predicted probabilities ranging from .45 to .84. But the presence of liberal House majorities during these eight terms constrained these probabilities to range between only .10 and .17.

The effect of the House median's preferences on the Court then disappears after the 1994 congressional elections, as a result of the median representative's rightward shift toward the most preferred rule of the median justice. Between 1994 and 2004 the constrained Rehnquist Court was as likely to issue conservative judgments in cases involving constitutional challenges to federal statutes as if it had been unconstrained by the preferences of House majorities; the effect of these preferences on the Court's judgments is small and insignificant at conventional thresholds during these terms.

But had the 1994 elections not changed the composition of Congress, we likely would have seen a very different Rehnquist Court in its last eleven terms. Figure 5.4 reports for the Rehnquist Court terms the two predicted probability series displayed in Figure 5.1, along with a predicted probability series for a "Liberally Constrained Court." This latter series reports the predicted probability of a conservative judgment between the 1994 and 2004 terms, had the House remained as liberal as the 1994 Democratic majority House. In all terms from 1994 through 2004 these predicted probabilities are distinct at conventional thresholds from both the "Counterfactual Unconstrained Court" and the "Actual Constrained Court" series also reported in Figure 5.4. During these terms the unconstrained Rehnquist Court is predicted to issue conservative judgments in cases involving constitutional challenges to federal statutes with probabilities ranging from .58 to .64. Although the House was slightly less conservative than the Court during these terms, the differences between the two institutions were insufficiently large to exert any detectable effect on the Court's decisions. But had the House remained as liberal as the 1994 Democratic majority House, the predicted probability of a conservative judgment in these terms would have ranged between only .12 and .18.

Figures 5.1 and 5.4 may help to explain many of the cases that puzzled observers during both the first and the second Rehnquist Courts. Recall from Chapter Four that the Rehnquist Court's decision in *Morrison v. Olson*, 487 U.S. 654 (1988), upholding the federal independent counsel statute, was one of the first prominent decisions to call into question the

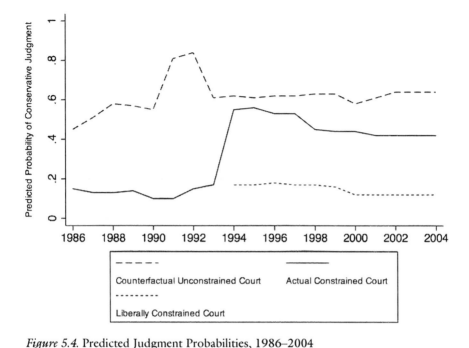

Figure 5.4. Predicted Judgment Probabilities, 1986–2004
Simulated from the estimates reported in Table 5.3. The "Actual Constrained Court" series uses the actual values of judicial and elected branch preferences; the "Counterfactual Unconstrained Court" series sets the preferences of the median representative to those of the median justice in each term; the "Liberally Constrained Court" series sets the preferences of the median representative to their 1994 value. Case-specific control variables remain at their sample values. The "Actual Constrained Court" and "Counterfactual Unconstrained Court" series are distinct with at least 90 percent confidence between the 1986 and 1993 terms; the "Liberally Constrained Court" series is distinct from the other two series with at least 90 percent confidence between the 1994 and 2004 terms.

Rehnquist majority's commitment to conservative principles. The case had resulted from the efforts of the Democratic majority in the House of Representatives to wield the independent counsel statute against prominent members of the Reagan administration. This statute had originated as a provision in the Ethics in Government Act of 1978, and had most recently been reauthorized in the Independent Counsel Reauthorization Act of 1987 by a unified Democratic Congress; the reauthorization is estimated to have moved the status quo in a liberal direction.[30] Court watchers assumed that the conservative majority on the Court, four of whose members had been directly appointed or promoted by the Reagan administration, would side with the administration's claim of executive power and strike the statute.[31]

And had the 1987 term Rehnquist Court been unconstrained by the considerably more liberal House, it is predicted to have struck liberal federal statutes with a probability of .51. But the Court rejected the constitutional challenge to the Independent Counsel Reauthorization Act of 1987 in a "crushing defeat" for the Reagan administration.[32] Although the Court's ruling in *Morrison* was characterized as "astonishing" by Court watchers, it was perhaps predictable. The Court was not unconstrained in its 1987 term; it was facing a considerably more liberal House of Representatives. Moreover, *Morrison* presented an explicit, overt conflict between the House, the body possessed of the powers to both punish and reward the justices, and the executive branch. Although the conservative justices owed their appointments to the executive branch, and likely shared the Reagan administration's policy preferences for the most part, that administration could neither save them from House impeachment investigations nor initiate appropriations measures increasing their salaries. Because of the presence of the liberal House majority, the actual predicted probability that the Court would strike a liberal federal statute in this term was only .13.

In its 1989 term the Court upheld the minority ownership preferences in awarding and transferring broadcast licenses that had been implemented by the Federal Communications Commission in 1978 (*Metro Broadcasting v. FCC*, 497 U.S. 547 [1990]). The FCC's regulations had been challenged on Fifth Amendment equal protection grounds. At issue in the case were not only the FCC's regulations, issued during the liberal Jimmy Carter administration, but also the efforts of the Democratic Congresses between 1987 and 1989 to prevent the Reagan-era FCC from revising those regulations. In each of these years the Congress had attached a rider to the FCC's appropriations bills, preventing the agency from altering the preferential treatment given to minority-owned businesses. The last of these, enacted in 1989 by a unified Democratic Congress, had been largely supported by Democrats and opposed by Republicans; the bill is estimated to have moved the status quo in a liberal direction.[33] Like *Morrison v. Olson* (1988), then, *Metro Broadcasting* directly implicated the conservative Rehnquist Court majority in a fight between the conservative Reagan administration and the liberal Democratic House of Representatives.

In the same term the Court also upheld Section 1 of the Sherman Antitrust Act, prohibiting anticompetitive practices such as horizontal price fixing, as applied to economic boycotts intended to affect the price paid for legal services (*FTC v. Superior Court Trial Lawyers Association (SCTLA)*, 493 U.S. 411 [1990]). Section 1 had been amended most immediately prior to *SCTLA* by a provision of the Consumer Goods Pricing Act of 1975, striking exemptions from Section 1's provisions for state fair trade laws; that Act had been passed by unified Democratic majorities and is estimated to have moved the status quo in a liberal direction. By upholding the application of Section 1 in *SCTLA*, the Court reversed a ruling by a conservative majority panel for the D.C. Circuit that had weakened the *per se* illegality of price fixing, a foundational principle in the Court's antitrust jurisprudence.[34] The appellate panel's opinion had been widely viewed with suspicion by those endorsing a robust application of antitrust statutes; many feared that Judge Douglas Ginsburg's opinion, if allowed to stand, would "open the door to economically-powerful bullies disrupting governments and markets."[35]

And had the Court been unconstrained by a liberal House majority, it might very well have invalidated the liberal statutes at issue in both *Metro Broadcasting* and *SCTLA*: the unconstrained predicted probability of a conservative judgment in this term was .57. But as a result of the presence of the sitting liberal House majority, the actual predicted probability that the Court would strike liberal statutes in this term was only .14. The Court upheld both statutes.

Only a few terms later, however, the political landscape changed dramatically. As we have seen, the House median shifted significantly to the right in the 1994 elections. Now House majorities no longer constrained the conservative Rehnquist Court majority from issuing conservative judgments.

Many of these conservative judgments involved strikes of liberal federal statutes previously enacted by Democratic Congresses. They included *U.S. v. Lopez*, 514 U.S. 549 (1995), striking the Gun-Free School Zones Act of 1990, as amended in 1994;[36] *Seminole Tribe of Florida v.*

Florida, 517 U.S. 44 (1996), striking the Indian Gaming Regulatory Act of 1988;[37] *Colorado Republican Federal Campaign Committee v. Federal Election Commission*, 518 U.S. 604 (1996), striking provisions of the Federal Election Campaign Act of 1971, as amended in 1976, imposing limits on political parties' independent expenditures on behalf of congressional candidates; *City of Boerne v. Flores*, 521 U.S. 507 (1997), striking the Religious Freedom Restoration Act of 1993; *Printz v. United States*, 521 U.S. 898 (1997), striking the Brady Handgun Violence Prevention Act of 1993;[38] *Eastern Enterprises v. Apfel*, 524 U.S. 498 (1998), striking the Coal Industry Retiree Health Benefit Act of 1992; *Alden v. Maine*, 527 U.S. 706 (1999), striking provisions of the Fair Labor Standards Act, as last amended in 1977;[39] *College Savings Bank v. Florida Prepaid*, 527 U.S. 666 (1999), striking provisions of the Trademark Remedy Clarification Act of 1992, making states liable for damages caused by unfair practices such as false advertising; *Florida Prepaid v. College Savings Bank*, 527 U.S. 627 (1999), striking provisions of the Patent and Plant Variety Protection Remedy Clarification Act of 1992, making states liable for damages caused by unremediated patent infringement; *Kimel v. Florida Board of Regents*, 528 U.S. 62 (2000), striking provisions of the 1977 amendments to the Fair Labor Standards Act, as applied in the context of the Age Discrimination in Employment Act; *U.S. v. Morrison*, 529 U.S. 598 (2000), striking provisions of the Violence Against Women Act of 1994;[40] and *Board of Trustees of the University of Alabama v. Garrett*, 531 U.S. 356 (2001), striking provisions of the Americans with Disabilities Act of 1990 (ADA), permitting state employees to sue their employers for disability-based discrimination.[41]

As we saw in Chapter Four, these rulings were generally characterized by observers as constituting large departures from the Court's prior jurisprudence. The Court's decision in *Lopez*, for example, was described by professional Court watchers as "extraordinary,"[42] "stunning,"[43] "radical,"[44] and "a distinct surprise."[45] *Seminole Tribe* was characterized as "shocking"[46] and "amazing."[47] *Boerne* was described as a "new departure" in the Court's Section 5 jurisprudence,[48] one that added "an entirely new" and "entirely alien" chapter to the Court's Section 5 precedents.[49] *Printz* was seen as "huge,"[50] as having "enormous consequences,"[51] and as a decision that "would have been inconceivable to many people only a few years ago."[52] The Court's rulings in *Alden*, *College Savings Bank*, and *Florida Prepaid* were characterized as decisions that "few would have predicted."[53] *Garrett* was described as signaling a conservative "revolution" on the Court.[54]

But the estimates reported in Table 5.3 suggest that perhaps these rulings should not have come as such a surprise. Given the preferences of the new Republican majority that assumed control of the House in January 1995, and that maintained this control throughout the remainder of the Rehnquist Court's terms, the Court's rulings in these cases were instead relatively predictable. Because these preferences were only slightly less conservative than those of the Rehnquist Court, the House now exercised no appreciable constraint on the Court's judgments. The Court was therefore free to strike liberal federal statutes, which it was predicted to do in these terms with unconstrained probabilities ranging between .58 and .63.

But, as reported in Figure 5.4, had the post-1994 House medians remained as liberal as that of the 1994 House, most of these statutes likely would have been upheld: the predicted probabilities of strikes in these cases would then have ranged only between .12 and .18. The Court appears to have struck these liberal federal statutes not because the justices had suddenly become more conservative, but because the House had suddenly become more conservative.

In short, the estimates reported here would appear to fully explain the puzzle of the break between the "two" Rehnquist Courts, a break characterized by many as of "historic importance."[55] The dramatic changes in the Rehnquist Court's jurisprudence in the mid-1990s, changes seen in several different areas of constitutional law, appear to have been the product not of changes in the preferences of the justices, but rather of changes in the preferences of House majorities.

The estimates reported in Table 5.3 can also be used to interrogate one of the more prominent claims made about the second Rehnquist Court, namely that it was the product of an apparently newfound interest by the conservative majority in federalism or states' rights. Presumably if the federalism interpretation were correct, the Rehnquist Court would have been equally likely to strike both liberal and conservative federal statutes. All federal statutes should have been similarly at risk during the second

Rehnquist Court, as the justices sought to free state governments from burdensome federal regulations.

But this interpretation is belied by the estimates reported in Table 5.3. The second Rehnquist Court was as likely to uphold conservative federal statutes between its 1994 and 2004 terms, as it was to strike liberal federal statutes. Examples of such conservative upholds included provisions of the Antiterrorism and Effective Death Penalty Act of 1996, restricting state prisoners' ability to file habeas corpus petitions in federal courts (*Felker v. Turpin*, 518 U.S. 651 [1996]),[56] provisions of the Prison Litigation Reform Act of 1996, as amended in 1997, limiting federal civil actions challenging the conditions of confinement in correctional facilities (*Miller v. French*, 530 U.S. 327 [2000]), the 1996 amendments to the Immigration and Nationality Act, permitting the Attorney General to detain aliens convicted of certain categories of crimes pending deportation hearings (*Demore v. Kim*, 538 U.S. 510 [2003]), the 2000 Children's Internet Protection Act, prohibiting public libraries from receiving federal funds for internet access unless they restricted access to obscene or pornographic imagery (*U.S. v. American Library Association*, 539 U.S. 194 [2003]), and the Schedule I classification of marijuana under the Controlled Substances Act, originally enacted in 1970 and most recently amended by the Hillory J. Farias and Samantha Reed Date-Rape Drug Prohibition Act of 2000, adding Gamma-Hydroxybutyric acid (GHB) to the list of Schedule I substances but leaving the Schedule I classification of marijuana untouched (*Gonzales v. Raich*, 545 U.S. 1 [2005]).

All these statutes had been passed by unified Republican Congresses, and all are estimated to have moved the status quo in a conservative direction. Had the second Rehnquist Court faced the liberal Democratic 1994 House, these statutes would have been upheld with predicted probabilities ranging from only .12 to .17. But because the Court was unconstrained by a liberal House, these conservative statutes were instead upheld with predicted probabilities ranging from .61 to .64.

These predicted probabilities suggest that the federalism explanation for the second Rehnquist Court does not hold much water. That Court had few problems with federal statutes enacted by Republican Congresses. It was only statutes enacted by liberal Democratic Congresses that the Court found objectionable.

Estimating Strike Probabilities

Our two strategies for measuring the Court's judgments objectively still have left out many cases involving constitutional challenges to federal statutes for which no roll call votes are available, and which were enacted during periods of divided government. One way to include these statutes in our analyses is to measure the average locations of statutes enacted by these Congresses, as predicted by prominent models of congressional behavior. Three of these models, namely a floor median model, a committee gatekeeping model under an open rule, and a party gatekeeping model under an open rule, specify the chamber medians as the pivotal legislators in determining the policy location of legislation.[57] We can then take the midpoint between the enacting chamber medians' estimated most preferred rules as a proxy for the rule embodied by any given statute.

We are still left with the question of how to code the Court's rulings on these statutes, however. Our previous strategies for coding the Court's judgments took advantage of the fact that we were measuring the direction in which a statute moved the status quo ex ante. We measured this movement directly with the roll call–based judgment measure, and indirectly with the partisan Congress-based judgment measure. When the Court upheld a statute's constitutionality it preserved the direction of this movement; when it struck a statute as unconstitutional it reversed the direction of this movement.

However, locating statutes at precise policy points complicates this measurement strategy. When the Court upholds a statute, it preserves a policy located at some precise point; we could take that point as a measure of the policy location of the Court's judgment. But when the Court strikes a statute, what value should be assigned to its judgment then?

One way out of this measurement conundrum is to code the Court's constitutional rulings on these statutes as simple strikes and upholds, and then to estimate the probability that the Court strikes a federal statute as a function of both judicial and elected branch preferences over that statute. Recall our assumption from Chapter Three that federal statutes embody standards of constitutionality endorsed by the enacting elected branches. When a constitutional challenge to a federal statute comes before the Court, the justices articulate the standard they will use to gauge the constitutionality of the challenged statute. They may accept the standard endorsed by the enacting elected branch majorities, as embodied in the statute, or they may move that standard in a liberal or conservative direction, as much or as little as they prefer.

The traditional view of an unconstrained, independent Court assumes that the Court is free to locate this standard at will, and *ceteris paribus* will apply the median justice's most preferred constitutional standard in every case. A model of elected branch constraint on the Court predicts instead that the Court will defer to the most preferred standards of pivotal elected officials.

We can think about the probability that any given statute is struck or upheld by the Court as a function of the distance between the constitutional standard embodied by the statute at issue, and the standard implemented by the Court in its majority opinion. Should the standard endorsed by the Court be identical to that embodied in the challenged statute, the statute will surely be upheld on constitutional grounds. But as the standard applied by the Court to a particular statute moves further away from that embodied by the statute, either to the left or to the right, then the probability that the statute will be upheld must surely decline.

If the constitutional rule or standard announced by the Court in its opinions is a function of judicial preferences, then we should find that a measure of the distance between the most preferred rule of the median justice and that embodied by a challenged statute is a good predictor of the probability that a statute is struck by the Court. If the location of the Court's rule is not responsive to elected branch preferences, then we should find that strike probabilities are not responsive to the inclusion of measures of the distances between the most preferred rules of pivotal elected officials and that embodied by a challenged statute. If, however, we do find that increases in the latter distances are associated with increases in the probability that statutes are struck, then we will have evidence that the Court's legal rules are in fact responsive to elected branch preferences.

Tables 5.5 and 5.6 report the results of these analyses, which include the same controls used in previous probit regressions, albeit coded for this new dependent variable. These controls include the lower court's disposition in a case (that is, whether the lower court struck or upheld

Table 5.5: Estimating the Probability of a Strike: Bailey XTI Judicial and
Elected Branch Preferences over Challenged Federal Statutes, 1953–2004

	Coefficient	SE	95% CI
SCOTUS Median/Statute Distance	1.60	.49	(.65, 2.55)
House Median/Statute Distance	2.50	1.44	(−.32, 5.32)
Senate Median/Statute Distance	−.08	1.35	(−2.72, 2.56)
President/Statute Distance	−.59	.30	(−1.18, −.01)
Lower Court Strike	.06	.20	(−.32, .45)
US Pro-Strike Party	.83	.47	(−.08, 1.75)
US Pro-Uphold Party	.35	.26	(−.17, .87)
Statute Age	−.01	.02	(−.05 .03)

N = 309
Wald chi^2 = 27.12

Note: Probit regression; robust standard errors reported, clustered by term. Intercept term not reported. Italicized variables are statistically significant at the .10 level (two-tailed).

Table 5.6: Estimating the Probability of a Strike: Judicial Common Space
Judicial and Elected Branch Preferences over Challenged Federal Statutes,
1953–2004

	Coefficient	SE	95% CI
SCOTUS Median/Statute Distance	1.90	.78	(.36, 3.43)
House Median/Statute Distance	3.85	1.50	(.91, 6.79)
Senate Median/Statute Distance	2.24	1.63	(−.96, 5.44)
President/Statute Distance	−1.71	.49	(−2.67, −.75)
Lower Court Strike	.04	.20	(−.34, .43)
US Pro-Strike Party	.99	.49	(.04, 1.95)
US Pro-Uphold Party	.30	.29	(−.27, .87)
Statute Age	−.01	.02	(−.04, .02)

N = 309
Wald chi^2 = 57.66

Note: Probit regression; robust standard errors reported, clustered by term. Intercept term not reported. Italicized variables are statistically significant at the .10 level (two-tailed).

the statutory provision at issue), whether the United States was a party to a case arguing against a statute's constitutionality, and whether the United States was a party to a case arguing in favor of the statute's constitutionality. These analyses also control for statute age; a statute may be less (or more) likely to be struck by the Court as time passes.[58]

These estimates of strike probabilities, using the largest possible sample of cases involving constitutional challenges to federal statutes between 1953 and 2004, are entirely consistent with the estimates of the probabilities of conservative judgments reported in Tables 5.1 through 5.4. In Tables 5.5 and 5.6 there are no effects in the predicted direction on the probability that the Court strikes a federal statute as a function of either the median senator's or the president's preferences over that statute, using either the Bailey XTI or the JCS preference estimates. There are clear effects on that probability from the preferences of the median justice; the Court was more likely to strike a federal statutory provision between 1953 and 2004 when those statutes were more distant from the preferences of the median justice. Using the Bailey XTI preference estimates, increasing the distance between the most preferred rule of the median justice and that embodied by a challenged statute from the smallest to the largest observed distance between 1953 and 2004 increases the probability of a strike from .13 to .81; using the Judicial Common Space estimates this probability increases from .16 to .45.[59] These predicted probabilities are distinct at conventional thresholds.

However, there are also large effects on strike probabilities from the preferences of the median representative over challenged statutes. Using the Bailey XTI preference estimates, the smallest distance between an enacted statute and the most preferred rule of the median representative is observed for statutes enacted in 1987 and reviewed during the 1988 term; the largest observed distance is for statutes enacted in 1976 and reviewed in the 1995 term. Using the JCS preference estimates, the smallest such distance is observed for statutes enacted in 1970 and reviewed in the Court's 1980 term; the largest such distance is observed for statutes enacted in 1976 and reviewed in the 1995 term. Moving from the smallest to the largest observed distance between the most preferred rule of the median representative and that embodied by a challenged statute increases the probability that the Court will strike a statute from .16 to .47

using the Bailey XTI preference estimates, and from .15 to .59 using the Judicial Common Space estimates. Again, these predicted probabilities are distinct at conventional thresholds.

These estimated effects of changes in the preferences of the median representative become even larger in magnitude when we isolate the Rehnquist Court terms, terms of particular interest for estimating the Court's responsiveness to changes in elected branch preferences. As reported in Tables 5.7 and 5.8, during these terms changes in the median justice's preferences over challenged statutes appear to have no effect on the predicted probability that a statute will be struck, regardless of the preference estimates used. There are also no effects on this probability from changes in the preferences of the median senator or the president. But moving from the smallest to the largest distance between the most preferred rule of the median representative and that embodied by a challenged statute increases the predicted probability of a strike from .06 to .96 using the Bailey XTI preference estimates, and from .15 to .68 using the Judicial Common Space preference estimates; these predictions are distinct at conventional thresholds.[60]

Table 5.7: **Estimating the Probability of a Strike: Bailey XTI Judicial and Elected Branch Preferences over Challenged Federal Statutes, 1986–2004**

	Coefficient	SE	95% CI
SCOTUS Median/Statute Distance	−1.74	1.40	(−4.49, 1.00)
House Median/Statute Distance	8.88	2.37	(4.23, 13.52)
Senate Median/Statute Distance	1.82	1.86	(−1.81, 5.46)
President/Statute Distance	−.57	.49	(−1.54, .40)
Lower Court Strike	.92	.28	(.37, 1.48)
US Pro-Strike Party	1.09	.77	(−.41, 2.60)
US Pro-Uphold Party	.21	.47	(−.72, 1.14)
Statute Age	−.05	.04	(−.14, .04)

N = 107
Wald chi^2 = 61.67

Note: Probit regression; robust standard errors reported, clustered by term. Intercept term not reported. Italicized variables are statistically significant at the .10 level (two-tailed).

Table 5.8: Estimating the Probability of a Strike: Judicial Common Space Judicial and Elected Branch Preferences over Challenged Federal Statutes, 1986–2004

	Coefficient	SE	95% CI
SCOTUS Median/Statute Distance	.15	2.03	$(-3.82, 4.12)$
House Median/Statute Distance	4.47	1.74	$(1.06, 7.88)$
Senate Median/Statute Distance	4.74	3.13	$(-1.41, 10.88)$
President/Statute Distance	-1.92	1.47	$(-4.80, .95)$
Lower Court Strike	.81	.29	$(.24, 1.37)$
US Pro-Strike Party	1.28	.78	$(-.25, 2.80)$
US Pro-Uphold Party	.27	.50	$(-.72, 1.25)$
Statute Age	$-.04$	.04	$(-.11, .04)$

N = 107
Wald chi^2 = 57.87

Note: Probit regression; robust standard errors reported, clustered by term. Intercept term not reported. Italicized variables are statistically significant at the .10 level (two-tailed).

We can use these estimates to characterize the alternative likelihoods that the Rehnquist Court would strike statutes enacted by a given Congress, as a function of both the actual judicial and elected branch preferences in each term, and the counterfactual preferences generated by assuming that the median representative's preferences were identical to those of the median justice in every term. The difference between these two series of predicted probabilities will reveal the magnitude of the effect of House preferences on the Court's dispositions of these statutes.

Figure 5.5 displays these two probability series for statutes enacted by the liberal 1965 Congress, using the Bailey XTI preference estimates. This is the Congress that enacted a number of landmark liberal statutes, including the Elementary and Secondary Education Act, the Social Security Act of 1965, establishing Medicaid and Medicare, the Voting Rights Act of 1965, and the Housing and Urban Development Act of 1965. Statute age is set at the correct value for each term, while case-specific control variables are held at their sample values.

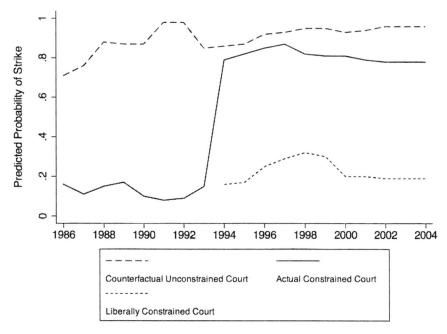

Figure 5.5. Predicted Strike Probabilities for Statutes Enacted in 1965
Simulated from the estimates reported in Table 5.7. The "Actual Constrained Court"
series uses the actual values of judicial and elected branch preferences; the "Counterfactual Unconstrained Court" series sets the preferences of the median representative
to those of the median justice in each term; the "Liberally Constrained Court" series
sets the preferences of the median representative to their 1994 value. Case-specific
control variables remain at their sample values. The "Actual Constrained Court" and
"Counterfactual Unconstrained Court" series are distinct with at least 90 percent
confidence between the 1986 and 1993 terms; the "Liberally Constrained Court"
series is distinct from the other two series with at least 90 percent confidence between
the 1994 and 2004 terms.

Had the median representative's preferences been identical to those of
the median justice in every term, as reported by the "Counterfactual Unconstrained Court" series, we can see that the probability of a strike of a
1965 statute would have ranged between .71 and .98 between 1986 and
2004. However, Figure 5.5 also reveals the degree to which a liberal House
protected these liberal statutes during the 1980s and early 1990s. As reported by the "Actual Constrained Court" series, the presence of liberal

House majorities held the predicted probability of a strike to between .08 and .17 between the 1986 and 1993 terms. The differences between these two series are distinct at conventional thresholds in every term.

After the 1994 elections, however, this congressional protection vanished. Now the Court was free to strike these statutes as a function of its own preferences. Between the 1994 and 2004 terms, the predicted probabilities reported in the "Actual Constrained Court" series are not significantly different from those reported in the "Counterfactual Unconstrained Court" series. But had the House not moved to the right after the 1994 elections, these liberal 1965 statutes would have remained under its protection. The "Liberally Constrained Court" series reported in Figure 5.5 reports the predicted probability of a strike of a 1965 statute under the counterfactual assumption that the House had remained as liberal as the 1994 Democratic majority House. Under this counterfactual assumption, the predicted probabilities of strikes of 1965 statutes range between only .16 and .32 between 1994 and 2004; these predicted probabilities are distinct from those reported in both the "Counterfactual Unconstrained Court" and the "Actual Constrained Court" series at conventional thresholds.

The estimates reported in Tables 5.7 and 5.8 can also help us to understand some of the cases from the Rehnquist Court involving federal statutes passed during periods of divided Congresses. For example, in its 1988 term the first Rehnquist Court upheld a federal statute on jurisprudential grounds that it would later reject after the 1994 elections. As we saw in Chapter Four, in *Pennsylvania v. Union Gas Co.*, 491 U.S. 1 (1989), the Court upheld the Superfund Amendments and Reauthorization Act of 1986 (SARA) against an Eleventh Amendment challenge. This statute had made explicit the congressional intention to render states liable in federal courts for damages caused by environmental harms. While statutory efforts to address environmental damage arising as a consequence of industrial activity were agreed to be a valid exercise of congressional powers under the Interstate Commerce Clause, the state of Pennsylvania argued that the Eleventh Amendment nonetheless prohibited the Congress from allowing states to be sued in federal courts for violating the provisions of such statutes.

Although SARA had been enacted by a divided Congress, we can nonetheless estimate the probability that a statute enacted in 1986 would be struck by the 1988 term Rehnquist Court. Using the estimates reported in Table 5.7, had the conservative majority on this Court been unconstrained by the preferences of the liberal majority in the House of Representatives, it is predicted to have struck statutes enacted in 1986 with a probability of .79. In other words, left to its own devices, the 1988 term Court likely would have accepted the Eleventh Amendment challenge to the Superfund Amendments and Reauthorization Act, and struck the statute. However, because of the presence of that liberal Democratic House majority, the actual predicted probability of such a strike in this term was only .22. The Court upheld the Superfund Amendments, rejecting Pennsylvania's Eleventh Amendment challenge.[61]

Only seven years later, however, the Court would overrule its Eleventh Amendment decision in *Union Gas.* As we have seen, in *Seminole Tribe of Florida v. Florida*, 517 U.S. 44 (1996), the Court reviewed an Eleventh Amendment challenge to the Indian Gaming Regulatory Act, enacted in 1988 by a Democratic-majority Congress. As in *Union Gas,* the congressional power to regulate Indian gaming under the Indian Commerce Clause was not at issue in the case. The issue in *Seminole Tribe* was whether, in the course of pursuing valid statutory goals under the Interstate and Indian Commerce Clauses, the Congress could make states liable in federal court for having violated such statutes. In *Union Gas* the Court had rejected such a challenge to the Superfund Amendments and Reauthorization Act. But in *Seminole Tribe* the Rehnquist Court overruled its decision in *Union Gas,* accepting the Eleventh Amendment challenge to the Indian Gaming Regulatory Act and striking the offending statutory provisions.

In *Seminole Tribe* the justices were not constrained by a liberal House majority. Using the estimates reported in Table 5.7, the unconstrained predicted probability that the 1995 term Rehnquist Court would strike a statute enacted by the 1988 Congress was .77; the preferences of the conservative 1996 Republican House were sufficiently similar to those of the justices to have no detectable impact on this Court's dispositions.[62] However, had the 1995 term Court instead reviewed the Indian Gaming

Regulatory Act while facing a House as liberal as the one faced by the 1988 term Rehnquist Court, the Court that had upheld the Superfund Amendments and Reauthorization Act, the Indian Gaming Regulatory Act would have been struck with a predicted probability of only .09. This probability is distinct at conventional thresholds from the unconstrained predicted probability.[63] Conversely, if the 1988 term Rehnquist Court had faced a House as conservative as the House faced by the 1995 term Rehnquist Court, it would no longer have been constrained in its constitutional rulings on federal statutes. Under this condition it would have struck the Superfund Amendments and Reauthorization Act with an unconstrained predicted probability of .79.[64]

In other words, the difference between the outcomes in *Union Gas* and *Seminole Tribe* was not a product of a change in the justices' preferences. Had the Rehnquist Court justices been unconstrained by a liberal House majority in their 1988 term, they likely would have accepted the Eleventh Amendment challenge to the Superfund Amendments and Reauthorization Act, and struck the relevant statutory provisions. Because they were unconstrained by a liberal House in their 1995 term, they were able to endorse the Eleventh Amendment challenge to the Indian Gaming Regulatory Act, and strike the offending statutory provisions, overruling their own recent Eleventh Amendment precedent. However, they most likely would not have taken this jurisprudential step, had they not faced a friendly majority in the House of Representatives. The second Rehnquist Court's dramatic turnabout in its Eleventh Amendment jurisprudence appears to have been a direct result of the similarly dramatic 1994 House elections.

Likewise, in its 1989 term the first Rehnquist Court upheld the National Trails System Act Amendments of 1983 in *Preseault v. ICC*, 494 U.S. 1 (1990). This statute had authorized the Interstate Commerce Commission to convert unused railroad lines into recreational trails. It had been challenged on the grounds that it exceeded congressional power under the Interstate Commerce Clause, the creation of bike trails not having much to do with the regulation of commerce across state lines. In its ruling, the Court had declared that the congressional power to regulate interstate commerce extended even to such noneconomic aims as the promotion of the "enjoyment and appreciation of the open-air, outdoor areas and historic resources of the Nation."[65]

Preseault was significant because only a few terms later the Court would reject this interpretation of the Interstate Commerce Clause in its landmark *Lopez* opinion. Understanding what changed between *Preseault* and *Lopez* is thus critical for understanding the Rehnquist Court's about-face on congressional power under this clause.

The National Trails System Act Amendments were enacted during a divided partisan Congress, and we do not have a final passage roll call vote for the statute. But we can estimate the probability that the 1989 term Rehnquist Court would strike statutes enacted by the 1983 Congress. Using the estimates reported in Table 5.7, had the Court been unconstrained by the liberal House in its 1989 term, there was a predicted probability of .73 that it would have struck the statute at issue in *Preseault*. But given the liberal House median sitting during this term, the actual predicted probability that the Court would strike this statute was only .12.[66] The Court upheld the statute.

However, had the 1989 term Court faced a House as conservative as that faced by the 1994 term Court, the Court that issued the ruling in *U.S. v. Lopez* (1995), the justices likely would not have endorsed such an expansive reading of the Interstate Commerce Clause. Under this condition, the preferences of the majority in the House of Representatives would have been insufficiently distinct from those of the majority on the Court to constrain the latter's decision making. The Court would have struck the National Trails System Act Amendments with an unconstrained predicted probability of .73.

Likewise, using the estimates reported in Table 5.7, the 1994 term Court is predicted to strike statutes enacted in 1994, like the amended Gun-Free School Zones Act, with a probability of .96; the preferences of the conservative Republican majority that assumed control of the House of Representatives in 1995 do not decrease this probability. However, had the 1994 term Court instead faced a House as liberal as the 1990 House, the House faced by the 1989 term Court that had upheld the National Trails System Act Amendments, this Court would have struck the Gun-Free School Zones Act with a predicted probability of only .17.[67]

In other words, the remarkable change in the second Rehnquist Court's interpretation of the Interstate Commerce Clause appears to have been directly related to the perhaps equally remarkable 1994 House elections. Left to their own devices, the conservative Rehnquist Court justices likely would have struck not only the Gun-Free School Zones Act in their 1994 term, but also the Trails System Act Amendments in their 1989 term. That they did not alter their Interstate Commerce Clause jurisprudence earlier seems largely due to the presence of liberal House majorities until the 1994 term.

We can also use the estimates reported in Tables 5.7 and 5.8 to further consider the "federalism" interpretation of the second Rehnquist Court. This interpretation suggests that the second Rehnquist Court began to strike federal statutes out of a newfound interest in states' rights. But the estimates reported in these tables suggest that the Rehnquist Court had quite different plans for federal statutes enacted by liberal Democratic majority Congresses, and those enacted by conservative Republican majority Congresses.

Figures 5.6 and 5.7 illustrate this differential treatment by using the estimates reported in Table 5.7 to simulate the predicted probabilities that statutes enacted in 1987 and 1995 would be struck by the Court, as a function of both actual and counterfactual values for the House median's preferences. In the 1986 midterm elections the Democrats won majorities in both the House and Senate, holding those majorities until the 1994 midterm elections. In both the Bailey XTI and the Judicial Common Space preference estimates the House and Senate medians shift markedly to the left as a result of the 1986 elections; the statutes enacted by the 1987 Congress thus measure as relatively liberal. By contrast, the statutes enacted by the Republican majority 1995 Congress measure as relatively conservative. In both Figures 5.6 and 5.7 the preferences of the median justice, the median senator, and the president are set at their actual values for each term, while case-specific controls are held at their sample values.

In Figure 5.6, the "Counterfactual Unconstrained Court" series reports predicted strike probabilities for 1987 statutes under the assumption that the House median shared the same most preferred rule as the Court median in every term. The "Actual Constrained Court" series re-

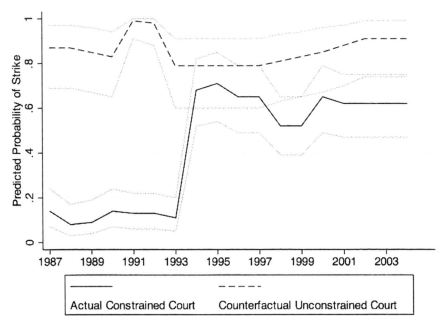

Figure 5.6. Predicted Strike Probabilities for Statutes Enacted in 1987
Simulated from the estimates reported in Table 5.7, with 95 percent confidence intervals. The "Actual Constrained Court" series uses the actual values of judicial and elected branch preferences; the "Counterfactual Unconstrained Court" series sets the preferences of the median representative to those of the median justice in each term. Case-specific control variables remain at their sample values.

ports predicted strike probabilities for these statutes while setting the median representative's most preferred rule to its actual value in each term. The 95 percent confidence intervals for these predicted probabilities are reported as well. We can see that between 1987 and 1993 these two series are distinct with at least 95 percent confidence in every term. Had the Court been unconstrained by the liberal House of Representatives during these terms, it would have struck a statute enacted in 1987 with predicted probabilities ranging from .79 to .99. But because of the constraint posed by the presence of the liberal House, these predicted strike probabilities ranged from only .08 to .14. After the 1994 elections, however, the Court was free to strike statutes enacted by this liberal Congress. Between its 1994 and 2004 terms an unconstrained Court would have struck statutes enacted in 1987 with probabilities ranging from .79 to .91. The only

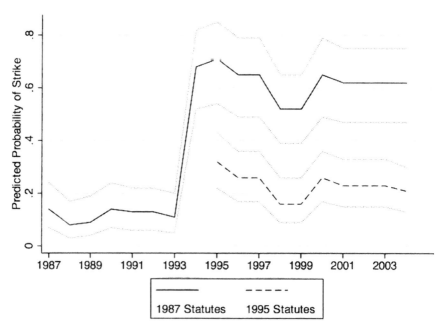

Figure 5.7. Predicted Strike Probabilities for Statutes Enacted in 1987 and 1995 Simulated from the estimates reported in Table 5.7, with 95 percent confidence intervals. Preference variables are set to their actual values, while case-specific control variables are held to their sample means.

slightly less conservative House median has no effect on these predicted strike probabilities; the 95 percent confidence intervals for the two series overlap in every term between 1994 and 2004.

So far, these results are consistent with the "federalism" story. Starting in the 1994 term, the Rehnquist Court began to take a much harder line on evaluating the constitutionality of federal statutes. But this hard line did not extend to all federal statutes. Figure 5.7 reports the predicted strike probabilities for both 1987 and 1995 statutes, along with the 95 percent confidence intervals, using the actual values of both judicial and elected branch preferences, while holding case-specific control variables at their sample values. The two series are clearly distinct in every term between the 1995 and 2004 terms. While the strike probabilities for 1987 statutes range between .52 and .71 between the 1995 and 2004 terms, the strike probabilities for 1995 statutes range between only .16 and .32 over the same period.

In short, the estimates of strike probabilities reported in Tables 5.5 through 5.8 are quite consistent with the estimates of the probabilities of conservative judgments reported in Tables 5.1 through 5.4. Both sets of estimates indicate that the Court's judgments in cases involving constitutional challenges to federal statutes between 1953 and 2004 were rather remarkably responsive to the preferences of majorities in the House of Representatives. We see that responsiveness most clearly during the Rehnquist Court terms, when a consistently conservative majority on the Court faced first a series of liberal Democratic House majorities, and then a series of conservative Republican House majorities. During these terms we appear to have observed two distinct Rehnquist Courts not because the justices' own preferences suddenly became more conservative in the 1994 term, nor because they one day discovered an interest in preserving federalism, nor because they abruptly got fed up with Congress. Instead, we appear to have observed two Rehnquist Courts because the Supreme Court is not, and perhaps was not designed to be, independent of congressional influence.

Constitutional Review of State Action

One limitation of the findings reported here is the narrowly defined sample from which they were estimated. Many prominent decisions made by the Court lie outside even the largest sample of cases used here. We have no estimates of the factors that affected the Court's rulings in these cases. These cases include, perhaps most importantly, those involving constitutional review of state and local action. Several of these cases, particularly those from the Warren Court, are frequently cited as evidence of the Court's independence. Ronald Dworkin, for example, after asserting the important role given to independent federal courts in the U.S. Constitution, cites *Brown v. Board of Education of Topeka*, 349 U.S. 294 (1954), finding a Fourteenth Amendment equal protection violation in racially segregated public schools, and *Griswold v. Connecticut*, 381 U.S. 479 (1965), finding a "right to privacy" violation in state statutes restricting access to contraceptives, as "shining examples of our constitutional structure working at its best."[68] Justice Stephen Breyer points to *Cooper v. Aaron*, 358 U.S. 1 (1958), ordering the immediate desegregation of Little Rock's schools, as an example of an "unpopular" decision that compelled the elected branches to respect the Court's desegregation rulings.[69] The Constitution Project also cites several prominent Warren Court cases as evidence for its claim that "[a] wide array of constitutional and civil rights have been recognized and upheld only because of an independent judiciary."[70] These cases include *Engel v. Vitale*, 370 U.S. 421 (1962), prohibiting organized prayer in public schools, *Gideon v. Wainwright*, 372 U.S. 335 (1963), holding that the constitutional right to counsel applies to state prosecutions, *Miranda v. Arizona*, 384 U.S. 436 (1966), holding that, prior to questioning, police must clearly advise suspects of their rights respecting custodial interrogation, *Loving v. Virginia*, 388 U.S. 1 (1967), nullifying state statutes prohibiting interracial marriage, and *Tinker v. Des Moines Independent Community School District*, 393 U.S. 503 (1969), affirming that symbolic speech is protected by the First Amendment.

In these cases some observers see a defiant and independent Court standing up to conservative elected branch preferences. Is it possible that our estimates of the Court's deference to elected branch preferences do not generalize to such cases?

It is possible, but perhaps not very likely. The powers of the elected branches to both discipline and reward the justices are not limited to cases involving constitutional rulings on federal statutes. We looked only at these cases simply because they presented easily measurable outcomes. But we have no obvious reason to think that the judicial deference to elected branch preferences we have observed is limited only to these cases.

Of course, low salience cases that elected branch majorities don't care about likely won't result in elected branch sanctions, no matter what the Court decides. But the cases frequently cited as evidence of the Court's independence would be hard to characterize in these terms. Instead, those convinced of the Court's independence cite cases that drew significant national attention and that had national policy impact. These cases probably drew more attention than did many cases involving constitutional review of federal statutes. It is difficult to imagine that the Court would have deferred to elected branch preferences in the latter cases, but not in the former.

Moreover, the state action cases typically cited to support the thesis of an independent Court tend to fit the pattern we have observed in cases involving federal statutes. The string of widely cited Warren Court state action cases starting with *Brown*, for example, all resulted in what are thought to be liberal rulings by a Court that, as we have seen, was generally predicted to issue liberal rulings even after factoring in the effects of slightly less liberal House majorities. However, we also saw that the Court's liberal rulings on federal statutes appear to have been contingent on the presence of a moderately liberal House: had the House been sufficiently more conservative, many of these liberal Warren Court rulings are predicted to have been conservative rulings instead. By extension, the famous liberal Warren Court rulings on state action, starting with *Brown*, were likely also contingent on the presence of a moderately liberal House.

This inference is strengthened by looking at some of the most prominent Rehnquist Court rulings involving state action. In its first eight terms the Court reaffirmed the fundamental right to an abortion established in *Roe v. Wade*, 410 U.S. 113 (1973) (*Webster v. Reproductive Health Services*, 490 U.S. 492 [1989]; *Hodgson v. Minnesota*, 497 U.S. 417 [1990]; *Planned Parenthood of Southeastern Pennsylvania v. Casey*, 505 U.S. 833 [1992]); struck state actions on the grounds that they violated the robust interpretation of the Establishment Clause articulated in *Lemon v. Kurtzman*, 403 U.S. 602 (1971) (*Allegheny County v. Greater Pittsburgh ACLU*, 492 U.S. 573 [1989]; *Lee v. Weisman*, 505 U.S. 577 [1992]); and ruled that federal judges could order local governments to increase taxes to remedy constitutional violations like race-segregated schools, "one of the major surprises of the [1989] term" (*Missouri v. Jenkins*, 495 U.S. 33 [1990]). These liberal rulings suggest that the first Rehnquist Court was pulling its punches not only in cases involving federal statutes, but also in cases involving state action.

But relieved of the need to defer to liberal House majorities after the 1994 congressional elections, the Court's rulings appear to have changed not only in the former cases, but also in the latter. In these post-1994 terms the Court backed off on its prior commitments to the Establishment Clause (*Rosenberger v. University of Virginia*, 515 U.S. 819 [1995]; *Agostini v. Felton*, 521 U.S. 203 [1997]; *Zelman v. Simmons-Harris*, 536 U.S. 639 [2002]); school desegregation (*Missouri v. Jenkins*, 515 U.S. 70 [1995]); and the role of racial composition in drawing congressional districts (*Miller v. Johnson*, 515 U.S. 900 [1995]).

Perhaps most famously, the second Rehnquist Court also reversed the Florida Supreme Court's order of a recount in the contested 2000 presidential election, effectively declaring George W. Bush to be the winner of that election (*Bush v. Gore*, 531 U.S. 98 [2000]). Many have criticized this decision as a naked assertion of power by the conservative Rehnquist Court majority.[71] But, if the evidence reported in this chapter is any guide, it was likely not only the conservative justices' preferences that were driving the outcome in that case. The five justices in the *Bush v. Gore* majority knew that they could anticipate an incoming Republican-majority House, a majority that surely would not seek to punish the justices for halting the Florida recount. Indeed, that incoming House majority presumably shared the conservative justices' apparent preference to end the uncertainty over Bush's election. But it is difficult to imagine that the Rehnquist Court would have been as willing to interfere in the Florida recount process had it instead faced an incoming liberal Democratic majority in the House. That counterfactual majority would have possessed not only divergent preferences over the Florida recount, but also the means to punish a Court that did not defer to those preferences. In other words, *Bush v. Gore*, along with other prominent conservative rulings from the second Rehnquist Court, was perhaps just as much a product of a conservative Republican House of Representatives, as of a conservative Court.

Of course, this narrative account of the Court's likely rulings in cases involving constitutional review of state action should perhaps be given little weight. There are no quantitative results reported here making use of the Court's judgments in such cases. It seems reasonable that the estimates reported here would extend at least to the Court's prominent rulings involving state action, the rulings we would expect members of Congress to care about. But we have no direct evidence to support that inference.

The Deferential Supreme Court

Existing empirical studies are nearly unanimous in supporting the conventional wisdom that the Supreme Court decides cases independently of elected branch preferences. But it looks as if those studies, far from providing rigorous confirmation of the truth of our beliefs, instead may have been inappropriately influenced by the power of those beliefs to shape what we see. Existing studies have almost uniformly relied on a subjectively coded measure of the direction of the Court's judgments, a measure that turns out to reflect not only how the justices actually decide cases, but also our expectations about how they decide cases. These expectations have perhaps permitted our belief in the Court's independence to color the very nature of the data we have used to test the veracity of that belief.

The results reported here may be misleading in different ways. While the judgment measures used here have been objectively coded, our samples have of necessity been relatively small, and limited to a particular kind of case. They have also been limited to the modern Supreme Court between 1953 and 2004. It is possible that the results reported in this chapter don't generalize beyond these limited samples, or this somewhat limited time frame.

But even if these results don't generalize, they would still seem to be worthy of note. In cases involving the constitutional review of federal statutes between 1953 and 2004, the justices of the Supreme Court of the United States appear to have been profoundly influenced by the preferences of majorities in the House of Representatives. The Court's deference to House majorities was sufficiently large over this period that, when the preferences of majorities on the Court diverged from those of majorities in the House, the Court was more likely to issue judgments that conformed to the latter than to the former.

These results suggest that the justices respond to the specific institutional incentives created by the U.S. Constitution. The consistent responsiveness of the justices to the preferences of the median representative, and not to the preferences of the median senator or the president, is particularly telling. The Constitution gives to the House the "sole" power to initiate impeachment investigations of the justices. Deterring these investigations may give the justices particularly compelling incentives to defer to the preferences of the median representative. The Constitution's Origination Clause likewise gives to the House a special role in initiating appropriations bills, a category of bills including those increasing judicial salaries. The justices need House majorities regularly to introduce and support judicial salary increases if their salaries are not to decrease every year in real terms; they thus have particular incentives to defer to the preferences of those majorities. Like other holders of public office, the justices appear to respond to the constituency with the power both to remove them from office and to financially reward their performance.

We might wonder, however, whether there aren't other factors that might be driving the justices' apparent responsiveness to these constitutionally specified incentives. Neither the justices nor members of the House of Representatives exist in hermetically sealed isolation from economic, social, and political currents. These currents may drive changes in both the preferences of House majorities, and the justices' choices in cases involving constitutional interpretation. Without identifying and controlling for these broader forces, we may be wrongly attributing the justices' choices in these cases to their deference to the preferences of House majorities, when in fact both the justices and members of the House are simply responding to broader trends. This is the problem to which the next chapter turns.

6

ELECTED BRANCH PREFERENCES, PUBLIC
OPINION, OR SOCIOECONOMIC TRENDS?

The estimates reported in Chapter Five suggest that, at least in cases involving constitutional challenges to federal statutes, the justices of the Supreme Court are surprisingly responsive to the preferences of majorities in the House of Representatives. This finding emerges even after taking into account the possible effects from other elected branch preferences, the justices' own preferences, and case-specific factors that may affect the justices' decisions. It is also evident across different samples of cases, different ways of measuring the Court's judgments, and different ways of measuring judicial and elected branch preferences.

This finding suggests that the Constitution's provisions subjecting the justices to elected branch oversight are not moribund. These provisions give to the House of Representatives a particularly prominent role in both the impeachment and the appropriations processes, two means by which elected branch majorities may conceivably seek to punish or reward the justices for their decisions. If the justices respond to either the potential threats posed by the impeachment process or the potential rewards posed by the appropriations process (or both), we would expect particular responsiveness to the preferences of majorities in the House of Representatives.

Still, we might wonder whether something else is really driving the apparent responsiveness of the justices' decisions to the preferences of House majorities. Neither the justices nor the members of the House of Representatives are isolated from broader political currents. Some of these currents must drive the results of elections for the House of Representatives, elections that produce the majorities to which the justices seem so responsive. Even after election, incumbent members of the House are still likely to be responsive to the political winds, at least insofar as these winds blow in their districts.

So perhaps the estimates reported in Chapter Five are misleading. Perhaps the justices are not in fact responding to the incentives posed by the impeachment and appropriations processes. Perhaps they are responding to other forces that simply happen to be correlated with the shifting preferences of House majorities. Because these forces were not identified, measured, and controlled for in the analyses of Chapter Five, perhaps we mistakenly attributed their effects to the preferences of House majorities.

A leading candidate for one such unidentified factor must surely be public opinion. Many have suggested that the justices may respond to popular preferences directly, not simply as mediated through elected branch preferences. In this account the justices are assumed to care about the extent to which their rulings meet with compliance by the general public. Because the Court lacks the institutional capacity to enforce unpopular rulings, the justices are said to tailor their opinions to come as close as possible to their own most preferred rules, while yet ensuring widespread voluntary compliance. As the rules that can induce such compliance change over time with shifts in public opinion, we should observe corresponding changes in the Court's judgment.

If the public opinion story is correct, then to the extent that popular preferences are correlated with elected branch preferences, without controlling for public opinion we might mistakenly attribute the direct effect of popular preferences on the Court's judgments to elected branch preferences. By the same token, once we control for popular preferences, we might find that there is no longer an association between elected branch preferences and the Court's judgments.

But public opinion is itself presumably driven by other, more fundamental, socioeconomic trends. Perhaps the justices are concerned neither with elected branch punishments and rewards, nor with the extent of popular compliance with their rulings. We might still find that their judgments appear to be associated with elected branch preferences and/or popular preferences, simply because the justices are affected by the same socioeconomic forces that drive changes in elected branch and popular preferences more generally. Because the justices live in the same society as do members of the elected branches and respondents to public opinion surveys, their decisions may be affected by the same socioeconomic trends that affect both elected officials' votes on policy choices, and citizens' preferences over those policy choices. The justices' decisions may appear to be affected by elected branch and/or popular preferences, when in fact those decisions are simply evolving along with those preferences.

This chapter closely examines these possible alternative explanations for the findings reported in Chapter Five. Because we are dealing with observational data, not experimental data, there is of course only so much one can do. We cannot run controlled experiments, manipulating treatments and subjects at will. Nonetheless, the consistency of the findings reported here is impressive. Even after controlling for public opinion and a variety of socioeconomic indicators that themselves appear to move public opinion, the preferences of House majorities emerge as the only clear and consistent influence on the judgments of the justices of the Supreme Court.

Public Opinion and the Supreme Court

As we saw in Chapter Two, many express skepticism about the efficacy of elected branch checks on the Supreme Court. But even some of these skeptics have nonetheless suggested that the justices may respond directly to public opinion, irrespective of elected branch preferences.[1] Indeed, Jeffrey Rosen has suggested that the justices may "represent the views of national majorities more precisely than Congress."[2]

Those who study the relationship between public opinion and the Court's judgments generally deemphasize the specific constitutional provisions discussed in Chapter Two, provisions that may incentivize judicial deference to elected branch preferences. Instead, these researchers have focused on the Court's lack of implementation and enforcement powers, a weakness shared by courts more generally. Because the justices cannot enforce their rulings, it is argued, these rulings will see widespread compliance by the general public only if that compliance is purely voluntary. In turn, only rulings that are widely supported will induce widespread

voluntary compliance. Consequently, if the justices care about maximiz-
ing compliance with their rulings, they must tether their rulings to popular support. We should then observe that the Court's judgments change
in response to changes in popular preferences.[3]

Numerous quantitative studies have in fact found that the justices' decisions are closely associated with public opinion.[4] These findings must
then raise questions about those reported in Chapter Five. Over the period analyzed there, public opinion trends were generally correlated with
elected branch preferences. For example, the dominant measure of public
opinion that has been used in the academic literature on the Court's
responsiveness to popular preferences is the time series of the public
"mood" that we encountered in Chapter Four.[5] This measure is constructed by political scientist James Stimson from 139 different domestic
social and economic policy questions that have been asked in identical
form in major public opinion polls in two or more years since 1952. From
these surveys an annual index of the public mood is generated; this index
is increasing in liberalism.[6] In order to look at correlations between this
measure of public opinion and the measures of elected branch preferences
used in Chapter Five, which are increasing in conservatism, we can rescale
the mood measure to be increasing in conservatism as well.

After rescaling, we find that this index of the conservative public mood
is positively correlated with the measures of elected branch preferences
used in Chapter Five, although not all correlations rise to the level of
statistical significance. For example, between 1953 and 2004 the public
mood index is correlated with the Bailey XTI estimates of the preferences
of the median representative at .20 (p = .15), with the preferences of the
median senator at .61 (p = .00), and with presidential preferences at .46
(p = .00). Using the Judicial Common Space estimates over the same
period, the public mood is correlated with the preferences of the median
representative at .30 (p = .03), with the preferences of the median senator at .60 (p = .00), and with presidential preferences at .20 (p = .17).

These correlations between the public mood index and measures of
elected branch preferences suggest that the findings reported in Chapter Five may simply have been spurious. If public opinion trends are
correlated with changes in elected branch preferences, then perhaps it
is really public opinion that is driving the apparent association of the

Court's judgments with changes in elected branch preferences. Perhaps the elected branches have no effect on the Court's judgments, after all.

On the other hand, there is also the possibility that studies documenting an effect of public opinion on the Court's judgments might themselves simply be reporting spurious results. With only a handful of exceptions, these studies have not controlled for elected branch preferences.[7] Given the correlations between those preferences and the most commonly used measure of public opinion, it is possible that elected branch preferences were driving the effects documented in these studies, rather than public opinion.

The few studies that have included measures of both public opinion and elected branch preferences in the same empirical model have all found that the Court's judgments are associated with changes in public opinion, but not with changes in elected branch preferences.[8] However, all of these studies suffer from a substantial threat to inference in that they have all used as their dependent variable the measure of the direction of the Court's judgments reported in the Supreme Court Database. As we saw in Chapter Five, this measure codes a judgment as liberal or conservative as a function of the disposition in the case and the prior subjective assignment of an "issue" code to the case. We have good reason to suspect that this measure can be inadvertently biased by coders' expectations about the kinds of judgments typically issued by more liberal and more conservative courts. The measure is thus inappropriate for detecting the existence of external influences on the Court's judgments.

Moreover, the findings reported in Chapter Five do not actually lend themselves very well to the "spurious association" hypothesis. Those findings were specific to the House of Representatives. Only increases in the conservatism of the median representative were consistently associated with increases in the conservatism of the Court's judgments. In no analyses were increases in the conservatism of the median senator or the president linked to increases in the conservatism of the Court's judgments. In fact, increases in the conservatism of both the median senator and the president were associated with *decreases* in the probability of a conservative judgment in Table 5.1, using the Bailey XTI preference estimates, although these perverse effects were not replicated using the JCS preference estimates.

The specificity of these findings suggests the relevance of the specific constitutional provisions giving the House of Representatives a powerful agenda-setting role in both the impeachment and the appropriations processes. The relevance of these specific constitutional provisions in turn suggests that the justices respond to well-defined incentives to avoid removal from office and to attract increased salaries and budgets.

By contrast, the public opinion hypothesis is relatively institution-free. The hypothesis proposes that the Supreme Court defers to public opinion because, like all courts, it lacks budgetary and police powers to implement and enforce its decisions. The justices are consequently said to seek voluntary compliance with their rulings, a goal requiring that they issue only those rulings meeting with widespread popular support. The Constitution's specific provisions giving the elected branches powers to induce judicial deference to elected branch preferences play virtually no role in the public opinion hypothesis; the justices are thought to respond only to their lack of implementation and enforcement powers, not to elected branch sanctions.

According to the public opinion hypothesis, then, if we find that changes in elected branch preferences are associated with changes in the Court's judgments, the likely explanation is that elected branch preferences are highly correlated with popular preferences. But this supposition does not do a very good job explaining the empirical prominence of the House of Representatives reported in Chapter Five. Over the period studied there, the preferences of House majorities were significantly less correlated with public opinion trends than were the preferences of Senate majorities, using both sets of preference estimates. In the Bailey XTI preference estimates, they were also less correlated with public opinion than were presidential preferences.

If public opinion were driving the results reported in Chapter Five, we wouldn't expect to find such a specific and prominent relationship between the preferences of the median representative and the Court's judgments. Instead we would likely expect to find strong relationships between the preferences of the median senator and the Court's judgments, using both sets of preference estimates, and possibly also between presidential preferences and the Court's judgments, using the Bailey XTI estimates. The House would be the elected branch we would expect to have the least relationship with the Court's judgments.

The particular impact of House majorities on the Court's judgments suggests instead that the justices are responding to the precise institutional incentives specified by the Constitution, not to a more generalized concern for public opinion. The empirical prominence of the House reported in Chapter Five is most easily explained by reference to the prominent constitutional role given to the House in the impeachment and appropriations processes. By implication, this finding suggests in turn that the justices care about the specific dangers and rewards posed by impeachment and appropriations.

We also saw in Chapter Four that the public mood index does not appear to fit the pattern in at least the Rehnquist Court's judgments particularly well. At the start of the Rehnquist Court the public mood was in the middle of a liberal trend, after having peaked in conservatism in 1980. It continued to move in a liberal direction until 1992, when it began to move in a conservative direction again. After 1994 this conservative movement leveled off. But while we see conservative movement in public opinion between 1992 and 1994, this movement simply restores popular preferences to where they were at the start of the Rehnquist Court. That is, public opinion during the second Rehnquist Court was no more conservative than it had been at the start of the first Rehnquist Court, and was considerably more liberal than it had been during the late 1970s and early 1980s. Yet the Rehnquist Court's jurisprudence in its second incarnation was by most accounts considerably more conservative than it had been under either the Burger Court or the first few terms of the Rehnquist Court.

There are thus several reasons to think that public opinion is not driving the results reported in Chapter Five. But we can subject these intuitions to empirical examination. First, we can simply add public opinion as an additional variable to the analyses reported in Chapter Five. The public mood index discussed earlier is available not only as an annual measure, but also, at least from 1958, as a quarterly estimate. We can thus match the date on which each of the Court's judgments was issued to the estimate of the conservative public mood for that quarter. Second, we can aggregate the Court's judgments into an annual time series in order to investigate the dynamic relationships between public opinion, elected branch preferences, and the Court's judgments.

Public Opinion and the Court's Judgments: A Case-Based Analysis

Tables 6.1 to 6.4 report replications of the analyses reported in Tables 5.1 to 5.4, but include the quarterly index of the conservative public mood as an additional independent variable. These comprise the analyses reported in Chapter Five using measures of the Court's judgments objectively coded as liberal or conservative. Because the analyses reported here cover only the period from 1958 to 2004, they use slightly fewer observations than do those reported in Chapter Five.

Tables 6.1 to 6.4 confirm our suspicions that public opinion trends, at least as measured by the quarterly index of the public mood, were not

Table 6.1: **Estimating the Probability of a Conservative Judgment: Bailey XTI Judicial and Elected Branch Preferences and the Public Mood, 1958–2004, Roll Call–Based Judgment Measure**

	Coefficient	SE	95% CI
Conservatism of SCOTUS Median	1.64	.52	(.63, 2.66)
Conservatism of House Median	5.08	1.54	(2.07, 8.10)
Conservatism of Senate Median	−3.29	1.19	(−5.63, −.95)
Conservatism of President	−.34	.13	(−.60, −.09)
Conservatism of Public Mood	.02	.02	(−.06, .03)
Liberal Lower Court Ruling	.42	.25	(−.07, .90)
US Liberal Party	−.17	.37	(−.89, .56)
US Conservative Party	.93	.34	(.25, 1.60)

N = 162
Wald chi² = 35.08

Note: Probit regression; robust standard errors reported, clustered by term. Intercept term not reported. Italicized variables are statistically significant at the .10 level (two-tailed).

Table 6.2: Estimating the Probability of a Conservative Judgment: Judicial Common Space Judicial and Elected Branch Preferences and the Public Mood, 1958–2004, Roll Call–Based Judgment Measure

	Coefficient	SE	95% CI
Conservatism of SCOTUS Median	2.43	.82	(.82, 4.05)
Conservatism of House Median	2.44	1.22	(.05, 4.84)
Conservatism of Senate Median	−.47	1.80	(−4.00, 3.06)
Conservatism of President	−.31	.28	(−.87, .24)
Conservatism of Public Mood	.02	.03	(−.07, .04)
Liberal Lower Court Ruling	.31	.23	(−.15, .77)
US Liberal Party	−.11	.38	(−.85, .64)
US Conservative Party	.98	.34	(.31, 1.65)

N = 162
Wald chi^2 = 41.13

Note: Probit regression; robust standard errors reported, clustered by term. Intercept term not reported. Italicized variables are statistically significant at the .10 level (two-tailed).

driving the results reported in Chapter Five. In none of these analyses does the public mood ever have an independent effect on the Court's judgments. For example, in the roll call–based sample of cases used to produce the estimates reported in Table 6.1, the public mood is observed at its liberal zenith in the second quarter of 1960, with about 72 percent of the population favoring liberal public policies. Using the estimates reported in this table, and holding all other variables at their sample values, the predicted probability that the Court would issue a conservative judgment when the public mood is this liberal is .32. The public mood reaches its most conservative point in the second quarter of 1981, with only about 51 percent of the population favoring liberal public policy outcomes. Again holding all other variables constant at their sample values, the predicted probability that the Court would issue a conservative judgment when the public mood is this conservative is .43. However, these two predictions are not distinct at conventional levels of statistical significance. Using the estimates reported in Table 6.2, this same movement increases the predicted probability of a conservative judgment from .31 to .45, but again the small increase is not significant at conventional levels.

We see similar results in Tables 6.3 and 6.4, using the partisan Congress-based judgment measure. In this larger sample of cases, the most liberal public mood is observed in the fourth quarter of 1960, and the most conservative public mood again in the second quarter of 1981. Using the estimates reported in Table 6.3 and holding other variables at their sample values, the predicted probabilities that the Court would issue a conservative judgment at these values for the public mood are .24 and .32, respectively, but these predictions are not distinct at conventional thresholds. Using the estimates reported in Table 6.4, these predicted probabilities are .31 and .27, but again these predictions are indistinguishable.

The preferences of Senate majorities and the president continue to have no association with the Court's judgments in the predicted direction. In Table 6.1, using the roll call–based judgment measure and the Bailey XTI

Table 6.3: **Estimating the Probability of a Conservative Judgment: Bailey XTI Judicial and Elected Branch Preferences and the Public Mood, 1958–2004, Partisan Congress-Based Judgment Measure**

	Coefficient	SE	95% CI
Conservatism of SCOTUS Median	−.36	.33	(−1.00, .29)
Conservatism of House Median	4.69	1.31	(2.11, 7.26)
Conservatism of Senate Median	.28	.91	(−1.49, 2.06)
Conservatism of President	−.17	.16	(−.47, .14)
Conservatism of Public Mood	.01	.02	(−.06, .04)
Liberal Lower Court Ruling	.07	.20	(−.33, .46)
US Liberal Party	.16	.29	(−.42, .74)
US Conservative Party	.66	.34	(−.01, 1.33)

N = 255
Wald chi² = 55.60

Note: Probit regression; robust standard errors reported, clustered by term. Intercept term not reported. Italicized variables are statistically significant at the .10 level (two-tailed).

Table 6.4: Estimating the Probability of a Conservative Judgment: Judicial Common Space Judicial and Elected Branch Preferences and the Public Mood, 1958–2004, Partisan Congress-Based Judgment Measure

	Coefficient	SE	95% CI
Conservatism of SCOTUS Median	−.57	.49	(−1.52, .39)
Conservatism of House Median	5.06	.99	(3.11, 7.01)
Conservatism of Senate Median	−.59	1.34	(−3.23, 2.04)
Conservatism of President	−.26	.19	(−.64, .12)
Conservatism of Public Mood	−.01	.02	(−.04, .05)
Liberal Lower Court Ruling	−.00	.22	(−.42, .42)
US Liberal Party	.12	.28	(−.43, .68)
US Conservative Party	.52	.35	(−.18, 1.21)

N = 255
Wald chi^2 = 67.23

Note: Probit regression; robust standard errors reported, clustered by term. Intercept term not reported. Italicized variables are statistically significant at the .10 level (two-tailed).

preference estimates, the preferences of both Senate majorities and the president are perversely associated with the probability of a conservative judgment, but these perverse effects disappear in Tables 6.2 through 6.4. Finally, the preferences of the median justice are only inconsistently related to the Court's judgments. While we see significant effects from the preferences of the median justice in the predicted direction in Tables 6.1 and 6.2, these effects are not present in Tables 6.3 and 6.4.

By contrast, in each of these analyses the preferences of majorities in the House of Representatives continue to have strong associations with the Court's judgments in the predicted direction. Holding all other variables in Table 6.1 at their sample values, moving from the most liberal House median (observed in both the 1965 and the 1975 terms in this sample of cases) to the most conservative (observed in the 1995 term) increases the predicted probability of a conservative judgment from .14 to .67; the difference between the two predictions is significant at conventional thresholds. Using the estimates reported in Table 6.2 and again holding other variables at sample values, moving from the most liberal

House median (observed in the 1975 term) to the most conservative (observed in the 2004 term) increases the predicted probability of a conservative judgment from .26 to .62, again the difference is significant at conventional thresholds.

For the sample of cases used to produce the estimates reported in Table 6.3, the most liberal House median is observed in the 1974 term, and the most conservative in the 1995 term. Holding other variables at sample values, moving from the most liberal to the most conservative House median increases the predicted probability of a conservative judgment from .09 to .55; the predictions are distinct at conventional thresholds. For the sample of cases used to produce the estimates reported in Table 6.4, the most liberal House medians are observed in the 1974 and 1975 terms, and the most conservative in the 2004 term. Again holding other variables at sample values, moving from the most liberal to the most conservative House median increases the predicted probability of a conservative judgment from .10 to .74; the predictions are distinct at conventional thresholds.

In short, there is no evidence in these analyses that the findings reported in Chapter Five were simply the spurious result of an association between elected branch preferences and the public mood. Those findings remain essentially unaltered after controlling for the public mood, which itself has no independent effect on the Court's judgments in cases involving constitutional challenges to federal statutes between 1958 and 2004.

Public Opinion and the Court's Judgments: A Time-Series Analysis

The analyses reported in Tables 6.1 to 6.4 use individual judgments as the unit of analysis, as did the analyses reported in Chapter Five. But it may also be helpful to aggregate the Court's judgments into an annual time series in order to investigate the dynamic nature of the relationships between the Court's rulings, judicial and elected branch preferences, and public opinion. These data can be highly serially correlated, meaning that their values in a given year can be strong predictors of their values in future years. Failing to account for these dynamics can produce misleading results, as well as obscure important and interesting features of the over-time relationships among judicial and elected branch preferences, public opinion, and the Court's judgments.

One of the most flexible ways to model dynamic relationships is to use an error correction model (ECM) framework. ECMs model the change in the value of a dependent variable as a function of lagged values of this variable, change in independent variables of interest, and lagged values of independent variables of interest. Compared to many other specifications employed in standard time-series analyses, the ECM is relatively agnostic about how shifts in predictor variables immediately affect dependent variables, and how these effects decay over time.[9]

To estimate the ECM, the dataset we used in Chapter Five is converted into an annualized time series. In this framework, the dependent variable is now the change in the percentage of cases each year in which the Supreme Court rules in a conservative direction; this variable is positively signed when the Court decides a greater proportion of cases in a conservative direction in a given term, relative to its prior term, and is negatively signed when the reverse is true.[10] The quarterly estimates of the conservative public mood are used to calculate an annualized mean that is weighted by the number of cases in each quarter of the year; the differenced and lagged values of this conservative mood index are included in the ECM.[11] Also included are the differenced and lagged values of the measures of the preferences of the Supreme Court median, the House and Senate medians, and the president. Case-specific variables are no longer relevant and are thus dropped from the analysis. Years when there are more judgments in the sample are given slightly more weight in the analyses.[12]

The ECM results are reported in Tables 6.5 and 6.6. These tables report no relationships in the predicted direction between either the differenced or the lagged values of the conservative public mood and changes in the proportion of the Court's judgments decided in a conservative direction. There are also no relationships in the predicted direction between changes in the direction of the Court's judgments and the preferences of Senate majorities or the president. Finally, the preferences of the median justice are only inconsistently related to changes in the proportion of conserva-

Table 6.5: **Estimating Increases in the Percent of Conservative Supreme Court Judgments per Year, 1958–2004, Roll Call–Based Judgment Measure, Error Correction Model**

	Bailey XTI Preference Estimates	Judicial Common Space Preference Estimates
Conservatism of SCOTUS Median		
Annual Change (Immediate Effect)	68.66**	247.45***
	(26.72)	(71.43)
Lagged Value (Long-Term Effect)	44.98**	131.40***
	(20.75)	(42.14)
Conservatism of House Median		
Annual Change (Immediate Effect)	93.84	113.67
	(70.57)	(100.31)
Lagged Value (Long-Term Effect)	251.01***	154.40**
	(68.19)	(59.21)
Conservatism of Senate Median		
Annual Change (Immediate Effect)	−50.97	−57.49
	(87.07)	(94.25)
Lagged Value (Long-Term Effect)	−167.95***	−134.52
	(44.88)	(94.58)
Conservatism of President		
Annual Change (Immediate Effect)	−3.14	6.80
	(7.86)	(10.49)
Lagged Value (Long-Term Effect)	−3.26	−9.96
	(7.24)	(12.35)
Conservatism of Public Mood		
Annual Change (Immediate Effect)	.66	−.33
	(1.72)	(1.83)

Lagged Value (Long-Term Effect)	1.60	1.27
	(1.07)	(1.35)
Error Correction Rate		
Lagged Value of % Conservative Judgments	−1.00***	−1.06***
	(.15)	(.15)
N	46	46
R-squared	.64	.63
p-value of Ljung-Box Q test for serial correlation	.96	.83

Note: Ordinary least squares regression; robust standard errors. Intercept term not reported. Estimates significantly different from zero at *p*<.10; **p*<.05; ***p*<.01 (two-tailed).

tive judgments. While both the differenced and the lagged values of the median justice's preferences are associated with changes in the proportion of conservative judgments in the predicted direction in Table 6.5, these findings are not generally replicated in Table 6.6.

However, across all four analyses reported in Tables 6.5 and 6.6, there are strong relationships in the predicted direction between the preferences of the median representative and changes in the proportion of the Court's judgments decided in a conservative direction. In Table 6.5, reporting results from analyses of the roll call–based judgment measure, this relationship appears between the value of the median representative's preferences in the immediately prior term and changes in the proportion of conservative judgments issued in the current term, relative to the prior term. Moving from a term wherein the House median's preferences in the prior term are set to their most liberal value, to a term wherein they are set to their most conservative value, while holding all other variables at their sample values, generates predicted increases in the proportion of judgments decided in a conservative direction of 78 percentage points using the Bailey XTI preference estimates, and 57 percentage points using the Judicial Common Space estimates. These predicted increases are significant at conventional thresholds.[13] The "error correction rates," or the

Table 6.6: Estimating Increases in the Percent of Conservative Supreme Court Judgments per Year, 1958–2004, Partisan Congress–Based Judgment Measure, Error Correction Model

	Bailey XTI Preference Estimates	Judicial Common Space Preference Estimates
Conservatism of SCOTUS Median		
Annual Change (Immediate Effect)	14.23 (24.93)	58.79* (32.83)
Lagged Value (Long-Term Effect)	−17.52 (14.86)	−25.44 (24.58)
Conservatism of House Median		
Annual Change (Immediate Effect)	178.02** (85.14)	284.77*** (71.80)
Lagged Value (Long-Term Effect)	163.69*** (59.21)	223.93*** (49.97)
Conservatism of Senate Median		
Annual Change (Immediate Effect)	−32.59 (77.25)	−133.44** (55.99)
Lagged Value (Long-Term Effect)	−1.47 (36.20)	−93.62 (67.01)
Conservatism of President		
Annual Change (Immediate Effect)	−12.96* (6.56)	−10.68 (8.01)
Lagged Value (Long-Term Effect)	−4.85 (7.37)	−11.56 (10.05)
Conservatism of Public Mood		
Annual Change (Immediate Effect)	−.05 (1.32)	−1.45 (1.37)

Lagged Value (Long-Term Effect)	1.81	.94
	(1.14)	(.87)
Error Correction Rate		
Lagged Value of % Conservative Judgments	−.89***	−1.05***
	(.15)	(.14)
N	46	46
R-squared	.59	.74
p-value of Ljung-Box Q test for serial correlation	.76	.57

Note: Ordinary least squares regression; robust standard errors. Intercept term not reported. Estimates significantly different from zero at *p<.10; **p<.05; ***p<.01 (two-tailed).

coefficients on the lagged values of the dependent variable, tell us that approximately 100 percent of these increases take place in the term of interest, rather than being distributed more slowly over time. In other words, the Court responds relatively quickly to changes in the preferences of the median representative.

In Table 6.6, reporting the ECM results for the partisan Congress-based judgment measure, we see two different effects from the preferences of the median representative. The significant coefficients on the differenced preferences of the House median tell us that, in terms wherein there are large increases in the conservatism of the median representative, relative to the prior term's value, there are corresponding large increases in the proportion of conservative judgments issued by the Court. For example, an increase in the conservatism of the median representative as large as that observed between the 1993 and 1994 terms produces a predicted increase in the proportion of conservative judgments issued by the Court of 40 percentage points using the Bailey XTI preference estimates, and of 78 percentage points using the Judicial Common Space estimates. These increases are significant at conventional thresholds.

Table 6.6 also reports large increases in the proportion of conservative judgments issued by the Court when the median representative in the immediately prior term was more conservative, relative to the sample average. Moving from a term wherein the House median's preferences in the prior term are set to their most liberal value, to a term wherein they are set to their most conservative value, while holding all other variables at their sample values, generates predicted increases in the proportion of judgments decided in a conservative direction of 51 percentage points using the Bailey XTI preference estimates, and of 82 percentage points using the Judicial Common Space estimates. These predicted increases are significant at conventional thresholds. Again, the estimated error correction rates reported in Table 6.6 tell us that these increases are virtually all realized in the term of interest, rather than being distributed more slowly over time.[14]

In short, the results reported in Tables 6.5 and 6.6 further indicate that the findings reported in Chapter Five were not simply the product of spurious associations between public opinion and the preferences of House majorities. In the ECM results the justices do not respond to changes in the public mood. Nor do they consistently respond to changes in the preferences of the median senator or the president, or even of the median justice. They consistently respond only to changes in the preferences of the median member of the House of Representatives.

Socioeconomic Trends and the Supreme Court

Still, there remains the possibility that the justices are responding to broad socioeconomic currents that are not captured, or not fully captured, in the public mood index. Public opinion does not move randomly; it appears to respond to identifiable and measurable economic, social, and political trends. If popular preferences are responsive to these socioeconomic trends, then perhaps the justices' decisions are likewise directly responsive to these societal currents, rather than simply to the resulting shifts in the public mood index. Because that index may only imperfectly reflect the dynamics of these socioeconomic trends, by including that index in Tables 6.1 through 6.6 we may not have adequately controlled for the possible effects of these trends on the justices' decisions. And because these socioeconomic trends, like the public mood index, may be correlated with elected branch preferences, their absence from the analyses reported in Chapter Five may present yet another reason to suspect the results of those analyses.

Identifying the forces that move public opinion is a project fraught with many methodological challenges. When socioeconomic indicators and public opinion move together over time, it is difficult to identify causality. Moreover, we don't always have good theory to explain why popular preferences would change in the observed direction, in response to changes in these indicators.

Still, we can perhaps leave these methodological concerns on the table for the present purposes. There are a series of economic, social, and policy indicators that have been found to be associated with the Stimson index of the public mood; these are presumably good candidates for inclusion in our analyses of the Court's judgments. For example, the public mood index appears to respond to changes in unemployment and inflation. Respondents in public opinion surveys express more support for liberal public policies after increases in unemployment, and express less support for liberal public policies after increases in inflation. Increases in unemployment thus cause liberal movements in the public mood index, while increases in inflation cause conservative movements in the public mood.[15] Perhaps the justices also respond directly to changes in unemployment and inflation, not simply as mediated through changes in the public mood. Perhaps without even realizing it, the justices decide fewer cases in a conservative direction after increases in unemployment, and more cases in a conservative direction after increases in inflation.

Others have found an association between the homicide rate and the public mood index: as the homicide rate increases, support for more liberal public policies decreases.[16] Again, perhaps the justices respond directly to the homicide rate, not simply as mediated through the public mood, deciding more cases in a conservative direction after increases in the homicide rate.

Finally, some researchers have found that certain indicators of public policy appear to cause movement in the public mood. Increases in the percent of the federal budget devoted to military spending are associated with increases in support for liberal policies,[17] while increases in the cumulative number of significant liberal federal statutes are associated with decreases in support for liberal policies.[18] Again, perhaps the justices respond to these public policy trends directly, decreasing the number of conservative judgments after increases in military spending, and increasing the number of conservative judgments after long stretches of liberal public policymaking.

Of course, all the reasons why we might not think that the findings reported in Chapter Five are simply the spurious result of an association with public opinion apply here as well. The specificity of those findings would seem to undercut a suspicion that they are being driven by more fundamental associations between broad economic, social, and policy trends and the Court's judgments. The fact that the Court's judgments appear to be related only to changes in the preferences of House majorities, and not to changes in the preferences of Senate majorities or the president, or indeed to the index of the public mood, would appear to indicate instead that the constitutional provisions endowing House majorities with particular powers to punish and reward the justices are driving the results reported in Chapter Five.

Still, we can add to both our case-based and time-series analyses the economic, social, and policy indicators that have been found to be associated with the public mood index, the full set of which is available only between 1958 and 2000.[19] These indicators include the annual percent unemployed and the percent change in the annual Consumer Price Index, both reported by the United States Bureau of Labor Statistics; the annual homicide rate, reported by the Bureau of Justice Statistics; the annual percent of the federal budget devoted to military spending, reported by the Policy Agendas Project;[20] and the "Policy Liberalism" series constructed by political scientists Robert Erikson, Michael MacKuen, and James Stimson, and extended by Nathan Kelly.[21]

Socioeconomic Trends and the Court's Judgments: A Case-Based Analysis

Tables 6.7 through 6.10 report the results from including these indicators in the case-based analyses reported in Tables 6.1 through 6.4. As is standard in the existing literature, the socioeconomic indicators are all lagged by one year to account for their delayed effects on the other variables in the analyses. Because of this lagging, and because the full

Table 6.7: Estimating the Probability of a Conservative Judgment: Bailey XTI Judicial and Elected Branch Preferences, the Public Mood, and Socioeconomic Indicators, 1958–2000, Roll Call–Based Judgment Measure

	Coefficient	SE	95% CI
Conservatism of SCOTUS Median	1.41	.95	(−.45, 3.27)
Conservatism of House Median	4.21	1.93	(.43, 7.99)
Conservatism of Senate Median	−.80	2.13	(−4.96, 3.37)
Conservatism of President	−.32	.17	(−.65, .02)
Conservatism of Public Mood	−.02	.05	(−.12, .08)
Lagged Unemployment	−.05	.09	(−.24, .13)
Lagged Inflation	−3.14	7.14	(−17.13, 10.85)
Lagged Homicide Rate	.06	.20	(−.34, .45)
Lagged Defense Spending	.00	.03	(−.06, .06)
Lagged Policy Liberalism	.03	.03	(−.02, .09)
Liberal Lower Court Ruling	.40	.27	(−.13, .93)
US Liberal Party	−.04	.42	(−.87, .79)
US Conservative Party	1.11	.38	(.38, 1.85)

N = 153
Wald chi^2 = 33.47

Note. Probit regression; robust standard errors reported, clustered by term. Intercept term not reported. Italicized variables are statistically significant at the .10 level (two-tailed).

set of socioeconomic indicators is available only through the 2000 term, these analyses contain slightly fewer observations than those reported earlier.

The results, however, are entirely consistent with those reported in Tables 6.1 through 6.4. In none of the analyses are any of the socioeconomic variables associated with the Court's judgments. The public mood also remains unassociated with the Court's judgments in all analyses. The preferences of the Senate median and the president are likewise unrelated to the Court's judgments in the predicted direction; although increasingly conservative presidential preferences are associated with a decreasing probability of a conservative judgment in Table 6.7, this perverse effect is not observed in Tables 6.8 through 6.10. Finally, the preferences of the median justice are associated with the Court's judgments in the

Table 6.8: Estimating the Probability of a Conservative Judgment: Judicial Common Space Judicial and Elected Branch Preferences, the Public Mood, and Socioeconomic Indicators, 1958–2000, Roll Call–Based Judgment Measure

	Coefficient	SE	95% CI
Conservatism of SCOTUS Median	2.64	1.53	(−.35, 5.63)
Conservatism of House Median	4.89	2.14	(.70, 9.08)
Conservatism of Senate Median	−.62	2.09	(−4.72, 3.48)
Conservatism of President	−.40	.34	(−1.06, .26)
Conservatism of Public Mood	−.00	.05	(−.10, .09)
Lagged Unemployment	−.03	.09	(−.20, .14)
Lagged Inflation	2.79	7.66	(−12.23, 17.81)
Lagged Homicide Rate	.06	.18	(−.30, .41)
Lagged Defense Spending	.02	.03	(−.05, .08)
Lagged Policy Liberalism	.03	.02	(−.01, .08)
Liberal Lower Court Ruling	.43	.27	(−.11, .96)
US Liberal Party	−.04	.42	(−.87, .79)
US Conservative Party	1.08	.37	(.35, 1.80)

N = 153
Wald chi^2 = 36.21

Note: Probit regression; robust standard errors reported, clustered by term. Intercept term not reported. Italicized variables are statistically significant at the .10 level (two-tailed).

predicted direction only in Table 6.8, but not in the remaining three analyses.

However, in all four analyses the preferences of the median representative are consistently associated with the Court's judgments in the predicted direction, at conventional levels of statistical significance. This is in fact the only variable, including the case-specific control variables, that is significantly related to the direction of the Court's judgments in all four analyses. Moreover, the magnitudes of the estimated effects of the preferences of House majorities are similar to those estimated in Tables 6.1 through 6.4. Moving from the most liberal median representative to the most conservative, while holding all other variables at their sample values, increases the predicted probability of a conservative judgment from .18

Table 6.9: Estimating the Probability of a Conservative Judgment: Bailey XTI Judicial and Elected Branch Preferences, the Public Mood, and Socioeconomic Indicators, 1958–2000, Partisan Congress–Based Judgment Measure

	Coefficient	SE	95% CI
Conservatism of SCOTUS Median	−.79	.59	(−1.95, .37)
Conservatism of House Median	3.26	1.62	(.09, 6.43)
Conservatism of Senate Median	.28	1.45	(−2.56, 3.11)
Conservatism of President	−.05	.14	(−.32, .23)
Conservatism of Public Mood	.01	.05	(−.08, .10)
Lagged Unemployment	−.10	.07	(−.23, .03)
Lagged Inflation	−6.78	5.74	(−18.03, 4.47)
Lagged Homicide Rate	.09	.13	(−.16, .34)
Lagged Defense Spending	−.02	.02	(−.07, .03)
Lagged Policy Liberalism	−.01	.02	(−.05, .03)
Liberal Lower Court Ruling	.01	.22	(−.43, .44)
US Liberal Party	.31	.30	(−.29, .91)
US Conservative Party	.66	.40	(−.12, 1.43)

N = 246
Wald chi^2 = 104.86

Note: Probit regression; robust standard errors reported, clustered by term. Intercept term not reported. Italicized variables are statistically significant at the .10 level (two-tailed).

to .63 using the estimates reported in Table 6.7, from .17 to .75 using the estimates reported in Table 6.8, from .13 to .45 using the estimates reported in Table 6.9, and from .11 to .63 using the estimates reported in Table 6.10. These predicted probabilities are all distinct at conventional levels of significance.[22]

In short, there is no evidence in the case-based analyses that the findings reported in Chapter Five were simply the spurious result of associations between elected branch preferences, public opinion, and socioeconomic trends. Those findings remain essentially unaltered after controlling for both public opinion and a variety of socioeconomic indicators, none of which have an independent effect on the Court's judgments in cases involving constitutional challenges to federal statutes between 1958 and 2000.

Table 6.10: Estimating the Probability of a Conservative Judgment: Judicial Common Space Judicial and Elected Branch Preferences, the Public Mood, and Socioeconomic Indicators, 1958–2000, Partisan Congress–Based Judgment Measure

	Coefficient	SE	95% CI
Conservatism of SCOTUS Median	.13	1.11	(−2.05, 2.31)
Conservatism of House Median	4.71	1.75	(1.28, 8.14)
Conservatism of Senate Median	−.31	1.56	(−3.36, 2.74)
Conservatism of President	−.17	.23	(−.62, .27)
Conservatism of Public Mood	.04	.05	(−.06, .14)
Lagged Unemployment	−.02	.08	(−.18, .13)
Lagged Inflation	−2.48	5.11	(−12.49, 7.53)
Lagged Homicide Rate	.00	.13	(−.24, .25)
Lagged Defense Spending	.02	.02	(−.03, .07)
Lagged Policy Liberalism	−.01	.02	(−.04, .02)
Liberal Lower Court Ruling	−.01	.23	(−.45, .44)
US Liberal Party	.32	.31	(−.29, .92)
US Conservative Party	.62	.40	(−.17, 1.41)

N = 246
Wald chi^2 = 99.26

Note: Probit regression; robust standard errors reported, clustered by term. Intercept term not reported. Italicized variables are statistically significant at the .10 level (two-tailed).

Socioeconomic Trends and the Court's Judgments: A Time-Series Analysis

We can also look for effects of these economic, social, and policy indicators using the aggregated time series of the Court's judgments. Because we have so few data points in this time series, we will first estimate the effects of the differenced and lagged values of these indicators on the change in the proportion of conservative judgments issued by the Court, without including any of the other covariates. Only those indicators that have a significant relationship with the Court's judgments will then be included in the final ECM models.

In the time series aggregated from the roll call–based judgment measure, only the differenced value of defense spending as a proportion of federal budget and the lagged value of the "Policy Liberalism" series are associated at conventional levels of significance with changes in the proportion of conservative judgments issued by the Court. In the series aggregated from the partisan Congress-based judgment measure, only the lagged value of the homicide rate and the lagged value of the "Policy Liberalism" series are similarly associated with changes in the Court's judgments. These indicators are then included in the time-series analyses reported earlier in Tables 6.5 and 6.6.

Tables 6.11 and 6.12 report these results. In Table 6.11, increases in the proportion of the federal budget allocated to defense spending are associated with decreases in the proportion of the Court's judgments decided in a conservative direction in the analysis using the Bailey XTI preference estimates, but this effect is not present in the analysis using the Judicial Common Space preference estimates. Similarly, a larger cumulative number of enacted liberal federal statutes in the immediately prior term is associated with an increase in the proportion of conservative judgments in the analysis using the Judicial Common Space preference estimates, but not in that using the Bailey XTI preference estimates. In Table 6.12 neither of the included socioeconomic indicators has a significant association with changes in the Court's judgments, once elected branch and judicial preferences are taken into account.

Public opinion also continues to be largely unassociated with changes in the Court's judgments. Although we do observe a weakly significant effect for the lagged value of the public mood in the analysis using the Bailey XTI preference estimates reported in Table 6.12, this effect is not evident in any of the other analyses. Changes in the proportion of judgments decided in a conservative direction are similarly unrelated in the predicted direction to the preferences of both Senate majorities and the president, and are only inconsistently related in the predicted direction to the preferences of the median justice.

However, as in all the other analyses reported here, changes in the direction of the Court's judgments are consistently related to changes in the preferences of House majorities. In the analyses reported in

Table 6.11: **Estimating Increases in the Percent of Conservative Supreme Court Judgments per Year, Roll Call–Based Judgment Measure, Error Correction Model, Controlling for Socioeconomic Indicators**

	Bailey XTI Preference Estimates	Judicial Common Space Preference Estimates
Conservatism of SCOTUS Median		
Annual Change (Immediate Effect)	55.99*	156.18***
	(27.46)	(56.16)
Lagged Value (Long-Term Effect)	30.95	94.75***
	(19.42)	(33.43)
Conservatism of House Median		
Annual Change (Immediate Effect)	102.86	113.74
	(82.11)	(98.88)
Lagged Value (Long-Term Effect)	282.46***	198.60**
	(61.37)	(77.08)
Conservatism of Senate Median		
Annual Change (Immediate Effect)	−3.91	−29.98
	(91.10)	(71.36)
Lagged value (Long-Term Effect)	−75.50	−4.73
	(63.98)	(87.50)
Conservatism of President		
Annual Change (Immediate Effect)	−6.56	−1.12
	(7.45)	(10.37)
Lagged Value (Long-Term Effect)	1.57	−10.36
	(6.88)	(13.37)
Conservatism of Public Mood		
Annual Change (Immediate Effect)	2.18	−.20
	(1.33)	(1.41)
Lagged Value (Long-Term Effect)	1.20	−.18
	(1.44)	(1.32)

Defense Spending as Percent of Federal Budget		
Annual Change (Immediate Effect)	−3.41**	−2.40
	(1.49)	(1.76)
Policy Liberalism		
Lagged Value (Long-Term Effect)	.84	1.64***
	.76	(.49)
Error Correction Rate		
Lagged Value of % Conservative Judgments	−1.08***	−1.26***
	(.14)	(.12)
N	42	42
R-squared	.76	.80
p-value of Ljung-Box Q test for serial correlation	.99	.83

Note: Ordinary least squares regression; robust standard errors. Intercept term not reported. Estimates significantly different from zero at *$p<.10$; **$p<.05$; ***$p<.01$ (two-tailed).

Table 6.11, using the time series of the Court's judgments aggregated from the roll call–based judgment measure, this effect is again observed through changes in the conservatism of the median representative in the immediately prior term. Moving from a term wherein the House median's preferences in the prior term are set to their most liberal value, to a term wherein they are set to their most conservative value, while holding all other variables at their sample values, generates predicted increases in the proportion of judgments decided in a conservative direction of 88 percentage points using the Bailey XTI preference estimates, and 66 percentage points using the Judicial Common Space estimates. These predicted increases are significant at conventional thresholds. The "error correction rates," or the coefficients on the lagged values of the dependent variable, again tell us that approximately 100 percent of these increases take place in the term of interest, rather than being distributed more slowly over time.

Table 6.12: Estimating Increases in the Percent of Conservative Supreme Court Judgments per Year, Partisan Congress–Based Judgment Measure, Error Correction Model, Controlling for Socioeconomic Indicators

	Bailey XTI Preference Estimates	Judicial Common Space Preference Estimates
Conservatism of SCOTUS Median		
Annual Change (Immediate Effect)	15.81	60.08
	(26.87)	(39.52)
Lagged Value (Long-Term Effect)	−14.26	−32.40
	(19.42)	(32.14)
Conservatism of House Median		
Annual Change (Immediate Effect)	178.91*	278.91***
	(95.52)	(85.88)
Lagged Value (Long-Term Effect)	158.02***	213.13***
	(56.41)	(55.57)
Conservatism of Senate Median		
Annual Change (Immediate Effect)	−48.30	−133.28*
	(76.44)	(69.59)
Lagged Value (Long-Term Effect)	−55.07	−83.76
	55.01	(70.66)
Conservatism of President		
Annual Change (Immediate Effect)	−10.33*	−9.06
	(5.95)	(8.98)
Lagged Value (Long-Term Effect)	−3.16	−7.39
	(7.71)	(10.65)
Conservatism of Public Mood		
Annual Change (Immediate Effect)	.69	-.44
	1.29	(1.32)
Lagged Value (Long-Term Effect)	2.39*	1.07
	(1.19)	(1.18)

Homicide Rate
  Lagged Value (Long-Term Effect)   .52   .39
                                          (4.48)   (3.99)

Policy Liberalism
  Lagged Value (Long-Term Effect)   -.79   -.18
                                          (.73)   (.40)

Error Correction Rate
  Lagged Value of % Conservative Judgments -.81***   -.98***
                                          (.16)   (.17)

N   42   42
R-squared   .61   .74
p-value of Ljung-Box Q test for serial   .95   .63
correlation

Note: Ordinary least squares regression; robust standard errors. Intercept term not reported.
Estimates significantly different from zero at *$p<.10$; **$p<.05$; ***$p<.01$ (two-tailed).

In Table 6.12, reporting the ECM results for the partisan Congress-based judgment measure, we again see two different effects from the preferences of the median representative. First, in terms wherein there are large increases in the conservatism of the median representative, relative to the prior term's value, there are corresponding large increases in the proportion of conservative judgments issued by the Court. An increase in the conservatism of the median representative as large as that observed between the 1993 and 1994 terms produces a predicted increase in the proportion of conservative judgments issued by the Court of 40 percentage points using the Bailey XTI preference estimates, and of 76 percentage points using the Judicial Common Space estimates. These increases are significant at conventional thresholds.

Second, there are also large increases in the proportion of conservative judgments issued by the Court when the median representative in the immediately prior term was more conservative, relative to the sample average. Moving from a term wherein the House median's preferences in the prior term are set to their most liberal value, to a term wherein they are set to their most conservative value, while holding all other variables at their sample values, generates predicted increases in the proportion of judgments decided in a conservative direction of 50 percentage points using the Bailey XTI preference estimates, and of 71 percentage points using the Judicial Common Space estimates. These predicted increases are significant at conventional thresholds. Again, the estimated error correction rates reported in Table 6.12 tell us that these increases are virtually all realized in the term of interest, rather than being distributed more slowly over time.

The Constitutionally Constrained Court

The findings reported here suggest that those reported in Chapter Five were not simply the product of spurious associations with more fundamentally causal trends in public opinion, economic and social conditions, or public policy. Even after controlling for public opinion and a variety of economic, social, and policy indicators, using both case-based and time-series specifications, the results reported in Chapter Five remain essentially unaltered. In cases involving constitutional challenges to federal statutes, the justices are largely unresponsive to public opinion trends or to changes in economic, social, or policy indicators. They are similarly unresponsive to changes in the preferences of majorities in the Senate and of the president. Even their own estimated preferences are only inconsistently related to their judgments in these cases. Instead, the justices consistently defer to the preferences of majorities in the House of Representatives, at substantively meaningful levels.

There may still be reasons to suspect these findings. We may have measured public opinion only imperfectly. We may have failed to identify and include the factors that are "really" driving the observed relationship between the preferences of House majorities and the Court's judgments in these cases. The most we can say is that this observed relationship is not being driven by the possibly confounding factors that were identified and included here. Still, the robustness of the findings reported in Chapter Five to the varying specifications reported here is striking.

There is a final objection that some may raise about the interpretation of these findings. The perhaps natural interpretation is an institutional one. The Constitution gives to the House the "sole" power to initiate impeachment investigations of the justices. Deterring these investigations may give the justices particularly compelling incentives to defer to the preferences of the median representative. The Constitution's Origination Clause likewise gives to the House a special role in initiating appropriations bills, a category of bills including those increasing judicial salaries and budgets. The justices need House majorities regularly to introduce and support judicial salary increases if their salaries are not to decrease every year in real terms; they thus have particular incentives to defer to the preferences of those majorities. The observed specificity of the justices' deference to the preferences of House majorities suggests that this deference is the product of these constitutionally defined incentives.

Some may object, however, that the pattern we observe in the Court's judgments, while real, could instead be explained by a normatively inspired "preference for deference."[23] That is, perhaps the justices, rather than trying to avoid congressional punishment and/or induce congressional rewards, simply believe that the most normatively defensible interpretive strategy, when reviewing federal statutes on constitutional grounds, is to defer to congressional preferences. Perhaps they believe that, in a representative democracy, the most appropriate role for the country's highest court is not to act as a countermajoritarian force, but rather to endorse majoritarian decisions. So perhaps the justices are not in fact influenced by the Constitution's provisions governing their tenures and salaries. Perhaps they just behave as if they are.

Yet again, the specificity of the justices' observed deference would seem to undermine this alternative causal story. That story suggests that the justices should defer relatively equally to the preferences of all the elected branches. But the justices do not defer to congressional preferences, broadly defined. They do not defer to presidential preferences. They defer narrowly and relatively precisely to the preferences of majorities in the House of Representatives. The story based on constitutionally specified incentives can explain the particularity of the justices' deference. The story based on a "preference for deference" cannot.

There is, however, a final complicating factor we have yet to address. In Chapter Five we noted that a belief in the Court's independence can affect the way that judgments are coded by academic researchers; the hypothesis of the Court's independence in effect may have been hard-wired into the data used to test that hypothesis. Many academic researchers have likewise assumed that the sample of cases heard by the Court in any given term has been selected without regard to elected branch preferences. That sample may then be used to test hypotheses about judicial deference to elected branch preferences, without correcting for any possible selection bias in the sample.

We have followed that practice in Chapters Five and Six. But it may not be a wise practice. After all, the Court chooses its own docket. If the justices defer to the preferences of House majorities when deciding cases on the merits, perhaps they also defer to those preferences when deciding whether to accept cases for review. Or perhaps litigants, anticipating the Court's likely deference on the merits, defer to the preferences of House majorities in deciding whether to appeal decisions to the Court. Either process could result in a docket biased in ways that may make it difficult to draw inferences from the cases that make it onto that docket. This is the question to which the next chapter turns.

7

RESTORING THE COURT'S MISSING DOCKET

We saw in Chapter Four that many observers found the pre-1994 Rehnquist Court to be considerably more moderate than they had expected it to be, even as increasingly conservative justices replaced moderate and liberal justices. We now know that these observers were correct: at least in cases involving the constitutional review of federal statutes, the first Rehnquist Court was indeed significantly more liberal than it would have been, had only the justices' preferences determined its judgments.

Another thing observers noticed about this first Rehnquist Court was that it appeared to be taking increasingly fewer cases involving important public policy issues. *New York Times* reporter Linda Greenhouse noted at the close of the 1991 term that the Court appeared to want to "withdraw, not completely but measurably, from roles it has played for many years."[1] At the start of the 1993 term the *Times* again drew attention to the Court's shrinking docket, pointing out that, "for reasons it has not explained," the number of cases accepted by the Court for review had declined by about one-third over the previous few years.[2] Somewhat ironically, given what was about to occur in the 1994 term, the *Times* reported, "There is little on the Court's docket these days that engages first principles."[3]

The Court's shrinking docket, as seen in the annual number of orally argued cases reported in Figure 7.1, soon attracted the attention of legal academics.[4] But it seemed that nobody could provide a good explanation for why the Court's docket began to contract in the 1986 term, the first

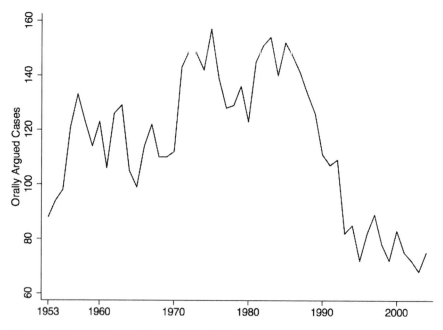

Figure 7.1. Orally Argued Cases, 1953–2004
Source: United States Supreme Court Database.

term of the Rehnquist Court. The number of certiorari petitions to the Court had remained relatively constant over the period of the contracting docket, as had the frequency of requests for review made to the Court by the Solicitor General's office.[5] Mandatory appellate review had been eliminated by Congress in 1988, but the decline in the Court's docket predated this development, and in any case was observed in the Court's discretionary certiorari docket as well. And while the justices appointed to the Court in the late 1980s voted for certiorari less frequently on average than did their predecessors, the decline in certiorari votes was also observed in the votes of those justices who had remained on the Court throughout the 1980s.[6]

The curious phenomenon of the Court's apparently disappearing docket attracted, and continues to attract, significant attention.[7] Yet despite this high level of scrutiny, we seem to be no closer to explaining the mystery of the Court's dwindling docket. There is, however, an explanation that has yet to be considered. As we saw in the last two chapters, when the preferences of majorities on the Court and in the House of Representatives diverge, the median justice appears to defer to the preferences of the median representative. When the divergence between the Court and the House is large, the median justice can end up endorsing legal rules that lie quite distant from her own preferences.

The Court's apparent deference to the preferences of House majorities raises an interesting question. When the preferences of the median justice and those of the median representative diverge, why would the median justice and those of her colleagues even more distant from the median representative want to take any cases in which the House might have an interest? After all, if the Court takes these cases, it will only wind up issuing opinions that the median justice and her more extreme colleagues won't like very much. So perhaps the median justice and her likeminded brethren use the Court's discretionary docket to take fewer cases, or fewer significant cases, when they face increasing constraint from House majorities.[8]

It may not have been coincidence, then, that the Court's docket began to decline in precisely the same period that the justices were facing increasing constraint from the House of Representatives, or that the docket's decline more or less halted in the mid-1990s, precisely when that constraint largely evaporated. Figure 7.2 reports again the Court's docket of orally argued cases for the 1953 through the 2004 terms, as well as the absolute value of the distance between the estimated most preferred rule of the median representative and that of the median justice in each term, using the Bailey XTI preference estimates.[9]

During the Warren Court there appears to be little association between the two series. Starting with the Burger Court, however, the two series appear to move in opposite directions. As the distance between the House and the Court shrank in the first terms of the Burger Court, the number of cases granted oral argument before the justices rose sharply. While the preferences of House and Court majorities remained similar through the 1970s and early 1980s, the size of the Court's orally argued docket likewise remained relatively large. But as the preferences of the median justice and the median representative diverged in the 1980s, the size of the Court's docket began to decline precipitously. The Court's docket of orally argued cases contracted in the 1986 term, the first term

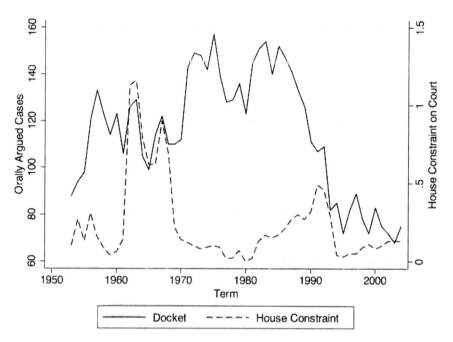

Figure 7.2. The Court's Docket and Congressional Constraint, 1953–2004
Source: United States Supreme Court Database, Bailey (2007). House constraint is
calculated as the absolute value of the distance between the estimated most preferred
rules of the median justice and the median representative in each term.

of the Rehnquist Court, and shrank in almost every year through the
1993 term. The decline in the Court's docket then more or less halted in
the 1994 term.

In other words, the Court's docket began to shrink at precisely the
same time that liberal House constraint on the Court began to bite, in
the mid-1980s. The decline in the Court's docket then ceased just as this
constraint on the Court dissipated after the 1994 elections.

The possible responsiveness of the Court's docket to the preferences of
House majorities has significance that extends well beyond simply providing an explanation for the Court's shrinking docket in the late 1980s. If
the Court's docket of potentially troublesome cases contracts when the
justices' preferences diverge from those of House majorities, then that
docket may mislead us. The Court's actual, realized docket may not fully

reveal the extent to which its dispositions respond to the preferences of House majorities. The cases that the Court *doesn't* take, and the dispositions that it *doesn't* make, may be just as important for estimating that responsiveness as the cases and dispositions that we actually observe.

In other words, the Court may have a missing docket, a docket that we don't see. This missing docket contains the cases that the Court would have taken, had it not faced hostile majorities in the House of Representatives. And we may only be able to uncover the true scope of the Court's deference to the preferences of those majorities by finding, and restoring, its missing docket.

This chapter proceeds by addressing a series of questions. First, why would the Court's docket be responsive to the degree of preference divergence between the House and the Court, and is there any evidence of such responsiveness? Second, if so, is there a way to estimate the number of cases that the Court would have heard, had it faced more friendly House majorities? Third, is there then a way to estimate what the Court's dispositions would have been in these missing cases? And finally, if we can restore the Court's missing docket, what does it tell us?

Friendly House Majorities, Hostile House Majorities, and the Court's Docket

Studies of the Court's dispositions routinely have assumed, at least implicitly, that the Court's docket is a reasonably random selection from the larger population of cases that could have been reviewed. Because the Court's cases have been chosen at random, we can be assured that our analyses of the dispositions in those cases will not be biased by any unusual characteristics of the particular sample of cases heard in any given term.[10]

But, of course, this is not how the Court's docket works at all. Each term the Court receives about eight thousand petitions for writs of certiorari, or grants of Supreme Court appellate review. The justices select from this pool of petitions the cases they want to review; it takes four "yes" votes to grant cert. Of late the justices have been granting cert to only about 80 cases per term, or approximately one percent of the possible cases.

Because the justices choose the cases they want to review, there is nothing random about the Court's docket. So how and why might the preferences of House majorities matter to the justices as they choose cases for review?

Recall from Chapter Five that when the justices review the constitutionality of federal statutes, we assume that they consider the implicit constitutional standards embodied by those statutes. In their majority opinions they may endorse those standards, or apply constitutional standards located to the right or the left of those embodied by challenged statutes. As the standard applied by the Court to a particular statute moves further away from that embodied by the statute, either to the right or the left, the probability that the statute will be struck increases.

Consider the situation facing the justices in the 1980s and early 1990s. As the Court moved to the right, there would have been an increasing number of federal statutes enacted by unified Democratic Congresses embodying standards located to the left of those preferred by the median justice and her four more conservative colleagues. For example, assuming for the sake of argument that federal statutes embody legal rules located somewhere near the midpoints between the most preferred rules of the enacting House and Senate medians, and using the Bailey XTI preference estimates, at least five justices on the Rehnquist Court between the Court's 1987 and 1993 terms would have preferred constitutional standards located to the right of those embodied by every single federal statute enacted between the 1986 and 1994 elections. Had the median justice been free to implement these more preferred standards, many of these statutes likely would not have survived constitutional review.

But at the same time that the median justice was moving in a conservative direction, the median representative in the House was moving in a liberal direction. The House median sitting during the Rehnquist Court's first eight terms would have been made worse off had the conservative majority on the Court sought to move any of the rules embodied by these statutes in a conservative direction. This implies that majorities in the House would have had incentives both to punish the justices should they attempt to move any of these rules rightward, and to reward them should they preserve the rules embodied in any of these liberal statutes. Meanwhile, the decreased opportunities for the Court's conservative majority to move policy rightward were not generally offset by greater opportunities for the more liberal justices to move policy leftward.[11]

So as the preferences of House majorities moved further to the left, away from the preferences of the conservative Rehnquist Court majority, the opportunities for the conservative justices to move liberal rules rightward would have contracted. While in some cases they still might have been able to move policy to the right, the magnitudes of these rightward movements would have been small. Thus as the magnitude of the gap between liberal House majorities and conservative Court majorities grew, the justices in the conservative majority would have had decreasing incentives to take cases involving challenges to liberal statutes.

There is, then, good reason to suspect that the Rehnquist Court's docket may have decreased in the late 1980s and early 1990s at least in part as a function of the increasing gap between the preferences of liberal House majorities and those of conservative Court majorities. This constraint would have decreased the incentives of the more conservative justices to hear cases challenging liberal policy outcomes prior to the 1994 term, including any challenges to statutes enacted by the liberal Congresses sitting between the 1986 and 1994 elections. And the more liberal the preferences of House majorities became, relative to those of the Court, the more these incentives would have decreased.

We can use the aggregate data from Figure 7.2 to examine the effects of this preference gap on the Court's docket. It turns out that our suspicions

Table 7.1: **Estimating the Annual Change in the Court's Docket, Bailey XTI Preference Estimates, 1981–2004**

	Coefficient	SE	95% CI
SCOTUS Median/House Median Distance	−35.69	15.48	(−67.81, −3.58)

N = 24
Root MSE = 9.88

Note: Ordinary least squares regression; robust standard errors. Intercept term not reported. Italicized variables are statistically significant at the .10 level. Distance variable is lagged one year.

have some support. From the Burger through the Rehnquist Courts the annual change in the Court's docket is negatively and significantly correlated with the size of the gap between the most preferred rules of the House and Court medians. In other words, the bigger the divergence between the preferences of the House and Court medians in any given term, the more the Court was likely to take fewer cases in the succeeding term. This negative correlation becomes even more pronounced for the 1981–2004 terms, after the Reagan appointees began to join the Court.[12]

Table 7.1 reports the results of a simple regression of the annual change in the Court's docket between 1981 and 2004 as a function of the degree of preference divergence between the House and Court medians. These results tell us that in the absence of any such divergence, as in the 1981 term, the Court's docket was likely to stay approximately the same size as it had been in the previous year. But at the highest level of divergence between the two medians, as in the 1992 term, the Court's docket was predicted to decrease by approximately thirteen cases relative to the preceding term's docket. These predictions are distinct with at least 95 percent confidence.[13]

There is suggestive evidence, then, that the Rehnquist Court in particular took fewer cases as the distance between the justices' preferences and those of House majorities began to increase. Between its 1986 and 1993 terms, the Court is predicted to have shrunk its docket by an average of nine cases in every term solely as a function of the large gap between the preferences of liberal House majorities and those of the conservative Court majority. Between its 1994 and 2004 terms, however, the Court's docket is predicted to remain essentially unchanged from term to term, as the preferences of House majorities approached those of the Court.[14]

Estimating the Court's Missing Docket

The aggregate analysis of the Court's docket suggests that the preferences of liberal House majorities may have reduced the size of the Rehnquist Court's docket in its pre-1994 terms. Given the analyses of the last two chapters, we might be especially interested in the effect of House preferences on the Court's docket of constitutional challenges to liberal federal statutes. If liberal House constraint on the Court reduced the number of such challenges heard during the pre-1994 terms, then analyses that do not take this selection bias into account, like those reported in Chapters Five and Six, may return misleading results.

One seemingly obvious strategy might be to start with the pool of appeals made to the Rehnquist Court, or requests for writs of certiorari, in cases involving constitutional challenges to liberal federal statutes. We might then ask whether increased liberal House constraint on the Court in any given term reduced the probability of certiorari being granted to such cases.

The problem with this particular strategy is that the pool of certiorari petitions is itself not a random sample. It represents the product of litigants' choices to appeal to the Court, as opposed to accepting lower courts' decisions. And if litigants believe that divergence in the preferences of majorities on the Court and in the House reduces the likelihood of writs of certiorari being granted in certain kinds of cases, they may be less likely to petition the Court for such writs when this divergence is large. We may then fail to accurately estimate the effects of preference divergence on the probability of certiorari being granted, because the pool of certiorari petitions itself has already been shaped by that divergence.[15]

In order to accurately estimate the number of constitutional challenges to liberal federal statutes that the Rehnquist Court did not hear because of the gap between the justices' preferences and those of liberal House majorities, we need to start with a population that itself has been unaffected by that gap. One such population may be a defined pool of federal statutes enacted by some set of liberal Congresses. We can follow these statutes over the Rehnquist Court terms, recording whether and when any constitutional challenges to their provisions are docketed by the Court. We can then ask whether the rate of docketed challenges is a function of the degree of preference divergence between majorities on the Court and in the House.

Of course, most federal statutes will never reach the Court's docket, irregardless of the preferences of House majorities. Many federal statutes may be insufficiently important to be challenged on constitutional grounds; they do not impact any constituency sufficiently negatively for that constituency to bear the costs of litigation. In order to address this concern we can restrict our attention only to "important" federal statutes.

While there are various definitions of importance when it comes to federal statutes, one widely used standard is the pool of "landmark" federal statutes identified by congressional historian Stephen Stathis. We can identify a liberal set of these landmark statutes and then follow this set over the course of the Rehnquist Court, identifying whether and when any constitutional challenges to these statutes are docketed by the Court.[16]

It is important to note that, in order to avoid the problem of selection bias in the certiorari pool, we have now shifted our question slightly. Instead of asking, "Does the likelihood that the justices grant certiorari to a constitutional challenge to a federal statute respond to divergence between the justices' preferences and those of House majorities?" we are now asking, "Does the likelihood of a docketed constitutional challenge to a federal statute respond to divergence between the justices' preferences and those of House majorities?" That is, our new question permits the possibility that the docketing of these constitutional challenges may be responsive to preference divergence either at the certiorari stage, or at the stage wherein litigants decide whether to file certiorari petitions, or even at earlier stages of the litigation process. The results that we will explore here will not permit us to distinguish between these varying causal mechanisms, although future research might be able to do so. However, our results will at a minimum tell us whether, at the end of the day, the Court's docket of these challenges varies as a function of the gap between the preferences of the justices and those of House majorities, as well as illuminate the magnitude of that variation, should it exist.

Constitutional Challenges to Liberal Landmark Federal Statutes, 1987–2004

We want to identify a set of relatively liberal landmark statutes that we can follow over the course of the Rehnquist Court. For this purpose we will narrow our focus to those landmark federal statutes enacted between 1987 and 1994. As we saw in Chapter Five, in the 1986 midterm elections the Democrats won majorities in both the House and Senate, holding those majorities until the 1994 midterm elections. In both the Bailey XTI and the Judicial Common Space preference estimates the House and Senate medians shift markedly to the left as a result of the

1986 elections, growing increasingly liberal until the 1994 elections. If we assume that statutes embody legal rules located at the midpoint between the enacting House and Senate medians, using the Bailey XTI preference estimates all of these statutes are located considerably to the left of the most preferred rule of the median justice between 1987 and 2004.

Happily, following these statutes through the last term of the Rehnquist Court, the degree of preference divergence between the Court and the House varies considerably. As we saw in Figure 3.1, using the Bailey XTI preference estimates the House median remains to the left of the Court median throughout the Rehnquist Court terms. But the magnitude of this liberal House divergence decreases dramatically as a function of the 1994 congressional elections. As a result we can observe the Court's docketing of these liberal landmark statutes during terms with both relatively high and relatively low levels of liberal House divergence.

Between 1987 and 1994 the Congress enacted eighty-five statutes that receive the "landmark" designation from congressional historian Steven Stathis. Following these statutes from the 1987 through the 2004 terms results in 1,233 statute-year observations. The Rehnquist Court reviews one of these liberal landmark statutes between its 1987 and 1993 terms and twelve liberal landmark statutes during its post-1993 terms.[17]

Even taking into account the increased availability of these statutes for review during the Court's post-1993 terms, there is still a large increase in the rate at which they are docketed by the Court after the 1994 elections.[18] Still, there is the possibility that this effect is being driven by statute age. Perhaps it takes time for constitutional challenges to federal statutes to mature in the lower courts before they are appealed to, or reviewed by, the Supreme Court. Perhaps these liberal federal statutes, enacted between 1987 and 1994, are being docketed with greater frequency in the post-1993 terms simply because they were only then ripe for constitutional litigation.

What we want to do, then, is to estimate the probability of a docketed constitutional challenge to one of these statutes, as a function of the distance between the preferences of the majorities on the Court and in the House, while controlling for statute age. We also want to control for the distances between the preferences of Senate majorities and the Court, and the president and the Court; perhaps the Court's docket is responsive to the distances between the preferences of the justices and these elected officials as well. Each of these distances will be measured as the most preferred rule of the median justice minus the most preferred rule of the respective elected official; these distances will be positive when the elected official is more liberal than the median justice, zero when the two have identical preferences, and negative when the elected official is more conservative than the median justice (true only for presidential preferences during some terms in our sample). We expect that as these distances become larger in the positive direction (indicating more liberal elected officials, relative to the median justice), the Court will be less likely to review liberal statutes. We will not be able to include any case-specific controls, as we did in previous chapters, as these controls are available only for docketed statutes. Our sample here, by contrast, includes both docketed and undocketed federal statutes.

Table 7.2 reports the results of this analysis. Only the preferences of House majorities have a significant effect on the Court's docketing of liberal landmark statutes; the preferences of Senate majorities and the president have no effect on the Court's docket at conventional significance levels.[19] The Court is less likely to review liberal landmark statutes as House majorities become more liberal, relative to the Court's majority. This effect is not being driven by statute age; Table 7.2 reveals that these liberal federal statutes were in fact less likely to reach the Court's docket under constitutional suspicion as time passed.[20] The statutes' increased probabilities of review after the House came under conservative Republican control in 1994 would have been even higher, had statute age not depressed post-1993 rates of review.

The magnitude of the effect of House majorities on the Rehnquist Court's docket is sizable. Holding other variables at their sample values, liberal landmark statutes are four and a half times more likely to be reviewed between the Rehnquist Court's 1994 and 2004 terms, relative to its pre-1994 terms, as a function of the increased conservatism of House majorities after the 1994 elections.[21] Aggregating the predicted rates of review over the available statute-year observations, we find that the Court is predicted to review only approximately one liberal landmark statute between its 1987 and 1993 terms, which is in fact the observed number. But, had statute age not depressed the post-1993 rates of review,

Table 7.2: Estimating the Probability of Review of Landmark Federal Statutes Enacted Between 1987 and 1994, Bailey XTI Preference Estimates, 1987–2004

	Coefficient	SE	95% CI
More Liberal House	−10.20	4.73	(−19.47, −.92)
More Liberal Senate	−2.93	2.50	(−7.82, 1.96)
More Liberal President	−.89	.45	(−1.77, .02)
Statute Age	−.23	.10	(−.43, −.02)

N = 1233
Wald chi^2 = 11.36

Note: Poisson regression; robust standard errors reported, clustered by term. Intercept term not reported. Italicized variables are statistically significant at the .05 level. The "More Liberal" variables subtract the estimated most preferred rules of the median representative, the median senator, and the president from that of the median justice. These variables are positive when the elected branches are more liberal than the Court, negative when the elected branches are more conservative than the Court, and zero when there is no preference divergence.

the Court is predicted to review approximately seventeen liberal landmark statutes during its post-1993 terms, rather than the twelve that we observe, as a result of the House's conservative majorities during these terms.[22]

We now know that the Court docketed fewer constitutional challenges to liberal landmark statutes when the median representative's most preferred rule was significantly more liberal than that of the median justice. This raises an interesting counterfactual question. How many such challenges *would* the Rehnquist Court have docketed between its 1987 and 1993 terms, had the preferences of House majorities not affected the Court's docket?

Because between its 1994 and 2004 terms the Rehnquist Court is largely unconstrained by the preferences of House majorities, we can essentially use the frequency with which it dockets liberal statutes during these terms to simulate the Court's docket during its pre-1994 terms. We will allow the preferences of the median justice, the median senator, and the president to retain their actual values between the 1987 and 1993 terms. We will also keep the number and age of liberal landmark statutes at their actual values during these terms. But we will assume counterfactually that the preferences of the House median during these terms were identical to those of the Court median. That is, we will assume that during these terms, the Court was completely unconstrained by House preferences (or that the value of *More Liberal House* in Table 7.2 is set to zero during these terms). We will then simulate the predicted probabilities of review for the pool of landmark statutes enacted between 1987 and 1993, under these conditions.

The results of this simulation are impressive. The Court actually reviewed only one constitutional challenge to a liberal landmark statute during these terms. But had the Court been unconstrained by liberal House majorities, it is predicted to have reviewed approximately fourteen constitutional challenges to liberal landmark statutes during those terms.[23] There are thus approximately thirteen "missing" constitutional challenges to liberal landmark statutes that we don't see on the Court's docket between the 1987 and 1993 terms, solely due to the effect, or the anticipated effect, of liberal House majorities on the Court's docketing decisions.

These estimates reveal just how substantially the preferences of House majorities can affect the Court's docket. According to these estimates, the Court's docket of constitutional challenges to liberal landmark statutes between its 1987 and 1993 terms was reduced by 93 percent as a result of the liberal preferences of Democratic House majorities. It was nearly reduced out of existence entirely.

The one liberal landmark statute reviewed during the Court's pre-1994 terms lies well outside the 95 percent confidence interval for the number of docketed landmark statutes that we would predict under perfectly convergent House and Court majorities. However, we don't find a substantial missing docket during the Rehnquist Court's remaining terms, after the preferences of House majorities had converged most of the way toward those of the median justice. Had the preferences of House and Court majorities been perfectly convergent during the post-1993 terms, the Court is predicted to have reviewed approximately 23 liberal landmark statutes. The twelve liberal landmark statutes actually docketed during these terms lie just within this prediction's 95 percent confidence interval.[24] That is, the difference between the Court's missing and real-ized dockets of constitutional challenges to liberal landmark statutes in its post-1993 terms is sufficiently small so as to be indistinguishable from the null hypothesis of no difference.

In short, there is a substantively large and statistically significant effect of liberal House majorities on the Court's docket between its 1987 and 1993 terms. During the terms that the conservative Rehnquist Court faced a liberal Democratic House, its docket of constitutional challenges to liberal landmark statutes is reduced by approximately 93 percent as a result of the preferences of liberal House majorities. Yet once the prefer-ences of House majorities approached those of the median justice after the 1994 elections, the Court's docket of these challenges becomes indis-tinguishable from the docket we would have observed in the presence of perfectly convergent preferences.

The Effects of the Court's Missing Docket

We are now in a position to consider in what ways the Court's actual, realized docket might mislead us. We know that constitutional challenges to liberal federal statutes were considerably less likely to be docketed during the Rehnquist Court's pre-1994 terms, when the con-servative majority on the Court faced significant constraint from the lib-eral House. How might the absence of these cases from the Court's real-ized docket affect our analyses of the Court's independence?

Figure 7.3 illustrates the problem, which is known more technically in the social science literature as selection bias. In each panel of Figure 7.3, we see hypothetical samples of cases heard by a conservative Supreme Court whose median justice's preferences remain constant across both samples. The horizontal axes represent the magnitude of the gap between the preferences of the median justice and those of a more liberal median representative; this gap is characterized as "Liberal House Constraint." The vertical axes plot the locations of the Court's rules as announced in its opinions, and are increasing in the liberalism of those rules. Each case involves a challenge to the constitutionality of a liberal statute. For illus-trative purposes we assume that this Court chooses more liberal rules as it faces larger values of liberal House constraint.

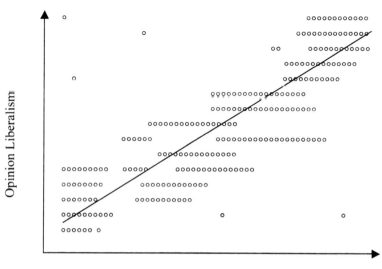

Figure 7.3a. Estimating the Effects of Congressional Preferences on the Court's Opinions, No Selection Bias

As the degree of liberal House constraint on the Court increases, so, too, does the liberalism of the Court's opinions.

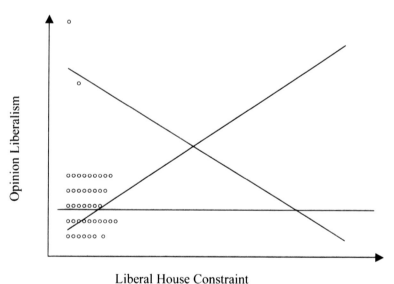

Figure 7.3b. Estimating the Effects of Congressional Preferences on the Court's Opinions, with Selection Bias

Although the true relationship between liberal House constraint and the liberalism of the Court's opinions is the same here as in Figure 7.3a, because the Court takes so few cases when it faces more severe liberal House constraint we do not observe this relationship.

Figure 7.3a shows a Court whose docket is unaffected by selection bias. This is a Court whose cases are assigned by some random case-generating process, like a lottery over all liberal statutes. As a result of the lottery this Court takes about as many cases in the terms when it faces significant liberal House constraint, as it does in the terms when it faces little constraint. By assumption, this Court issues significantly more liberal rules when it faces increasing liberal House constraint. If we estimated the relationship between liberal House constraint and the location of the Court's rules, we would find the nice regression line plotted in Figure 7.3a: as liberal House constraint on the Court increases, the Court's rules get more liberal.

Figure 7.3b shows us a different sample of cases from the same underlying population of possible cases, a sample that has been affected by selection bias. The Court in Figure 7.3b was allowed to choose its own docket, and it chose to hear many fewer challenges to liberal statutes during the periods when it faced liberal House constraint. In the cases that went undocketed, the conservative median justice would have faced pressure from liberal House majorities to endorse rules that were significantly to the left of her own most preferred rule. She and the justices to her right would have had little to gain by accepting such cases for review.

Because the sample of cases from the terms with liberal constraint is so reduced, it is now hard to see whether there is any relationship between liberal House constraint and the Court's decisions. We can see that the conservative Court issues conservative opinions when it faces no liberal House constraint. But what does the Court do when it faces a high degree of liberal constraint? Does the regression line plotting that relationship slope upward, as in Figure 7.3a? Well, maybe. Is it instead a flat line, indicating no relationship between constraint and the Court's opinions? Could be. Is it even downwardly sloping, telling us that as liberal House constraint on the Court increases, the Court is actually more likely to issue *conservative* decisions? Possibly.

When we estimate relationships from data, we require relatively low levels of prediction error in order to have confidence that our estimated relationships aren't just due to chance association. But any prediction we might make from the data plotted in Figure 7.3b would have a very large degree of associated error. This error might even lead us to reject the hypothesis of a relationship between liberal House constraint and the Court's opinions, despite the stipulation that such a relationship actually exists.

We can see the potential problem created by selection bias in the actual Supreme Court docket by looking at the constitutional challenges to landmark federal statutes docketed by the Rehnquist Court. Congressional historian Stephen Stathis identifies landmark statutes enacted only through 2002. Between 1987 and 2004, the Court reviewed the constitutionality of twenty-five of the landmark statutes that were enacted between 1987 and 2002. Between its 1987 and 1993 terms, it reviewed only one liberal landmark statute enacted between 1987 and 1993, striking the challenged statute. The Court also struck ten of the twelve liberal landmark statutes it reviewed between the 1994 and 2004 terms, and four of the twelve conservative landmark statutes it reviewed between the 1995 and 2004 terms.

Unsurprisingly, given these numbers, a probit regression on the Court's propensity to strike landmark statutes as a function of judicial and elected branch preferences, controlling for statute age, does not confirm the findings reported in Chapters Five and Six. As can be seen in Table 7.3,

Table 7.3: **Estimating the Probability of a Strike of Docketed Landmark Statutes Enacted Between 1987 and 2002, Bailey XTI Preference Estimates, 1987–2004**

	Coefficient	SE	95% CI
SCOTUS Median/Statute Distance	−1.10	5.06	(−11.03, 8.83)
House Median/Statute Distance	1.55	4.40	(−7.07, 10.17)
Senate Median/Statute Distance	5.29	5.56	(−5.61, 16.19)
President/Statute Distance	6.49	2.75	(1.11, 11.88)
Statute Age	−.14	.09	(−.31, .04)

N = 25
Wald chi^2 = 12.84

Note: Probit regression; robust standard errors reported, clustered by term. Intercept term not reported. Italicized variables are statistically significant at the .10 level.

there are no apparent effects from the preferences of House majorities on the probability that the Court will strike one of these statutes. There is, however, an apparent and surprising association between presidential preferences and this propensity; the Court is more likely to strike a landmark federal statute, the further is the statute's estimated location from the president's most preferred legal rule.[25] This is an estimated effect that has appeared in none of the many previous analyses reported in Chapters Five and Six.

If we were restricted to considering only the cases on the Court's revealed docket, we might be compelled to conclude that, in contrast to its dispositions of ordinary federal statutes, the Court's dispositions of landmark federal statutes are unaffected by the preferences of House majorities. Yet they are surprisingly and unaccountably affected by presidential preferences. However, we already know that there were many constitutional challenges to liberal landmark statutes enacted between 1987 and 1993 that were kept off the Court's docket apparently because of the preferences of liberal House majorities. And so we may be in a situation like that represented in Panel 2 of Figure 7.3: we may be unable accurately to estimate the effect of liberal House constraint on the Court's dispositions of landmark statutes because we have too few cases (only one, to be exact) from terms wherein the Court experienced high levels of such constraint.

The question then arises, what would happen if we could restore the missing constitutional challenges to the Court's docket? Would the estimated relationship between liberal House constraint and the Court's dispositions then look something like the relationship pictured in Panel 1 of Figure 7.3?

To answer this question we need to have a good sense of what the Court's dispositions would have been in these missing cases. Of course, we don't actually observe the Court's dispositions in these missing cases. We observe its dispositions only in the cases it actually dockets. One strategy to address this problem is to take advantage of two features of cases involving constitutional challenges to landmark federal statutes enacted between 1987 and 2004. The first is that we have access to the full population of potential cases from which the Court's docketed cases are drawn, namely the full set of landmark federal statutes enacted during this time period. The second is what we might call the liquidity of the market for the litigation of these statutes. That is, any federal statute sufficiently consequential to impose significant policy costs on some group or groups, as is likely the case for these landmark statutes, should have no shortage of potential litigants both to challenge and to defend its constitutionality. Appeals of lower court rulings on these statutes should presumably continue to the Supreme Court, unless potential appellants anticipate that the Court will not rule in their favor.

In other words, if a majority of the justices is inclined to strike a consequential federal statute, there is no reason to think that this majority will not have the opportunity to review a constitutional challenge to that statute. We should observe these statutes as docketed strikes. When there is not a majority to strike a consequential statute, we should observe that these statutes are not struck by the Court. Some of these "not struck" statutes may be found on the Court's docket as cases wherein constitutional challenges were explicitly rejected by the justices. Other "not struck" statutes may never make it onto the Court's docket, either because the justices do not vote to accept cases wherein their constitutionality is challenged, or because litigants anticipate that the justices won't take these cases in the first place.

We can then use the full population of enacted federal landmark statutes to estimate the Court's propensity to strike one of these statutes (as opposed to "not striking" the statute), as a function of judicial and elected branch preferences, controlling for statute age. In other words, we can perform the same kind of analysis as reported in Table 7.3, but without being tethered to the Court's docket. Once we have estimated these strike propensities, free from any distortions induced by the evident selection bias in the Court's docket, we can then apply these estimated strike propensities to the statutes on the Court's "missing" docket.

Of course, there may be landmark statutes in our sample that remain "not struck" simply because nobody cared enough to litigate them. But we don't expect the proportion of these statutes to vary systematically as a function of either judicial or elected branch preferences. As a result, their presence should not affect our analysis. Instead, we are looking for statutes that remain "not struck" while elected branch preferences protect them, but that are struck once that protection dissipates.

Table 7.4: Estimating the Probability of a Strike of Landmark Statutes Enacted Between 1987 and 2002, Bailey XTI Preference Estimates, 1987–2004

	Coefficient	SE	95% CI
SCOTUS Median/Statute Distance	−6.24	4.08	(−14.23, 1.76)
House Median/Statute Distance	8.18	3.61	(1.11, 15.25)
Senate Median/Statute Distance	2.38	2.65	(−2.81, 7.57)
President/Statute Distance	.44	1.37	(−2.25, 3.12)
Statute Age	−.18	.10	(−.38, .02)

N = 1663
Wald chi^2 = 13.82

Note: Poisson regression; robust standard errors reported, clustered by term. Intercept term not reported. Italicized variables are statistically significant at the .05 level.

As noted previously, Stephen Stathis identifies landmark statutes enacted only through 2002. Including the statutes enacted after the 1994 congressional elections, there are 151 landmark statutes enacted between 1987 and 2002. Following each of these statutes through the 2004 term yields a total of 1,663 statute-year observations.

Table 7.4 reports the estimated propensity of the Court to strike these statutes, as a function of Bailey XTI judicial and elected branch preferences over the statutes, controlling for statute age. These estimates are much more consistent with those reported in Chapters Five and Six. The justices' preferences and those of the median senator and the president are not associated with the probability that the Court strikes a landmark federal statute between the 1987 and 2004 terms. However, and in stark contrast to the estimates reported in Table 7.3 using only the docketed sample, this probability does respond sharply to the preferences of House majorities. Setting the preferences of those majorities to their actual values but holding other variables at their sample means, the Court's post-1993 rate of striking liberal landmark statutes is more than three times higher than its pre-1994 rate, solely as a function of changes in the preferences of House majorities.[26] The Court's predicted strike rate for liberal landmark statutes during its post-1993 terms is also more than three times its strike rate for conservative landmark statutes during those same terms, again solely as a function of the preferences of House majorities.[27]

We can use these estimates to simulate strike probabilities for each statute enacted between 1987 and 1993 in each of the Court's terms during this period, as a function of actual judicial and elected branch preferences over each statute, and the statute's age. Aggregating these predicted strike probabilities over all statute-year observations between the 1987 and 1993 terms, the Court is predicted to strike approximately three liberal landmark statutes during those terms.[28]

As we have seen, the Court actually heard only one constitutional challenge to a liberal landmark statute during these terms, striking the challenged statute. But recall that we estimated that the Court would have heard an additional thirteen challenges to liberal landmark statutes between its 1987 and 1993 terms, had it not been constrained by the preferences of liberal House majorities. We have now estimated that the Court would have struck two of these undocketed statutes and upheld eleven of them. The Court's total observed and unobserved docket between its 1987 and 1993 terms would have included fourteen constitutional challenges to liberal landmark statutes, of which three would have been accepted and eleven rejected.

Restoring the Court's Missing Docket, 1987–2004

The results reported in Table 7.3, using only the Court's docketed cases involving constitutional challenges to federal landmark statutes enacted between 1987 and 2002, indicate that the preferences of House majorities had no effect on the Court's rulings in these cases. However, we can now restore the Court's missing docket of such cases between its 1987 and 1993 terms. We have estimated that, had the Court's docket been unaffected by liberal House constraint, the justices would have reviewed an additional thirteen liberal landmark statutes between the 1987 and 1993 terms, for a total of fourteen docketed statutes. We also estimated that the Court would strike three of these fourteen statutes. One of these statutes is already recorded as a strike, the one disposition that we actually observe on the Court's docket. So we will add two struck and eleven upheld liberal landmark statutes to the Court's docket between its 1987 and 1993 terms.[29]

Table 7.5: **Estimating the Probability of a Strike of "Restored" Docket of Landmark Statutes Enacted Between 1987 and 2002, Bailey XTI Preference Estimates, 1987–2004**

	Coefficient	SE	95% CI
SCOTUS Median/Statute Distance	−3.61	1.98	(−7.49, .27)
House Median/Statute Distance	14.17	4.35	(5.63, 22.70)
Senate Median/Statute Distance	−4.41	5.52	(−15.23, 6.41)
President/Statute Distance	2.51	2.16	(−1.71, 6. 74)
Statute Age	−.16	.08	(−.32, −.00)

N = 38
Wald chi^2 = 18.70

Note: Probit regression; robust standard errors reported, clustered by term. Intercept term not reported. Italicized variables are statistically significant at the .10 level.

When we restore these thirteen missing dispositions to the Court's docket, we now have thirty-eight instances of constitutional challenges to landmark federal statutes on the Court's docket between the 1987 and 2004 terms. Table 7.5 reports the results of a probit regression of the effects of judicial and elected branch preferences on strike probabilities for this "restored" docket, controlling for statute age. Now we see no effects from the preferences of the median justice, the median senator, or the president on the probability that the Court strikes a landmark federal statute. However, there is a large effect of House majorities on this probability. Holding other variables at their sample values, moving from the smallest distance between a landmark statute and the median representative's most preferred rule to the largest increases the probability of a strike from .12 to .95.[30] Holding other variables at their mean values, but setting the preferences of the median representative to their actual values, the average probability that one of the fourteen liberal landmark statutes on the Court's "restored" docket between the 1987 and 1993 terms will be struck is only .20, but rises to .89 for the twelve liberal landmark statutes docketed between the 1994 and 2004 terms, solely as a function of the increased distance between these statutes and the median representative's most preferred rule.[31] Meanwhile, holding all other variables at their mean values but setting the preferences of the median representative to the observed values, the predicted probability that one of the twelve docketed conservative statutes will be struck between the 1995 and 2004 terms averages only .25.[32] Once we address the selection bias in the Court's docket of constitutional challenges to landmark statutes, we can see that, just as we saw in Chapters Five and Six, when the justices' preferences diverge from those of majorities in the House of Representatives, the Court's rulings are more likely to conform to the latter than to the former.

In sum, when we analyzed only the Rehnquist Court's realized docket of constitutional challenges to federal landmark statutes enacted between 1987 and 2002, we found no support for the hypothesis of judicial deference to the preferences of House majorities in the Court's dispositions of those challenges. But we can now see that our failure to reject the null hypothesis of judicial independence from those majorities was entirely due to the selection bias in the Court's realized docket. That realized docket contained too few challenges to liberal landmark statutes, during the terms when the Rehnquist Court experienced the greatest liberal House constraint, for us to be able to accurately estimate the effects of that constraint on the Court's dispositions. And these cases were not missing at random, but rather as a result of a systematic process by which the conservative Rehnquist Court heard fewer constitutional challenges to liberal landmark statutes during the terms that it faced liberal majorities in the House of Representatives. Facing considerable pressure to uphold such statutes during these terms, the conservative majority on the Court presumably saw little upside to hearing these cases, and conservative litigants presumably saw little upside to bringing these cases to the Court in the first place.

Selection Bias and Its Consequences

When we test hypotheses about the Court's independence using only its actual, realized, docket, we are assuming that the cases that the Court didn't take are irrelevant to our inferences from the cases that it did. We are assuming that the Court's silences in these missing cases do not convey important and useful information. Without taking these silences into account, we may very well fail to reject the null hypothesis that elected branch preferences have no effect on the Court's dispositions.

But the Court's silences do convey important information. They tell us that the Court's docket seriously underrepresents critical cases from periods of significant elected branch constraint, cases that could illustrate the Court's responsiveness to that constraint. And they tell us that before we can draw valid inferences from the justices' dispositions in docketed cases, we have to look at the selection bias in that docket.

Certainly it is easier to analyze the Court just by looking at the cases it accepts for review. Those cases are available online in an easily searchable format, with pre-coded judgments nonetheless. But our analyses of the selection bias on the Court's docket suggest that ignoring this bias may lead to very misleading results.

So it turns out that getting an objective measure of the Court's judgments, while necessary, might not in and of itself be sufficient to get accurate estimates of the extent of the justices' deference to elected branch preferences. Even with such a measure, we may still fail to accurately estimate the extent to which the Court defers to elected branch preferences in its dispositions of constitutional challenges to federal statutes. Before we can see the full scope of that deference, we need to take into account the extent to which the Court's docket is also responsive to those preferences.

We saw in the last chapter that our subjective measure of the Court's judgments appears to have been profoundly influenced by our expectation that, since the Court is surely independent of the elected branches, the primary influence on the Court's judgments must be the justices' own preferences. Analogously, we may see a similar effect of our prior expectations in studies of the Court that fail to take into account the selection bias in the Court's docket. If you believe that the Court does not need to fear elected branch retaliation, then you likely also believe that there is no reason for the justices (or litigants anticipating the justices' decisions) to take elected branch preferences into account at the certiorari stage. You would believe yourself to be on safe ground in assuming that the sample of cases heard by the Court is randomly generated, at least with respect to elected branch preferences.

But it turns out that our expectations may have misled us. The Court's judgments in cases involving constitutional challenges to federal statutes are not only a function of the justices' preferences. The subjectively coded judgment measure reported in the Supreme Court Database thus fails to accurately represent the Court's judgments, at least during periods of significant elected branch constraint on the Court. Likewise, during these same periods, the Court's docket fails to reflect a representative sample of cases. Our empirical analyses may thus have been doubly undermined by our prior belief in the Court's independence.

Some may object that our empirical analyses have focused too heavily on the Rehnquist Court. Perhaps there was something unusual about the Rehnquist Court. Perhaps the median justice on that Court, widely reputed (and estimated) to be Justice Sandra Day O'Connor, was particularly sensitive to the preferences of House majorities. It is true that the analyses in Chapter Five and Six included cases from the Warren and Burger Courts as well. But perhaps things have changed. The Rehnquist Court's successor, the Court led by Chief Justice John Roberts, is widely reputed to be a significantly more conservative Court. Perhaps the days of judicial deference to House majorities are over. Perhaps the justices on the Supreme Court no longer care what our elected representatives think. This is the question to which the next chapter turns.

8

MISREADING THE ROBERTS COURT

We have seen that the widespread belief in the Supreme Court's independence can give rise to very misleading expectations about its jurisprudence, particularly when the justices' preferences diverge from those of majorities in the House of Representatives. These expectations may appear to be confirmed in quantitative studies relying on the subjectively coded Supreme Court Database judgment measure, when in fact that measure may simply be reflecting only the self-confirming power of our own expectations. Close observers of the Court who find its judgments not to conform to their prior expectations, or to the picture painted by these quantitative studies, can understandably be quite confused.

We saw this series of events unfold over the course of the first eight terms of the Rehnquist Court. That Court had been widely expected to be significantly more conservative than its predecessor, the relatively moderate Burger Court. Quantitative analyses using the Supreme Court Database judgment measure appeared to confirm these expectations. But close observers of the Court during these first eight terms, the terms wherein it faced liberal Democratic Congresses, were instead struck by its apparent moderation.

We also know how this story ended. Just as observers had become accustomed to the Rehnquist Court's relative moderation, in its 1994 term it suddenly became the Court they had finally stopped expecting. Explanations for this abrupt change of heart were generally unsatisfying, and few linked the Court's about-face to the 1994 congressional elections. But as we saw in the analyses of Chapters Five, Six, and Seven, those elections, and the continued Republican dominance of the House through the 2004 term, were in fact associated with the dramatic changes in the second Rehnquist Court's jurisprudence.

History appears to have repeated itself. Professional commentators expected the Rehnquist Court's successor, the Court led by Chief Justice John Roberts, to move even further to the right. Quantitative characterizations of that Court using the subjectively coded Supreme Court Database measure seemed to confirm those expectations. But close observers of the Roberts Court were repeatedly struck by its apparent moderation in many important cases in its first four full terms, those occurring between 2006 and 2010. In searching for explanations for this moderation, those observers pointed neither to the congressional elections of 2006, which produced Democratic House majorities for the first time since 1994, nor to those of 2008, which extended those majorities. But perhaps they should have.

Although the numbers are small, analysis of the roll call–based measure of the Roberts Court's judgments in cases involving constitutional challenges to federal statutes during its first four full terms, all terms wherein it faced liberal House majorities, supports the impression of moderation. First, as in the case of the first Rehnquist Court when it faced an oppositional House, the Roberts Court heard few cases involving constitutional challenges to liberal federal statutes. In its first four full terms the Roberts Court heard only 42 percent of the number of constitutional challenges to liberal federal statutes heard by the second Rehnquist Court during its first four terms. Second, the Roberts Court was not aggressively conservative in its dispositions of the docketed challenges to these statutes. The Roberts Court during these terms struck only 40 percent of the number of liberal federal statutes struck by the second Rehnquist Court during its first four terms. These differences are nonrandom. By this objectively coded measure, the Roberts Court was not the ultra-conservative Court it had been expected to be. And the perhaps obvious explanation for its moderation was sitting across First Street in the U.S. Capitol building.

"A Walking Constitutional Amendment"

Justice Sandra Day O'Connor's resignation from the Court at the close of the 2004 term was a momentous occasion. Justice O'Connor was widely believed to have been the median justice on the Rehnquist Court, the justice whose vote could make—or break—a five-vote majority.[1] Her departure thus gave the Republican Party the opportunity to shift the Court's jurisprudence to the right.[2] As Democratic Senator Dianne Feinstein said, "This is the pivotal appointment. This is enormous."[3]

The *New York Times* predicted that Justice O'Connor's retirement would "trigger an enormous political collision."[4] Ralph G. Neas, president of the liberal group People for the American Way, said, "This is one of those moments in American history. No matter what side you're on, everything you've believed in, everything you've cared about, everything you've fought for is at stake. It's such a closely divided court."[5] Dr. James C. Dobson, founder and chairman of the conservative group Focus on the Family, agreed, observing, "Today marks a watershed moment in American history: the resignation of a swing-vote justice on the Supreme Court and the opportunity to change the court's direction."[6]

The death of Chief Justice Rehnquist on September 3, 2005, and the nomination and confirmation of his successor, D.C. Circuit Judge John G. Roberts, delayed the arrival of this "watershed moment." Judge Roberts, originally proposed for Justice O'Connor's seat, had clerked for Rehnquist and served in both the Reagan and George H. W. Bush Justice Departments. Although he was perceived to be a devoted conservative, his renomination for the Chief Justice's seat was also seen as "a swap [of] one reliable conservative for another."[7] Liberal interest groups, who had vociferously opposed Roberts for the O'Connor seat, remained united in their opposition but appeared to ratchet down the rhetoric.[8] Roberts was confirmed to the position of Chief Justice with a 78–22 vote and began his service on the Court on October 3, 2005.

The Bush administration then nominated Third Circuit Judge Samuel Alito Jr. for Justice O'Connor's seat after Harriet Miers failed to satisfy both senators and interest groups on the right.[9] Alito was widely perceived to be a significantly more conservative jurist than Justice O'Connor; a longtime colleague of his predicted, "Make no mistake: he will move the court to the right, and this confirmation process is really going to be a question about whether Congress and the country wants to move this court to the right."[10]

And so the rhetoric heated back up.[11] Emily's List characterized Judge Alito as "one of the most conservative jurists in the country" and predicted that *Roe v. Wade* was in danger.[12] Ralph Neas of People for the American Way warned of a "constitutional catastrophe" should Alito be confirmed: "He is a walking constitutional amendment who would undo precedents that protect fundamental rights and liberties that Americans think are theirs forever. The American people could wake up one morning and those liberties would no longer be there. It's that dramatic."[13] Senator Edward Kennedy predicted that an Alito confirmation would "fundamentally alter the balance of the court and push it dangerously to the right,"[14] while Senator John Kerry denounced the nomination as pandering to "the far right wing."[15] Even constitutional theorist Bruce Ackerman of Yale Law School said, "The confirmation of Samuel Alito carries a clear and present danger of a constitutional revolution on a very broad front, well beyond *Roe v. Wade*."[16]

The savviest Court watchers focused not so much on Judge Alito's likely impact on the Court, but rather on that of Justice Anthony Kennedy. Kennedy was perceived to be the next most conservative justice after O'Connor; with Alito's confirmation his would become the pivotal vote on the Court. And there was little doubt among the Court's observers that Kennedy was significantly more conservative than O'Connor. As Steven G. Calabresi of Northwestern University Law School said, "Kennedy is very much the median justice now, as Justice O'Connor was, and he is to her right."[17]

Alito's eventual confirmation with a 58–42 vote in the Senate on January 31, 2006, thus led to dire forecasts. Constitutional theorist Erwin Chemerinsky predicted a "decisive" change in the Court's jurisprudence.[18] Journalist Jan Crawford Greenburg asserted that "George W. Bush and his team of lawyers will be shaping the direction of American law and culture long after many of them are dead."[19] The *New York Times* predicted a conservative shift in the Court's jurisprudence that would last for "decades."[20] Some liberal intellectuals seemed to simply give up hope that the Roberts Court could be anything but an instrument for conservative ideas. Laurence H. Tribe of Harvard Law School said, "The idea that one can regroup and come back at the court is not realistic for the foreseeable future." Rather, says Tribe, liberals should shift their focus to "20, 30 or 40 years from now."[21]

Quantitative analyses of the Roberts Court's judgments using the subjectively coded Supreme Court Database measure appeared to confirm these expectations. These analyses reported a Court that was "the most conservative one in living memory," moving sharply to the right as a result of the replacement of O'Connor with Alito.[22] For example, in the Supreme Court Database fully 65 percent of the Court's decisions in its 2008 term were assigned conservative judgment codes, "the highest number in any year since at least 1953."[23]

But, as had been the case with the Rehnquist Court, the Supreme Court Database's characterization of the Roberts Court did not match the observations of many journalists and legal academics. During the first flush of expectations about the Court's likely move to the right, much of the initial commentary on the Roberts Court did point to evidence that seemed to support those expectations. Thus many focused, for example, on the Court's 2007 ruling that the issuance of a paycheck to an employee whose salary had been reduced by unlawful discrimination did not in itself constitute a discriminatory act, thereby precluding the employee from filing a discrimination complaint under federal statutory filing deadlines (*Ledbetter v. Goodyear Tire and Rubber Company*, 05-1074 [2007]). However, few noted that this case raised no constitutional questions, with the opinion turning rather on the Court's interpretation of Title VII of the Civil Rights Act of 1964. The Court's decision could therefore be overturned with new statutory language. And in fact this occurred in January 2009; the very first federal statute signed into law by President Barack Obama was the Lilly Ledbetter Fair Pay Act, restoring the state of the law to the status quo obtaining before *Ledbetter*.[24]

Others focused on the Chief Justice's opinion in *Parents Involved in Community Schools v. Seattle School District No. 1* (2007), invalidating school assignment plans in Seattle and Louisville on the grounds that they unconstitutionally sorted individual children by race. The Chief's opinion asserted, "The way to stop discrimination on the basis of race is to stop discriminating on the basis of race."[25] Many read this opinion as a

conservative manifesto precluding almost every racially based effort to re-
mediate prior discrimination.[26] But here few noted that the Chief's opinion was signed by only three other Justices. The fifth vote to strike the
school assignment plans at issue came from Justice Kennedy, who wrote
his own opinion concurring in the judgment. As the fifth and pivotal vote
to create a judgment majority, Kennedy's was the controlling opinion.[27]
And Justice Kennedy's opinion was considerably more sympathetic to
racially targeted efforts to remedy school segregation. He criticized the
majority opinion's "all-too-unyielding insistence that race cannot be a
factor in instances when, in my view, it may be taken into account," arguing that "avoiding racial isolation" and addressing "de facto resegrega-
tion in schooling" are "compelling interests" that a school district can
constitutionally pursue while taking race "into account."[28] Moreover, in
a surprising yet little-discussed move, Justice Kennedy, who had dissented
from the 2003 *Grutter v. Bollinger* decision permitting the use of race as a
factor in admissions at the University of Michigan Law School, went out
of his way to endorse that decision in *Parents Involved*.[29] After the decision, Charles J. Ogletree Jr. of Harvard Law School said, "The hidden
story in the decision today is that Justice Kennedy refused to follow the
lead of the other four justices in eviscerating the legacy of *Brown*."[30] The
general counsel for the Seattle Public Schools observed, "The heartening
thing is that a majority of the Supreme Court affirmed the principle of
diversity in public education."[31]

Still others pointed to the Court's decision in *Gonzales v. Carhart*
(2007), upholding the federal Partial-Birth Abortion Ban Act of 2003.
But again few drew attention to the fact that, despite the entreaties of
Justices Scalia and Thomas in their concurring opinion, Justice Kennedy's
majority opinion in *Carhart* affirmed the "fundamental right" to an
abortion extended in *Roe v. Wade* (1973), and reaffirmed in *Planned
Parenthood v. Casey* (1992), dealing abortion opponents a major disappointment. Some perhaps more expert observers saw *Carhart* as being
quite limited in impact. Dr. Isaac Schiff, chairman of the department of
obstetrics and gynecology at Massachusetts General Hospital in Boston,
noted, "This law by itself, if it were the only law passed, would be a non-
occurrence."[32] Even Justice Stevens, who had dissented from the decision, agreed with this assessment, noting in an interview, "The statute is

a *silly* statute. It's a *silly* statute. It's just a distressing exhibition by Congress, but what we decided isn't all that important."[33]

These early efforts by liberal observers to read the Roberts Court's decisions as heralding a new ultra-conservative jurisprudence came under pressure as time progressed. As observers saw more cases from the Roberts Court, they increasingly came to focus on what appeared to be that Court's moderation. During the Court's 2007 term, for example, its rulings in several employment discrimination cases produced a "five for five sweep for employees' rights in workplace discrimination cases that was little short of astonishing."[34] The Court then invalidated the Military Commissions Act of 2006 in a ruling characterized by the *New York Times* as "a stirring defense of habeas corpus" and "a major victory for civil liberties" (*Boumediene v. Bush* [2007]).[35] This was followed by a prohibition on the use of the death penalty for the crime of child rape (*Kennedy v. Louisiana* [2008]); the *Times* editorialized as a result that the Roberts Court "exemplified . . . decency and restraint," and that its decisions constituted "evidence of a new tone and direction from the court."[36] Linda Greenhouse was moved to write, "Something is happening, clearly. The question is what."[37]

At the close of the 2007 term the *Times* characterized the Court as one that "defied labeling," noting that, "the more liberal justices won their share of high-profile cases."[38] These instances of "undeniable good news" included the "critically important decision in favor of the detainees being held in Guantanamo Bay," a decision characterized as providing an "important defense of basic liberties"; the Court's "wise" decision prohibiting the death penalty for child rape; a ruling granting additional procedural rights to immigrants facing deportation; "several welcome rulings in favor of workers"; and "a number of favorable rulings for criminal defendants."[39] Linda Greenhouse opined, "The more muted and centrist tone of the term that just ended has made me less persuaded that the court is on a collision course with mainstream public opinion."[40]

In its 2008 term, the term characterized by the Supreme Court Database as the most conservative term since 1953, the Court neatly evaded what had been expected to be a major conservative ruling, surprising even those who were willing to describe the Court as "muted and centrist." The Congress in 2006 had enacted a twenty-five-year extension of the Voting Rights Act of 1965, including the preclearance provisions that were bitterly resented by many in the Southern states still subject to federal oversight under the Act. A suit was quickly brought challenging congressional authority to enact the extension under Section 5 of the Fourteenth Amendment (*Northwest Austin Municipal Utility District No. 1 v. Holder* [2009]).

Linda Greenhouse predicted that the Court's resolution of the case "promises to tell us more than almost any other about John G. Roberts Jr."[41] She noted that opponents of the extension "understood recent trends at the court to be working in their favor," and reminded readers of Roberts's strongly worded opinions in two earlier decisions involving governmental efforts to address racial inequities (although she failed to note that these opinions had not attracted majority support on the Court).[42] Adam Liptak wrote that the case was "widely considered the most important of the term."[43]

But the Court ducked the constitutional issue in *Northwest Austin*, suggesting that the statute's language enabled the sewer district bringing the constitutional challenge to evade its provisions; its disposition preserved the key provisions of the Voting Rights Act extension.[44] Debo P. Adegbile of the NAACP Legal Defense and Educational Fund observed, "This case was brought to tear the heart out of the Voting Rights Act, and today that effort failed."[45] The *Times* characterized the decision as "very good news," while its legal writers puzzled that "almost all of the signs in this case" had "suggested that the court was steeling itself to make a major pronouncement about the role of race in American democracy."[46] Linda Greenhouse characterized the Court's ruling as "surprising" and a "mystery."[47]

Liberals found many other decisions to like during the Court's 2008 term. There were rulings enabling consumers to sue cigarette manufacturers for fraud (a "welcome departure" and a "major and well-deserved setback" for tobacco companies),[48] protecting those who complained of sexual harassment at work ("a strong ruling . . . in favor of employees"),[49] preserving a broad reading of a federal statute prohibiting gun ownership by those convicted of domestic violence ("good sense on gun violence"),[50] refusing to find that federal regulatory actions preempted stricter state regulations ("a wise and surprising decision"),[51] prohibiting prosecutors from using an identity theft statute as a tool in immigration cases (the Court upheld "a guiding principle in American law"),[52] requiring elected judges to recuse themselves from cases involving major donors to their campaigns ("a crucial statement that judges and justices are not for sale"),[53] and invalidating a school's invasive search of a thirteen-year-old girl ("an important victory for students' rights").[54] Adam Liptak characterized the term as ending with "restraint."[55]

Likewise, during the Roberts Court's 2009 term it issued rulings striking a federal statute criminalizing the possession or distribution of materials depicting cruelty to animals (the Court "wisely declined to create another category of expression outside of the First Amendment's protection"),[56] preventing juveniles from being imprisoned for life without parole for crimes short of murder (a "welcome" and "particularly heartening" decision),[57] freeing claims of "disparate impact" employment discrimination from onerous filing deadlines (an "important victory" for workers),[58] subjecting the National Football League to federal antitrust statutes ("the public won"),[59] permitting the submission of a federal habeas corpus petition despite a missed statutory deadline ("in the highest legal tradition" and demonstrating "why society invests so much hope in the wisdom of judges"),[60] narrowing the ability of federal immigration authorities to seek the deportation of those convicted of minor drug offenses (expressing "that same spirit of understanding"),[61] failing to find Fifth Amendment "takings" violations in Florida's efforts to restore its public beaches ("a blow to the property rights movement"),[62] requiring a narrow reading of the federal criminal statute requiring the provision of "honest services" ("a favorite [statute] of prosecutors"),[63] and permitting the Hastings College of the Law to deny recognition to a Christian student group that barred from membership non-Christian and gay and lesbian students ("denying government support for intolerance").[64]

At the close of the 2009 term the Times praised these "many welcome decisions."[65] Thomas Goldstein of SCOTUSblog observed that the Chief Justice appeared to care about "the position of the court in American life. He is not pressing every ideological question but is willing to cross over."[66] But while this seemed like a reasonable characterization in 2010, it was certainly not what had been expected in 2005. What had happened to the early expectations for an ultra-conservative Roberts Court? What could have occurred to lead the *New York Times* to editorialize that the Roberts Court's decisions illustrated "why society invests so much hope in the wisdom of Judges"![67]

The Moderate Roberts Court, 2006–2009

As had happened with the Rehnquist Court, nobody thought to look to the results of congressional elections to find the source of the Roberts Court's surprising moderation. But just as the Roberts Court had begun its first full term, the Democrats had swept the 2006 midterm elections, winning majorities in both chambers. For the first time since the party's founding, Republicans had won no Democratic seats in either chamber, while the Democrats had won thirty seats from Republicans in the House (also picking up the Vermont Independent seat formerly held by Representative Bernie Sanders) and had taken six seats in the Senate. It had been the largest seat gain for House Democrats since the 1974 elections.

Although their importance was not acknowledged by professional Court watchers, the 2006 elections significantly changed the Roberts Court's situation. Instead of facing supportive Republican House majorities, the Roberts Court now faced potentially hostile Democratic House majorities. The justices' incentives would now have been to moderate their decisions, to cabin their preferences.

Just as in our analyses of the Rehnquist Court, we want to look at the Roberts Court's judgments without letting our expectations get in the way. In order to do this we need to use an objectively coded judgment measure that is free from confirmation bias. One such measure can be found in the Roberts Court's treatment of constitutional challenges to federal statutes, the same kinds of cases that we looked at in Chapters Five through Seven. These cases are few, but our objective measurements of the Court's judgments in them are of high quality.

One of the first things to note about these cases is how just how few of them there are. During its first four full terms (2006–2009), all terms wherein the Court faced Democratic House majorities, the Roberts Court heard only 57 percent of the number of constitutional challenges to federal statutes heard by the second Rehnquist Court during its first four terms facing Republican House majorities (1994–1997). Despite the small numbers involved, this difference is significant at conventional thresholds.[68] The congressionally constrained Roberts Court was significantly less likely to review constitutional challenges to federal statutes, relative to the largely unconstrained second Rehnquist Court.

Moreover, using the roll call–based measure of the direction in which a statute moves the status quo ex ante, the Roberts Court was even less likely to hear constitutional challenges to *liberal* federal statutes, relative to the post-1993 Rehnquist Court. During its first four full terms, the Roberts Court heard only 42 percent of the number of constitutional challenges to liberal federal statutes heard by the second Rehnquist Court during its first four terms. Again, this difference is significant at conventional thresholds.[69]

Recall from Chapter Seven that when preferences diverge, we expect the Court to take fewer cases that might arouse the attention of hostile House majorities. We found that when the conservative Rehnquist Court faced liberal House majorities between the 1987 and 1993 terms, it was significantly less likely to docket constitutional challenges to liberal statutes, relative to the terms wherein it faced friendly conservative House majorities. Had the Rehnquist Court been forced to docket more of these cases, we predicted that it largely would have upheld the challenged statutes. Avoiding the cases avoided those outcomes. Likewise, the conservative Roberts Court, during the terms that it faced Democratic House majorities, appeared to docket significantly fewer cases likely to arouse the anger of those majorities, relative to the congressionally unconstrained second Rehnquist Court. *Northwest Austin Municipal Utility District No. 1 v. Holder* (2009), wherein the Roberts Court dodged a constitutional challenge to the liberal extension to the Voting Rights Act, is emblematic of this pattern.

Finally, the Roberts Court in its first four full terms struck only 40 percent of the number of liberal federal statutes struck by the second Rehnquist Court in its first four terms after the 1994 congressional elections.[70] Again, the difference is significant at conventional thresholds. Moreover, most of the Roberts Court strikes came in cases involving different provisions of the same campaign finance statute. The one strike of a liberal federal statute not regulating campaign finance came in *U.S. v. Stevens* (2010), involving a 1999 statute that had criminalized the commercial use of depictions of animal cruelty.[71] The Court struck the statute on First Amendment grounds to little public outcry. Indeed, the 8–1 ruling (with Justice Alito in dissent) generated praise from many liberal media organizations, whose editorial boards lauded the justices' unwillingness to criminalize a new category of expression. The *New York Times*, for example, called the Court's decision "wise," "welcome," and "gratifying."[72]

The remaining cases wherein the Roberts Court struck liberal federal statutes during these terms all involved different provisions of the McCain-Feingold Bipartisan Campaign Reform Act of 2002 (BCRA).[73] In *Federal Election Commission v. Wisconsin Right To Life*, 06-969 (2007), the Court held that the statute's ban on corporate- and union-financed "issue" advertisements mentioning a candidate for federal office within a pre-election window could not apply to ads that had a "reasonable interpretation other than as an appeal to vote for or against a specific candidate."[74] In *Davis v. Federal Election Commission* (2008), the Court struck the "Millionaire's Amendment" of the BCRA, conferring special fundraising privileges on candidates whose opponents spent at least $350,000 of their own money on their campaigns. And in *Citizens United v. Federal Election Commission* (2010), the Court struck in their entirety the BCRA's prohibitions on corporate- and union-financed independent campaign ads during specified pre-election windows, extending its ruling in *Wisconsin Right to Life*.

The primary impact of the Roberts Court's constitutional limits on liberal Congresses during these four terms, then, came in the area of federal campaign finance legislation. What is interesting, and perhaps revealing, about this fact is that there is a considerable amount of disagreement even among liberals as to the policy impact of campaign finance statutes. Empirical research has found few effects of campaign spending on the choices made by either voters or legislators; one effect that has been documented is that campaign finance limits disproportionately hurt challengers.[75] Thus some liberal observers opined that the Court's judgments in these cases would have little impact, while others hailed these rulings as promoting electoral competition, arguing that ultimately voters would benefit from them.[76]

These few decisions limiting the powers of liberal Congresses to regulate campaign spending should be put in the context of the rulings of the second Rehnquist Court in its first four terms. In these terms that Court not only limited the congressional ability to regulate campaign finance (*Colorado Republican Federal Campaign Committee v. FEC*, 518 U.S. 604 [1996], striking provisions of the Federal Election Campaign Act of 1971, as amended in 1976, limiting political parties' "independent" campaign expenditures) but also restricted federal efforts to regulate guns (*U.S. v. Lopez*, 514 U.S. 549 [1995], striking provisions of the Gun-Free School Zones Act of 1990, as amended in 1994, criminalizing possession of a firearm within a defined radius of a school, and *Printz v. U.S.*, 521 U.S. 898 [1997], striking provisions of the Brady Handgun Violence Prevention Act of 1993, requiring local law enforcement officers to conduct background checks on prospective handgun purchasers); prevent governmental corruption (*U.S. v. National Treasury Employees Union*, 514 U.S. 527 [1995], striking provisions of the Ethics Reform Act of 1989, prohibiting the apparently widespread practice of interest group payment of "honoraria" to officers and employees of the federal government); regulate the cable industry (*Denver Area Education Telecommunications Consortium v. FCC*, 518 U.S. 727 [1996], striking provisions of the Cable Television Consumer Protection and Competition Act of 1992 regulating the broadcasting of "patently offensive" programming); require states to negotiate in good faith with Indian tribes (*Seminole Tribe of Florida v. Florida*, 517 U.S. 44 [1996], striking provisions of the Indian Gaming Regulatory Act of 1988, permitting tribes to sue states in federal court to compel good faith negotiations over the establishment of gaming operations); provide pension funds for miners (*Eastern Enterprises v. Apfel*, 524 U.S. 498 [1998], striking provisions of the Coal Industry Retiree Health Benefit Act of 1992, requiring coal operators to contribute to pension funds for their former employees); and tax commercial shippers (*U.S. v. U.S. Shoe*, 523 U.S. 360 [1998], striking a provision of the Internal Revenue Code, last amended in 1990, imposing a Harbor Maintenance Tax on commercial cargo shipped through one of the nation's ports). The scale and breadth of the second Rehnquist Court's attack on liberal federal statutes, even in just its first four terms, would appear to overshadow the Roberts Court's few campaign finance rulings.

Moreover, the Roberts Court's campaign finance rulings should also be set against its ruling in *Boumediene v. Bush* (2008). In *Boumediene* the Court struck the conservative Military Commissions Act of 2006, ruling that it was prohibited by the Constitution's directive that the writ of habeas corpus "shall not be suspended, unless when in Cases of Rebellion or Invasion the public Safety may require it."[77] The Roberts Court's ruling in *Boumediene* was nearly universally hailed by liberals as a momentous victory for civil liberties. Ronald Dworkin, for example, characterized the Court's decision in *Boumediene* as a "great victory" and a "landmark change in our constitutional practice," noting that "American law has never before recognized that aliens imprisoned by the United States abroad have [habeas corpus] rights."[78]

By way of comparison, the second Rehnquist Court also struck two provisions of conservative statutes during its first four full terms. In *U.S. v. IBM*, 517 U.S. 843 (1996), the Court struck a provision of the Internal Revenue Code, last amended in 1976, imposing a tax on premiums paid for insuring exports; in *Reno v. ACLU*, 521 U.S. 844 (1997), the Court struck provisions of the Communications Decency Act of 1996, regulating the communication of indecent or offensive messages to minors over the internet. But these rulings did not produce nearly as much liberal enthusiasm as did *Boumediene v. Bush* (2008).

The Immoderate Roberts Court, 2010–2012?

And so there is very little evidence that the Roberts Court, during the four terms that it faced liberal Democratic Congresses, was the conservative juggernaut that so many had feared in 2005. Instead, that Court was almost precisely the mirror image of the Rehnquist Court in its first four terms after the 1994 congressional elections. In both cases, two justices of similar ideological proclivities had just been appointed to the Court. Observers fully expected those justices to move the Court in a direction consistent with their own views. And yet, precisely the opposite phenomenon happened. In the case of the Rehnquist Court, the Court shifted dramatically rightward in the terms immediately following the 1994 congressional elections. In the case of the Roberts Court, the

Court appears to have moderated leftward in the terms immediately following the 2006 congressional elections.

But the Court's political context changed again in the 2010 congressional elections, with the Republican Party regaining a majority in the House of Representatives; this majority was retained in the 2012 elections. Our experience with the Rehnquist Court suggests that the Roberts Court's relative moderation between its 2006 and 2009 terms may have been a product of the liberal House majorities sitting between the 2006 and 2010 elections. We may now see a considerably less moderate Roberts Court. While as of this writing it is still too early to systematically assess the post-2010 Roberts Court, there are indeed signs of immoderation. As noted in the Preface, in *National Federation of Independent Business v. Sebelius* (2012) the Roberts Court struck a federal statute on Spending Clause grounds for the first time in seventy-five years. Not since the early days of the New Deal, during the terms dominated by the conservative Four Horsemen, had the Court struck a federal statute on Spending Clause grounds.[79] Its ruling not only endangered the expansion of Medicaid that had anchored the Affordable Care Act, but it also significantly handicapped the ability of the federal government to initiate or expand federally funded programs providing other valued public goods. It remains to be seen whether, under the condition of continued Republican domination of the House of Representatives, the Roberts Court will continue its more aggressively conservative jurisprudence.

9

WHAT'S SO GREAT ABOUT INDEPENDENT COURTS, ANYWAY?

It is widely believed that the Supreme Court of the United States decides constitutional cases independently of elected branch preferences. If the evidence reported here survives further scrutiny, this belief is not correct. At least in its constitutional rulings on federal statutes, the Court is extraordinarily deferential to the preferences of majorities in the House of Representatives. By implication, given the position of the Supreme Court at the top of the appellate hierarchy, the same may very well be true of federal courts in the United States more generally.

This empirical finding leaves us with a question. Are we better or worse off because of the Court's apparent deference to House majorities? The fact that our Constitution creates incentives for this deference does not necessarily imply that it produces better outcomes. In fact, given the conventional belief that independent courts are superior to deferential courts, particularly in the protection of individual rights and liberties, many may be quite troubled by the finding of the Court's deference.

But perhaps they should not be. Perhaps we are in fact better off with federal courts that defer to the majoritarian House of Representatives. After all, we know that we are better off when our political leaders are compelled to defer to electoral majorities. Our economies grow more, our armies go to war less, we achieve higher levels of literacy and health, and we have more protections for individual rights and liberties.[1] Perhaps we are similarly better off when our judges are also compelled to defer to elected majorities.

Indeed, looking only at the findings reported in Chapters Five through Seven, there is little evidence to suggest that rights and liberties would have been more protected had the Court been more independent of House majorities. During many of the terms between 1953 and 2004, the preferences of majorities on the Court were not sufficiently different from those of majorities in the House to indicate that the Court would have decided cases much differently had it been more independent of House majorities. During the Warren and early Burger Courts, for example, majorities on both the House and the Court generally favored extending rights protections in a variety of areas. While before the 1974 midterm elections Democratic majorities in the House were perhaps slightly less committed to this project than were those on the Court, they were nonetheless sufficiently supportive of the Court's efforts during this period that, even after factoring in the effects of House preferences, the Court was still predicted to endorse landmark federal civil rights statutes. In other words, a more independent Court likely would not have ruled much differently during these terms than the Court we actually observed.

Likewise, after the 1994 elections, the preferences of majorities on the Court and in the House were sufficiently similar that the Court's rulings between its 1994 and 2004 terms were virtually indistinguishable from the rulings it likely would have issued, had it been independent of the preferences of House majorities. Those Republican House majorities were not generally disposed to continue the project of extending federal rights guarantees. But then neither was the majority on the second Rehnquist Court. Again, a more independent Court likely would have looked very similar to the deferential Court we actually observed during these terms.

When the preferences of majorities on the Court and in the House did diverge significantly, the direction of this divergence was not that predicted by the conventional story. During the 1970s and 1980s, majorities on the Court grew increasingly conservative, and thereby less committed to the protection and extension of the civil rights and liberties guaranteed by the landmark federal statutes of the 1960s and their later extensions. But, at least until the 1994 elections, liberal Democrats continued to maintain majorities in the House of Representatives. The findings reported in Chapter Five through Seven suggest that these liberal majorities restrained the increasingly conservative Court from striking liberal federal statutes, including the landmark civil rights statutes of the 1960s and their later extensions. During this period, in other words, civil rights and liberties likely would have been *less* protected, had the Court been more independent of House majorities.

What we see very little of, at least during the period observed here, are instances of a Court committed to the protection and extension of civil rights and liberties, but restrained from doing so by majorities in the House of Representatives. Only under this scenario would increasing the Court's independence from the elected branches plausibly lead to greater protections for economic and political rights. But, at least in these data and over this period, we don't see this scenario. Instead, we see a Court that, had it been free to decide cases independently of the preferences of House majorities, mostly likely either would have endorsed the actions of those majorities, or would have reversed those actions in the direction of fewer rights protections. On net, at least in the data analyzed here, we most likely would have had fewer protections for civil rights and liberties, had the Supreme Court been more independent between 1953 and 2004.

But perhaps the data analyzed here are simply too limited to speak to the question of the merits of more independent courts. After all, several cross-national empirical studies report that more independent courts are in fact associated with increased protections for civil rights and liberties.[2] Perhaps these findings suggest that, despite the evidence reported here, we would see even more extensive protections for civil rights and liberties in the United States, were our federal judges more independent of elected majorities.

Upon closer examination, however, there are important limitations to the existing cross-national studies of judicial independence. And when we address these limitations, initial results appear to support the findings reported in Chapters Five through Seven. At least in democratic countries like the United States, more independent courts seem to actually reduce protections for individual rights and liberties. We would likely be worse off with more independent federal courts. We could perhaps even be better off were we to prohibit those courts from exercising judicial review altogether.

Measuring Judicial Independence

One critical limitation of existing quantitative analyses of judicial independence concerns measurement. Many measures of judicial independence have been based on purely subjective assessments.[3] As we saw in Chapter Five, subjective assessments may be inappropriately influenced by coders' expectations. For example, believing that more independent courts lead to high levels of rights protections, and observing high levels of rights protections in a particular country, a coder may inadvertently give that country's courts a higher score on a subjective measure of judicial independence than might otherwise have been the case. By contrast, objective measures of judicial independence code the constitutional provisions that regulate the institutional relationships between courts and policymaking branches. However, most of these objective measures combine multiple constitutional features that may or may not actually condition courts' independence.[4]

Economists studying the effects of legal institutions have measured judicial independence more simply by coding the tenure of the judges on a country's highest courts.[5] Longer tenures are thought to lead to greater independence, and hence to higher levels of rights protections. Common law countries inheriting their legal institutions from the United Kingdom are particularly singled out as guaranteeing long-tenured and thus independent courts.[6] In this narrative the 1701 Act of Settlement that we saw in Chapter Two plays an important role; the Act is said to have granted British judges "independence from Parliament," ensuring that the principle of judicial independence from majoritarian legislatures would then be transplanted into Britain's colonies.[7] On the tenure-based measure all common law constitutions are coded as ensuring lifelong judicial tenure, and thus as providing the highest level of judicial independence. The greater protections for economic and political rights observed in common law countries are then said to be at least in part a function of these high levels of judicial independence.[8]

This tenure-based measure has the virtue of objectively coding isolated constitutional provisions affecting judicial independence. However, as we saw in Chapters Five through Seven, the length of tenure alone may be insufficient to measure a court's independence from policymaking branches. Many judges with nominal "life" tenure are still dependent upon those branches for their survival in office. For example, the tenure-based measure codes Supreme Court justices under the common law U.S. Constitution as having life tenure, and thus as enjoying the highest level of judicial independence. But as we saw in Chapter Two, the justices do not in fact have "life" tenure. Their continued tenures in office, like many other aspects of their positions, are conditional on the continuing support of majorities in the House of Representatives. As reported in Chapters Five, Six, and Seven, this conditionality appears to be effective at incentivizing the justices' deference to the preferences of House majorities.

Many other common law constitutions that permit nominally long judicial tenures, and that are coded as guaranteeing the highest level of judicial independence on the tenure-based measure, likewise allow policy-making branches to remove judges from office for only vaguely defined offenses. For example, while these tenure-based studies cite the 1701 Act of Settlement as having ensured that British judicial tenure would no longer be dependent on the pleasure of the king, we saw in Chapter Two that this Act also secured the dependence of judicial tenure on the pleasure of the Parliament, codifying the parliamentary right to remove judges via either impeachment proceedings or "upon the Address of both Houses of Parliament" (legislative address).[9] Under the constitutions of Australia and Ireland, judges on the highest courts may likewise be removed for "misbehaviour" by majority votes in both legislative chambers.[10] Most other common law constitutions have incorporated provisions for judicial impeachment or removal by legislative address; presumably we might expect judicial deference under these constitutions as well.[11]

Some constitutions also prohibit long-tenured judges from striking, altering, or in any way changing the policies issued by the legislative and executive branches. Regardless of the length of judicial tenure in these countries, we would not expect their courts to be able to significantly change levels of rights protections. In the United Kingdom, for example, a country coded on the tenure-based measure as having the highest level of judicial independence, and cited in the studies using this measure as the exemplar of a country wherein independent courts have restrained predatory legislative majorities, courts are in fact explicitly prohibited from voiding parliamentary enactments on the grounds that they violate economic or political rights.[12] As a recent illustration, the UK's Human Rights Act of 1998 directs that a declaration of a statutory provision's incompatibility with a specified right "does not affect the validity, continuing operation, or enforcement of the provision . . . and is not binding on the parties to the proceedings in which it is made."[13] This prohibition on judicial review has also been adopted in several of the common law countries also coded on the tenure-based measure as granting to their courts the highest level of independence from the policymaking branches.[14] But the prohibition on judicial review in these countries renders their judges' tenures somewhat beside the point.

More generally, incorporating information about both judicial removal and judicial review into the tenure-based measure of judicial independence should improve our ability to accurately measure that concept. Using this information, we can group the constitutions used in the tenure-based studies into three roughly drawn categories.[15] Some constitutions do not permit courts to review the actions of the policymaking branches, or to engage in judicial review. We should expect the smallest effect of courts on rights protections in these countries, irregardless of the provisions for judicial tenure and judicial removal made in their constitutions.[16]

Some constitutions empower courts to check the policymaking branches, but through a wide variety of mechanisms render the judges on these courts at least partially dependent on those branches for their survival in office. For example, some of these constitutions do not specify judicial tenure and/or removal procedures, leaving both to the discretion of the policymaking branches. Others provide for relatively short judicial tenures, lying between 4 and 10 years; under several of these constitutions judicial terms are renewable at legislative or executive discretion. Finally, some of these constitutions, like that of the United States, permit judges to continue to serve as long as they satisfy some vaguely defined standard of conduct, with the power to define that standard of conduct more precisely given to the policymaking branches. All these constitutions arguably provide an intermediate judicial check on policymaking; courts operating under these constitutions should have a greater effect on rights provisions, relative to the first category of constitutions.[17]

Finally, some constitutions fully protect judges from the policymaking branches. Under these constitutions judges are guaranteed life tenure, and may be removed under extraordinary circumstances only by other life-tenured judges.[18] We would expect the greatest effect of courts on rights in these countries, relative to countries in the first two categories.

The Conditional Benefits of Judicial Independence

Another difficulty for crossnational empirical studies of judicial independence has been explaining precisely why we should expect more independent courts to increase rights protections, rather than to decrease those protections (or to have no effect at all). As we saw in Chapter One, few have given this explanation much sustained consideration. Instead, it is generally simply assumed that judges prefer greater protections for economic and political rights, relative to their counterparts in the policymaking branches, and that more independence from those branches allows them to act on their sincere preferences. But why we should expect judges to prefer greater rights protections in the first place, relative to executives and legislators, is generally left unexplored.

Recently a group of development economists have suggested that the beneficial effects of independent judges may be a function of their relatively greater insulation from the pressures that induce legislators and executives to predate economic and political rights. Because of their uncertain tenures, legislators and executives face incentives to give preferential treatment to their supporters and to silence their opponents. Expropriating the private property of their opponents and redistributing it to their supporters may prolong these leaders' tenures in office, as may suppressing both individual dissent and collective protest. But judges whose tenures are relatively more secure presumably face these incentives to a lesser degree. More certain tenures should lessen the perceived need to take actions such as these, actions that generally have the effect of undermining economic and political rights, to prolong a hold on public office. As a result, we should observe that judges generally appear to prefer greater protections for rights, relative to their counterparts in the policymaking branches.[19]

Importantly, this causal story does not assume that judges sincerely prefer more robust rights protections, relative to legislators and executives.[20] Legislators, executives, and judges within any given country are all assumed to have sincere preferences over rights protections drawn from the same country-specific distribution. The parameters of this distribution may be affected by factors such a country's level of socioeconomic development and/or its degree of ethnic conflict. But within any single country, the mechanisms by which some individuals are selected to be legislators, others to be executives, and still others to be judges, are not thought to produce systematic differences in sincere rights preferences by office.[21] On average, controlling for country-specific characteristics, there is then no reason to expect sincere judicial rights preferences to be any different from sincere legislative and/or executive rights preferences.

But the institutional rules governing these officials' survival in office are thought to induce significant office-specific differences in *revealed* rights preferences. Legislators and executives, whose tenures in office are dependent upon cultivating supporters and undermining opponents, are incentivized to choose lower levels of rights protections, regardless of their sincere preferences. Judges whose tenures in office are in turn dependent upon retaining the support of legislators and/or executives will likewise be induced to endorse these rights choices, again regardless of their sincere preferences. But independent judges with guaranteed tenures will be insulated from the need to cultivate support, and will therefore be relatively freer to decide cases on the basis of their sincere preferences. On average, controlling for country-specific characteristics, they should choose higher levels of rights protections, relative to those chosen by survival-constrained legislators and executives.

This story has the virtue of not requiring that judges inexplicably have sincere preferences for greater rights protections, relative to their counterparts in the policymaking branches. The causal story focuses our attention instead on the revealed rights preferences of legislators and executives. It is really the effect of uncertain tenures on the rights choices of legislators and executives that produces a predicted effect of more independent courts. The uncertain tenures of policymakers shift their revealed preferences away from their sincere preferences, in the direction of choosing to protect fewer rights. Judges with certain tenures are simply freer to decide cases on the basis of their sincere preferences. Relative to the revealed preferences of executives and legislators for fewer rights protections, judicial sincere preferences should be in the direction of more rights protections.

But surprisingly, those who tell this causal story do not distinguish between the threats to rights posed by policymakers operating under more or less democratic political institutions. Both nondemocratic and democratic policymakers are thought to equally endanger economic and political rights. For example, independent courts are said to protect rights by resisting policies enacted by and benefiting "democratic majorities," thereby preventing the "tyranny of the majority."[22] Supposedly independent courts in the English common law countries are said to have protected rights, and spurred economic development, largely by defying legislative majorities.[23] Apparently reflecting this assumption that more majoritarian political leaders are as dangerous to individual rights as their less majoritarian counterparts, empirical studies testing this argument do not control for policymaking institutions in their empirical analyses, nor do they permit the effects of independent courts on rights to vary across different policymaking institutions.[24]

Yet rights are not equally threatened by political leaders in North Korea and by those in the United Kingdom. More generally, legislators and executives face varying incentives to predate individual rights. Political leaders in nondemocratic countries generally need to retain the support of only a small number of powerful elites in order to secure their hold on office. In these countries, the uncertain tenures of legislators and executives most likely have the effect predicted by the economists' model: these nondemocratic political leaders can most efficiently extend their tenures in office by showering their cronies with private goods not available to those outside their inner circles, while expropriating the property and suppressing the speech and assembly rights of the latter. Regardless of their sincere rights preferences, these nondemocratic leaders face powerful incentives to predate the rights of the vast majority of their countries' citizens in order to prolong their uncertain tenures in office.[25]

But under more democratic constitutions, political leaders must secure larger numbers of supporters in order to stay in office. Rewarding those supporters with private goods becomes increasingly expensive, relative to public goods, as the required number of supporters increases. Eventually a democratic leader will likely trade off private goods for public goods as the most efficient means to attract and maintain supporters. Policies that protect economic and political rights are among the public goods that democratic leaders may seek to provide to maintain the support of large numbers of backers. That is, the widespread expropriation of private property and suppression of dissent are not likely to attract large numbers of supporters in national elections. Policies that instead provide for the security of private property as well as the protection of speech and assembly rights are likely to be considerably more popular. Regardless of their sincere rights preferences, then, democratic leaders may face powerful incentives to protect the economic and political rights of at least majorities of their countries' citizens.[26]

There is in fact considerable empirical evidence that more democratic legislators and executives are significantly more protective of rights than their less democratic counterparts. Moving from the least to the most majoritarian policymaking institutions increases civil liberties by approximately 4 points and political rights by approximately 5.5 points on the 7-point Freedom House scales.[27] As political scientist Bruce Bueno de Mesquita and his colleagues have written, "Whatever else is found in the basket of public goods provided by government, the benefits of civil liberties [and] political rights . . . seem to be of universal desirability among residents of a state."[28] At a minimum our analyses of the effects of judicial independence on rights need to control for the evident effects of policymaking institutions. If more independent courts are typically found in countries with more democratic policymaking institutions, then the increases in rights protections associated with those courts may simply be a spurious finding.

But the logic of the argument linking more independent courts to increased rights protections also implies that the effects of such courts will vary as a function of a country's policymaking institutions. For the subset of countries with the least democratic policymaking institutions, the story told by the economists should be correct. Controlling for country-specific characteristics, judges' sincere rights preferences should not differ significantly from those of legislators and/or executives. Nondemocratic policymaking institutions should incentivize policymakers to predate rights more extensively than they might otherwise prefer. Independent courts should insulate judges from these incentives, allowing them to more frequently decide cases on the basis of their sincere rights preferences. On average independent judges in these countries should choose more rights protections, relative to survival-constrained executives and legislators.

But the logic of this argument should actually work in the opposite direction under more democratic constitutions. Democratic policymaking institutions should incentivize policymakers to protect rights more extensively than they might otherwise prefer. Independent courts should then insulate judges from these incentives, allowing them to more frequently decide cases on the basis of their sincere rights preferences. On average independent judges in these countries should then choose *fewer* rights protections, relative to survival-constrained executives and legislators.

Thomas Jefferson actually made precisely this prediction in 1816. Reflecting on the widespread adoption of good behavior tenure in the state and federal constitutions after independence, Jefferson wrote that protecting judicial tenure probably leads to beneficial outcomes under nondemocratic constitutions. But those same protections for judicial tenure likely have the opposite effect under democratic constitutions: "Where judges were named and removable at the will of an hereditary executive, from which branch most misrule was feared, and has flowed, it was a great point gained, by fixing them for life, to make them independent of that executive. But in a government founded on the public will, this principle operates in an opposite direction, and against that will."[29] Jefferson thus suggested that the colonists had been mistaken to maintain their support for good behavior judicial tenure after the break with Great Britain. The time was ripe, he argued, to eliminate good behavior judicial tenure in favor of the popular election of judges, or, at the very least, to make those judges "removable on a concurrence of the executive and legislative branches."[30] Jefferson wrote, "I am not among those who fear the people. They . . . are our dependence for continued freedom."[31]

Perhaps Jefferson was right, and the effects of more independent courts are conditional on the nature of a country's policymaking institutions. Certainly it is not hard to find examples of positive effects from more independent courts in less democratic countries. The experience of Ghana in the mid-1990s may illustrate these positive effects. In 1992 Ghana's military dictator, Flight Lieutenant Jerry Rawlings, won the Ghanaian presidency in the first elections held since his 1981 coup; his party also won virtually every seat in the parliamentary elections held later that year after a boycott by opposition parties. Rawlings's victory was not generally viewed by international observers as the result of a free and fair electoral process; there were widespread reports that fear of violence had suppressed an effective opposition.[32] As a result, for several years after 1992 Ghana continued to receive only a 1 on the 10-point Polity IV democracy scale (with 10 being the most democratic regime).[33]

Rawlings's military regime had been marked by widespread reports of human rights abuses, and the post-1992 Rawlings administration continued to predate the rights of Ghanaian citizens.[34] This administration denied its political opponents access to the state-controlled Ghana Broadcasting Corporation,[35] prevented those opponents from holding public protests over the government's proposed policies,[36] required that December 31st, the anniversary of Rawlings's 1981 coup, be celebrated as a public holiday,[37] required all political organizations to register with the government,[38] monopolized appointments to state-controlled media organizations despite constitutional provisions requiring parliamentary participation,[39] and immunized itself from any legal challenges arising from its disposition of previously expropriated properties.[40]

But the 1992 Ghanaian Constitution had also instituted a partially independent Supreme Court. Justices on this court, appointed by the president with the approval of the Ghanaian Parliament, served until the age of 70, and could be removed only for "misbehavior or incompetence or on ground of inability to perform the functions of his office."[41] Associate justices could be removed only by a committee of judges appointed jointly by an independent Judicial Council and the Chief Justice; the Chief Justice could be removed by a presidentially appointed tribunal.[42] This partially independent court struck on constitutional grounds each of the Rawlings administration's policies noted in the prior paragraph.[43]

Perhaps at least in part as a result of the Supreme Court's decisions, Ghanaian civil liberties in the mid-1990s were considerably more protected than we might have predicted from the country's low Polity IV democracy score. Using the dataset compiled by economist Rafael La Porta and his colleagues, which measures rights levels as of 1995, countries receiving a 0 or 1 Polity IV democracy score in 1995 averaged 6.2 on the 7-point Freedom House civil liberties scale in 1995 (with 7 being the lowest level of civil liberties). Ghana received a 4 on this scale, the highest score received by any of these countries.

The absence of effective electoral competition after 1992 appears to have given Ghana's former military dictator and his deputies few incentives to satisfy popular demands for political and economic rights.

Extending stronger guarantees for the freedoms of speech and assembly, and greater protections for property rights, would only have empowered the Rawlings administration's potential opponents. Even if many offi cials in this administration sincerely preferred greater rights protections, they faced compelling incentives to continue to predate rights in order to maintain their public offices. But the justices on the Ghanaian Supreme Court faced few such incentives. They would likely survive in office even were Rawlings to lose power. As a result they were perhaps freer to ex press their sincere preferences for greater rights protections.

The example of Turkey during approximately the same time period, however, may illustrate the very different effects of an independent court in a country with relatively democratic policymaking institutions. Follow ing a military coup in 1980, democratic elections were restored to Turkey in the post-coup constitution of 1982. By 1989 Turkey was receiving a 9 on the Polity IV democracy scale, indicating the presence of generally open and competitive elections.[44]

The post-1982 democratic governments took several steps to restore rights lost under the previous military regime. For example, the military government had implemented a ban on the female headscarf on university campuses. Numerous female students who wore the headscarf in this pre dominantly Muslim country were expelled, while several of their counter parts on the faculty and staff saw their positions terminated.[45] The ban was widely criticized by human rights groups; Human Rights Watch declared that, "this restriction of dress, which applies only to women, is discrimina tory and violates their right to education, freedom of thought, conscience, religion, and privacy."[46] On three occasions between 1988 and 2008 the Turkish Parliament sought to lift the headscarf ban using both statutory and constitutional means; the 2008 constitutional amendments were sup ported by approximately 80 percent of the members of Parliament.[47]

The prior Turkish military regime had also implemented a policy pro tecting military personnel from trial by civilian courts, requiring that cur rent and former military personnel be tried for all charges only in military courts. This policy was widely believed to protect military leaders from prosecution by civilian authorities, undermining the rule of law.[48] In 2009 the Turkish Parliament enacted legislation reversing this policy, allowing military personnel to be tried in civilian courts.[49]

However, the post-coup 1982 constitution had also institutionalized strict independence for the Turkish Constitutional Court. A judge appointed to this court served until the age of 65 (for a maximum possible 25-year term) and could only be removed from the bench either automatically, upon conviction for a serious criminal offense, or "by a decision of an absolute majority of the total number of members of the Constitutional Court if it is definitely established that he is unable to perform his duties on account of ill-health."[50] In other words, judges on the Turkish Constitutional Court could not be removed under any circumstances by the democratic elected branches.

While electoral competition apparently incentivized Turkey's elected officials to extend more protections for individual rights after 1982, judges on the Turkish Constitutional Court were insulated from these incentives. After each occasion on which the Turkish Parliament sought to lift the headscarf ban on university campuses, for example, the Constitutional Court overturned the Parliament's actions.[51] The last of these decisions was characterized by Human Rights Watch as "a blow to freedom of religion and other fundamental rights."[52] Likewise, in 2010 the Constitutional Court struck the statute permitting military personnel to be tried in civilian courts; the decision was widely criticized in both the domestic and international press.[53] Finally, the Court actively interfered in Turkey's electoral politics, banning 18 political parties between 1983 and 2008 on the grounds that these parties' platforms were inconsistent with the values embodied by the Turkish Constitution. These actions drew criticism from many sources, including from the European Commission.[54]

Perhaps not unrelatedly, Turkish civil liberties in the mid-1990s were considerably less protected than we might have predicted on the basis of the country's high Polity democracy score. In the La Porta data, the average 1995 Freedom House civil liberties score for those countries receiving a 1995 Polity democracy score of 9 or 10 is 1.9 on a 7-point scale. Turkey's 1995 Freedom House civil liberties score is 5, the lowest in the group (and the only 5 in the group). Likewise, the average human rights score for these same countries on the scale developed by Charles Humana is 86.3; the scale ranges from 0 to 99, with 99 being the highest level of rights protections.[55] Turkey's Humana score is 44, again the lowest in the group by far.

In post-1982 Turkey, effective electoral competition appears to have given legislators and presidents strong incentives to satisfy popular demands for increased rights protections. Even if many Turkish elected officials sincerely preferred fewer rights protections, they faced compelling incentives to extend popular rights in order to maintain voter support. But the justices on the Turkish Constitutional Court faced no such incentives. They would survive in office even if current incumbents were to lose elections. As a result they were perhaps freer to express their sincere preferences for relatively fewer rights protections.

We can make reasonably clear predictions about the effects of independent courts in countries whose institutions provide compelling incentives for policymakers either to extensively suppress or to extensively promote rights. Among those countries whose policymaking institutions are located between these two extremes, it is less clear what to expect from more independent courts. Uncertainly tenured policymakers in these countries face incentives to provide some rights protections, and some preferential treatment to political cronies; their survival incentives do not clearly pull their rights choices in one direction, relative to their sincere rights preferences. More independent judges in these countries will be freer to decide cases on the basis of their sincere rights preferences, but their decisions may either increase or decrease rights protections, relative to the decisions of the policymaking branches. We would not then predict any consistent effect from more independent courts in this intermediate category of policymaking institutions.

In sum, because existing empirical analyses fail to condition their estimates of the effects of judicial independence on the nature of a country's policymaking institutions, they may have reported misleading results. The analyses to follow instead permit the effects of judicial independence to vary as a function of those policymaking institutions.

Reestimating the Effects of Independent Courts

We will then do two things differently when we look at the effects of more independent courts, relative to the existing empirical work. First, we will use an alternative measure of judicial independence, incorporating constitutional provisions permitting the policymaking branches to remove judges from office, and prohibiting courts from exercising judicial review, into the tenure-based measure of judicial independence.[56] Second, we will allow the effects of more independent courts to vary as a function of a country's policymaking institutions. The direction of the effects of more independent courts on economic and political rights protections may be very different, depending on whether rights are more or less protected ex ante.

We will look at the effects of our measure of judicial independence on five different measures of civil and economic rights. Civil rights are measured using the 100-point scale reported by Charles Humana; the Humana index is increasing in the protection of civil rights, as defined by 37 criteria derived from the rights enumerated in three U.N. treaties: the 1948 Universal Declaration of Human Rights, the International Covenant on Civil and Political Rights, and the International Covenant on Economic, Social, and Cultural Rights. Civil liberties are measured using the 7-point Freedom House measure of civil liberties, which is inverted so that it also is increasing in greater protections for civil liberties. Property rights are measured using a subjectively coded 5-point index of property rights; increases in this index indicate stronger guarantees for property rights.[57] The security of private property from governmental expropriation is also measured using the share of the assets of the top ten banks in a given country that are owned by the government of that country in 1995. Increases in this measure indicate weaker property rights and higher likelihoods of governmental expropriation.[58] Finally, economic rights are also measured using the number of governmentally required procedures that a new firm must complete in order to begin legal operations. Increases in the number of mandated startup procedures indicate weaker guarantees for economic freedoms and more opportunities for governmental extraction of rents.[59]

We will allow the effects of the alternative measure of judicial independence to vary as a function of the nature of a country's policymaking institutions, which are grouped into three categories based on their openness to democratic influence.[60] Finally, we will control for a country's level of economic development, average value of ethnolinguistic fractionalization, and absolute latitude. Higher levels of economic development, lower levels of ethnolinguistic heterogeneity, and greater distances from the equator could be associated with greater protections for individual rights.[61] These country-specific factors may affect the parameters of the distributions from which judicial, legislative, and executive rights preferences are drawn.

Table 9.1 reports the results of ordinary least squares regressions on the measures of economic and political rights as a function of policy-making institutions, judicial independence, and country-specific controls. These results first illuminate the ex ante distribution of rights as a function of policymaking institutions, prior to any judicial intervention. We can identify this distribution using the coefficient on *Majoritarian Policy-making Institutions*, which reports the effects of democratizing policymaking institutions among those countries that prohibit courts from exercising judicial review. For four out of the five rights measures these effects are substantively large, in the predicted direction, and significant at conventional thresholds. Among the countries that prohibit judicial review, moving from the least to the most democratic policymaking institutions increases civil rights on the 100-point Humana index by approximately 68 points, increases civil liberties on the 7-point Freedom House index by more than 5 points, increases property rights on the 5-point Holmes et al. index by approximately 1.5 points, and reduces the share of governmentally owned banking assets by approximately 57 percentage points. The same institutional reform is also predicted to reduce mandated startup procedures by 1 procedure, although this effect is not significant at conventional thresholds.

These effects, which are consistent with those reported elsewhere, indicate that policymakers in fact face very different incentives to protect economic and political rights, as a function of the rules governing their survival in office. Those policymakers dependent for their survival in office on only small numbers of powerful elites generally predate rights; those who must seek the support of large numbers of citizens in order to stay in office generally protect rights.

This variation in the ex ante protection of rights by the policymaking branches, prior to any judicial intervention, implies that we should then expect the effects of more independent courts to be conditional on this variation. Where policymakers are induced to depart from their sincere preferences by predating rights, we should expect judges free from these

Table 9.1: **Estimating Levels of Rights Protections**

	Humana Human Rights Index	Freedom House Civil Liberties Index, 1995	Property Rights Index	Government-Owned Bank Assets	Startup Procedures
Judicial Independence	15.01*** (5.68)	1.14*** (0.37)	1.32*** (0.471)	−0.24** (0.12)	−0.78 (0.98)
Majoritarian Policymaking Institutions (MPI)	34.04*** (3.00)	2.59*** (0.22)	0.72** (0.34)	−0.28*** (0.08)	−.50 (1.62)
Judicial Independence * MPI	−13.38*** (3.11)	−0.96*** (0.23)	−0.80*** (0.29)	0.25*** (0.08)	1.65* (0.90)
Log GDP pc	1.07 (1.30)	0.14 (0.10)	0.59*** (0.08)	−0.12*** (0.03)	−1.81** (0.77)
ELF	−4.64 (5.70)	0.27 (0.54)	0.97** (0.46)	−0.30** (0.15)	−7.95*** (1.98)
Latitude	−1.47 (10.49)	1.04 (0.82)	0.02 (0.57)	0.53** (0.22)	−5.72* (3.22)***
N	63	69	66	60	54
R^2	0.83	0.85	0.75	0.44	0.45

Note: Ordinary least squares regression; robust standard errors reported. Intercept term not reported. Estimates significantly different from zero at *p<.10; **p<.05; ***p<.01 (two-tailed).

pressures to be less likely to choose rights predation. Where policymakers are induced to depart from their sincere preferences by protecting rights, we should expect judges free from these pressures to be less likely to choose rights protections. Where policymakers are not clearly impelled to choose either greater or lesser rights predation, relative to their sincere preferences, we do not expect more independent judges to have any consistent effects on rights outcomes.

The effects of the alternative measure of judicial independence are reported as conditional coefficients in the first column of Table 9.2; they are largely consistent with these expectations.[62] On four out of five rights measures more independent courts increase rights protections among the countries with the least democratic policymaking institutions. On only one measure do more independent courts have any effect on rights among the countries with moderately democratic policymaking institutions. And on all five measures, more independent courts actually *reduce* rights protections among the countries with the most democratic policymaking institutions.

Substantively, the rights-increasing effects of more independent courts are modest. Among the countries with the least democratic policymaking institutions, moving from a constitution that prohibits judicial review to one that permits judicial review but does not fully insulate courts from the policymaking branches increases human rights on the 100-point Humana scale by approximately 15 points, increases civil liberties on the 7-point Freedom House scale by approximately 1 point, increases property rights on the 5-point Holmes et al. scale by approximately 1.3 points, and decreases the share of government-owned bank assets by approximately 24 percentage points; more independent courts have no effect on the number of procedures required of startup companies.[63] While these increases in rights are significant at conventional thresholds, they are clearly dominated by those that could be realized from retaining deferential courts in these countries, and instead democratizing policymaking institutions.

Among the countries with moderately majoritarian policymaking institutions, we see no effects from instituting more independent courts on the Humana civil rights index, the Freedom House civil liberties index, the share of government-owned bank assets, or the number of mandated

Table 9.2: **Estimating Levels of Rights Protections: Conditional Coefficients for Judicial Independence Controlling for Log GDP pc, ELF, Latitude**

Policymaking Institutions	Full Sample	Full Sample with Continent Dummies	Constitutions Unamended After 1980	Former Colonies
		Humana Human Rights Index		
Least Majoritarian	15.00*** (5.68)	12.44** (6.01)	15.61** (7.13)	18.68*** (6.12)
More Majoritarian	1.62 (3.74)	1.44 (3.65)	3.41 (4.16)	−3.70 (5.79)
Most Majoritarian	−11.76*** (3.89)	−9.57*** (3.49)	−8.79*** (3.13)	−26.07** (11.87)
N	63	63	45	40
		Freedom House Civil Liberties Index, 1995		
Least Majoritarian	1.14*** (.37)	0.92** (0.43)	0.99** (0.46)	1.06** (0.43)
More Majoritarian	0.19 (0.25)	0.16 (0.27)	0.17 (0.28)	−0.11 (0.37)
Most Majoritarian	−0.77*** (0.30)	−0.60** (0.31)	−0.65*** (.29)	−1.27** (.74)
N	69	69	48	42
		Property Rights Index		
Least Majoritarian	1.32*** (0.47)	1.26*** (0.50)	1.43** (0.70)	1.53*** (0.55)
More Majoritarian	0.52*** (0.20)	0.45** (0.22)	0.59** (0.33)	0.51*** (0.23)

(continued)

Table 9.2: (continued)

Policymaking Institutions	Full Sample	Full Sample with Continent Dummies	Constitutions Unamended After 1980	Former Colonies
Most	−0.28**	−0.37***	−0.25*	−0.50*
Majoritarian	(0.15)	(0.15)	(0.16)	(0.40)
N	66	66	46	41

Government-Owned Bank Assets

Least	−0.24**	−0.28*	−0.16	−0.22
Majoritarian	(0.12)	(0.15)	(0.171)	(0.15)
More	0.00	-0.03	0.04	0.02
Majoritarian	(0.06)	(0.08)	(0.09)	(0.11)
Most	0.25***	0.23***	0.25***	0.26*
Majoritarian	(0.07)	(0.08)	(0.08)	(0.18)
N	60	60	47	36

Startup Procedures

Least	−0.78	−1.17	−1.82	−0.95
Majoritarian	(0.98)	(1.35)	(1.32)	(1.02)
More	0.87	0.27	0.42	0.25
Majoritarian	(0.68)	(0.81)	(0.78)	(0.94)
Most	2.52**	1.71*	2.65**	1.45
Majoritarian	(1.26)	(1.23)	(1.33)	(1.83)
N	54	54	39	33

Note: Robust standard errors reported. Estimates significantly different from zero at *p<.10; **p<.05; ***p<.01 (two-tailed).

startup procedures. Only for the property rights index is there any effect of increasing judicial independence; moving from a constitution that prohibits judicial review to one that both permits judicial review and fully insulates courts from the policymaking branches increases property rights by approximately 1 point on the 5-point property rights index. By contrast, on every measure except for mandated startup procedures these countries could realize substantively large increases in rights protections by retaining deferential courts and democratizing policymaking institutions. Again, this reform appears to dominate that of instituting more independent courts.

In the most democratic countries, independent courts actually have a *negative* effect on rights on every measure of rights protections. Moving from a constitution that prohibits judicial review to one that both permits judicial review and fully insulates courts from the policymaking branches decreases human rights by approximately 23.5 points on the 100-point Humana index, decreases civil liberties by approximately 1.5 points on the 7-point Freedom House scale, decreases property rights by approximately .5 points on the 5-point Holmes et al. index, increases the share of government-owned bank assets by approximately 50 percentage points, and increases the number of mandated startup procedures by approximately 5 procedures. Again, all effects are significant at conventional thresholds.

These results suggest that judges insulated from accountability are perhaps not the unconditional protectors of economic and political rights they have been reputed to be. At least in this sample, only in the countries with the least democratic policymaking institutions do we see any consistent rights-increasing effects from more independent courts. However, even these judicially induced increases in rights are quite modest relative to the gains that could be realized by retaining deferential courts, and instead democratizing these countries' policymaking institutions. Overall, rights appear to be maximally protected by democratic policymakers who are unchecked by courts.

Robustness Checks

Some may have concerns about the robustness of these results. Perhaps there are factors not included in the analyses reported here that are actually driving the apparently conditional effects of more independent courts on levels of rights protections. For example, perhaps cultural beliefs affect levels of rights protections, in ways that stymie our efforts to estimate the effects of more independent courts on those protections. While the analyses reported here do control for a country's level of economic development, ethnolinguistic composition, and climate, perhaps these control variables do not capture the effects of cultural beliefs on rights.

Another possible concern is that a country's constitutional choices, for example the choice to institute more independent courts possessed of the power of judicial review, and its policy choices, for example the choice to have fewer rights protections, are both being driven by the same unidentified variable or variables. Then the apparent association we document between more independent courts and lower levels of rights protections in democracies would not be a causal association. It is true that the measure of judicial independence used here is coded from constitutional rules; constitutions are generally harder to change than the policy decisions that contribute to a country's level of rights protections. It thus seems reasonable to assume that sticky constitutional rules are not being affected by the same forces that affect countries' current rights policies. But some may think this is not a reasonable assumption.

Following existing work, there are three strategies we can pursue to address these two concerns. The first strategy, addressing the concern about omitted variables like cultural beliefs, involves including regional indicator variables to control for regional fixed effects. These indicator variables will control for every omitted factor common to a given region, eliminating the need to individually identify and measure these factors. The conditional coefficients resulting from these estimations are reported in the second column of Table 9.2.[64] While the magnitudes of the effects of judicial independence are overall somewhat reduced, we still observe the same pattern of effects on all rights indices: independent courts generally increase rights protections only in the least majoritarian countries, have no effect in more majoritarian countries (except on the property rights index), and reduce rights protections in the most majoritarian countries. These effects all remain significant at conventional levels.

The second strategy to test the robustness of these results, addressing the concern about unidentified causes common to both constitutional and policy choices, involves reducing the sample to only those countries whose constitutions have not been amended since 1980. In these countries, the factors that affected policy decisions about rights in the mid-1990s are less likely to have been the same factors that affected a country's pre-1980 constitutional choices. The third column of Table 9.2 reports the conditional coefficients from this estimation; again the results follow the same pattern as in the larger sample and remain significant at conventional levels. The one exception is that we no longer observe a significant rights-increasing effect of judicial independence on the share of government-owned banking assets in the least majoritarian countries.

Finally, we can reduce the sample to only those countries that were former colonies. Because these countries inherited many if not all of their constitutional rules well before the mid-1990s, we should perhaps be less troubled by concerns about the endogeneity of constitutions for this set of countries. The conditional coefficients estimated for this sample are reported in the last column of Table 9.2. Again, we see the same pattern in these coefficients as observed in the larger sample, as well as continued significance at conventional thresholds. The only exceptions are that in this sample more independent courts do not reduce governmentally owned banking assets in the least majoritarian countries, and have no apparent effect on the number of startup procedures required in the most majoritarian countries.

The results reported in the first column of Table 9.2, then, largely withstand these robustness tests. They are only initial findings. Considerably more work will need to be done before they can be said to have been validated, perhaps with more refined measures of judicial independence and larger samples of constitutions. Until then they remain only preliminary results. But they are nonetheless striking. They suggest that Thomas Jefferson may have been correct. Under nondemocratic constitutions, making judges more independent of the legislative and executive branches may be "a great point gained" for those seeking increased protections for economic and political rights (although "great" may be a little too strong to characterize the benefits of more independent courts in this context). But under democratic constitutions, the effect of more independent courts may operate "in an opposite direction, and against . . . the public will."[65]

Rethinking the Value of Judicial Independence

At least in these initial results, independent courts don't appear to be such a great idea. Although this is not what most of us were taught in school, we should perhaps not be too surprised. At some level the question is perhaps why anyone ever would have believed that independent courts would unconditionally lead to increased rights in the first place. Certainly advocates of judicial reform in seventeenth- and eighteenth-century England and colonial North America did not appear to share this belief. The English Act of Settlement of 1701 did protect judges from removal at the pleasure of the sovereign, a power widely believed to enable the Crown to undermine the economic and political rights of the growing commercial class. But it also enabled judicial removal at the pleasure of the Parliament, a power used by parliamentary majorities at least in part to remove judges insufficiently protective of their constituents' rights.[66] The Act of Settlement institutionalized the principle not of judicial independence, but rather of judicial accountability to democratically elected majorities.[67] The ascendant English Parliament also never gave courts the right to override or set aside parliamentary enactments.[68]

The American colonists continued the struggle for legislative control over executive-appointed judges, a struggle eventually culminating in the Declaration of Independence. Given the chance to design their own judicial institutions, first in state constitutions and later in the federal constitution, they chose to make judges dependent on majoritarian legislatures for their tenures and salaries.

Reformers apparently fought for legislative control over judicial tenures and salaries because they believed that these institutional rules would affect the way that judges decided cases. In their absence, when judges served at the pleasure of the Crown, could not be removed by legislative majorities, and received their salaries directly from the Crown's agents, it was generally assumed that judges would not adequately protect individual rights and liberties. Recall the Massachusetts Bay Assembly's declaration in 1774 that such a judge "will discover to the world, that he has not a due sense of the importance of an impartial administration of justice; that he is an enemy to the constitution, and has it in his heart to promote the establishment of an arbitrary government in the province."[69] But the solution to this problem was not to insulate judges from any form of accountability, including accountability to popular preferences. After all, the Crown was insulated from popular accountability; that was precisely the problem. As Madison wrote in Federalist 51, "A power independent of the society may as well espouse the unjust views of the major as the rightful interests of the minor party, and may possibly be turned against both parties."[70] Instead, the solution was to make judges dependent for their tenures and salaries upon the people's representatives.

Importantly, prior to the codification of legislative control over judicial tenures and salaries, occurring in England at least as early as 1701 but in the colonies only after independence, judicial decisions were suspect even when the King or his agents did not exercise their powers of removal. That is, judicial decisions were not believed to be fair, impartial, and protective of individual rights unless and until a judge was removed by the monarch or his appointed governor. Indeed, removal by the Crown was, if anything, a signal that a judge was *not* deferring to royal preferences, that he was in fact too protective of individual rights, and insufficiently protective of the Crown's interests. Judicial removal was not a sign that "at pleasure" tenure was having the desired effect (from the point of view of the Crown), but rather that it had been insufficiently effective. Instead, it was the judges who remained in office who were largely seen first by parliamentary reformers, and later by their counterparts in the colonies, as the Crown's most effective agents.

Shifting the object of compelled judicial deference from the Crown to the legislature was expected to work in largely the same way. Judges were expected to respond to the new institutional rules by deferring to majoritarian legislative preferences for greater protections for economic and political rights. State legislative and congressional majorities would only need to remove those judges who clearly were *not* deferring to their preferences. And these were expected to be few. As Alexander Hamilton said in Federalist 81, "There never can be danger that the judges, by a series of deliberate usurpations on the authority of the legislature, would hazard the united resentment of the body entrusted with it, while this body was possessed of the means of punishing their presumption by degrading them from their stations."[71]

The evidence reported in Chapters Five, Six, and Seven suggests that Hamilton may have been right. The House of Representatives apparently does not need to actually initiate impeachment proceedings against the justices, or to explicitly promise salary increases in return for favorable decisions, in order to compel judicial deference to the preferences of House majorities. We see this most perhaps clearly with the late Burger and early Rehnquist Courts. These conservative courts seem to have deferred to liberal House majorities, preserving the power of those majorities to investigate allegations of wrongdoing by the executive, ameliorate environmental harms, diversify the airwaves, and preserve land for public recreational use. These same courts also preserved abortion rights and robustly enforced the Establishment Clause against errant state and local governments. And the House did not need to impeach a single justice or promise quid pro quo salary increases in return for this apparent deference.

Perhaps the Constitution's majoritarian checks on the federal courts have worked too well. Because they have needed to be invoked so rarely, we now seem to think that they do not work at all. And so we have constructed elaborate, if perhaps implausible, theories to explain why our apparently antidemocratic, autocratic, unaccountable federal judges are generally so solicitous of our preferences for civil rights, liberties, and other public goods. They are men and women of superior character, we say. They would never abuse their seemingly limitless power. They are better than the rest of us. They are certainly better than the venal, ambitious, power-hungry inhabitants of the Capitol Building.

But when Madison wrote about remedying "the defect of better motives" in Federalist 51, he did not add, "except for the judges, who of course have nothing but better motives."[72] Apparently we are fortunate that it was men like Madison who drafted our Constitution, rather than today's advocates of independent courts. For it looks as if we may have been better off precisely because our federal judges have been incentivized to defer to the majoritarian House of Representatives. We might have enjoyed fewer protections for our rights and liberties, had those judges been left to their own devices.

Rethinking the Value of Judicial Review

And yet, as Jefferson pointed out in 1816, those who drafted our federal constitution (and many of our state constitutions) were not fully committed democrats. James Madison was not alone in fearing majority "factions" who might agitate "for paper money, for an abolition of debts, for an equal division of property, or for any other improper or wicked project."[73] Many features of the Constitution's design were clearly intended to thwart the efficacy of such majorities. One of these features was undoubtedly the existence of long-tenured judges who were not explicitly prohibited from voiding legislative enactments not "made in pursuance" to the Constitution.[74] The Constitution leashed these judges; the House of Representatives holds the leash. But the leash undoubtedly has some slack in it. Even a leashed Court can presumably do more damage to the policy agenda of the elected branches than a Court that is constitutionally prohibited from vetoing those branches' enactments.

The Roberts Court's campaign finance decisions between its 2006 and 2009 terms may illustrate the perils of slack in the Court's leash. Recall that during these four terms, the conservative majority on this Court faced liberal Democratic majorities in the House of Representatives. And the Court appears generally to have deferred to those majorities' preferences in favor of liberal federal statutes. The Court largely eschewed reviewing liberal federal statutes during these terms, and largely upheld those statutes whose constitutionality it did review. There were only a few exceptions to this pattern, and aside from *U.S. v. Stevens* (2010) (wherein the Court struck a statute prohibiting commercial depictions of animal cruelty), these exceptions all involved different provisions of the same liberal campaign finance statute, the McCain-Feingold Bipartisan Campaign Reform Act of 2002 (BCRA). These campaign finance rulings culminated in *Citizens United v. Federal Election Commission*, 558 U.S. 50 (2010), wherein the Roberts Court struck the BCRA's prohibitions on corporate- and union-financed independent campaign ads.

Exceptions to the Roberts Court's deference to liberal House majorities may have been few. But these few exceptions may nonetheless give us pause. The Roberts Court's repeated strikes of the BCRA during these terms, culminating in *Citizens United* (2010), were not endorsed by sitting Democratic House majorities. These rulings were in that sense counter-majoritarian. Given the widespread evidence that populations are better off when democratically elected majorities are permitted to extend public goods, we may very well want to question the wisdom of allowing our federal courts to strike public goods endorsed by sitting elective majorities. That is, we may want to question the wisdom of the practice of judicial review, even when exercised by apparently democratically accountable courts such as our own.

The exercise of judicial review, even by democratically accountable courts, may endanger valued public goods for yet another reason. The practice of judicial review involves the nullification of statutes rather than their enactment. Even democratically accountable courts can more easily respond to elective majorities' preferences to repeal previously enacted public goods than to their preferences to enact new public goods. This asymmetric responsiveness may have particular bite under a constitution such as that of the United States, which makes public goods both hard to enact and hard to repeal. Enacting a federal statute under the U.S. Constitution requires mustering a majority in the House, a supermajority in the Senate, and either the assent of the president or two-thirds majorities in both congressional chambers. Repealing a federal statute requires the same. Given that elected officials in these three institutions have different constituencies, different electoral clocks, and terms of different lengths, coordinating support across all three institutions is notoriously difficult. But the Supreme Court is also possessed of the power to repeal statutes, at least in part, by striking their provisions as unconstitutional. And the Constitution incentivizes the justices to respond largely to only one of the three policymaking branches, namely the House of Representatives. In effect, the Constitution provides a fast track for majorities in the House to induce the repeal of federal statutes, via the exercise of judicial review by the Supreme Court. But our constitutional design does not provide an analogous fast track for the enactment of federal statutes.

The exercise of judicial review under the U.S. Constitution, then, even by the apparently democratically accountable Supreme Court, may bias public goods provision downward, relative to the level of public goods provision we would expect to see in the absence of judicial review. The Court's ruling in *National Federation of Independent Business* (2012) may illustrate this bias. In that case, the Court struck provisions of the Patient Protection and Affordable Care Act enabling the federal government to withhold all Medicaid funds from states refusing to participate in a dramatic expansion of Medicaid's coverage to previously uninsured low-income individuals. The Court ruled that only the new funds available to fund Medicaid's expansion could be withheld from these states, making it much more attractive for states to refuse to participate in that expansion.

As noted in the Preface, the Court's ruling in this case appears to have been induced by the Republican Party's impressive victories in the 2010 House elections. These victories brought to power a vocal Republican House majority committed to the repeal of the Affordable Care Act. The Court's apparent responsiveness to this majority, despite ex ante predictions that the Medicaid expansion surely would be upheld, appears to illustrate its democratic accountability.

But the Court's ruling, responsive though it may have been, likely will have a significantly negative effect on public goods provision. States that sued the federal government to prevent Medicaid's expansion include those with some of the largest populations of low-income uninsured individuals. Many of the governors of these states have already committed to refuse the federal funds available under the proposed Medicaid expansion. Ironically, while those with higher incomes may still receive subsidies to purchase health insurance under other provisions of the Affordable Care Act, those below the federal poverty line will receive nothing if their states do not participate in Medicaid's expansion. In the words of one observer, the Court's ruling may result in "the poorest Americans in the poorest states in the nation excluded from any health coverage under the Affordable Care Act."[75]

The post-2010 Republican House majority had attempted to repeal the Affordable Care Act on numerous occasions. But while these repeal attempts generally had passed the House, they just as generally had failed to pass the Democratic-majority Senate, or to receive support from President Obama. By exercising judicial review, then, the Court was able to repeal an instance of public goods provision that could not have been repealed by the policymaking branches, in the absence of judicial review. And while the Court appears to have been responding to a democratically elected majority in the House, the nature of judicial review prevents the justices from similarly responding to this majority's preferences to enact new policies providing different public goods (whatever those may be).

The presence of judicial review, even as exercised by democratically responsive courts, may then work more generally to lower levels of public goods provision. We appear to see this effect in the estimates reported in Tables 9.1 and 9.2: although democracies with democratically accountable courts have higher levels of rights protections than those with more independent courts, the democracies with the most robust protections for economic and political rights appear to be those that simply prohibit their courts from overruling the policies enacted by their elected branches. These findings are consistent with others suggesting that it is the most democratic institutions that are consistently the best for human welfare. Nondemocratic institutions that get in the way of majorities appear to only make outcomes worse.[76]

Perhaps this is what our only imperfectly democratic Founders wanted. As we saw in Chapter Two, many of those who participated in the drafting and ratification of the Constitution feared the exercise of power by completely independent, unaccountable, anti-majoritarian courts. They appear to have designed a series of elected branch checks on the federal courts precisely in order to prevent this unfettered exercise of judicial power, implementing Jefferson's advice to "Let mercy be the character of the law-giver, but let the judge be a mere machine."[77] If the evidence reported here withstands further scrutiny, these checks appear to work as designed. The Supreme Court, at least, does appear to function largely as a "mere machine," endorsing the preferences of democratically elected majorities in the House of Representatives.

But many of these same Founders also feared the unfettered exercise of power by elective majorities bent on redistribution. They designed a series of checks on the elected branches as well, checks that hinder elective majorities from enacting policies providing public goods. One of these checks appears to be the exercise of judicial review by the federal courts.

Jefferson suggested, perhaps more charitably, that the drafters of the early constitutions had been influenced by their struggles against the British Crown to endorse many provisions that were less than democratic, but that had seemed democratic by comparison with absolute monarchy: "In truth, the abuses of monarchy had so much filled all the space of political contemplation, that we imagined everything republican which was not monarchy."[78] He particularly singled out the institution of good behavior judicial tenure as having been the product of "prejudice . . . derived from a monarchical institution," and warned that this institution would operate against "the public will."[79] We should trust our elected representatives to protect our rights, argued Jefferson, not unelected judges.

Jefferson rued the many anti-democratic provisions present in both the state and federal constitutions. But he also encouraged each generation to revisit these constitutions, which he cautioned against treating with "sanctimonious reverence . . . like the arc of the covenant, too sacred to be touched."[80] Instead, he argued, "laws and institutions must go hand in hand with the progress of the human mind." Each generation has "a right to choose for itself the form of government it believes most promotive of its own happiness; consequently, to accommodate to the circumstances in which it finds itself, that received from its predecessors."[81]

The findings reported here are only preliminary. But, in the spirit of Jefferson's advice to future generations, they may be worth further pursuit. Perhaps, as evidence accumulates, we may find ourselves reevaluating the wisdom of allowing even our democratically accountable federal courts to exercise judicial review. Perhaps we may become willing to consider institutional reforms leashing those courts even more tightly to majoritarian preferences. Perhaps, like the United Kingdom, New Zealand, the Netherlands, and Switzerland before us, we may one day tell our federal courts that they can no longer overturn policies enacted by the federal elected branches.[82] If those statutes encroach on our rights, we would be free to throw the incumbents out and demand statutory repeals. But it would no longer be the job of unelected judges to decide which rights we deserve, and which we do not. We might then find that the mercy of the elected lawgiver really does exceed that of the unelected judge.

Preface

1. *National Federation of* Independent *Business (NFIB) et al. v. Sibelius* (2012). The Court's most recent prior ruling striking a federal statute as exceeding congressional powers under the Spending Clause was *U.S. v. Butler*, 297 U.S. 1 (1936), striking provisions of the Agricultural Adjustment Act of 1933 providing payments to farmers that reduced their production of certain crops.

2. The Urban Institute, "Making the Medicaid Expansion an ACA Option," June 29, 2012, http://www.urban.org/UploadedPDF/412606-Making-the-Medicaid-Expansion-an-ACA-Option.pdf.

3. Michael Cooper, "Many Governors Are Still Unsure About Medicaid Expansion," *New York Times*, July 14, 2012.

4. Sarah Kliff, "Forget States Opting Out; What Happens to Medicaid If They Opt-In?" *Washington Post*, July 16, 2012.

5. Michael A. Bailey, "Welfare and the Multifaceted Decision to Move," *American Political Science Review* 99 (February 2005): 125–135.

6. Stephanie Kirchgaessner, "U.S. Hospitals Face Financial Problems," *Financial Times*, July 10, 2012.

7. "Making the Medicaid Expansion an ACA Option."

8. David Kopel, "Major Limits on the Congress's Powers, in an Opinion Worthy of John Marshall," SCOTUSblog (Jun. 28, 2012, 6:33 PM), http://www.scotusblog.com/2012/06/major-limits-on-the-congresss-powers-in-an-opinion-worthy-of-john-marshall/.

9. Ibid. The relevant precedents were *Steward Machine Company v. Davis*, 301 U.S. 548 (1937), and *South Dakota v. Dole*, 483 U.S. 203 (1987).

10. William E. Forbath, "Workingman's Constitution," *New York Times*, July 5, 2012; Dahlia Lithwick, "Where Is the Liberal Outrage?" http://www.slate.com/articles/news_and_politics/jurisprudence/2012/07/06.

11. Julie Rovner, "Medicaid Expansion Goes Overlooked in Supreme Court Antic-ipation," http://www.npr.org/blogs/health/2012/06/27/155861308/medicaid-expansion-goes-overlooked-in-supreme-court-anticipation.

12. More technically, four of the Republican-appointed justices on the Court voted to strike the entire Medicaid expansion, a more radical alternative than that proposed in Roberts's controlling opinion, joined in relevant part by Justices Breyer and Kagan.

Chapter One. The Supreme Court, Congress, and American Democracy

1. William Rehnquist, *The Supreme Court* (New York: Knopf, 2001), 209.

2. Sandra Day O'Connor, "Fair and Independent Courts," *Daedalus* (Fall 2008): 8–10, 8.

3. Stephen Breyer, "Serving America's Best Interests," *Daedalus* (Fall 2008): 139–143, 143.

4. Cass R. Sunstein, *One Case at a Time: Judicial Minimalism on the Supreme Court* (Cambridge: Harvard University Press, 1999), 239.

5. Ronald Dworkin, *Law's Empire* (Cambridge: Harvard University Press, 1986), 244, 356. Also see Dworkin, *Freedom's Law: The Moral Reading of the American Constitution* (Cambridge: Harvard University Press, 1996), 34–35.

6. "Report to ABA Commission on Separation of Powers and Judicial Indepen-dence," February 21, 1997, 44.

7. "The Newsroom Guide to Judicial Independence," The Constitution Project, http://www.constitutionproject.org/pdf/37.pdf.

8. Eugene V. Rostow, "The Democratic Character of Judicial Review," 66 *Har-vard Law Review* 193 (1952): 197.

9. Robert G. McCloskey, *The American Supreme Court* (Chicago: University of Chicago Press, 1960), 29, 250.

10. Charles Black Jr., "The Supreme Court and Democracy," *Yale Review* 50 (1961): 199.

11. Alexander Bickel, *The Least Dangerous Branch: The Supreme Court at the Bar of Politics* (New York: Bobbs-Merrill, 1962), 25.

12. Philip B. Kurland, *Politics, the Constitution, and the Warren Court* (Chicago: University of Chicago Press, 1970), 172, 204.

13. See James F. Spriggs II and Thomas G. Hansford, "Explaining the Overrul-ing of U.S. Supreme Court Precedent," *Journal of Politics* 63 (2001): 1091–1111; Brian R. Sala and James F. Spriggs II, "Designing Tests of the Supreme Court and the Separation of Powers," *Political Research Quarterly* 57 (2004): 197–208; An-drew D. Martin, "Statutory Battles and Constitutional Wars: Congress and the Su-preme Court," in *Institutional Games and the U.S. Supreme Court*, ed. Jon R. Bond, Roy B. Flemming, and James R. Rogers (Charlottesville: University of Virginia Press, 2006); Jeffrey Segal, Chad Westerland, and Stefanie A. Lindquist, "Congress, the Supreme Court, and Judicial Review: Testing a Constitutional Separation of Powers

Model," *American Journal of Political Science* 55 (2011): 89–104; and Tom S. Clark, *The Limits of Judicial Independence* (New York: Cambridge University Press, 2011).

14. Breyer (2008), 142.

15. *New York Times*, December 10, 1998.

16. Sandra Day O'Connor, "Remarks on Judicial Independence," 58 *Florida Law Review* 1 (January 2006): 6. Similarly, the late Chief Justice William H. Rehnquist asserted, "We want our federal courts, and particularly the Supreme Court, to be independent of popular opinion when deciding the particular cases or controversies that come before them." Rehnquist (2001), 210.

17. Richard A. Posner, "Judicial Autonomy in a Political Environment," 38 *Arizona State Law Journal* 1 (2006): 1.

18. Steven P. Croley, "The Majoritarian Difficulty: Elective Judiciaries and the Rule of Law," 62 *University of Chicago Law Review* 689 (1995): 708.

19. Erwin Chemerinsky, *Interpreting the Constitution* (New York: Praeger, 1987), 119.

20. Martin Redish, "Judicial Discipline, Judicial Independence, and the Constitution: A Textual and Structural Analysis," 72 *Southern California Law Review* 673 (1999): 683.

21. Dworkin (1996), 16.

22. Bruce Fein and Burt Neuborne, "Why Should We Care About Independent and Accountable Judges?" *Judicature* 84 (2000): 3, 10.

23. United Nations Department of Public Information DPI/1837/HR—August 1996. Judicial independence had already been made a provision in both the Universal Declaration of Human Rights and the International Covenant on Civil and Political Rights. In 1985 the UN adopted a set of standards known as "Basic Principles on the Independence of the Judiciary."

24. "Guidance for Promoting Judicial Independence and Impartiality," Revised Edition, January 2002, Office of Democracy and Governance, Bureau for Democracy, Conflict, and Humanitarian Assistance, U.S. Agency for International Development.

25. See http://www.ced.org/issues/democratic-institutions/judicial-independence-and-selection.

26. Friedrich A. Hayek, *The Constitution of Liberty* (Chicago: University of Chicago Press, 1960). Douglass C. North and Barry R. Weingast suggest, for example, that, after the English 1701 Act of Settlement, "the political independence of the courts limited potential abuses by Parliament . . . the creation of a politically independent judiciary greatly expanded the government's ability credibly to promise to honor its agreements." "Constitutions and Commitment: The Evolution of Institutions Governing Public Choice in Seventeenth-Century England," *Journal of Economic History* 49 (1989): 803–832, 819. Edward L. Glaeser and Andrei Shleifer assert that "parliamentary control over lay justice . . . as Hayek (1960) so clearly emphasized, is likely to undermine the freedoms inherent in the Magna Carta." "Legal Origins," *Quarterly Journal of Economics* 117 (2002): 1193–1229, 1210. Rafael La Porta, Florencio Lopez-de-Silanes, Cristian Pop-Eleches, and Andrei Shleifer claim

that independent courts may protect rights by resisting policies enacted by and benefiting "democratic majorities," thereby preventing the "tyranny of the majority." "Judicial Checks and Balances," *Journal of Political Economy* 112 (2004). 445, 447; also see Rafael La Porta, Florencio Lopez-de-Silanes, and Andrei Shleifer, "The Economic Consequences of Legal Origins," *Journal of Economic Literature* 46 (2008): 285–332.

27. See, e.g., La Porta et al. (2004), La Porta et al. (2008).

28. Jeffrey Toobin, *The Nine* (New York: Doubleday, 2007), 2.

29. Scott Douglas Gerber, *A Distinct Judicial Power: The Origins of an Independent Judiciary, 1606–1787* (New York: Oxford University Press, 2011), xiv.

30. Morris P. Fiorina, Paul E. Peterson, Bertram Johnson, and D. Stephen Voss, *The New American Democracy*, 7th ed. (New York: Pearson Longman, 2011), 433.

31. Article III, Section I.

32. Raoul Berger, *Impeachment: The Constitutional Problems* (Cambridge: Harvard University Press, 1973), 187; Saikrishna Prakash and Steven D. Smith, "How to Remove a Federal Judge," 116 *Yale Law Journal* 72 (2006): 128. Also see Raoul Berger, "Impeachment of Judges and 'Good Behavior' Tenure," 79 *Yale Law Journal* 1475 (1970); Michael J. Gerhardt, "The Constitutional Limits to Impeachment and Its Alternatives," 68 *Texas Law Review* 1 (1989); and Maria Simon, "Note: Bribery and Other Not So 'Good Behavior': Criminal Prosecution as a Supplement to Impeachment of Federal Judges," 94 *Columbia Law Review* 1617 (1994).

33. Article II, Section IV.

34. Article III, Section I.

35. *The Federalist Papers*, ed. Clinton Rossiter (New York: NAL Penguin, 1961), 485.

36. Ibid., 473.

37. John Ferejohn, "Independent Judges, Dependent Judiciary: Explaining Judicial Independence," 72 *Southern California Law Review* 353 (1999): 358; Michael Gerhardt, *The Federal Impeachment Process*, 2nd ed. (Chicago: University of Chicago Press, 2000), 103; Saikrishna Prakash and Steven Smith, "Reply: (Mis)Understanding Good-Behavior Tenure," 116 *Yale Law Journal* 159 (2006): 161.

38. While the Origination Clause specifies merely that bills for "raising Revenue" must originate in the House of Representatives, House majorities have historically interpreted this provision as applying to appropriations bills as well. James V. Saturno, "The Origination Clause of the U.S. Constitution: Interpretation and Enforcement," Congressional Research Service, March 15, 2011, http://www.fas.org/sgp/crs/misc/RL31399.pdf.

39. Article III, Section 2.

40. Article III, Section 1.

41. Gerber (2011), 24. Also see Breyer (2008), 141, pointing to Alexander Hamilton's support for "the independence of the judiciary."

42. Alexander Hamilton, "Federalist 81," in Rossiter (1961), 485.

43. James Madison, "Federalist 51," in ibid., 324.

44. Ibid.

45. Thomas Jefferson to Edmund Pendleton, August 26, 1776, in *The Papers of Thomas Jefferson Volume 1*, ed. Julian P. Boyd (Princeton: Princeton University Press, 1950).

46. John Adams, *Thoughts on Government* (1776), reprinted in *The Works of John Adams*, ed. Charles Francis Adams, vol. 4 (Boston: Little, Brown, 1851), 193–200.

47. Ibid.; Constitution of Massachusetts 1780, accessed at http://www.nhinet .org/ccs/docs/ma-1780.htm. It is thus difficult to see in Adams's writing the "final step in the political theory of an independent judiciary" seen by Gerber (2011), 24.

48. Sandra Day O'Connor, "Remarks on Judicial Independence," 58 *Florida Law Review* 1 (2005): 4; Charles G. Geyh, *When Courts and Congress Collide* (Ann Arbor: University of Michigan Press, 2006).

49. "Federalist 81," in Rossiter (1961), 485.

50. See James F. Spriggs II and Thomas G. Hansford, "Explaining the Overruling of U.S. Supreme Court Precedent," *Journal of Politics* 63 (2001): 1091–1111; Brian R. Sala and James F. Spriggs II, "Designing Tests of the Supreme Court and the Separation of Powers," *Political Research Quarterly* 57 (2004): 197–208; Andrew D. Martin, "Statutory Battles and Constitutional Wars: Congress and the Supreme Court," in Bond, Flemming, and Rogers, *Institutional Games and the U.S. Supreme Court*; Segal, Westerland, and Lindquist, "Congress, the Supreme Court, and Judicial Review"; and Clark (2011).

51. See, e.g., Thomas W. Merrill, "The Making of the Second Rehnquist Court: A Preliminary Analysis," 47 *Saint Louis University Law Journal* 569 (2003).

52. These probabilities are simulated from the estimates reported in Table 5.3 and are displayed in Figure 5.4.

53. The estimates and predicted probabilities supporting these claims are reported in Table 5.3 and Figures 5.1–5.3.

54. The estimates and predicted probabilities supporting this claim are reported in Table 5.3 and Figure 5.2.

55. Toobin (2007), 2.

56. The estimates and predicted probabilities supporting this claim are reported in Table 5.3 and Figure 5.3.

57. "Landmark" federal statutes are those identified by congressional historian Stephen W. Stathis and reported in *Landmark Legislation, 1774–2002* (Washington, DC: Congressional Quarterly, 2003).

58. See, e.g., Toobin (2007).

59. Dworkin (1996), 12–13.

60. Breyer (2008), 142. *Cooper v. Aaron* is also cited as a prominent example of the Court's independence by Saikrishna Prakash, "America's Aristocracy," 109 *Yale Law Journal* 541 (1999): 575.

61. These cases include *Heart of Atlanta Motel v. U.S.*, 379 U.S. 241 (1964), upholding provisions of the Civil Rights Act of 1964 prohibiting racial discrimination in hotels and motels serving interstate travelers; *Katzenbach v. McClung*, 379 U.S.

294 (1964), upholding provisions of the same Act prohibiting racial discrimination by restaurants serving food that had moved in interstate commerce; *South Carolina v. Katzenbach* 383 U.S. 301 (1966), upholding key provisions of the Voting Rights Act of 1965; and *Katzenbach v. Morgan*, 384 U.S. 641 (1966), upholding that Act's ban on literacy tests as applied to former residents of Puerto Rico.

62. These cases include *Briscoe v. Bell*, 432 U.S. 404 (1977), upholding the 1975 amendments to the Voting Rights Act of 1965, extending that Act's protections to language minorities, and *Grove City College v. Bell*, 465 U.S. 555 (1984), upholding Title IX of the Education Amendments of 1972, prohibiting sex discrimination in any educational institution receiving federal funds as applied to students' receipt of federal financial aid.

63. Empirical studies showing a positive relationship between judicial independence and rights protections include Kathleen Pritchard, "Comparative Human Rights: An Integrative Explanation," *Policy Studies Journal* 15 (1986): 110–122; Gerald Blasi and David Cingranelli, "Do Constitutions and Institutions Help Protect Human Rights?" in *Human Rights and Developing Countries*, ed. David Cingranelli (Greenwich, CT: JAI, 1996); Frank Cross, "The Relevance of Law in Human Rights Protection," *International Review of Law and Economics* 19 (1999): 87–98; Witold J. Henisz, "The Institutional Environment for Economic Growth," *Economics and Politics* 12 (2000): 1–31; Linda Camp Keith, "Judicial Independence and Human Rights Protection Around the World," *Judicature* 85 (2002): 195–200; Lars P. Feld and Stefan Voigt, "Economic Growth and Judicial Independence: Cross-Country Evidence Using a New Set of Indicators," *European Journal of Political Economy* 19 (2003): 497–527; Robert M. Howard and Henry F. Carey, "Is an Independent Judiciary Necessary for Democracy?" *Judicature* 87 (2004): 284–290; Clair Apodaca, "The Rule of Law and Human Rights," *Judicature* 87 (2004): 292–299; La Porta et al. (2004); La Porta et al. (2008); and Emilia Powell and Jeffrey Staton, "Domestic Judicial Institutions and Human Rights Treaty Violations," *International Studies Quarterly* 53 (2009): 149–174.

64. La Porta et al. (2004); La Porta et al. (2008).

65. Bruce Bueno de Mesquita, Alastair Smith, Randolph M. Siverson, and James D. Morrow, *The Logic of Political Survival* (Cambridge: MIT Press, 2003), 182. Also see James D. Morrow, Bruce Bueno de Mesquita, Randolph M. Siverson, and Alastair Smith, "Retesting Selectorate Theory: Separating the Effects of W from Other Elements of Democracy," *American Political Science Review* 102 (2008): 393–400. Bueno de Mesquita et al. (2003) and Morrow et al. (2008) report the effects of increases in the size of a leader's "winning coalition," or the number of individuals whose support is necessary to secure the leader's survival in office. Their results include controls for income, population, constraints on executive authority, and regional and temporal fixed effects. Some analyses also include country-specific fixed effects.

66. Bueno de Mesquita et al. (2003), 179.

67. Bickel (1962), 25.

68. Fein and Neuborne (2000), 3.

69. Charles Gardner Geyh, "Why Judicial Elections Stink," 64 *Ohio State Law Journal* 43 (2003): 71.

70. "Report to ABA Commission on Separation of Powers and Judicial Independence," February 21, 1997, iv.

71. Quoted by U.S. District Court Judge Joseph H. Rodriguez in ibid., 20. John Ferejohn has likewise noted that the normative ideal of judicial independence requires that "judges can be counted on, for the most part, to act as impartial and morally autonomous agents who share the values that underlie our constitutional democracy." Ferejohn, "Independent Judges, Dependent Judiciary: Explaining Judicial Independence," 72 *Southern California Law Review* 353 (1999): 354.

72. Frank B. Cross, "Thoughts on Goldilocks and Judicial Independence," 64 *Ohio State Law Journal* 195 (2003): 198.

73. Saikrishna Prakash, "America's Aristocracy," 109 *Yale Law Journal* 541 (1999): 578.

74. Dworkin (1996), 32.

75. La Porta et al. write, "Judges are not intrinsically more supportive of private property than the executive or the legislatures, but are merely more insulated from immediate political pressures when they are independent." La Porta et al. (2004), 447, n. 2.

76. See La Porta et al. (2004) and La Porta et al. (2008).

77. Thomas Jefferson to Samuel Kercheval, July 12, 1816, in *The Writings of Thomas Jefferson*, ed. Paul Leicester Ford, vol. 10 (New York: G. P. Putnam's Sons, 1899), 38.

78. Federalist 51, 322.

Chapter Two. The Supreme Court, the Elected Branches, and the Constitution

1. Fiorina et al., *New American Democracy*, 7th ed., 433.

2. In the popular press see, e.g., Edward Lazarus, "Life Tenure for Federal Judges: Should It Be Abolished?" CNN.com, December 10, 2004; Stuart Taylor Jr., "Life Tenure Is Too Long for Supreme Court Justices," *Atlantic*, June 2005; Fred Graham, "In Need of Review: Life Tenure on the U.S. Supreme Court," *USA Today*, January 15, 2006; Linda Greenhouse, "New Focus on the Effects of Life Tenure," *New York Times*, September 10, 2007; and Nathan Koppel, "For 'Maverick' Federal Judges, Life Tenure Is Largely Unfettered License," *Wall Street Journal*, August 8, 2008. In the legal academy see, e.g., John O. McGinnis, "Justice Without Justices," 16 *Constitutional Commentary* 541 (1999): 542 (characterizing the justices as "vested for life with the awesome power to make final decisions with wide-ranging consequences for the nation"); Martin Redish, "Judicial Discipline, Judicial Independence, and the Constitution: A Textual and Structural Analysis," 72 *Southern California Law Review* 673 (1999): 685 ("Article III's provision of life tenure is quite

obviously intended to insulate federal judges from undue external political pressures on their decision-making"); L. A. Powe, "Go Geezers Go: Leaving the Bench," 25 *Law and Social Inquiry* 1227 (2000): 1234 ("Life tenure for judges is the stupidest provision of the 1787 Constitution"); Ward Farnsworth, "The Regulation of Turnover on the Supreme Court," 2005 *University of Illinois Law Review* 407, 411 ("Life tenure is due for a fresh defense"); and Steven G. Calabresi and James Lindgren, "Term Limits for the Supreme Court: Life Tenure Reconsidered," *Harvard Journal of Law and Public Policy* 29 (2006): 769.

3. Article III, Section 1. Subsequently I shall use the common spelling of "behavior."

4. Article I, Sections 2 and 3, further specify that "the House of Representatives . . . shall have the sole power of impeachment . . . The Senate shall have the sole power to try all impeachments. When sitting for that purpose, they shall be on oath or affirmation . . . no person shall be convicted without the concurrence of two thirds of the members present. Judgment in cases of impeachment shall not extend further than to removal from office, and disqualification to hold and enjoy any office of honor, trust or profit under the United States: but the party convicted shall nevertheless be liable and subject to indictment, trial, judgment and punishment, according to law."

5. Martin Redish has characterized the Good Behavior Clause as "the most mysterious provision in the United States Constitution—and that, of course, is really saying something." Martin H. Redish, "Response: Good Behavior, Judicial Independence, and the Foundations of American Constitutionalism," 116 *Yale Law Journal* 139 (2006): 139

6. The Necessary and Proper Clause, Article I, Section 8, gives Congress the power to "make all Laws which shall be necessary and proper for carrying into Execution the foregoing Powers, and all other Powers vested by this Constitution in the Government of the United States, or in any Department or Officer thereof." See Raoul Berger, *Impeachment: The Constitutional Problems* (Cambridge: Harvard University Press, 1973), 187: "It is open to the Congress, and I consider it highly desirable, to enact legislation under its 'necessary and proper' power which would give effect of the implications of 'good behavior' and confirm and facilitate judicial removal of judges for 'misbehavior.'" Also see Saikrishna Prakash and Steven D. Smith, "How to Remove a Federal Judge," 116 *Yale Law Journal* 72 (2006): 128: "Using its Necessary and Proper authority, Congress may provide means for determining violations of good behavior." Also see Raoul Berger, "Impeachment of Judges and 'Good Behavior' Tenure," 79 *Yale Law Journal* 1475 (1970); Michael J. Gerhardt, "The Constitutional Limits to Impeachment and Its Alternatives," 68 *Texas Law Review* 1 (1989); and Maria Simon, "Note: Bribery and Other Not So 'Good Behavior': Criminal Prosecution as a Supplement to Impeachment of Federal Judges," 94 *Columbia Law Review* 1617 (1994).

7. See, e.g., Martha Andes Ziskind, "Judicial Tenure in the American Constitution: English and American Precedents," 1969 *Supreme Court Review* 135; Philip B. Kurland, "The Constitution and the Tenure of Federal Judges: Some Notes from

History," 36 *University of Chicago Law Review* 665 (1969); Sam J. Ervin Jr., "Separation of Powers: Judicial Independence," 35 *Law and Contemporary Problems* 108 (1970); Stephen B. Burbank, "Alternative Career Resolution: An Essay on the Removal of Federal Judges," 76 *Kentucky Law Journal* 643 (1988); Harry T. Edwards, "Regulating Judicial Misconduct and Divining 'Good Behavior,'" 87 *Michigan Law Review* 765 (1989); Peter Shane, "Who May Discipline or Remove Federal Judges? A Constitutional Analysis," 142 *University of Pennsylvania Law Review* 209 (1993); Suzanna Sherry, "Judicial Independence: Playing Politics with the Constitution," 14 *Georgia State University Law Review* 795 (1998); Redish (1999); and Laurence Claus, "Constitutional Guarantees of the Judiciary: Jurisdiction, Tenure, and Beyond," 54 *American Journal of Comparative Law* 459 (2006).

8. Prakash and Smith (2006), 86: "There is no reason to suppose that all departures from good behavior would necessarily constitute 'high Crimes and Misdemeanors.'" Redish (2006) suggests that permitting removal under the Good Behavior Clause would enable judges to be removed for decisions that "offend those in political power" or that do not "comport with the political and constitutional views of the majoritarian branches." Redish (2006), 156–157.

9. Prakash and Smith write, "With impeachment, a judge can be removed by officials who act and are expected to act as politicians, under a standard that (as Gerald Ford famously remarked) can as a practical matter mean whatever Congress wants it to mean, and without any possibility of appeal." Saikrishna Prakash and Steven Smith, "Reply: (Mis)Understanding Good-Behavior Tenure," 116 *Yale Law Journal* 159 (2006): 161. Michael Gerhardt notes that "Ford's observation captures the practical reality of impeachment, and subsequent attempts to circumscribe the scope of impeachable offenses have not succeeded in eliminating any role for political factors." *The Federal Impeachment Process*, 2nd ed. (Chicago: University of Chicago Press, 2000), 103. John Ferejohn has likewise pointed out that nothing in the Constitution prevents the Congress from setting the impeachment bar to include "actions taken on the bench in good faith." "Independent Judges, Dependent Judiciary: Explaining Judicial Independence," 72 *Southern California Law Review* 353 (1999): 358.

10. "Article VII," *Impeachable Offenses: A Documentary History from 1787 to the Present*, ed. Emily Field Van Tassel and Paul Finkelman (Washington, DC: Congressional Quarterly, 1999), 165.

11. "Final Report by the Special Subcommittee on H. Res. 920 of the Committee on the Judiciary, House of Representatives, Ninety-First Congress, Second Session," Van Tassel and Finkelman (1999), 67–73, 68, 70.

12. Ibid., 304–308.

13. Ibid.

14. *Nixon v. U.S.*, 506 U.S. 224 (1993), 235. Michael Gerhardt notes that "the Court has left the federal impeachment process for over two centuries to the complete, unreviewable discretion of the Congress." Gerhardt (2000), 132.

15. Article III, Section 1.

16. Article III, Section 2.

17. Article III, Section 1.

18. Gerber (2011).

19. In the 1761 instructions to the royal governors forbidding any further judicial appointments in the colonies made on the condition of good behavior tenure, the Crown characterized appointments "granted during pleasure only" as "the ancient practice and usage in our said colonies and plantations." Gerber (2011), 49. Also see Wood (1969), 160, 294–296; Ervin (1970), 112; Berger (1973), 1492, 1494; Joseph H. Smith, "An Independent Judiciary: The Colonial Background," 124 *University of Pennsylvania Law Review* 1104 (1976); Peter Charles Hoffer and N. E. H. Hull, *Impeachment in America, 1635–1805* (New Haven: Yale University Press, 1984), 9; David P. Currie, "Separating Judicial Power," 61 *Law and Contemporary Problems* 3 (1998): 7; Prakash and Smith (2006); and Gerber (2011), 24.

20. Leonard W. Labaree, *Royal Government in America* (New Haven: Yale University Press, 1930), 394–395; Klein (1960), 448–449; Hoffer and Hull (1984), 27–56.

21. William Henry Drayton, "A Letter from Freeman of South Carolina" (Charleston, 1774), 10, quoted in Wood (1969), 160.

22. Berger (1973), 132–141.

23. Colonial assemblies passed bills providing for good behavior judicial tenure in 1756 in North Carolina and in 1761 in New York. In 1769 the New Hampshire Assembly petitioned that colony's governor to make judicial appointments "in the same form, as to their continuance, as the Commissions of the Judges of Westminster Hall." Gerber (2011), 108, 192–193.

24. The governors of North Carolina and New York refused to sign their assemblies' bills providing for good behavior tenure; New Hampshire's governor likewise refused his assembly's request for the same. Gerber (2011), 108, 192–193. Also see Klein (1960), 450–445; Wood (1969), 294–295; Smith (1976), 1119; Black (1985), 112; and Hoffer and Hull (1984), 10–11.

25. In 1733, for example, James DeLancey was appointed Chief Justice of the New York Supreme Court with good behavior tenure by Governor George Clinton. His successor was appointed with at pleasure tenure in 1762 by New York's Acting Governor Cadwallader Colden. Milton M. Klein, "Prelude to Revolution in New York: Jury Trials and Judicial Tenure," *William and Mary Quarterly*, 3rd ser., 17 (1960): 439–462.

26. Board of Trade to King George III, November 11, 1761, as quoted in Gerber (2011), 194, and Klein (1960), 448.

27. Gerber (2011), 49; "Order of the King in Council," November 23, 1761, as cited in Klein (1960), 453. Governor Josiah Hardy of New Jersey was in fact removed by the Crown in 1762 for having violated this instruction. Gerber (2011), 235–236.

28. Letters from a Farmer, in Ford, *Writings of Dickinson*, 367, as quoted in Wood (1969), 160.

29. Berger (1973), 151, 1495; Smith (1976); Hoffer and Hull (1984), 59–95.

30. "William III, 1700 & 1701: An Act for the further Limitation of the Crown and better securing the Rights and Liberties of the Subject [Chapter II. Rot. Parl.

12 & 13 Gul. III. p. 1. n. 2.]," *Statutes of the Realm: Volume 7: 1695–1701* (1820), 636–638, http://www.british-history.ac.uk/report.aspx?compid=46986.

31. Ibid.

32. Sam J. Ervin Jr., "Separation of Powers: Judicial Independence," 35 *Law and Contemporary Problems* 108 (1970): 111. David Currie argues that the assent of the sovereign to legislative address eventually became pro forma, rendering both impeachment and legislative address means of judicial removal possessed exclusively by the Parliament. David P. Currie, "Separating Judicial Power," 61 *Law and Contemporary Problems* 3 (1998): 8.

33. Berger (1973), 27, 62–63; M. V. Clarke, "The Origin of Impeachment," in *Oxford Essays in Medieval History*, ed. Frederick Maurice Powicke (Oxford: Clarendon Press, 1934), 164; Hoffer and Hull (1984), 3–14.

34. See Berger (1973) and Gerhardt (2000).

35. Berger (1973), xiii, refers to the "familiar English categories" of impeachable offenses under the standard of "high crimes and misdemeanors": "'subversion of the Constitution' (usurpation of power), 'abuse of power,' 'betrayal of trust,' 'neglect of duty,' and the like." Also see 21, 35, 46, 62, 65. Blackstone cited "maladministration" as the first "high misdemeanor" that constituted an impeachable offense. Berger (1973), 65.

36. Berger (1973), 53–102.

37. Gerhardt (2000), 103.

38. Richard Wooddeson, *Laws of England*, vol. 2 (Dublin: E. Lynch, 1792), 611.

39. Berger (1973), 46, reports for example a Parliamentary declaration in the context of the impeachment of the Earl of Clarendon that the "discretion of parliament . . . is, and ought to be unconfined for the safety and preservation of the whole." Also see 48–49, 65.

40. Ibid., 2. Berger claims that Parliament's use of impeachment during this period "played a mighty role in the achievement of English liberty" (7). Also see Hoffer and Hull (1984), 3–14.

41. Berger (1973), 3, reports, for example, that in the seventeenth-century impeachments of Justices Robert Berkley and John Finch, ostensibly pursued under charges of "subversion of fundamental law and the like, their real sin was to exert pressure in favor of the 'Ship-Money Tax.'" Berger, 55, n. 253, quotes a declaration by the seventeenth-century House of Lords that impeachments represented "the groans of the people." Also see 76.

42. Ibid., 35.

43. See Wood (1969), 160, 294–296; Ervin (1970), 112; Berger (1973), 1492, 1494; Hoffer and Hull (1984), 9; and Gerber (2011), 24.

44. In 1732 the Massachusetts Bay Colony's assembly protested to the royal governor their inability to remove royally appointed judges from office: "The Representatives who raise the money and whose constituents pay for it, have no sort of remedy . . . for we cannot impeach, as is the usage of the House of Commons in such

cases." Hoffer and Hull (1984), 32. In 1740 the North Carolina assembly sought to impeach that colony's chief justice for abuse of power. Gerber (2011), 191. In 1774, the Massachusetts Bay Colony assembly attempted to impeach the colony's chief justice for abuse of power. Hoffer and Hull (1984), 27–56, survey several such episodes.

45. Berger (1973), 149. Also see Mary Clarke, *Parliamentary Privilege in the American Colonies* (New Haven: Yale University Press, 1943), 220; and Hoffer and Hull (1984), 11–56.

46. *Boston Gazette*, January 4, 1768, reprinted in *Quincy's Mass. Reports, 1761– 1772*, vol. 4, 581, 583, 584 (1865), as quoted in Berger (1973), 32, n. 107.

47. Hoffer and Hull (1984), 41–56, term these "revolutionary impeachments."

48. Board of Trade to King George III, November 11, 1761, as quoted in Gerber (2011), 194.

49. One of the recorded purposes of the Townshend Revenue Act of 1767 was to pay judicial salaries from revenues raised by Parliament, and so to remove this power from the colonial legislatures. Hoffer and Hull (1984), 49–59.

50. Adams, *Works of John Adams*, vol. 3 (1856), 514–515.

51. As quoted in Gerber (2011), 84. Also see Smith (1976), 1150, and Black (1985), 117, 128.

52. See Judith Resnik, "Interdependent Federal Judiciaries: Puzzling About Why and How to Value the Independence of Which Judges," *Daedalus* (Fall 2008): 28–47.

53. Wood (1969), 298; also see 300–302.

54. Thomas Paine, *Common Sense* (1776), http://www.gutenberg.org/files/147/ 147-h/147-h.htm.

55. *The People the Best Governors; or, A Plan of Government Founded on the Just Principles of Natural Freedom* (Hartford, 1776), as quoted in Jack N. Rakove, *Original Meanings: Politics and Ideas in the Making of the Constitution* (New York: Random House, 1996), 305.

56. Thomas Jefferson to Edmund Pendleton, August 26, 1776, in *The Papers of Thomas Jefferson*, ed. Julian P. Boyd, vol. 1 (Princeton: Princeton University Press, 1950), 504.

57. Ibid., 505.

58. Berger (1973), 151, 1495; Smith (1976); Hoffer and Hull (1984), 59–95.

59. *The Creation of the American Republic, 1776–1787* (Chapel Hill: University of North Carolina Press, 1969), 161.

60. Constitution of Massachusetts 1780, Article V, accessed at http://www.nhinet .org/ccs/docs/ma-1780.htm.

61. See Wood (1969).

62. Rossiter, *Federalist Papers*, 466.

63. Ibid.

64. Ibid., 472.

65. Ibid., 324.

66. Ibid., 308.

67. Ibid., 324.

68. Madison's Observations on Jefferson's Draft of a Constitution for Virginia, as quoted in Wood (1969), 304.

69. "Rudiments of Law and Government Deduced from the Law of Nature" (1783), as quoted in Wood (1969), 303.

70. Jefferson to Philip Mazzei, November 1785, as quoted in Wood (1969), 304.

71. *Providence Gazette*, May 12, 1787, as quoted in Wood (1969), 456.

72. Max Farrand, ed., *The Records of the Federal Convention of 1787*, vol. 1 (New Haven, Yale University Press, 1911), 337, insert added.

73. Max Farrand, *The Records of the Federal Convention of 1787*, vol. 2 (New Haven: Yale University Press, 1911), 550.

74. Ibid.

75. Michael J. Gerhardt, "The Lessons of Impeachment History," 67 *George Washington Law Review* 603 (1999): 610. For example, "maladministration" was thought to be an instance of a "high Crime or Misdemeanor." Gerhardt (2000), 6, 9.

76. Gerhardt (2000), 7; Hoffer and Hull (1984), 101.

77. Federalist 65, in Rossiter (1961), 397.

78. Ibid., 396 (capitals in original). According to Indiana University Professor of Law Charles Gardner Geyh, "There appears to have been general agreement in the convention and ratification debates that impeachment ought to reach 'political' offenses not recognized as conventional crimes at common law." ABA Report from Commission on Separation of Powers and Judicial Independence, 10, Appendix A, 71.

79. Federalist 65, 398.

80. Federalist 81, in Rossiter (1961), 484, 482.

81. Ibid.

82. Federalist 79, in Rossiter (1961), 474.

83. Federalist 81, 485.

84. Farrand, *The Records of the Federal Convention of 1787*, rev. ed., vol. 2 (New Haven: Yale University Press, 1937), 44–45.

85. Charles Gardner Geyh and Emily Field Van Tassel, "Independence of the Judicial Branch in the New Republic," 74 *Chicago-Kent Law Review* 31 (1998): 42.

86. Federalist 79, 473.

87. Ibid., 472. Some contemporary observers concur with Hamilton's prediction of dependence. See, e.g., Frank B. Cross and Blake J. Nelson, "Strategic Institutional Effects on Supreme Court Decisionmaking," *Northwestern University Law Review* 95 (2001): 1437–1493, and William M. Landes and Richard A. Posner, "The Independent Judiciary in an Interest-Group Perspective," *Journal of Law and Economics* 18 (1976): 875–901, 885. Hamilton also made note of the elected branches' power to set the courts' budgets. Cross and Nelson (2001) likewise note the possible effects from the elected branches' refusal to appropriate sufficient funds for the Court's supporting personnel, including the clerks who are critical to the justices' ability to manage their caseload.

88. Rossiter (1961), 481.

89. Federalist 81, 491, 488.

90. Ibid., 490.

91. Ibid., 495.

92. Walter Hartwell Bennett, ed., *Letters from the Federal Farmer to the Republican* (Tuscaloosa: University of Alabama Press, 1978), 99.

93. Federalist 78, in Rossiter (1961), 465.

94. Ibid.

95. Gerber (2011), 56.

96. John Adams, *Thoughts on Government* (1776), reprinted in Adams (1851), vol. 4, 193–200, emphasis added.

97. Ibid.; Constitution of Massachusetts, 1780, accessed at http://www.nhinet .org/ccs/docs/ma-1780.htm. It is difficult to see in Adams's writing the "final step in the political theory of an independent judiciary" seen by Gerber (2011), 24.

98. Wood (1969), 161.

99. Prakash (1999), 571, 580.

100. Federalist 81, 482.

101. Federalist 78, 465–466.

102. Patrick Henry, "Statement at the Virginia Ratification Convention (June 12, 1788)," in *The Debates in the Several State Conventions on the Adoption of the Federal Constitution*, ed. Jonathan Elliot, vol. 3 (New York: J. B. Lippincott, 1863), 313.

103. Wilson, "Lectures on Law," in Wilson, *Works of Wilson*, vol. 1, 398–399, as quoted in Wood (1969), 598.

104. Prakash and Smith (2006), 88.

105. *Rules of the House of Representatives*, LIII, Section 603. Vehicles for initiating impeachment procedures include the request of a member of the House, a memorial submitted by private citizens, a presidential message, or charges transmitted from a state legislature or from a grand jury.

106. Eleanore Bushnell, *Crimes, Follies, and Misfortunes: The Federal Impeachment Trials* (Urbana: University of Illinois Press, 1992), reports several instances of such fishing expeditions.

107. This is not to imply that there have not been instances wherein conviction of a federal judge has failed of a two-thirds vote in the Senate after impeachment in the House. There have been several such instances. There have also been many more in-stances wherein federal judges have resigned just prior to, during, or just after House impeachment investigations. The question raised in the text concerns judicial incen-tives, and can only be answered with the data analyses of subsequent chapters.

108. Hoffer and Hull (1984), 4.

109. Some changes to the English institution of impeachment were made in the American context. For example, under the U.S. Constitution the punishment for im-peachment may extend no further than to removal from office, while in the English context the House of Lords has greater discretion over punishment in the case of conviction (Berger 1973). However, these differences between English and American impeachment should not affect the question of whether in either context judges have

incentives to defer to the lower legislative chamber, irrespective of the composition of the upper legislative chamber.

110. Dumas Malone, *Jefferson and His Time*, vol. 4 (Boston: Little, Brown, 1970), 459, 462; Hoffer and Hull (1984), 194–195.

111. James V. Saturno, "The Origination Clause of the U.S. Constitution: Interpretation and Enforcement," Congressional Research Service, March 15, 2011, http://www.fas.org/sgp/crs/misc/RL31399.pdf.

112. See Robert A. Dahl, "Decision-Making in a Democracy: The Supreme Court as a National Policy-Maker," 6 *Journal of Public Law* 279 (1957); Terri Jennings Peretti, *In Defense of a Political Court* (Princeton: Princeton University Press, 1999), 100, 130; Jeffrey A. Segal and Harold J. Spaeth, *The Supreme Court and the Attitudinal Model Revisited* (New York: Cambridge University Press, 2002), 94, 110; and Neal Devins, "Smoke, Not Fire," 65 *Maryland Law Review* 197 (2006).

113. Sandra Day O'Connor, "Remarks on Judicial Independence," 58 *Florida Law Review* 1 (2005): 4.

114. Testimony before the American Bar Association's Commission on Separation of Powers and Judicial Independence, October 11, 1996, "Report on an Independent Judiciary," ABA Commission on Separation of Powers and Judicial Independence, February 21, 1997, 12.

115. Raoul Berger likewise suggested that in the British context "the disuse of impeachment testifies not so much to the abandonment of an outmoded instrument of government as to the flexible good sense . . . of English administration." Raoul Berger, *Impeachment: The Constitutional Problems* (Cambridge: Harvard University Press, 1973), 3, n. 15.

116. Hoffer and Hull (1984), 146

117. Ibid., 149.

118. Ibid., 262, 261.

119. This list is drawn from Bushnell (1992), 14–15; Geyh (2006); and news reports for the most recent impeachments.

120. The House of Representatives has investigated many more federal judges than it has actually impeached. During the first two decades of the nineteenth century, for example, between 11 percent and 13 percent of federal judges were investigated by the Jeffersonian majority in the House. The frequency of House investigations of federal judges was also high during the 1870s and during the 1920s and 1930s. Emily Field Van Tassel, "Resignations and Removals: A History of Federal Judicial Service—and Disservice—1789–1992," 142 *University of Pennsylvania Law Review* 333 (1993): 370–371. More than fifty federal judges have resigned during the course of House impeachment investigations. Joseph Borkin, *The Corrupt Judge: An Inquiry into Bribery and Other High Crimes and Misdemeanors in Federal Courts* (New York: Clarkson Potter, 1962).

121. For histories of these impeachments, see Hoffer and Hull (1984); Bushnell (1992); Van Tassel and Finkelman (1999); and Geyh (2006).

122. Hoffer and Hull (1984), 188.

123. Report of the National Commission on Judicial Discipline and Removal (August 1993), 4. The absence of partisanship in these impeachments with respect to the impeaching House majorities does not, however, preclude the possibility that the decisions made by the judicial councils of the federal circuits were affected by partisanship in other ways.

124. Ruth Marcus, "Booting the Bench," *Washington Post*, April 11, 2005.

125. David Barton pamphlet (1996), 53, quoted in *Report of the ABA Commission on Separation of Powers and Judicial Independence*, 15.

126. Tom DeLay, "Impeachment Is a Valid Answer to a Judiciary Run Amok," *New York Times*, April 6, 1997.

127. Ralph Z. Hallow, "Republicans Out to Impeach 'Activist' Jurists," *Washington Times*, March 12, 1997.

128. Greg McDonald, "Some Republicans Mull Impeachment," *Houston Chronicle*, January 30, 1998.

129. Stephen B. Burbank, "Judicial Independence, Judicial Accountability, and Interbranch Relations," Daedalus 4 (Fall 2008): 4, citing editorial, *San Antonio Express*, January 12, 2004.

130. H. Res. 568, http://thomas.loc.gov/cgi-bin/bdquery/z?d108:h.res.00568:.

131. Linda Greenhouse, *New York Times*, January 1, 2005.

132. Jennifer Loven, "DeLay: Those Responsible for Schiavo's Death Will Answer for It," Associated Press, April 1, 2005.

133. Ruth Marcus, "Booting the Bench," *Washington Post*, April 11, 2005.

134. Ibid.

135. Ibid.

136. *Newdow v. United States Congress et al.*, 328 F.3d 466 (9th Cir. 2003).

137. Newt Gingrich, *Winning the Future* (Washington, DC: Regnery, 2005), 78.

138. *New York Times*, January 1, 2004.

139. Ibid.; Linda Greenhouse, "Rehnquist Resumes His Call for Judicial Independence," *New York Times*, January 1, 2005. In January 2005 the Court ruled the Sentencing Guidelines only "advisory," thereby eliminating the force of the Feeney Amendment. *U.S. v. Booker* (2005).

140. Testimony from December 13, 1996, in ABA Report, 19.

141. Ibid., 19, n. 43.

142. Remarks at Kalamazoo College, November 21, 1996, quoted in ABA Report, 22–23.

143. *New York Times*, December 10, 1998.

144. "Ginsburg Recalls Florida Recount Case," *New York Times*, February 4, 2001.

145. *New York Times*, January 1, 2004.

146. *New York Times*, January 1, 2005.

147. Charles Lane, "Ginsburg Faults GOP Critics, Cites a Threat from 'Fringe,'" *Washington Post*, March 17, 2006.

148. *Miami Herald*, April 18, 2005. Also see Jeffrey Jackson, "Judicial Independence, Adequate Court Funding, and Inherent Judicial Power," 52 *Maryland Law Review* 217 (1993).

149. December 13, 1996, as quoted in ABA Report, 28. Also see the October 11, 1996, testimony of Andrew Coats, then Dean, University of Oklahoma College of Law, and President, American College of Trial Lawyers, ABA Report, 29, n. 99.

150. December 13, 1996, as quoted in ibid., 28.

151. February 21, 1997, in ibid., 29.

152. "Money, or the Relations of the Judicial Branch with the Other Two Branches, Legislative and Executive," 40 *Saint Louis University Law Journal* 19 (1996).

153. "Remarks on Judicial Independence," 58 *Florida Law Review* 1 (January 2006).

154. *New York Times*, July 22, 2005.

155. For historical examples of congressional jurisdiction stripping, see Walter Murphy, *Congress and the Court* (Chicago: University of Chicago Press, 1962); Donald Morgan, *Congress and the Constitution: A Study of Responsibility* (Cambridge: Harvard University Press, 1966), 246–291; Rosenberg (1992), 377, 385, 387, 390; McNollgast (1995), 1664; Lucas A. Powe Jr., *The Warren Court and American Politics* (Cambridge: Harvard University Press, 2000), 134–136; Cross and Nelson (2001); Segal and Spaeth (2002), 230; and Neal Devins, "Constitutional Avoidance and the Roberts Court," 32 *University of Dayton Law Review* 339 (2007).

156. *New York Times*, October 27, 1996. The restrictions on judges' power to issue preliminary injunctions were upheld by the Supreme Court in June 2000. *New York Times*, June 20, 2000.

157. *New York Times*, October 27, 1996.

158. *New York Times*, January 1, 2005. Generally see Neal Devins, "Should the Court Fear Congress?" 90 *Minnesota Law Review* 1337 (2006), and Neal Devins, "Smoke, Not Fire," 65 *Maryland Law Review* 197 (2006).

159. O'Connor (2006), 2.

160. "2004 Year-End Report on the Federal Judiciary," January 1, 2005.

161. Friedman (1998), 743, 746.

162. As quoted in O'Connor (2006), 5.

163. For the story of Roosevelt's Court-packing proposal see most recently Jeff Sheshol, *Supreme Power: Franklin Roosevelt vs. the Supreme Court* (New York: W. W. Norton, 2010).

164. Senator Gouverneur Morris, in Charles S. Hyneman and George W. Carey, *A Second Federalist* (Columbia: University of South Carolina Press, 1970), 195–197.

165. For other historical examples of congressional manipulation of the number, composition, and jurisdiction of the lower federal courts, see Landes and Posner (1976), 885; Rosenberg (1992), 380–381; McNollgast (1995), 1648, 1663; Cross and Nelson (2001); and Segal and Spaeth (2002), 226, n. 8, 227–228, 236, 236, n. 34.

166. Jonathan D. Glater, "Lawmakers Trying Again to Divide Ninth Circuit," *New York Times*, June 19, 2005.

167. *Washington Post*, April 7, 2005.

168. "Term Limits for the Supreme Court: Life Tenure Reconsidered," 29 *Harvard Journal of Law and Public Policy* 769 (2006): 810, n. 109.

169. Saikrishna Prakash, "America's Aristocracy," 109 *Yale Law Journal* 541 (1999): 571, n. 141.

170. http://en.wikipedia.org/wiki/Supreme_Court_of_the_United_States.

171. Charles G. Geyh, "Judicial Independence, Judicial Accountability, and the Role of Constitutional Norms in Congressional Regulation of the Courts," 78 *Indiana Law Journal* 153 (2003): 220; Geyh (2006). Also see Segal and Spaeth (2002), 94: "Overall, the negative political consequences, electoral or otherwise, of limiting judicial independence far outweigh whatever short-run policy gains Congress might gain by reining in the Court."

172. Calabresi and Lindgren (2006), 810, n. 109.

173. Federalist 81, 485.

174. Arthur Conan Doyle, "The Adventure of Silver Blaze," *Strand* 4 (July–December 1892): 645–660. Holmes later explains, "I had grasped the significance of the silence of the dog, for one true inference invariably suggests others . . . Obviously the midnight visitor was someone whom the dog knew well."

175. November 2005 speech to the American Academy of Appellate Lawyers. This speech was also given at the University of Florida's Levin College of Law and reprinted in "Remarks on Judicial Independence," 58 *Florida Law Review* 1 (2006): 1–6, and in Daedalus (Fall 2008).

176. Federalist 81, 485.

Chapter Three. Estimating the Effect of Elected Branch Preferences on Supreme Court Judgments

1. Clark (2011) estimates the impact on Supreme Court decisions of congressional bill introductions imposing sanctions on the federal courts. Bill introductions are interpreted not as credible threats against the federal courts, but rather as signals about the level of public support for those courts; the justices are assumed to respond to these signals. The plausibility of this model is bolstered by results showing that the justices respond directly to public opinion as measured by the Stimson (1999) measure of the public "mood." However, using objective measures of the Court's judgments there is no evidence of responsiveness to the public mood, as reported in Chapter Six.

2. For example, conventional accounts of the Warren Court suggest that it boldly defied the more conservative elected branches: Morton J. Horwitz, *The Warren Court and the Pursuit of Justice* (New York: Hill and Wang, 1998), 3; Cass Sunstein, *Radicals in Robes* (New York: Basic Books, 2005), 36; and Toobin (2007), 2. This account has been challenged in Gerald Rosenberg, *The Hollow Hope* (Chicago: University of Chicago Press, 1991); Lucas A. Powe Jr., *The Warren Court and American Politics* (Cambridge: Harvard University Press, 2000); Mary Dudziak, *Cold War Civil Rights* (Princeton: Princeton University Press, 2002); Michael Klarman, *From Jim Crow to Civil Rights* (New York: Oxford University Press, 2004); and Corinna Barrett Lain, "Countermajoritarian Hero or Zero? Rethinking the Warren Court's Role

in the Criminal Procedure Revolution," 152 *University of Pennsylvania Law Review* 1451 (2004). Friedman (2009) provides an overview of the historiographical debates.

3. Segal and Spaeth (2002), 346, 110.

4. Lewis A. Kornhauser, "Modeling Collegial Courts II: Legal Doctrine," *Journal of Law, Economics and Organization* 8 (1992): 441–470; Jeffrey R. Lax, "Constructing Legal Rules on Appellate Courts," *American Political Science Review* 101 (2007): 591–604.

5. Majority opinions endorsing approximately these legal rules include, respectively, *A.L.A. Schechter Poultry Corporation v. United States*, 295 U.S. 495 (1935); *National Labor Relations Board v. Jones & Laughlin Steel Corporation*, 301 U.S. 1 (1937); *United States v. Lopez* 514 U.S. 549 (1995).

6. More technically, both justices and legislators are assumed to have single peaked preferences in a single policy dimension. See Lax (2007) for the generalization of this framework to a multidimensional space.

7. For discussions of the estimation of congressional preferences from roll call votes, see Keith T. Poole and Howard Rosenthal, *Congress: A Political-Economic History of Roll Call Voting* (New York: Oxford University Press, 1997), and Michael A. Bailey, "Comparable Preference Estimates across Time and Institutions for the Court, Congress, and Presidency," *American Journal of Political Science* 51 (2007): 433–448. For discussions of the estimation of judicial preferences from votes in cases, see Andrew D. Martin and Kevin M. Quinn, "Dynamic Ideal Point Estimation via Markov Chain Monte Carlo for the U.S. Supreme Court, 1953–1999," *Political Analysis* 10 (2002): 134–153, and Bailey (2007). The Martin-Quinn revealed preference estimates, which assume a single dimension of preferences, correctly predict 76 percent of the justices' votes from 1953 to 1999 (Martin and Quinn [2002]). For the Burger Court between 1981 and 1985, approximately 93 percent of votes on cases fell on a single dimension (Martin and Quinn [2002]). Another study, not using revealed preference estimates, found that from 80 percent to 93 percent of the variation in the justices' votes could be explained by a single underlying dimension of preferences; Bernard Grofman and Timothy J. Brazill, "Identifying the Median Justice on the Supreme Court through Multidimensional Scaling: Analysis of 'Natural Courts,' 1953–1991," *Public Choice* 112 (2002): 55. Lawrence Sirovich found only two dimensions in Supreme Court voting behavior: one corresponding to unanimous opinions and another to left-right divisions over policy. Lawrence Sirovich, "A Pattern Analysis of the Second Rehnquist U.S. Supreme Court," *Proceedings of the National Academy of Sciences* 100 (2003): 7432–7437.

8. See Poole and Rosenthal (1997), and Simon Hix, Abdul G. Noury, and Gerard Roland, *Democratic Politics in the European Parliament* (New York: Cambridge University Press, 2007).

9. A review of these concerns may be found in Joshua B. Fischman and David S. Law, "What Is Judicial Ideology, and How Do We Measure It?" 29 *Washington University Journal of Law and Policy* 133 (2009).

10. Ibid.

11. Median voter models date to the work of Duncan Black: "On the Rationale of Group Decision-Making," 56 *Journal of Political Economy* 23 (1948), and *The Theory of Committees and Elections* (New York: Cambridge University Press, 1958). For a recent review of median voter models as applied to the Supreme Court, see Andrew D. Martin, Kevin M. Quinn, and Lee Epstein, "The Median Justice on the United States Supreme Court," 83 *North Carolina Law Review* 1275 (2005).

12. For a discussion of these issues, see Jeffrey R. Lax and Charles M. Cameron, "Bargaining and Opinion Assignment on the U.S. Supreme Court," *Journal of Law, Economics and Organization* 23 (2007): 276–302.

13. See, e.g., John Ferejohn and Charles Shipan, "Congressional Influence on Bureaucracy," *Journal of Law, Economics and Organization* 6 (1990): 1–20; Rafael Gely and Pablo T. Spiller, "A Rational Choice Theory of Supreme Court Statutory Decisions with Applications to the State Farm and Grove City Cases," *Journal of Law, Economics, and Organization* 6 (1990): 263–300; William N. Eskridge Jr., "Overriding Supreme Court Statutory Interpretation Decisions," 101 *Yale Law Journal* 331 (1991); William N. Eskridge Jr., "Reneging on History? Playing the Court/Congress/President Civil Rights Game," 79 *California Law Review* 613 (May 1991); Pablo T. Spiller and Rafael Gely, "Congressional Control or Judicial Independence: The Determinants of U.S. Supreme Court Labor-Relations Decisions, 1949–1988," *RAND Journal of Economics* 23 (1992): 463–492; John Ferejohn and Barry Weingast, "A Positive Theory of Statutory Interpretation," *International Journal of Law and Economics* 12 (1992): 263–279; and Mario Bergara, Barak Richman, and Pablo T. Spiller, "Modeling Supreme Court Strategic Decision Making: The Congressional Constraint," *Legislative Studies Quarterly* 28 (2003): 247–280.

14. For an overview of these models, see Jeffrey A. Segal, "Separation-of-Powers Games in the Positive Theory of Congress and Courts," *American Political Science Review* 91 (1997): 28–44; Jeffrey A. Segal, "Correction to 'Separation-of-Powers Games in the Positive Theory of Congress and Courts,'" *American Political Science Review* 92 (1998): 923–926; and Timothy Groseclose and Sara Schiavoni, "Rethinking Justices' and Committees' Strategies in Segal's Separation of Powers Game," *Public Choice* 106 (2001): 131–135.

15. Spiller and Gely (1992) found support for the constrained Court hypothesis in statutory labor relations cases between 1949 and 1988, and Bergara, Richman, and Spiller (2003) found support in statutory civil liberties cases between 1947 and 1992. But Segal (1997) and Segal and Spaeth (2002) found no such support in the same latter set of statutory civil liberties cases. Thomas G. Hansford and David F. Damore found only mixed support for a constrained Court in statutory cases ("Congressional Preferences, Perceptions of Threat, and Supreme Court Decision Making," *American Politics Quarterly* 28 [2000]: 490–510), and James F. Spriggs II and Thomas G. Hansford found no effect from congressional preferences on the likelihood that the Supreme Court overruled statutory precedents ("Explaining the Overruling of U.S. Supreme Court Precedent," *Journal of Politics* 63 [2001]: 1091–1111). Clark (2011) found no effect of congressional preferences on the Court's decisions in statutory cases.

16. Constitutional amendments are a possible response to the Court's constitutional decisions; see Rafael Gely and Pablo T. Spiller, "The Political Economy of Supreme Court Constitutional Decisions: The Case of Roosevelt's Court-Packing Plan," *International Review of Law and Economics* 12 (1992): 45–67. The hurdles accompanying the amendment process, however, make this an unlikely avenue of elected branch constraint.

17. See Lee Epstein and Jack Knight, *The Choices Justices Make* (Washington, DC: Congressional Quarterly, 1998), 150–154; Lee Epstein, Jack Knight, and Andrew D. Martin, "The Supreme Court as a Strategic National Policymaker," 50 *Emory Law Journal* 583 (2001; Andrew D. Martin, "Statutory Battles and Constitutional Wars: Congress and the Supreme Court," in *Institutional Games and the U.S. Supreme Court*, ed. Jon R. Bond, Roy B. Flemming, and James R. Rogers (Charlottesville: University of Virginia Press, 2006).

18. Epstein, Knight, and Martin (2001) reported descriptive evidence supporting the proposition that moderate justices adjust their voting behavior in constitutional civil rights cases to take account of the preferences of presidents and median senators, but Martin (2006), using a more sophisticated methodology, found no such adjustment to congressional preferences. Spriggs and Hansford (2001) found no effect from congressional preferences on the likelihood that the Court overturned constitutional precedent, and Brian R. Sala and James F. Spriggs, II, "Designing Tests of the Supreme Court and the Separation of Powers," *Political Research Quarterly* 57 (2004): 197–208, found no evidence of congressional constraint in constitutional decisions between 1946 and 1999. Stefanie A. Lindquist and Rorie Spill Solberg found that congressional closeness to a statute decreased the likelihood that the statute would be struck by the Court ("Judicial Review by the Burger and Rehnquist Courts: Explaining Justices' Responses to Constitutional Challenges," *Political Research Quarterly* 60 [2007]: 71–90), but Jeffrey Segal, Chad Westerland, and Stefanie A. Lindquist, "Congress, the Supreme Court, and Judicial Review: Testing a Constitutional Separation of Powers Model," *American Journal of Political Science* 55 (2011): 89–104, found no such effects. Clark (2011) likewise found no effect of congressional preferences over statutes on the probability that the Court strikes a federal statute. But see Barry Friedman and Anna Harvey, "Electing the Supreme Court," *Indiana Law Journal* 78 (2003): 123–151; Anna Harvey and Barry Friedman, "Pulling Punches: Congressional Constraints on the Supreme Court's Constitutional Rulings, 1987–2000," *Legislative Studies Quarterly* 31 (2006): 533–562; Anna Harvey and Barry Friedman, "Ducking Trouble: Congressionally-Induced Selection Bias in the Supreme Court's Agenda," *Journal of Politics* 71 (2009): 574–592; Anna Harvey and Michael Woodruff, "Confirmation Bias in the United States Supreme Court Judicial Database," *Journal of Law, Economics and Organization* (2011), doi: 10.1093/jleo/ewr003; and Anna Harvey, "The Will of the Congress," 3 *Michigan State Law Review* 729 (2010).

19. Keith Krehbiel, "Why Are Congressional Committees So Powerful?" *American Political Science Review* 81 (1987): 929–935; Keith Krehbiel and Douglas Rivers, "The Analysis of Committee Power: An Application to Senate Voting on the

Minimum Wage," *American Journal of Political Science* 32 (1988): 1151–1174; Keith Krehbiel, "Cosponsors and Wafflers from A to Z," *American Journal of Political Science* 39 (1995): 906–923; Keith Krehbiel, "Restrictive Rules Reconsidered," *American Journal of Political Science* 41 (1997): 919–944; Keith Krehbiel, *Pivotal Politics: A Theory of U.S. Lawmaking* (Chicago: University of Chicago Press, 1998). In other work I have tested alternative models of congressional decision making, with consistent results across all models (see Friedman and Harvey [2003], Harvey and Friedman [2006], Harvey and Friedman [2009], Harvey [2010], and Harvey and Woodruff [2011]).

20. Bailey (2007). The Bailey cross-institutional preference estimates also link votes over time on related legal rules, such that when the justices cite with approval or disapproval previously decided cases, or directly overturn prior precedent, these are treated as comparable "votes" in the earlier cases. This "bridging" of votes over time allows the analyst to at least partially control for the fact that the Court's agenda may change over time, allowing the estimates to more precisely represent intertemporal preferences rather than intertemporal agenda change.

21. Lee Epstein, Andrew D. Martin, Jeffrey A. Segal, and Chad Westerland, "The Judicial Common Space," *Journal of Law, Economics, and Organization* 23 (2007): 303–325.

22. More specifically, the Martin-Quinn preference estimates from the fifteen unconstrained nominees' first year of service are assumed to be equivalent to the Poole-Rosenthal Common Space preference estimates of their appointing presidents. Other justices' Martin-Quinn preference estimates are then algebraically transformed into Common Space preference estimates using this equivalence (Epstein et al. [2007]).

23. Bryon J. Moraski and Charles R. Shipan, "The Politics of Supreme Court Nominations: A Theory of Institutional Constraints and Choices," *American Journal of Political Science* 43 (1999): 1069–1095.

24. Epstein et al. (2007).

25. See Fischman and Law (2009) for a discussion of this issue.

26. The estimated most preferred rule of the median justice in term *t* is paired with the estimated most preferred rules of these elected officials in year $t + 1$. The Bailey (2007) XTI measures are available only for the period 1950–2002. However, because the membership of the Court does not change during the 2003 and 2004 terms, we can reasonably assume that the median justice during these terms continued to be Justice O'Connor, and can perhaps without too much difficulty continue her estimated most preferred rule through these two terms. The composition of the House of Representatives also remained largely unchanged from 2003 to 2005; the Republican majority picked up eight seats in the 2002 elections, and another three seats in the 2004 elections. These seat changes would likely not have made large changes in the preferences of the median representative. It is thus not unreasonable to continue the estimated most preferred rule of the House median from 2002 through 2005. All analyses reported here have also been performed using just the Bailey XTI preference estimates through the 2001 term, with no substantive changes in the results.

27. See Poole and Rosenthal (1997), Appendix A, for a discussion of the analogous problem of identifying bill locations from congressional roll call votes alone.

28. See http://Supreme Court Databaseb.wustl.edu/. Studies using this measure include Segal (1997), Hansford and Damore (2000), Spriggs and Hansford (2001), Segal and Spaeth (2002), Sala and Spriggs (2004), Martin (2006), and Clark (2011). Some studies have looked at the effect of congressional preferences on judicial "activism," or the propensity of the Court to strike federal statutes. See, e.g., Jeffrey A. Segal and Chad Westerland, "The Supreme Court, Congress, and Judicial Review," 83 *North Carolina Law Review* 1323 (2005); Tom S. Clark, "The Separation of Powers, Court Curbing, and Judicial Legitimacy," *American Journal of Political Science* 53 (2009): 971–989; Jeffrey A. Segal, Chad Westerland, and Stefanie A. Lindquist, "Congress, the Supreme Court, and Judicial Review: Testing a Constitutional Separation of Powers Model," *American Journal of Political Science* 55 (2011): 89–104; and Clark (2011). However, without knowing anything about the legal rules embodied by these statutes, it is impossible to connect a model based on the predicted location of the Court's rule in a given case with the justices' decision to strike or uphold the statute at issue in that case.

29. See Harvey and Woodruff (2011).

30. See, e.g., Segal (1997).

31. All 6,929 cases between the 1953 and 2004 terms for which a judgment code is reported in the Supreme Court Database were included in Figures 3.3 and 3.4.

32. The p-value for the correlation coefficient is .13, for 52 observations.

33. The correlation coefficient is only .01 for these two series, with a p-value of .92.

34. Using the Bailey XTI estimates the correlation coefficient is –.07 for these two series, with a p value of .60, using the JCS estimates the correlation coefficient is .26, with a p-value of .06.

35. Using the Bailey XTI estimates the correlation coefficient is .47 for these two series, with a p-value of .00; using the JCS estimates the correlation coefficient is .22, with a p-value of .12.

36. See, e.g., Epstein and Martin 2011.

37. See, e.g., Jeff Yates, *Popular Justice: Presidential Prestige and Executive Success in the Supreme Court* (New York: State University of New York Press, 2002).

38. The 95 percent confidence intervals for these point predictions are (.23, .31) and (.55, .62), respectively. All predicted probabilities reported in this chapter hold all other variables constant at their actual values. Because these predicted probabilities take into account how all variables in the model actually covary in a dataset, they are more representative estimates of the size of a variable's effect than those generated by the approach of holding all variables constant at their means or other values. Andrew Gelman and Jennifer Hill, *Data Analysis Using Regression and Multilevel/Hierarchical Models* (New York: Cambridge University Press, 2006), 101–103. Probabilities are simulated using the *margins* command in Stata 12.

39. The 95 percent confidence intervals for these point predictions are (.28, .38) and (.53, .59), respectively.

40. This sample is restricted to those cases coded by the Supreme Court Database as involving constitutional analysis (AUTHDEC1 or AUTHDEC2 < 3) that also have directional judgment codes assigned for the 1953–2004 terms for the judgments of both the lower court and the Supreme Court.

41. The 95 percent confidence intervals for the Bailey XTI predicted probabilities are (.13, .29) and (.56, .67), and for the JCS predicted probabilities are (.20, 33) and (.57, .64).

42. This sample is restricted to those cases from the previous sample that are coded by the Supreme Court Database as involving constitutional review of federal action (AUTHDEC1 or AUTHDEC2 = 1). The 95 percent confidence intervals for the Bailey XTI predicted probabilities are (.16, .53) and (.62, .81), and for the JCS predicted probabilities are (.28, .56) and (.64, .76).

43. This sample is restricted to those cases in the previous sample that involve constitutional review of a federal statute. To construct this sample, cases from the previous sample were discarded if no entry in the LAW variable for any record referred to a federal statute. Cases were then read to ensure that each involved a constitutional challenge to a federal statute. There were 309 constitutional challenges to federal statutes between 1953 and 2004 identified through this method; 294 of these challenges are assigned directional judgment codes in the Supreme Court Database. The 95 percent confidence intervals for the Bailey XTI predicted probabilities are (.01, .16) and (.68, .86), and for the JCS predicted probabilities are (.07, .34) and (.63, .83).

44. Segal and Spaeth (2002), 110.

45. Ibid., 349.

46. There remains the possibility that, as discussed earlier, available judicial preference estimates already incorporate the effects of congressional preferences on the Court's judgments. As we will see in Chapter Five, however, that is not the reason, or at least not the only reason, we find no effects from congressional preferences here.

Chapter Four. The Puzzle of the Two Rehnquist Courts

1. Columbia University Professor of Law Thomas W. Merrill appears to have been the first to use the terminology of the "first" and "second" Rehnquist Courts in "The Making of the Second Rehnquist Court: A Preliminary Analysis," 47 *Saint Louis University Law Journal* 569 (2003).

2. Friedman (2009), 280–330.

3. Vincent Blasi, ed., *The Burger Court: The Counter-Revolution That Wasn't* (New Haven: Yale University Press, 1983).

4. *New York Times*, July 10, 1986.

5. *New York Times*, June 22, 1986; also see *New York Times*, June 18, 1986.

6. *New York Times*, June 19, 1986.

7. Ibid.

8. *New York Times*, June 18, 1986; also see *New York Times*, January 24, 1987. New York University Professor of Law Barry Friedman writes that "people expected

conservatives to prevail on a broad range of social issues" and to form "a solid con-servative majority." Friedman (2009), 325. Friedman notes that these expectations are captured in David G. Savage's 1992 book, *Turning Right: The Making of the Rehnquist Supreme Court* (New York: John Wiley and Sons).

9. *New York Times*, January 24, 1987.

10. *New York Times*, March 30, 1987.

11. *New York Times*, June 28, 1987.

12. See, e.g., *New York Times*, April 26, June 27, 28, 1987.

13. *New York Times*, June 27, 28, 1987.

14. The first quotation is from the *New York Times*, November 15, 1987. The sec-ond is from Bruce Fein, adjunct scholar at the Heritage Foundation, *New York Times*, February 7, 1988.

15. *New York Times*, June 12, 1988.

16. *New York Times*, September 11, 1988.

17. Ibid.

18. Ibid.

19. Ibid. Justice Kennedy joined the Court too late to participate in the case proceedings.

20. Ibid.

21. Ibid.

22. *New York Times*, July 1, 3, 1988.

23. *New York Times*, July 3, 1988.

24. Ibid.

25. Five justices in *Webster* were, however, in favor of permitting restrictive state statutes that did not place an "undue burden" on the right to an abortion promised in *Roe*.

26. 462 U.S. 416.

27. 476 U.S. 747 at 814.

28. The story of the Rehnquist Court's preservation of abortion rights has been told, in varying forms, by James F. Simon, *The Center Holds: The Power Struggles inside the Rehnquist Court* (New York: Simon and Schuster, 1995), 156; Edward P. Lazarus, *Closed Chambers* (New York: Crown, 1998), 449–450; and Merrill (2003), 634–635.

29. *Fitzpatrick v. Bitzer*, 427 U.S. 445 (1976).

30. *New York Times*, July 1, 1990.

31. *New York Times*, July 3, 1992.

32. Savage (1992).

33. *New York Times*, June 26, May 31, 1992.

34. Lazarus (1998), 406–407.

35. *New York Times*, May 31, 1992.

36. The vote in *Wright v. West* was actually unanimous on the judgment, but the justices divided over the question of the standard of review the federal courts should have applied in the case.

37. Lazarus (1998), 471; Merrill (2003), 636–637.

38. 492 U.S. 573 at 656.

39. 492 U.S. 573 at 604.

40. *New York Times*, June 26, 1992.

41. Ibid.

42. *New York Times*, July 1, 1992.

43. Ibid.

44. *New York Times*, July 5, 1, 1992.

45. *New York Times*, July 5, 1992.

46. *New York Times*, November 8, 1992.

47. *New York Times*, March 20, 1993.

48. Ibid.

49. *New York Times*, July 4, 1993.

50. Linda Greenhouse, "Supreme Court Faces a Docket Heavy with Unfinished Rights Cases," *New York Times*, October 1, 1993.

51. "And Now There Are 2: Justice Ginsburg Is Seated," *New York Times*, October 2, 1993.

52. *New York Times*, July 3, 1994.

53. Jeffrey Toobin, *The Nine* (New York: Doubleday, 2007).

54. *New York Times*, May 22, July 14, 1994.

55. *New York Times*, July 14, 1994.

56. Ibid.

57. Friedman (2009), 325.

58. 18 U.S.C. 922(q)(1)(A).

59. Merrill (2003), 585.

60. See, e.g., *Katzenbach v. McClung*, 379 U.S. 294 (1964), at 303–304: "Where we find that the legislators, in light of the facts and testimony before them, have a rational basis for finding a chosen regulatory scheme necessary to the protection of commerce, our investigation is at an end"; *Maryland v. Wirtz*, 392 U.S. 183 (1968), citing with approval the previous quotation; and *Hodel v. Virginia Surface Mining and Reclamation Association, Inc.*, 452 U.S. 264 (1981), at 276: "The court must defer to a congressional finding that a regulated activity affects interstate commerce, if there is any rational basis for such a finding."

61. Laurence H. Tribe, *American Constitutional Law*, 3rd ed. (New York: Foundation, 2000), 816.

62. 514 U.S. 549.

63. Ibid.

64. Ibid.

65. Ibid.

66. *New York Times*, April 27, 1995.

67. Christopher H. Schroeder, "Causes of the Recent Turn in Constitutional Interpretation," 51 *Duke Law Journal* 307 (2001), 318.

68. Tribe (2000), 816–822.

69. *New York Times*, May 24, 1995.

70. *New York Times*, May 28, 1995.

71. *New York Times*, April 28, 1995. The case referred to is *Garcia v. San Antonio Metropolitan Transit Authority*, 469 U.S. 528 (1985).

72. "Chicken Supreme: The Rehnquist Court Is Political in Every Way," *New Yorker*, August 14, 1995.

73. Jonathan L. Entin, "The New Federalism after *United States vs. Lopez*: Introduction," 46 *Case Western Reserve Law Review* 635 (1995–1996): 636.

74. *New York Times*, June 13, 1995.

75. Ibid.

76. *New York Times*, June 30, 1995.

77. Ibid.

78. *New York Times*, July 2, 1995.

79. Charles Fried, "Foreword: Revolutions?" 109 *Harvard Law Review* 13 (1995).

80. John G. Kester, "The Bipolar Supreme Court," *Wall Street Journal*, May 31, 1995; Timothy M. Phelps, "Judicial Revolution; Recent Cases Slant towards States," *Newsday*, May 29, 1995.

81. *New York Times*, July 3, 1995.

82. *Pennsylvania v. Union Gas Co.*, 491 U.S. 1 (1989).

83. 517 U.S. 44.

84. *New York Times*, March 28, 1996.

85. Ibid.

86. Ibid.

87. *New York Times*, July 3, 1996.

88. *New York Times*, April 14, 1996.

89. *New York Times*, May 26, 1996, quoting Clint Bolick, vice president of the Institute for Justice, a conservative think tank and law firm.

90. Section 2 of the Fifteenth Amendment, protecting the right to vote from state action, is an identical enforcement clause ("The Congress shall have power to enforce this article by appropriate legislation").

91. See *Katzenbach v. Morgan*, 384 U.S. 641 (1966), at 653: "It is not for us to review the congressional resolution . . . It is enough that we be able to perceive a basis upon which the Congress might resolve the conflict as it did"; *South Carolina v. Katzenbach*, 383 U.S. 301 (1966), at 324: Congress may use "any rational means" to enforce the Fifteenth Amendment.

92. *Katzenbach v. Morgan*, 384 U.S. 641 (1966), at 648–649: To restrict the Congress to only judicially approved applications of the Fourteenth Amendment would "depreciate both congressional resourcefulness and congressional responsibility for implementing the Amendment."

93. See *South Carolina v. Katzenbach*, 383 U.S. 301 (1966), upholding a statute suspending literacy tests in covered jurisdictions despite a prior Supreme Court ruling that such tests were facially constitutional, and *City of Rome v. United States*, 446 U.S. 156 (1980), upholding a seven-year extension of the preclearance requirements of the Voting Rights Act for changes in voting procedures in covered jurisdictions

that might have discriminatory impact, despite a prior Supreme Court ruling that had required proof of discriminatory intent for judicial determinations of unconstitutional conduct.

94. 521 U.S. 507.

95. Ibid.

96. *New York Times*, June 26, 1997.

97. Ruth Colker and James J. Brudney, "Dissing Congress," 100 *Michigan Law Review* 80 (2001): 127. Also see Steven A. Engel, "The McCulloch Theory of the Fourteenth Amendment: *City of Boerne v. Flores* and the Original Understanding of Section 5," 109 *Yale Law Journal* 115 (1999); Samuel Estreicher and Margaret H. Lemos, "The Section 5 Mystique, *Morrison*, and the Future of Federal Antidiscrimination Law," 2000 *Supreme Court Review* 109 (2000); and Evan H. Caminker, "'Appropriate' Means-Ends Constraints on Section 5 Powers," 53 *Stanford Law Review* 1127 (2001).

98. Robert C. Post and Reva B. Siegel, "Legislative Constitutionalism and Section Five Power: Policentric Interpretation of the Family and Medical Leave Act," 112 *Yale Law Journal* 1943 (2003): 1952, 1964.

99. *New York Times*, June 28, 1997.

100. *New York Times*, July 1, 1997.

101. Ibid.

102. Ibid.

103. Ibid.

104. *New York Times*, March 28, 1999.

105. *New York Times*, June 24, 1999.

106. Ibid.

107. Ibid.

108. Ibid.

109. Schroeder (2001), 317.

110. *New York Times*, June 27, 29, 1999.

111. *New York Times*, July 6, 1999.

112. *New York Times*, January 12, 2000.

113. *New York Times*, May 16, 2000.

114. *New York Times*, May 17, 2000.

115. Ibid.

116. *New York Times*, July 2, 2000.

117. Barry Friedman of the New York University Law School characterized the decision as "remarkable"; Michael Dorf of Columbia Law School predicted liberal "outrage." *New York Times*, December 13, 2000. Alan Dershowitz characterized the decision as "the single most corrupt decision in Supreme Court history." Dershowitz, *Supreme Injustice* (New York: Oxford University Press, 2001).

118. *New York Times*, February 22, 2001.

119. Ibid.

120. *New York Times*, June 30, 2001.

121. *New York Times*, July 15, 2001.

122. 535 U.S. 743.

123. *New York Times*, May 31, 2002.

124. *New York Times*, June 28, 2002.

125. Ibid.

126. *New York Times*, July 2, 2002.

127. John T. Noonan, *Narrowing the Nation's Power* (Berkeley: University of California Press, 2002).

128. *New York Times*, August 21, 2002.

129. *New York Times*, May 29, 2003.

130. Ibid.

131. *New York Times*, June 22, 2003.

132. Neal Devins, "Congress, the Supreme Court, and Enemy Combatants: How Lawmakers Buoyed Judicial Supremacy by Placing Limits on Federal Court Jurisdiction," 91 *Minnesota Law Review* 1562 (2007).

133. *New York Times*, June 12, 2005.

134. See, e.g., the chapters in Craig Bradley, ed., *The Rehnquist Legacy* (New York: Cambridge University Press, 2006).

135. See, e.g., Lynn A. Baker, "Conditional Federal Spending after *Lopez*," 95 *Columbia Law Review* 1911 (1995): 1919; Rachel Elizabeth Smith, "*United States v. Lopez*: Reaffirming the Federal Commerce Power and Remembering Federalism," 45 *Catholic University Law Review* 1459 (1996): 1490, n. 178; Jonathan L. Entin, "The New Federalism After *United States vs Lopez*: Introduction," 46 *Case Western Reserve Law Review* 635 (1995–1996); John C. Yoo, "The Judicial Safeguards of Federalism," 70 *Southern California Law Review* 1311 (1997); George D. Brown, "Should Federalism Shield Corruption? Mail Fraud, State Law and Post-*Lopez* Analysis," 82 *Cornell Law Review* 225 (1997): 280; Toni M. Massaro, "Reviving Hugo Black? The Court's 'Jot for Jot' Account of Substantive Due Process," 73 *New York University Law Review* 1086 (1998): 1112; H. Geoffrey Moulton Jr., "The Quixotic Search for a Judicially Enforceable Federalism," 83 *Minnesota Law Review* 849 (1999): 850–851; Frank Cross, "Realism About Federalism," 74 *New York University Law Review* 1304 (1999); Mark Tushnet, "The Supreme Court, 1998 Term—Foreword: The New Constitutional Order and the Chastening of Constitutional Aspiration," 113 *Harvard Law Review* 29 (1999); Daniel J. Meltzer, "State Sovereign Immunity: Five Authors in Search of a Theory," 75 *Notre Dame Law Review* 1011 (2000): 1038–1063; Robert Post and Reva Siegel, "Equal Protection by Law: Federal Antidiscrimination Legislation After *Morrison* and *Kimel*," 110 *Yale Law Journal* 441 (2000); Michael J. Gerhardt, "Federal Regulation in a Post-*Lopez* World: Some Questions and Answers," 30 *Environmental Law Reporter* 10980 (2000); Erik R. Neusch, "Medical Marijuana's Fate in the Aftermath of the Supreme Court's New Commerce Clause Jurisprudence," 72 *University of Colorado Law Review* 201 (2001), 239; John O. McGinnis, "Reviving Tocqueville's America: The Rehnquist Court's Jurisprudence of Social Discovery," 90 *California Law Review* 485 (2001); Christopher Bryant

and Timothy J. Simeone, "Remanding to Congress: The Supreme Court's New 'On the Record' Constitutional Review of Federal Statutes," 86 *Cornell Law Review* 328 (2001): 337–354, 369–388; Jack Balkin and Sanford Levinson, "Understanding the Constitutional Revolution," 87 *Virginia Law Review* 1045 (2001); Christopher H. Schroeder, "Causes of the Recent Turn in Constitutional Interpretation," 51 *Duke Law Journal* 307 (2001): 315; Keith Whittington, "Taking What They Give Us: Explaining the Court's Federalism Offensive," 51 *Duke Law Journal* 477 (2001); Neal Devins, "Congress as Culprit: How Lawmakers Spurred on the Court's Anti-Congress Crusade," 51 *Duke Law Journal* 435 (2001); Colker and Brudney (2001); Larry Kramer, "Foreword: We the Court," 115 *Harvard Law Review* 4 (2001); Seth Waxman, "Defending Congress," 79 *North Carolina Law Review* 1073 (2001): 1075–1076; Herman Schwartz, "The Supreme Court's Federalism: Fig Leaf for Conservatives," 574 *Annals of the American Academy of Political and Social Sciences* 119 (2001): 123–129; Ruth Colker and Kevin M. Scott, "Dissing States? Invalidation of State Action during the Rehnquist Era," 88 *Virginia Law Review* 1301 (2002); Richard Fallon, "Conservative Paths of the Rehnquist Court's Federalism Decisions," 69 *University of Chicago Law Review* 429 (2002); Louis D. Bilionis, "The New Scrutiny," 51 *Emory Law Journal* 481 (2002); Thomas W. Merrill, "The Making of the Second Rehnquist Court: A Preliminary Analysis," 47 *Saint Louis University Law Journal* 569 (2003); Jim Chen, "Judicial Epochs in Supreme Court History: Sifting through the Fossil Record for Stitches in Time and Switches in Nine," 47 *Saint Louis University Law Journal* 677 (2003); Ernest A. Young, "The Rehnquist Court's Two Federalisms," 83 *Texas Law Review* 1 (2004); Peter J. Smith, "Federalism, Instrumentalism, and the Legacy of the Rehnquist Court," 74 *George Washington Law Review* 906 (2006).

136. Gerhardt (2000), 10980.

137. Waxman (2001), 1075–1076.

138. Tushnet (1999).

139. Reported in Schroeder (2001), 319, n. 70; Whittington (2001), 487.

140. Baker (1995), 1919, referring to the "post-*Lopez* era"; Smith (1996), 1490, n. 178, referring to the "post-*Lopez* era"; Brown (1997), 280, referring to the "post-*Lopez* era"; Gerhardt (2000), 10980, referring to the "post-*Lopez* era"; Massarro (1998), 1112, referring to the "*Lopez* era"; Neusch (2001), 239, referring to the "pre-*Lopez* era." Some questioned the extent of the sharp break in the 1994 term. See "Understanding the Rehnquist Court: An Admiring Reply to Professor Merrill," 47 *Saint Louis University Law Journal* 659 (2003); Richard J. Lazarus, "*Rehnquist's* Court," 47 *Saint Louis University Law Journal* 861 (2003); and John O. McGinnis, "Continuity and Coherence in the Rehnquist Court," 47 *Saint Louis University Law Journal* 875 (2003).

141. See Jack Balkin and Sanford Levinson, "Understanding the Constitutional Revolution," 87 *Virginia Law Review* 1045 (2001): 1066–1083; Keith Whittington, "Taking What They Give Us: Explaining the Court's Federalism Offensive," 51 *Duke Law Journal* 477 (2001): 504; Colker and Brudney (2001), 111; and McGinniss (2001).

142. Schroeder (2001), 327.

143. *New York Times*, June 27, 29, 1999; McGinnis (2001); Schroeder (2001); Whittington (2001); Neal Devins, "Smoke, Not Fire," 65 *Maryland Law Review* 197 (2006); Friedman (2009), 354–357. Merrill (2003) varies this story slightly by focusing on the appointment of Clarence Thomas in 1991 as providing an important pro-federalism voice, and on the "conversion" of Scalia to the federalism revolution.

144. These cases were identified through the legal provisions reported by the United States Supreme Court Database (Supreme Court Database). This reporting is based on whether a particular legal provision is mentioned in the opinion summaries reported in the *Lawyer's Edition* of the *United States Reports* or the opinion syllabi reported in the official *United States Reports*. The figures in the text were computed from all cases between the 1986 and 2004 terms whose majority opinions were coded by the Supreme Court Database as involving one of these three constitutional provisions. The Supreme Court Database also reports whether a challenged statute is struck or upheld under each constitutional provision. In *New York v. U.S.*, 505 U.S. 144 (1992), the challenged statute is coded by the Supreme Court Database as upheld on Interstate Commerce Clause grounds; the main record in the case (the case citation record) also records the judgment as upholding the challenged statute. It is included here as an upheld statute even though some statutory provisions were struck on Tenth Amendment grounds. In both *Kimel v. Florida Board of Regents*, 528 U.S. 62 (2000), and *Board of Trustees of University of Alabama v. Garrett*, 531 U.S. 356 (2001), the challenged statutes are coded as upheld on Section 5 grounds but struck on Eleventh Amendment grounds. In both cases the case citation record records the judgment as striking the challenged statute; these cases are both included here as strikes.

145. Friedman (2009), 354, 357.

146. Federal statutes are frequently amended. The enacting Congress of each federal statute challenged in the cases retrieved from the Supreme Court Database under the procedures described in Chapter Three was identified as the most recent enacting or amending Congress for the specific provision at issue in a case. This method is described in greater detail in Chapter Five.

147. *New York Times*, July 6, 1999. The "federalism" explanation is also questioned by Frank Cross, "Realism about Federalism," 74 *New York University Law Review* 1304 (1999); Herman Schwartz, "The Supreme Court's Federalism: Fig Leaf for Conservatives," 574 *Annals of the American Academy of Political and Social Sciences* 574 (2001): 123–129; Colker and Scott (2002); and Peter J. Smith, "Federalism, Instrumentalism, and the Legacy of the Rehnquist Court," 74 *George Washington Law Review* 906 (2006).

148. Schroeder (2001), 325.

149. James A. Stimson, *Public Opinion in America: Moods, Cycles, and Swings, Second Edition* (Boulder: Westview, 1999). This index is used in Mishler and Sheehan (1993), Link (1995), Stimson et al. (1995), Mishler and Sheehan (1996), Flemming and Wood (1997), Erikson et al. (2002), McGuire and Stimson (2004), and Giles et al. (2008).

150. Stimson (1999) estimates two dimensions to the public mood, but the first dimension captures the majority of the opinion variance. Figure 4.2 reports the first dimension mood index estimated from the two-dimensional model. Stimson reports a liberal public mood ranging between 0 and 100; in Figure 4.2 this index is subtracted from 100 to create a conservative public mood index.

151. Schroeder (2001), 325, n. 89, also points out that the proportion of respondents self-identifying as "conservative" in the National Election Studies has stayed very stable over time, varying between only 51 percent and 54 percent between 1964 and 1998.

152. Colker and Brudney (2001).

153. Ibid., 83; Christopher Bryant and Timothy J. Simeone, "Remanding to Congress: The Supreme Court's New 'On the Record' Constitutional Review of Federal Statutes," 86 *Cornell Law Review* 328 (2001): 332–354, 369–388 (noting the Supreme Court's increased scrutiny of legislative records in its recent rulings on the constitutionality of federal statutes, and concluding, ultimately, that this approach is an unwarranted intrusion into the congressional sphere).

154. Kramer (1999).

155. Neal Devins, 51 *Duke Law Journal* 435 (2001); Neal Devins, "Congress, the Supreme Court, and Enemy Combatants: How Lawmakers Buoyed Judicial Supremacy by Placing Limits on Federal Court Jurisdiction," 91 *Minnesota Law Review* 1562 (2007).

156. Merrill (2003).

157. Chen (2003).

158. See Whittington (2001), 493; Merrill (2003), 576; and Neal Devins, "Congress and the Making of the Second Rehnquist Court," 47 *Saint Louis University Law Journal* 773 (2003).

159. Whittington (2001) dismissed the importance of the 1994 elections on the grounds that those elections did not seem to be primarily about federalism, and that in any case "realigning" elections are a thing of the past. Merrill (2003) argued that, if the Court cared about congressional preferences, it should have been more deferential to the Bush administration's statutory interpretations than to those of the Clinton administration. However, this claim does not follow. Devins (2003) suggested that the Court may have deferred to Congress between the 1986 and 1993 terms but in other articles (Devins [2001], [2006], [2007]) argued that Congress is not sufficiently motivated or organized to be able to discipline the Court.

160. Schroeder (2001), 327.

Chapter Five. Explaining the Puzzle of the Two Rehnquist Courts

1. These predicted probabilities are represented graphically in Figures 3.5 and 3.6. The comparable predicted probabilities of a conservative judgment using the Judicial Common Space preference estimates range from .50 to .67 between the 1986

and 2004 terms. The average predicted probability of a conservative judgment between the 1986 and 1993 terms using the JCS estimates is .63, and between the 1994 and 2004 terms is .57.

2. See Fischman and Law (2009) for a discussion of revealed preference estimation.

3. Lee Epstein, Jack Knight, and Andrew D. Martin, "The Childress Lecture Symposium: The Political (Science) Context of Judging," 47 *Saint Louis University Law Journal* 783 (2003)L 812. Epstein et al. note that between 1991 and 2000, seven of nine articles on judicial behavior in the leading political science journal used the Supreme Court Database, while it was used in fifteen of seventeen such articles in the number two journal.

4. These studies include Segal (1997), Hansford and Damore (2000), Spriggs and Hanford (2001), Segal and Spaeth (2002), Sala and Spriggs (2004), Martin (2006), and Clark (2011).

5. Some have raised isolated concerns about the Supreme Court Database judgment measure. Landes and Posner (2009) object to the Supreme Court Database decision rules for coding judgments in several issue areas but do not question the validity of the Supreme Court Database issue or judgment codes more generally; William M. Landes and Richard A. Posner, "Rational Judicial Behavior: A Statistical Study," *Journal of Legal Analysis* 1 (2009): 775. Shapiro (2009) suggests that the Supreme Court Database issue codes may fail to adequately reflect the doctrinal issues involved in a case as understood by legal academics, but does not address the more general problems raised by subjective issue coding; Carolyn Shapiro, "Coding Complexity: Bringing Law to the Empirical Analysis of the Supreme Court," 60 *Hastings Law Journal* 477 (2009). Gillman (2003) and Young (2005) suggested problems of circularity in the Supreme Court Database judgment codes, but did not pursue these suggestions; Howard Gillman, "Separating the Wheat from the Chaff in the Supreme Court and the Attitudinal Model Revisited," 13 *Law and Courts* 12 (2003); Ernest Young, "Just Blowing Smoke? Politics, Doctrine, and the Federalist Revival after Gonzales v. Raich," 2005 *Supreme Court Review* 1. Some researchers cite as justification for their lack of concern about the Supreme Court Database codes the reliability tests performed on a random sample of Supreme Court Database cases from the Warren and Burger Courts, which resulted in relatively high rates of inter-coder reliability (Supreme Court Database Documentation, Appendix I). These reliability tests do not, however, address the issue of validity.

6. Although it is possible for a case to be assigned more than one issue code, Harvey and Woodruff (2011) calculate that about 93.7 percent of cases in the database are assigned a single issue code. Anna Harvey and Michael Woodruff, "Confirmation Bias in the United States Supreme Court Judicial Database," *Journal of Law, Economics and Organization* (2011), doi: 10.1093/jleo/ewr003.

7. Supreme Court Database Documentation, 42.

8. The primary coder for the Supreme Court Database, Harold Spaeth, has written, for example, "Not only are [the justices] independent of the other branches, but their lifetime appointment also insulates them from factious electoral pressures . . .

Members of the Supreme Court can further their policy goals because they lack electoral or political accountability." Segal and Spaeth (2002), 21, 92.

9. Harvey and Woodruff (2011).

10. Poole and Rosenthal (1997).

11. Ibid.; Keith Krehbiel, Adam Meirowitz, and Jonathan Woon, "Testing Theories of Law-making," in *Social Choice and Strategic Decisions: Essays in Honor of Jeffrey S. Banks*, ed. David Austen-Smith and John Duggan (Berlin: Springer, 2005).

12. The Poole-Rosenthal estimates also report estimated bill and status quo locations. Although some recent papers have used the estimated bill location as a measure of policy location, e.g., Sala and Spriggs (2004), these estimates are highly dependent upon model specification in the DW-NOMINATE estimation procedure; Poole and Rosenthal (1997), Krehbiel et al. (2005). Here we will use simply the relative positions of these estimated bill and status quo locations, namely whether the estimated bill location lies to the left or the right of the estimated status quo location.

13. There are 309 such challenges in the sample.

14. These statutes have been frequently amended. The decision rule used was to first identify the specific section or sections of the statute actually being reviewed by the Court, and then to identify both the original enacting date and all reenactments of or amendments to this section or sections. As long as the challenged language of the statute remained substantially intact through all amendments and/or reenactments, the most recent reenacting or amending Congress was adopted as the enacting Congress. Cases involving multiple statutes were divided into separate observations, one for each statute.

15. The House of Representatives is used because there are more nonunanimous roll call votes in the House for these statutes, relative to the Senate.

16. This measure could be constructed for 166 challenged statutes during these terms.

17. There are 265 statutes reviewed by the Court between 1953 and 2004 enacted by unified partisan Congresses sitting between 1950 and 2004.

18. Harvey and Woodruff (2011).

19. Coding unified Democratic Congresses as liberal and unified Republican Congresses as conservative, this indicator matches the Poole-Rosenthal dichotomous statute measure in 74 percent of the 133 observations for which both measures are available between 1953 and 2004; an exact binomial test returns a .00 probability of a random association between the two measures.

20. The 95 percent confidence intervals are (.00, .13) and (.48, .69), respectively. All predicted probabilities reported in this chapter hold all other variables constant at their actual values. Because these predicted probabilities take into account how all variables in the model actually covary in a dataset, they are more representative estimates of the size of a variable's effect than those generated by the approach of holding all variables constant at their means or other values. Gelman and Hill (2007), 101–103. Probabilities are simulated using the *margins* command in Stata 12.

21. The 95 percent confidence intervals are (.03, .31) and (.42, .64).

22. The 95 percent confidence intervals are (.10, .29) and (.49, .75).

23. The 95 percent confidence intervals are (.19, .41) and (.37, .78).

24. The 95 percent confidence intervals are (.02, .19) and (.38, .68).

25. The 95 percent confidence intervals are (.05, .16) and (.58, .90).

26. These effects are also significant during the 1954, 1956, and 1957 terms, when more conservative House majorities appear to have increased the likelihood of conservative judgments, relative to the unconstrained likelihood, with at least 90 percent confidence.

27. Toobin (2007), 2.

28. See, e.g., Morton J. Horwitz, *The Warren Court and the Pursuit of Justice* (New York: Hill and Wang, 1998), 3; and Cass Sunstein, *Radicals in Robes* (New York: Basic Books, 2005), 36.

29. Revisionist accounts of the Warren Court include Gerald Rosenberg, *The Hollow Hope* (Chicago: University of Chicago Press, 1991); Lucas A. Powe Jr., *The Warren Court and American Politics* (Cambridge: Harvard University Press, 2000); Mary Dudziak, *Cold War Civil Rights* (Princeton: Princeton University Press, 2002); Michael Klarman, *From Jim Crow to Civil Rights* (New York: Oxford University Press, 2004); and Corinna Barrett Lain, "Countermajoritarian Hero or Zero? Rethinking the Warren Court's Role in the Criminal Procedure Revolution," 152 *University of Pennsylvania Law Review* 1451 (2004).

30. Seventy-four percent of the votes for passage in the House came from Democrats; 97 percent of the votes opposed came from Republicans.

31. *New York Times*, July 1, 3, September 11, 1988.

32. *New York Times*, September 11, 1988.

33. Eighty percent of those supporting the bill in the House were Democrats, while 73 percent of those opposing the bill were Republicans.

34. The panel was composed of Reagan appointees Douglas Ginsburg and Lawrence Silberman and Johnson appointee Spottswood Robinson III.

35. Donald I. Baker, "The *Superior Court Trial Lawyers Case*—A Battle on the Frontier Between Politics and Antitrust," in *Antitrust Stories*, ed. Eleanor M. Fox and Daniel A. Crane (New York Foundation Press, 2007), 257–286, 258.

36. Eighty percent of the votes in the House in support of the 1994 amendments came from Democrats; 67 percent of the votes opposed came from Republicans.

37. Sixty-two percent of the votes in favor of the statute came from Democrats in the House, while 51 percent of opposing votes came from Republicans.

38. Seventy-seven percent of the bill's support in the House came from Democrats; 62 percent of the votes in opposition came from Republicans.

39. Ninety-two percent of the Act's votes in support came from Democrats; 66 percent of the votes opposed came from Republicans.

40. Eighty percent of the votes in favor of the Violence Against Women Act came from Democrats; 67 percent of the votes in opposition came from Republicans.

41. Sixty-two percent of the votes in support of the Americans With Disabilities Act came from Democrats; 82 percent of the votes in opposition came from Republicans.

42. Justice John Paul Stevens, in *New York Times*, April 27, 1995.

43. *New York Times*, April 28, 1995.

44. Jeffrey Toobin, "Chicken Supreme: The Rehnquist Court Is Political in Every Way," *New Yorker*, August 14, 1995.

45. Jonathan L. Entin, "The New Federalism After *United States vs. Lopez*: Introduction," 46 *Case Western Reserve Law Review* 635 (1995–1996): 636.

46. Justice John Paul Stevens, in *New York Times*, March 28, 1996.

47. Justice David Souter, in ibid.

48. *New York Times*, June 26, 1997.

49. Robert C. Post and Reva B. Siegel, "Legislative Constitutionalism and Section Five Power: Policentric Interpretation of the Family and Medical Leave Act," 112 *Yale Law Journal* 1943 (2003): 1952, 1964.

50. Senator Charles Schumer (D-NY), in *New York Times*, June 28, 1997.

51. Yale Professor of Law Paul Gewirtz, in *New York Times*, July 1, 1997.

52. *New York Times*, July 1, 1997.

53. Schroeder (2001), 317.

54. *New York Times*, July 15, 2001.

55. Gerhardt (2000), 10980.

56. House Republicans had contributed 64 percent of the votes in favor of the Act, while House Democrats had contributed 65 percent of the votes in opposition.

57. See Krehbiel (1998).

58. Testing for nonlinear relationships between statute age and the probability of a strike did not produce significant improvements over the linear measure reported in Tables 5.5 and 5.6.

59. Using the Bailey XTI preference estimates, the smallest distance between an enacted statute and the most preferred rule of the median justice is observed for statutes enacted in 1970 and reviewed during the 1971 term; the largest observed distance is for statutes enacted in 1952 and reviewed in the 1963 term. Using the JCS preference estimates, the smallest such distance is observed for statutes enacted in 1999 and reviewed in the Court's 1999 term; the largest such distance is observed for statutes enacted in 1954 and reviewed in the 1967 term.

60. Using the Bailey XTI preference estimates, the smallest distance between an enacted statute and the most preferred rule of the median representative is observed for statutes enacted in 1987 and reviewed during the 1988 term; the largest observed distance is for statutes enacted in 1976 and reviewed in the 1995 term. Using the JCS preference estimates, the smallest such distance is observed for statutes enacted in 1989 and reviewed in the Court's 1989 term; the largest such distance is observed for statutes enacted in 1976 and reviewed in the 1995 term.

61. These simulations set statute age at two years and hold all other variables at sample values. The two predictions are distinct with at least 90 percent confidence.

62. Statute age is held at seven years and all other variables are held at sample values.

63. Statute age is held at seven years and all other variables are held at sample values.

64. Statute age is held at two years and all other variables are held at sample values.

65. 494 U.S. 1, 17–18 (quoting the statute).

66. These simulated probabilities hold the statute's age at six years and all other variables at their sample values. The predictions are distinct with at least 90 percent confidence.

67. Statute age is held at zero years; all other variables are held at sample values.

68. *Freedom's Law: The Moral Reading of the American Constitution* (Cambridge: Harvard University Press, 1996), 12–13. The justices in *Griswold* were not united in identifying the constitutional source of the privacy right endorsed in that case.

69. "Serving America's Best Interests," *Daedalus* (Fall 2008): 139–143, 142. *Cooper v. Aaron* is also cited as a prominent example of the Court's independence by Saikrishna Prakash, "America's Aristocracy," 109 *Yale Law Journal* 541 (1999): 575.

70. "The Newsroom Guide to Judicial Independence," The Constitution Project, http://www.constitutionproject.org/pdf/37.pdf.

71. See the comments of legal academics in *New York Times*, December 13, 2000. Also see Alan Dershowitz, *Supreme Injustice* (New York: Oxford University Press, 2001).

Chapter Six. Elected Branch Preferences, Public Opinion, or Socioeconomic Trends?

1. William Mishler and Reginald S. Sheehan, "The Supreme Court as a Countermajoritarian Institution? The Impact of Public Opinion on Supreme Court Decisions," *American Political Science Review* 87 (1993): 87–101; Michael W. Link, "Tracking Public Mood in the Supreme Court: Cross-Time Analyses of Criminal Procedure and Civil Rights Cases," *Political Research Quarterly* 48 (1995): 61–78; James A. Stimson, Michael B. MacKuen, and Robert S. Erikson, "Dynamic Representation," *American Political Science Review* 89 (1995): 543–565; William Mishler and Reginald S. Sheehan, "Public Opinion, the Attitudinal Model, and Supreme Court Decision Making: A Micro-Analytic Perspective," *Journal of Politics* 58 (1996): 169–200; Roy B. Flemming and B. Dan Wood, "The Public and the Supreme Court: Individual Justice Responsiveness to American Policy Moods," *American Journal of Political Science* 41 (1997): 468–498; Kevin T. McGuire and James A. Stimson, "The Least Dangerous Branch Revisited: New Evidence on Supreme Court Responsiveness to Public Preferences," *Journal of Politics* 66 (2004): 1018–1035; Micheal W. Giles, Bethany Blackstone, and Richard L. Vining Jr., "The Supreme Court in American Democracy: Unraveling the Linkages Between Public Opinion and Judicial Decision Making," *Journal of Politics* 70 (2008): 293–306; Christopher J. Casillas, Peter K. Enns, and Patrick C. Wohlfarth, "How Public Opinion Constrains the U.S. Supreme Court," *American Journal of Political Science* 55 (2011): 74–88; Lee Epstein and Andrew D. Martin, "Does Public Opinion Influence the Supreme Court? Possibly Yes (But We're Not Sure Why)," 13 *University of Pennsylvania Journal of Constitutional Law* 263 (2011); and Clark (2011).

2. Jeffrey Rosen, *The Most Democratic Branch* (New York: Oxford University Press, 2006), 5.

3 Mishler and Sheehan (1993), 89, draw our attention to "the limitations of the Court's power and its dependence on voluntary acquiescence to its decisions", Link (1995), 63, refers to the justices' concern for the "efficacy" of their decisions; Stimson, MacKuen, and Erikson (1995), 555, suggest that "the justices must consider the possibility that their decisions will be overridden or indifferently enforced"; Flemming and Wood (1997), 494, suggest that "the justices must always consider the possibility that their decisions will be overturned or indifferently enforced"; McGuire and Stimson (2004), 1019, observe, "While the Court is certainly not electorally accountable, those responsible for putting its rulings into effect frequently are"; and Casillas et al. (2010), 2, observe, "With little formal institutional capability to enforce the Court's decisions and to compel the elected branches . . . to respect its judgments, justices must often act strategically in their opinion writing." A somewhat more circular version of this story suggests that increasing the Court's legitimacy increases compliance with its rulings; the justices defer to popular preferences in order to increase the Court's legitimacy. Mishler and Sheehan (1993), Link (1995), Stimson, Mackuen, and Erikson (1995), McGuire and Stimson (2004), Giles, Blackstone and Vining (2008), and Casillas et al. (2010).

4. Mishler and Sheehan (1993), Link (1995), Stimson et al. (1995), Mishler and Sheehan (1996), Flemming and Wood (1997), Erikson et al. (2002), McGuire and Stimson (2004), Giles et al. (2008), Casillas et al. (2011), Epstein and Martin (2011), and Clark (2011).

5. James A. Stimson, *Public Opinion in America: Moods, Cycles, and Swings*, 2nd ed. (Boulder: Westview, 1999). This index is used in Mishler and Sheehan (1993), Link (1995), Stimson et al. (1995), Mishler and Sheehan (1996), Flemming and Wood (1997), Erikson et al. (2002), McGuire and Stimson (2004), Giles et al. (2008), Casillas et al. (2011), Epstein and Martin (2011), and Clark (2011).

6. Stimson (1999) estimates two dimensions to the public mood, but the first dimension captures the majority of the opinion variance. Throughout this chapter I use the first dimension public mood estimates, available at http://www.unc.edu/~jstimson/Data.html.

7. The exceptions include Mishler and Sheehan (1993), Link (1995), Flemming and Wood (1997), Martin and Epstein (2011), and Clark (2011).

8. Mishler and Sheehan (1993), Link (1995), Flemming and Wood (1997), Martin and Epstein (2011), and Clark (2011).

9. Suzanna De Boef and Luke Keele, "Taking Time Seriously," *American Journal of Political Science* 52 (2008): 184–200.

10. Data for years wherein there were no Supreme Court judgments (as was the case for three years in the roll call–based sample but for no years in the Congress-based sample) were estimated via linear interpolation.

11. Similar results to those reported here are yielded by using the annual estimates of mood corresponding to Court terms employed by Casillas et al. (2011).

12. Specifically, each term is given a sampling weight equal to ln(number of judgments in term + 2), chosen because it yields weights that are all greater than zero and that are increasing in the annual number of judgments at a diminishing rate. The range of weights in the roll call–based sample is [.69, 2.71]; the range in the partisan Congress-based sample is [1.10, 2.83]. Similar results are obtained when models are estimated without weights.

13. Using the Bailey XTI preference estimates, the term with the most liberal median representative in the prior term is the 1975 term; that with the most conservative median representative in the prior term is the 1996 term. Using the Judicial Common Space preference estimates, the terms with the most liberal median representatives in the prior terms are the 1975 and 1976 terms; those with the most conservative median representatives in the prior terms are the 2003 and 2004 terms.

14. Another result that can be of interest in an ECM is the value of the "long run multiplier," or LRM, calculated by dividing the coefficient on a variable's lagged value by the coefficient on the lagged value of the dependent variable, or the error correction rate. The absolute value of this ratio is the LRM, which reports the total influence of a predictor variable over time, incorporating both its short- and long-run effects. Because in the results reported here the error correction rate is close to 1 in all analyses, the LRMs do not convey significant additional information beyond that reported in the text.

15. Robert S. Erikson, Michael B. MacKuen, and James A. Stimson, *The Macro Polity* (New York: Cambridge University Press, 2002), 232–234.

16. J. Tobin Grant and Philip Habel, "The Sophisticated Macro Polity: Public Opinion and Responses to Policy Outcomes," typescript, Southern Illinois University, Carbondale.

17. Christopher Wlezien, "The Public as Thermostat: Dynamics of Preferences for Spending," *American Journal of Political Science* 39 (1995): 981–1000.

18. Erikson et al. (2002); Nathan J. Kelly, "Political Choice, Public Policy, and Distributional Outcomes," *American Journal of Political Science* 49 (2005): 865–880.

19. The policy liberalism data end in 2000. The socioeconomic data used here may be found at http://dvn.iq.harvard.edu/dvn/dv/Enns.

20. Information about the Policy Agendas Project may be found at http://www.policyagendas.org/datasets/index.html.

21. See Erikson, MacKuen, and Stimson (2002) and Kelly (2005).

22. In the sample used to produce the estimates reported in Table 6.7 the most liberal median representative is observed in the 1965 and 1975 terms, and the most conservative in the 1995 term; for Table 6.8 the most liberal representative is observed in the 1975 term and the most conservative in the 1994 and 1995 terms; for Table 6.9 the most liberal representative is observed in the 1974 term and the most conservative in the 1995 term; and for Table 6.10 the most liberal representative is observed in the 1974 and 1975 terms and the most conservative in the 1994 and 1995 terms.

23. See Lawrence Baum, *The Puzzle of Judicial Behavior* (Ann Arbor: University of Michigan Press, 1997), and Robert M. Howard and Jeffrey A. Segal, "A Preference

for Deference? The Supreme Court and Judicial Review," *Political Research Quarterly* 57 (2004): 131–143.

Chapter Seven: Restoring the Court's Missing Docket

1. *New York Times*, July 7, 1991.

2. *New York Times*, September 10, 1993.

3. Ibid.

4. Arthur D. Hellman, "The Shrunken Docket of the Rehnquist Court," 1996 *Supreme Court Law Review* 403 (1996); David M. O'Brien, "Join-3 Votes: The Rule of Four, the Cert. Pool, and the Supreme Court's Shrinking Plenary Docket," 13 *Journal of Law and Politics* 779 (1997); Margaret Meriwether Cordray and Richard Cordray, "The Supreme Court's Plenary Docket," 58 *Washington and Lee Law Review* 737 (2001); Kenneth W. Starr, "The Supreme Court and Its Shrinking Docket: The Ghost of William Howard Taft," 90 *Minnesota Law Review* 1363 (2006); David R. Stras, "The Supreme Court's Declining Plenary Docket: A Membership-Based Explanation," *Constitutional Commentary* (2010). Using the full set of appeals granted plenary review by the Court, or only those generating signed opinions, produces a very similar docket series.

5. While Cordray and Cordray (2001) point to a gradual decline in the frequency of requests for review made by the Solicitor General's office, Stras (2010) notes that these requests were relatively constant during the period of the docket's greatest decline, namely from the 1991 through the 1993 terms.

6. Stras (2010).

7. See Adam Liptak, "The Case of the Plummeting Supreme Court Docket," *New York Times*, September 28, 2009.

8. Since certiorari requires only four votes, as discussed below, it is possible that the four justices closest to the divergent House median will try to vote cases onto the Court's docket in order to move outcomes to the most preferred rule of the median representative. However, as we will see, the conditions necessary for this strategy to make sense largely did not exist for the set of federal statutes enacted during the Rehnquist Court's first eight terms.

9. Throughout this chapter I report only results using the Bailey XTI (2007) preference estimates; using the JCS preference estimates produces very similar results. Because of the timing of the construction of the Court's docket (certiorari is typically granted in the term preceding the term in which a case is docketed), in Figure 7.2 the Court's docket in a given term is paired with the degree of House constraint faced by the Court in the *preceding* term.

10. Those who have pointed out that the Court's docket may violate this assumption of randomness include Doris Marie Provine, *Case Selection in the United States Supreme Court* (Chicago: University of Chicago Press, 1980), 54–62; Lee Epstein, Jeffrey A. Segal, and Jennifer Nicoll Victor, "Dynamic Agenda-Setting on the United States Supreme Court: An Empirical Assessment," *Harvard Journal on Legislation* 39 (2002): 395–434; and Jonathan P. Kastellec and Jeffrey R. Lax, "Case Selection and

the Study of Judicial Politics," *Journal of Empirical Legal Studies* 5 (2008): 407–446; Harvey and Friedman (2009).

11. Only in cases involving statutes enacted in 1987 or 1998 and reviewed in the 1993 term would there have been any chance for the four more liberal justices to gain by voting to hear these cases. These potential gains would, however, have been very small.

12. For the 1969–2004 terms the correlation coefficient for the two series is −.31 (p = .07); it increases to −.44 (p = .03) for the 1981 through the 2004 terms.

13. The simulations are made using the *margins* command in Stata 12 from the estimates reported in Table 7.1. The point prediction for the assumption of zero preference divergence is 4; the 95 percent confidence interval is (−2, 10). The 95 percent confidence interval for the assumption of maximum preference divergence is (−24, −3).

14. The 95 percent confidence interval for the average predicted change between the 1986 and 1993 terms is (−13.4, −.9). The average predicted change for the 1994 to 2004 terms is an increase of 1.2 cases per year; the 95% confidence interval is (−3.6, 6.3).

15. McGuire et al. (2009) make the point that petitioners appeal only when they expect to win, although these authors do not analyze the potential effect of elected branch preferences on petitioners' decisions. Kevin T. McGuire, Georg Vanberg, Charles E. Smith Jr., and Gregory Caldeira, "Measuring Policy Content on the U.S. Supreme Court," *Journal of Politics* 71 (2009): 1305–1321. Owens (2010) begins with a sample of certiorari petitions, assumes this sample is unbiased, and finds no effect of elected branch preferences on the Court's certiorari decisions. Ryan J. Owens, "The Separation of Powers and Supreme Court Agenda Setting," *American Journal of Political Science* 54 (April 2010): 412–427.

16. Stathis (2003).

17. Enactment dates for docketed landmark statutes were identified as follows. First, minor amendments to landmark bills, i.e., amendments which themselves were not entitled to "landmark" status, were ignored. Similarly, if a landmark bill only incidentally amended an existing statute without changing the substance of that statute, and if that original statute was then reviewed by the Court, this was not counted as judicial review of a landmark bill. But if a bill identified as a landmark bill included as a subsection a separate act, which was then reviewed by the Court, this was treated as judicial review of a landmark bill.

18. There are 78 liberal landmark statutes enacted between 1987 and 1993, for a total of 298 statute-year observations between the 1987 and 1993 terms. Since only one of these observations resulted in a docketed case of judicial review, the average rate of review during this period is .003. Including the 1994 liberal landmark statutes, there are 85 liberal statutes available for review between the 1994 and 2004 terms, for a total of 935 statute-year observations. Because 12 of these observations resulted in docketed cases of judicial review, the average rate of review is .013. The rate of increase is 333 percent.

19. For the analyses reported in Tables 7.2 and 7.4, using large numbers of observations, the threshold for statistical significance is set at .05.

20. It would be ideal to estimate age-specific fixed effects in the analysis reported in Table 7.2. However, in this sample there are too many terms wherein the Court did not review any statutes of a given age, so that an age-specific fixed effect is perfectly correlated with a failure to review. In Table 7.2 I estimate age using a linear age counter; adding squared or cubed age terms did not improve the ability to estimate statute age.

21. Holding other variables at sample values, the average predicted probability of review for a liberal statute is .004 (95 percent confidence interval = .001, .010) between the 1987 and 1993 terms and is .018 (95 percent confidence interval = .011, .026) between the 1994 and 2004 terms.

22. The 95 percent confidence interval for the first prediction is (.3, 2.9), and for the second is (10.5, 24.2).

23. The 95 percent confidence interval is (7.4, 25.3). A predicted probability of review is simulated for each liberal landmark statute in each term between 1987 and 1993 by assuming that the value of *More Liberal House* is zero for each statute in each term, but that all other variables retain their actual values. The predicted probabilities of review are then summed over all the liberal landmark statute-year observations during these terms.

24. The 95 percent confidence interval is (11.5, 43.5).

25. Adding case-based covariates does not change this result. These case-based covariates are omitted here to permit comparison of the docket-level estimates with the population-level estimates reported later in this chapter.

26. The average predicted strike probability for a liberal landmark statute between the 1987 and 1993 terms, holding other variables at sample means, is .004 (95 percent confidence interval = .001, .008), and is .013 (95 percent confidence interval = .008, .018) between the 1994 and 2004 terms.

27. Holding other variables at sample means, the average predicted strike probability for a conservative landmark statute between the 1995 and 2004 terms is .004 (95 percent confidence interval = .001, .009).

28. The 95 percent confidence interval is (.9, 6.0).

29. The Court's missing docket is reconstructed by simulating the probability of review in each term for each landmark statute enacted between 1987 and 1993, assuming the median justice can set the legal rule in each case at her own most preferred rule, and using the actual values for statute age. These probabilities are then summed by term and year of enactment. A statute is brought onto the Court's docket from each of the term/enacting year groups with the thirteen highest summed probabilities of review. All thirteen statutes added to the Court's missing docket in this way come from term/enacting year groups for which the summed probability of review is greater than 50 percent. Strike probabilities are simulated in an analogous way. The two term/enacting year groups with the highest summed strike probabilities are then coded as strikes on the missing docket.

30. The landmark statute closest to the median representative's most preferred rule in this sample is a 1997 statute reviewed during the 2001 term; that furthest away is a 1992 statute reviewed during the 1995 term. The 95 percent confidence interval for the first prediction is (.02, .33) and for the second is (.65, .99).

31. The 95 percent confidence interval for the first prediction is (.07, .39) and for the second is (.65, .99).

32. The 95 percent confidence interval is (.11, .44).

Chapter Eight. Misreading the Roberts Court

1. "O'Connor Held Balance of Power," *New York Times*, July 2, 2005. The Bailey XTI estimates support this interpretation, as we saw in Chapter Three.

2. Ibid.

3. Ibid.

4. "Justice O'Connor," *New York Times*, July 2, 2005.

5. "Court in Transition," *New York Times*, July 2, 2005.

6. Ibid.

7. "President Names Roberts as Choice for Chief Justice," *New York Times*, September 6, 2005.

8. "In Pursuit of Conservative Stamp, President Nominates Roberts," *New York Times*, July 20, 2005; "Groups Gird for the Battle Over What Can Be Asked," *New York Times*, July 20, 2005; "The Strategy for a Successful Nomination: Disarm Opposition," *New York Times*, July 20, 2005; "An Advocate for the Right," *New York Times*, July 28, 2005; "Senate Democrats Increase Resistance to Roberts," *New York Times*, August 17, 2005; "Anxious Liberal Groups Try to Rally Opposition Against Supreme Court Nominee," *New York Times*, September 2, 2005; "Senate Democrats Are Shifting Focus from Roberts to Other Seat," *New York Times*, September 9, 2005; "Among Democratic Activists, Little Indecision on Roberts," *New York Times*, September 22, 2005.

9. "Conservatives Are Wary Over President's Selection," *New York Times*, October 4, 2005.

10. Larry Lustberg quoted in "Alito Is Seen as a Methodical Jurist with a Clear Record," *New York Times*, January 1, 2006.

11. "2 Camps, Playing Down Nuances, Stake Out Firm Stands," *New York Times*, January 1, 2006.

12. "G.O.P. Reaches to Other Party on Court Pick," *New York Times*, January 2, 2006.

13. "Armageddon! Measuring the Power of a New Justice," *New York Times*, January 6, 2006.

14. "Ideology Serves as a Wild Card on Court Pick," *New York Times*, January 4, 2006.

15. "Potentially, the First Shot in All-Out Ideological War," *New York Times*, January 1, 2006.

16. Ibid.

17. Linda Greenhouse, "In Steps Big and Small, the Supreme Court Moved Right," *New York Times*, July 1, 2007. Also see *New York Times*, July 2, 2005.

18. "Alito Vote May Be Decisive in Marquee Cases This Term," *New York Times*, February 1, 2006.

19. Jan Crawford Greenburg, *Supreme Conflict: The Inside Story of the Struggle for Control of the United States Supreme Court* (New York: Penguin, 2007), 315.

20. "Hearings a Test for Democrats and Alito," *New York Times*, January 8, 2006.

21. Linda Greenhouse, "On the Wrong Side of 5 to 4, Liberals Talk Tactics," *New York Times*, July 8, 2007.

22. Adam Liptak, "Court under Roberts Is Most Conservative in Decades," *New York Times*, July 24, 2010.

23. Ibid.

24. *New York Times*, January 28, 2009.

25. *Parents Involved in Community Schools v. Seattle School District No. 1*, 05-908, (2007).

26. See, e.g., Jeffrey Toobin, "No More Mr. Nice Guy," *New Yorker*, May 25, 2009.

27. *Marks v. U.S.*, 430 U.S. 188 (1977).

28. *Parents Involved in Community Schools v. Seattle School District No. 1*, 05-908, (2007).

29. Ibid.

30. Adam Liptak, "The Same Words, but Differing Views," *New York Times*, June 29, 2007.

31. Tamar Lewin, "Across U.S., a New Look at School Integration Efforts," *New York Times*, June 29, 2007.

32. Gina Kolata, "Anger and Alternatives on Abortion," *New York Times*, April 21, 2007.

33. Jeffrey Rosen, "The Dissenter, Justice John Paul Stevens," *New York Times Magazine*, September 23, 2007. *Carhart* also does not appear to have opened the door for other, more broadly written, late term abortion statutes. In May 2008, in fact, a panel of the Fourth Circuit struck a partial birth abortion ban enacted by the Virginia legislature because it criminalized all abortions meeting the anatomical benchmarks defined for partial birth abortions, not just those that a physician had intended from the outset to meet those benchmarks. The appellate panel ruled that this statute was not permissible under *Carhart*. *New York Times*, May 21, 2008.

34. *New York Times*, June 20, 2008.

35. "Justice 5, Brutality 4," *New York Times*, June 13, 2008.

36. "Anger and Restraint," *New York Times*, June 26, 2008. Also see *New York Times*, May 28, 29, 2008.

37. Greenhouse observed both a decline in the number of 5–4 decisions and opinions from the conservative majority in three high-profile cases that hewed very closely to the facts of each case. *New York Times*, May 28, 2008.

38. *New York Times*, July 3, 2008.

39. Ibid.

40. Ibid.

41. Linda Greenhouse, "The Chief Justice on the Spot," *New York Times*, January 8, 2009.

42. The cases were *Parents Involved in Community Schools* (2007) and *League of United Latin American Citizens v. Perry* (2006).

43. Adam Liptak, "On Voting Rights, Test of History v. Progress," *New York Times*, April 27, 2009.

44. Linda Greenhouse, "Down the Memory Hole," *New York Times*, October 2, 2009.

45. Adam Liptak, "Justices Retain Oversight by U.S. on Voting," *New York Times*, June 22, 2009.

46. "The Voting Rights Act Survives," *New York Times*, June 22, 2009; Liptak, "Justices Retain Oversight.

47. Greenhouse, "Down the Memory Hole."

48. "Big Loss for Big Tobacco," *New York Times*, December 15, 2008.

49. *Crawford v. Metropolitan Government of Nashville and Davidson County, Tenn.* (2009). "Workers Who Speak Out," *New York Times*, January 29, 2009.

50. "Gun Sense and Nonsense," *New York Times*, February 27, 2009.

51. *Wyeth v. Levine* (2009). "A Win for Injured Patients," *New York Times*, March 4, 2009.

52. *Flores-Figueroa v. United States* (2009). "Making the Punishment Fit the Crime," *New York Times*, May 5, 2009.

53. *Caperton v. A.T. Massey Coal Company* (2009). "Honest Justice," *New York Times*, June 8, 2009.

54. *Safford Unified School District v. Redding* (2009). "An Unreasonable Search," *New York Times*, June 25, 2009.

55. Adam Liptak, "Roberts Court Comes of Age," *New York Times*, June 30, 2010.

56. *United States v. Stevens* (2010). "The Court and Free Speech," *New York Times*, April 23, 2010.

57. *Graham v. Florida* (2010). "A New Standard of Decency," *New York Times*, May 17, 2010.

58. *Lewis et al. v. City of Chicago* (2010). "The Supreme Court Opens a Door for Workers," *New York Times*, May 24, 2010.

59. *American Needle, Inc. v. National Football League et al.* (2010). "Throwing the Rule Book at the N.F.L.," *New York Times*, May 26, 2010.

60. *Holland v. Florida* (2010). "A Good Day for Judicial Discretion," *New York Times*, June 14, 2010.

61. *Carachuri-Rosendo v. Holder* (2010). "A Good Day for Judicial Discretion," *New York Times*, June 14, 2010.

62. *Stop the Beach Renourishment, Inc. v. Florida Department of Environmental Protection* (2010). "Common Sense and Private Property," *New York Times*, June 17, 2010; "The Court's Aggressive Term," *New York Times*, July 4, 2010.

63. *Skilling v. United States* (2010). "Balance of Prosecutorial Power," *New York Times*, June 24, 2010; "The Court's Aggressive Term," *New York Times*, July 4, 2010.

64. *Hastings Christian Fellowship v. Martinez et al.* (2010). "Denying Government Support for Intolerance," *New York Times*, June 28, 2010.

65. "The Court's Aggressive Term," *New York Times*, July 4, 2010.

66. Liptak, "Roberts Court Comes of Age."

67. "A Good Day for Judicial Discretion," *New York Times*, June 14, 2010.

68. The Roberts Court heard 13 constitutional challenges to federal statutes during these terms, for an average rate of 3.25 per term. Between the 1994 and 1997 terms the Rehnquist Court heard 23 constitutional challenges to federal statutes, for an average of 5.75 per term. The one-tailed p-value from a t-test of the means is .09 (assuming unpaired data with either equal or unequal variances).

69. The Roberts Court heard 5 constitutional challenges to liberal federal statutes during its first four full terms. The second Rehnquist Court heard 12 constitutional challenges to liberal statutes during its first four terms. The one-tailed p-value from a t-test of the means is .03 (assuming unpaired data with either equal or unequal variances).

70. The Rehnquist Court struck provisions of 10 liberal statutes between the 1994 and 1997 terms, for a mean of 2.5 per term; the Roberts Court struck provisions of only 4 liberal statutes between the 2006 and 2009 terms, for a mean of only 1 per term. The one-tailed p value is .03.

71. The statute had been opposed by seven Democrats and thirty-five Republicans in the House; it is estimated to have moved the status quo in a liberal direction.

72. "The Court and Free Speech," *New York Times*, April 23, 2010.

73. Only 12 Democrats had voted against the Act in the House, but 176 Republican representatives had been in opposition.

74. *Federal Election Commission v. Wisconsin Right to Life*, 06-969 (2007).

75. See Steven Levitt, "Using Repeat Challengers to Estimate the Effect of Campaign Spending on Election Outcomes in the U.S. House," *Journal of Political Economy* 102 (August 1994): 777-798; Stephen Ansolabehere, John M. De Figueiredo, and James M. Snyder, "Why Is There So Little Money in U.S. Politics?" *Journal of Economic Perspectives* 17 (March 2003): 105-130.

76. See Rick Pildes's 2004 *Harvard Law Review* Supreme Court Foreword; Christopher Cotton, "Help for Challengers?" *New York Times*, January 22, 2010; Heather K. Gerken, "A Silver Lining," *New York Times*, January 22, 2010; and Nathaniel Persily, "The Floodgates Were Already Open," *Slate*, January 25, 2010.

77. Article I, Section 9, Clause 2. The Military Commissions Act had only 7 Republicans voting against it in the House but 162 Democrats voting nay; it is estimated to have moved the status quo in a conservative direction.

78. Ronald Dworkin, "Why It Was a Great Victory," *New York Review of Books*, August 14, 2008. Also see *New York Times*, June 13, 14, 15, 2008.

79. The case was *U.S. v. Butler*, 297 U.S. 1 (1936).

Chapter Nine. What's So Great About Independent
Courts, Anyway?

1. Bueno de Mesquita et al. (2003), Bueno de Mesquita et al. (2008).

2. Empirical studies showing a positive relationship between judicial indepen-
dence and rights protections include Kathleen Pritchard, "Comparative Human
Rights: An Integrative Explanation," *Policy Studies Journal* 15 (1986): 110–122;
Gerald Blasi and David Cingranelli, "Do Constitutions and Institutions Help Protect
Human Rights?" in *Human Rights and Developing Countries*, ed. David Cingranelli
(Greenwich, CT: JAI, 1996); Frank Cross, "The Relevance of Law in Human Rights
Protection," *International Review of Law and Economics* 19 (1999): 87–98; Witold J.
Henisz, "The Institutional Environment for Economic Growth," *Economics and Poli-
tics* 12 (2000): 1–31; Linda Camp Keith, "Judicial Independence and Human Rights
Protection Around the World," *Judicature* 85 (2002): 195–200; Lars P. Feld and Ste-
fan Voigt, "Economic Growth and Judicial Independence: Cross-Country Evidence
Using a New Set of Indicators," *European Journal of Political Economy* 19 (2003):
497–527; Robert M. Howard and Henry F. Carey, "Is an Independent Judiciary
Necessary for Democracy?" *Judicature* 87 (2004): 284–290; Clair Apodaca, "The
Rule of Law and Human Rights," *Judicature* 87 (2004): 292–299; Rafael La Porta
et al., "Judicial Checks and Balances," *Journal of Political Economy* 112 (2004): 445;
La Porta et al. (2008); Emilia Powell and Jeffrey Staton, "Domestic Judicial Institutions and Human Rights Treaty Violations," *International Studies Quarterly* 53
(2009): 149–174.

3. These subjectively coded *de facto* measures include the 4-point scale of judicial independence reported by Charles Humana in his *World Human Rights Guide*
(New York: Oxford University Press, 1992), used by Cross (1999); the "Law and
Order" measure reported by the Political Risk Services (PRS) group, which assesses
inter alia "the strength and impartiality of the legal system," used by Henisz (2000);
the survey measure of judicial independence constructed by Feld and Voigt (2003);
the three-point measures of judicial independence coded from U.S. State Department annual country reports by Howard and Carey (2004), Tate and Keith (2007),
and Cingranelli and Richards (2008); the 10-point measure of judicial independence
coded from country expert reports and reported in the Bertelsmann Transformation
Index (BTI) (http://www.bertelsmann-transformation-index.de/en/bti/); and the
Fraser Institute's measure of judicial independence that is coded from the PRS country assessments, the Global Competitiveness Report (GCR), and the World Bank's
Doing Business datasets, both generated from surveys of firms doing business in given
countries (http://www.freetheworld.com/).

4. These measures include those used in Pritchard (1986); Keith (2002); and
Apodaca (2004). A more recent objective measure of judicial independence measures
the proportion of a country's total money supply that is the subject of contractual obligations. This "Contract Intensive Money" (CIM) measure purports to assess the degree to which a country's judicial institutions are trusted to enforce those contractual

obligations. The measure does not distinguish between those courts that are more or less dependent on the policymaking branches and is thus not particularly helpful for the empirical debate over judicial independence, Powell and Staton (2009).

5. La Porta et al., "Judicial Checks and Balances," *Journal of Political Economy* 112 (2004): 445. Their measure first separately codes the tenure of the judges serving on a country's "highest court" and those on its highest-ranked administrative court. It assigns a value of 2 to judges with life tenure, a value of 1 to judges with tenure longer than six years but less than life, and a value of 0 to judges with tenure of less than six years. They also code a dummy variable taking the value of 1 if judicial decisions in a country are a source of law, and 0 if otherwise. They then generate a normalized sum of these three measures that lies between 0 and 1. They note that excluding the "case law" indicator variable from this measure does not substantially affect results.

6. La Porta et al. (2004) assert that judicial independence is "the defining characteristic of common law." Also see Friedrich A. von Hayek, *The Constitution of Liberty* (Chicago: University of Chicago Press, 1960), 169, 171; Douglass C. North and Barry R. Weingast, "Constitutions and Commitment: The Evolution of Institutions Governing Public Choice in Seventeenth-Century England," *Journal of Economic History* 49 (December 1989): 803–832; and Edward L. Glaeser and Andrei Shleifer, "Legal Origins," *Quarterly Journal of Economics* 117 (2002): 1193–1229.

7. La Porta et al. (2004), 447. Glaeser and Shleifer (2002), 1200, likewise assert that the Act of Settlement established "judicial independence from both king and Parliament . . . Starting in the eighteenth century, judicial independence was an undisputed element of the English legal system." These claims echo those made by Hayek, among others, that during the English Civil War "an effort was made for the first time to secure the independence of the judges" and that the Act of Settlement of 1701 represented "the final confirmation of the independence of the judges." Hayek (1960), 169, 171.

8. La Porta et al. (2004), 447, 449. North and Weingast (1989), 819, likewise assert that after the Act of Settlement of 1701, "the political independence of the courts limited potential abuses by Parliament . . . the creation of a politically independent judiciary greatly expanded the government's ability credibly to promise to honor its agreements."

9. "William III, 1700 & 1701: An Act for the further Limitation of the Crown and better securing the Rights and Liberties of the Subject [Chapter II. Rot. Parl. 12 & 13 Gul. III. p. 1. n. 2.]," *Statutes of the Realm: Volume 7: 1695–1701* (1820), 636–638; http://www.british-history.ac.uk/report.aspx?compid=46986. Currie (1998), 8, argues that the assent of the sovereign to legislative address eventually became pro forma, rendering both impeachment and legislative address means of judicial removal possessed exclusively by the Parliament.

10. Constitution of Ireland, 1937, Article 35, *CCW Online*; Commonwealth of Australia Constitution Act, 1900, Article 72, *CCW Online*.

11. Judges on the Indian Supreme Court serve until the age of sixty-five but may be removed for "misbehavior" by majorities in both legislative chambers (conditional on these majorities comprising at least two-thirds of those voting). The Constitution of India, as amended to 1995, Article 124, *CCW Online*. Judges serving on the Supreme Court of the Kingdom of Nepal may be removed by a two-thirds vote in the lower chamber of the Nepalese legislature for "misbehaviour, or failure to discharge the duties of his office in good faith." The Constitution of the Kingdom of Nepal, 1990, Part 11, Section 87, *CCW Online*. In Nigeria the Chief Justice of the Supreme Court may be removed by a two-thirds vote in the upper legislative chamber; the Chief is then responsible for overseeing removal proceedings against the other justices serving on that court. Constitution of the Federal Republic of Nigeria (Promulgation) Decree, 1999, Articles 153, 155, 292, Schedule III Part I, *CCW Online*. In Liberia judges serve on the condition of "good behavior" and may be removed for "misconduct" by a majority vote in the lower legislative chamber and a two-thirds vote in the upper chamber. The Constitution of the Republic of Liberia, Articles 71 and 43, *CCW Online*. Under the common law constitutions of Malaysia, Singapore, Kenya, Uganda, Zambia, and Zimbabwe, judges on the highest courts may be removed for "misbehaviour" by presidentially appointed tribunals. Federal Constitution of Malaysia, 1957, Article 125, *CCW Online*, The Constitution of the Republic of Singapore, Article 98, *CCW Online*, The Constitution of the Republic of Kenya, 1963, Article 62, *CCW Online*, Constitution of the Republic of Uganda, 1995, Article 144, *CCW Online*, Constitution of Zambia, 1991, Article 98, *CCW Online*, The Constitution of the Republic of Zimbabwe, as amended to 1996, Article 87, *CCW Online*. In Ghana the Chief Justice on its Supreme Court may be removed for misbehavior via a presidentially appointed tribunal; the Chief is then responsible for overseeing removal proceedings against the remaining justices on that court. Constitution of the Fourth Republic of Ghana (Promulgation) Law, Article 146, *CCW Online*. The common law constitution of Canada leaves judicial tenure entirely to the discretion of legislative majorities (The Constitution Act, 1867, Article 101, *CCW Online*)

12. Robert L. Maddex, *Constitutions of the World* (Washington, DC: Congressional Quarterly, 1995), 296.

13. The Human Rights Act 1998, Chapter 42, Section 4, *Constitutions of the Countries of the World Online (CCW Online)*, Max Planck Institute for Comparative Public Law and International Law, Oceana Publications.

14. These countries include New Zealand (see Maddex [1995], 190), Israel (see Maddex [1995], 136), and Saudi Arabia (see Maddex [1995], 244). New Zealand's Bill of Rights Act of 1990, for example, directs that "No court shall, in relation to any enactment . . . hold any provision of the enactment to be impliedly repealed or revoked, or to be in any way invalid or ineffective, or decline to apply any provision of the enactment, by reason only that the provision is inconsistent with any provision of this Bill of Rights." The Bill of Rights Act 1990, Article 4, *CCW Online*.

15. La Porta et al. (2004) and La Porta et al. (2008) sample the seventy-one countries covered in Maddex (1995) that were not "transition economies," or those whose constitutions were rapidly changing. I follow La Porta et al. (2004) in using the version of each country's constitution in force as of 1994.

16. These are the constitutions coded by La Porta et al. as not permitting judicial review, as derived from Maddex (1995).

17. Given sufficient data it should be possible to separately estimate the effects of each of these mechanisms. However, estimating the effects of judicial independence conditional on the nature of a country's policymaking institutions, as I do below, reduces sample size below the threshold necessary to distinguish the effects of these varying mechanisms.

18. Examples include the common law constitutions of both Bangladesh and Pakistan (The Constitution of the People's Republic of Bangladesh, 1972, as amended to 1996, Article 96, *CCW Online*; The Constitution of the Islamic Republic of Pakistan, 1973, as amended to 1990, Article 179, Article 209, *CCW Online*).

19. Hayek (1960); La Porta et al. (2004); La Porta et al. (2008).

20. "Judges are not intrinsically more supportive of private property than the executive or the legislatures, but are merely more insulated from immediate political pressures when they are independent." La Porta et al. (2004), 447, n. 2.

21. Presumably the justification for this assumption is that typically judges are appointed by executives and/or legislators; there is no evident reason why these public officials would select judges with sincere rights preferences significantly different from their own.

22. La Porta et al. (2004), 447. Glaeser and Shleifer (2002), 1210, also claim that "parliamentary control over lay justice . . . as Hayek (1960) so clearly emphasized, is likely to undermine the freedoms inherent in the Magna Carta."

23. La Porta et al. (2004), 449; North and Weingast (1989), 819.

24. La Porta et al. (2004); La Porta et al. (2008).

25. Bueno de Mesquita et al. (2003); Morrow et al. (2008).

26. Civil liberties and political rights are not necessarily pure public goods; rights policies can of course be designed to protect the rights of some more than others, or to have varying degrees of "publicness." The argument is, however, robust to such mixed or club goods, in that we would expect policymakers operating under more majoritarian institutions to provide economic and political rights protections with fewer exceptions, or with more "publicness," than their counterparts operating under less majoritarian institutions. Bueno de Mesquita et al. (2003), 31, n. 5.

27. Bueno de Mesquita et al. (2003); Morrow et al. (2008).

28. Bueno de Mesquita et al. (2003), 179.

29. Thomas Jefferson to Samuel Kercheval, July 12, 1816, in *The Writings of Thomas Jefferson*, ed. Paul Leicester Ford, vol. 10 (New York: G. P. Putnam's Sons, 1899), 37–38.

30. Ibid., 39.

31. Ibid.

32. See, e.g., Mike Oquaye, "The Ghanaian Elections of 1992—A Dissenting View," *African Affairs* 94 (1995): 259–275.

33. Polity IV Project, http://www.systemicpeace.org/polity/polity4.htm.

34. Between 1981 and 1992 Ghana averaged only 5.6 on the 7-point Freedom House civil liberties scale (with 7 being the lowest level of civil liberties). Freedom in the World Comparative and Historical Data, http://www.freedomhouse.org.

35. *New Patriotic Party v. Ghana Broadcasting Corporation* [1992–1993] 2 GLR 354.

36. *New Patriotic Party v. Inspector-General of Police* [1993–94] 2 GLR 459.

37. *New Patriotic Party v. Attorney-General (31st December Case)* [1993–1994] 2 GLR 35.

38. *New Patriotic Party v. Attorney-General (CIBA Case)* [1996–1997] SCGLR 729.

39. *National Media Commission v. Attorney-General* [2000] SCGLR 1.

40. *Sam (No. 2) v. Attorney General* [2000] SCGLR 305.

41. Constitution of the Fourth Republic of Ghana (Promulgation) Law, Article 146, *CCW Online*.

42. The Ghanaian Supreme Court is thus not fully independent of the Ghanaian president; the president may threaten the Chief Justice with removal, and his leverage over the Chief Justice may influence the Chief's oversight of removal proceedings against Associate Justices. However, as will be discussed in the next section, no countries scoring this low on the Polity IV democracy scale fully guarantee judicial independence; many prohibit judicial review altogether. Instituting even partially independent courts may have some effect on rights protections, relative to prohibiting courts from making any changes to rights policies.

43. *New Patriotic Party v. Ghana Broadcasting Corporation* [1992–1993] 2 GLR 354; *New Patriotic Party v. Inspector-General of Police* [1993–1994] 2 GLR 459; *New Patriotic Party v. Attorney-General (31st December Case)* [1993–1994] 2 GLR 35; *New Patriotic Party v. Attorney-General (CIBA Case)* [1996–1997] SCGLR 729; *National Media Commission v. Attorney-General* [2000] SCGLR 1; *Sam (No. 2) v. Attorney General* [2000] SCGLR 305.

44. Polity IV Project, http://www.systemicpeace.org/polity/polity4.htm.

45. "Memorandum to the Turkish Government on Human Rights Watch's Concerns With Regard to Academic Freedom in Higher Education, and Access to Higher Education for Women Who Wear the Headscarf," Human Rights Watch Briefing Paper, June 29, 2004.

46. Ibid.

47. Ibid.; Case no. 1989/1; judgment no. 1989/12; "Turkey: Constitutional Court Ruling Upholds Headscarf Ban," June 5, 2008, www.hrw.org.

48. "Turkey's Constitutional Court Rules Against Civil Trials for Military," January 22, 2010, Bloomberg News Service.

49. Ibid.

50. The Constitution of the Republic of Turkey, 1982, as amended to 2002, Article 147, *CCW Online*.

51. "Memorandum to the Turkish Government . . . ," Human Rights Watch Briefing Paper, June 29, 2004; Case no. 1989/1; judgment no. 1989/12; "Turkey: Constitutional Court Ruling Upholds Headscarf Ban," June 5, 2008, www.hrw.org.

52. "Turkey: Constitutional Court Ruling Upholds Headscarf Ban," June 5, 2008.

53. "Turkey's Constitutional Court Rules Against Civil Trials for Military," January 22, 2010.

54. H. Shambayatti, "The Guardian of the Regime: The Turkish Constitutional Court in Comparative Perspective," in *Constitutional Politics in the Middle East*, ed. S. Arjomand (2008), 99; European Commission, "Turkey 2008 Progress Report," November 5, 2008.

55. Humana, *World Human Rights Guide*.

56. This alternative measure is coded 0 for those countries prohibiting the exercise of judicial review, 1 for those countries with partially independent courts, and 2 for those countries with strictly independent courts.

57. Kim R. Holmes, Bryan T. Johnson, and Melanie Kirkpatrick, *1997 Index of Economic Freedom* (Washington, DC: Heritage Foundation, 1997).

58. This measure is reported in Rafael La Porta, Florencio Lopez-de-Silanes, and Andrei Shleifer, "Government Ownership of Banks," *Journal of Finance* 57 (2002): 265–301.

59. This measure is reported in Simeon Djankov, Rafael La Porta, Florencio Lopez-de-Silanes, and Andrei Shleifer, "The Regulation of Entry," *Quarterly Journal of Economics* 117 (2002): 1–37.

60. Countries' policymaking institutions are coded using the BDM et al. (2003) measure of the size of a country's "winning coalition." This measure is available in five categories; due to the small numbers of less majoritarian countries in the sample, the three least majoritarian categories are combined.

61. Stanley L. Engerman and Kenneth L. Sokoloff, "Factor Endowments, Institutions, and Differential Paths of Growth Among New World Economies: A View from Economic Historians of the United States," in *How Latin America Fell Behind: Essays on the Economic Histories of Brazil and Mexico, 1800–1914*, ed. Stephen Harber (Stanford, CA: Stanford University Press, 1997); William Easterly and Ross Levine, "Africa's Growth Tragedy: Policies and Ethnic Divisions," *Quarterly Journal of Economics* 112 (1997): 1203–1250; Alberto Alesina, Reza Baqir, and William Easterly, "Public Goods and Ethnic Divisions," *Quarterly Journal of Economics* 114 (1999): 1243–1284; Rafael La Porta, Florencio Lopez-de-Silanes, Andrei Shleifer, and Robert W. Vishny, "The Quality of Government," *Journal of Law, Economics and Organization* 15 (1999): 222–279.

62. The conditional coefficients are calculated as $\text{\ss}_1 + \text{\ss}_3(MPI)$, in which $\text{\ss}_1$ is the coefficient on *Judicial Independence* and $\text{\ss}_3$ is the coefficient on *Judicial Independence* * *MPI*. The conditional standard errors are calculated as $\text{sqrt}(\text{var}\text{\ss}_1 + \text{var}\text{\ss}_3(MPI^2) + 2\text{covar}\text{\ss}_1\text{\ss}_3(MPI))$.

63. None of the countries with the least majoritarian policymaking institutions provide full independence to their courts.

64. These region dummies were coded by La Porta et al. (2004) and include North America, Central America, South America, Europe, Asia, Africa, and Oceania.

65. Thomas Jefferson to Samuel Kercheval, July 12, 1816, in Ford, *Writings of Jefferson*, vol. 10 (1899), 37–38.

66. Berger (1973), 3, reports for example that while the seventeenth-century impeachments of Justices Robert Berkley and John Finch were ostensibly pursued under charges of "subversion of fundamental law and the like," "their real sin was to exert pressure in favor of the 'Ship-Money Tax.'" Also see Clarke (1934) and Gerhardt (2000).

67. The 1660 "Declaration of Parliament Assembled at Westminister" asserted that there is "nothing more essential to the freedom of a state, than that the people should be governed by the laws, and that justice be administered by such only as are accountable for mal-administration." Hayek (1960), 169.

68. A. V. Dicey, *Introduction to the Study of the Law of the Constitution* (1885).

69. As quoted in Gerber (2011), 84.

70. Rossiter (1961), 324.

71. Federalist 81, in ibid., 485.

72. Federalist 51, in ibid., 322.

73. Federalist 10, in ibid., 84.

74. Article VI, Section 2, states that "This Constitution, and the Laws of the United States which shall be made in pursuance thereof . . . shall be the supreme Law of the Land."

75. Gordon Whitman, "Governors Who Refuse Medicaid Expansion Put Politics Ahead of People," http://www.huffingtonpost.com/gordon-whitman/politics-ahead-of-people_b_1695396.html.

76. BDM et al. (2003) ; Morrow et al. (2008).

77. Jefferson to Pendleton, August 26, 1776, in Boyd, *Papers of Thomas Jefferson*, vol. 1 (Princeton: Princeton University Press, 1950), 505.

78. Jefferson to Kercheval, July 12, 1816, 37.

79. Ibid., 40, 38.

80. Ibid., 42.

81. Ibid., 42–43.

82. Harvard University Professor of Law Mark Tushnet has likewise called for the elimination of judicial review in the United States, on similar although not identical grounds. Tushnet (1999), chap. 7.

INDEX

Figures, notes, and tables are indicated by f, n, and t, respectively, following page numbers.

Federation of Independent Business),
xi, 298*n*12
Briscoe v. Bell (1977), 302*n*62
British judges, 9, 40–42, 56, 267,
268–269, 288, 299*n*26, 307*nn*40–
41, 310*n*109, 311*n*115, 349*n*66. *See
also* Impeachment power
Brown v. Board of Education of Topeka
(1954), 22, 155, 185, 187, 254
Bueno de Mesquita, Bruce, 26, 273
Burbank, Stephen, 60
Bureau of Justice Statistics, 210
Burger Court (1969–1985), 160–163;
conservative frustration with, 154;
"Conservatively Constrained Court,"
161, 162*f;* "Counterfactual Unconstrained Court," 160–163, 162*f;*
docket and House constraint in, 225;
docket change annually (1981–1985),
229*t,* 230; early Burger Court
(1969–1973 terms) divergences
from elected branches, 90, 153–154;
House majority, effect on, 12, 154,
160–161, 163; late Burger Court
(1982–1985 terms) deference to
liberal House, 290; late Burger Court
(1982–1985 terms) divergences from
elected branches, 90–91, 153–154;
likelihood of conservative judgments,
153, 160; median justice's move to
conservatism, 89*f,* 160; median justice
vs. congressional most preferred legal
rule in, 90; moderate liberalism of,
16, 17; Rehnquist on, 108; and rights
protection, 24, 265
Bush, George H. W., 114, 155
Bush, George W., 253
Bush v. Gore (2000), 129, 188
Butler, United States v. (1936), 297*n*1

Calabresi, Steven, 73, 74, 252
Campaign finance regulation, xv,
260–261, 291

Carter, Jimmy, 92
Case-based analysis: of public opin-
ion hypothesis, 198–202, 198*t;* of
socioeconomic trends, 18, 210–214,
211–214*t*
Chase, Samuel, impeachment of, 11,
60, 61
Chemerinsky, Erwin, 3, 252
Chen, Jim, 138
Children's Internet Protection Act
(2000), 170
*Citizens United v. Federal Election Com-
mission* (2010), xv, 260, 291
City of. See name of city
Civil rights. *See* Rights protection
Civil Rights Act (1964), 24, 157, 158,
253, 301–302*n*61
Clinton, Bill, 92, 117
Coal Industry Retiree Health Benefit
Act (1992), 168, 261
Coburn, Tom, 67
Coding of Court's judgments. *See*
United States Supreme Court
Database
College Savings Bank v. Florida Prepaid
(1999), 127, 168, 169
Colonial judges, 9, 40–42, 61, 63, 267,
274, 289, 306*n*19, 306*nn*23–25
*Colorado Republican Federal Campaign
Committee v. FEC* (1996), 261
Commerce Clause. *See* Interstate Com-
merce Clause
Communications Decency Act (1996),
262
Compensation Clause. *See* Article III;
Salaries of judges
Conservative judgments. *See* Bailey XTI
estimates; Judicial Common Space
(JCS) estimates; Probability of con-
servative judgment
"Conservatively Constrained Court"
series of probabilities: Burger Court,
161, 162*f;* Warren Court, 156, 157*f*

CPSIA information can be obtained at www.ICGtesting.com
Printed in the USA
LVOW07s0434291014

410932LV00003B/137/P